THE MUMMY'S CURSE

# the Mummy's Curse

## The True History of a Dark Fantasy

ROGER LUCKHURST

OXFORD
UNIVERSITY PRESS

# OXFORD
### UNIVERSITY PRESS

Great Clarendon Street, Oxford, OX2 6DP,
United Kingdom

Oxford University Press is a department of the University of Oxford.
It furthers the University's objective of excellence in research, scholarship,
and education by publishing worldwide. Oxford is a registered trade mark of
Oxford University Press in the UK and in certain other countries

British Library Cataloguing in Publication Data
Data available

Library of Congress Cataloging in Publication Data
Data available

ISBN 978–0–19–969871–4

Printed in Great Britain on acid-free paper by
Clays Ltd, St Ives plc

*For Julie*
*&*
*i. m. Sally*

# ACKNOWLEDGEMENTS

M ANY THANKS TO the team at Oxford University Press for their support of this project. The book was completed with a six-month research fellowship from the Arts and Humanities Research Council. At a time of severe threat to the survival of humanities research in the university, to receive an individual grant felt like a great act of faith. I am therefore grateful to the staff and grant assessors for making the completion of this project possible. The resolutely unfactional and unconditionally supportive environment of the Department of English at Birkbeck College continues to make research work a joy in an era of the quantification of outputs and the immiseration of the universities.

I would like to thank the following for archival assistance: staff at Birkbeck Library; Malcolm Barres-Barker at Brent Archives for information on the British Empire Exhibition collection; the many librarians who have assisted me at the University of London Library over the years; the staff of the British Library in St Pancras and Colindale; Joanna Bowring, Head of Libraries at the British Museum, for many leads, not least introductions to Nigel Tallis in the Department of the Middle East Archive and Patricia Usick in the Department of Ancient Egypt and Sudan at the British Museum; Stephen Quirke and Rachel Sparkes at the Institute of Archaeology at UCL; the staff of the London Metropolitan Archives; the staff of the National Art Library at the Victoria and Albert Museum; the staff of the special collections at the School of Oriental and African Studies; the staff of the Victoria and Albert Archive at Blythe House for access to files on Captain H. B. Murray; librarians of the special collections at the Wellcome Institute for access to the Pettigrew Papers; and to Freda Wilkins-Jones at the Norfolk Record Office for steering me through the Haggard Papers. I also thank the librarians at the Courtauld Institute of Art and at the Eaton Collection, University of Riverside, for helpful access to rare materials. For queries rapidly answered, I would like to thank staff at the Society of Antiquaries, the British Film Institute, the Egyptian Exploration Society, the Flinders Petrie Museum, the Reform Club, the Carlton Club, the Royal Geographical Society, Lincoln's Inn Library, the Rhode Island School of Design, Treadwell's bookshop and the College of Psychic Science.

I particularly want to thank Anne Bricknell, great-granddaughter of Walter Herbert Ingram, who at a late stage provided lots of new concrete details, many startling leads, some very weird objects and a host of family legends. She also makes a fine Eton mess.

I should perhaps also take the opportunity to thank any Egyptian elementals that might still be hanging around, for deciding not to kill me off in some bizarre or comical manner during the writing of this book.

At the early stage, when this project needed impetus to build critical mass, I received some crucial invitations to lecture and these forced me to push the project on. Thanks to Josephine McDonagh for an invitation to speak in Oxford, Jarmila Mildorf in Stuttgart, and Gauri Viswanathan in New York. Surekha Davies invited me to join a closed seminar of anthropologists and historians to present material on this project, an intimidating but ultimately very productive occasion. Later, Rosemary Ashton asked me to contribute to the splendid 'Bloomsbury People' project at University College London and the local context for this project was deepened considerably by the wealth of collaborative scholarship at work there. Thanks also for the many invitations to speak on this subject over the years in university departments in Belfast, Birmingham, Brussels, Dublin, Glasgow, Keele, Strathclyde, Westminster and York.

What are essentially early and incomplete outlines of this project have been published in *Magic, Science, Technology and Literature*, edited by Jarmila Mildorf, Hans Ulrich Seeber and Martin Windisch (Münster: LIT Verlag, 2006) and in *Critical Quarterly* and in *History and Anthropology*. My thanks to the editors for letting me work out my ideas in these pieces.

Individuals who have helped along the way include David Amigoni, Isobel Armstrong, John Arnold, Anthony Bale, Mark Blacklock, Mark Bould, Peter Brooker, Ailise Bulfin, Carolyn Burdett, Claire Burton, Andy Butler, Luisa Cale, Jan Campbell, Fiona Candlin, Elliott Colla, Steve Connor, Victoria Coulson, Surekha Davies, Hilary Fraser, Stephen Frosh, David Glover, Jo Hutchings, Salima Ikram, Matthew Ingleby, Colin Jones, Cora Kaplan, John Larson, Rob Latham, Alex Lembert, Colin MacCabe, Scott McCracken, Edward Meyer, Jim Mussell, Alex Owen, Crispin Paine, Gill Partington, Christina Riggs, Laura Salisbury, Justin Sausman, Michael Slater, Paul Spiring, John Sutherland, Michael Taussig, Tony Venezia, Sherryl Vint, Minna Vuohelainen, Marina Warner, Nicholas Warner, Alex Warwick, Neil Whitehead, Martin Willis, Jo Winning, Sue Wiseman and Anne Witchard.

I've been lucky enough to develop some of the ideas in this book after invitations from the BBC producers Stephen Hughes and Laura Thomas for various radio pieces, and have also written on the area for the *Times Higher Education*. My thanks to them all.

I'm very grateful to scholars who have shared their unpublished work with me, including Ailise Bulfin, Elliott Colla, Gabriel Moshenska, Beverley Rogers and Alex Warwick. Those working on the history of Egyptology have proved a remarkably patient and generous bunch.

I am grateful to the many organizations that have granted permission to reproduce images: they are listed separately below.

The first half of this book was drafted in lively conversation with my friend and colleague Sally Ledger. The latter half was written in the wake of her sudden death, the dialogue brutally cut off. It is undoubtedly a poorer book for that, but nonetheless I offer up this work in memory of an inspiring friend.

This book is also, as always, for Julie, who much prefers mummies to all that other rubbish I write about. Julie has been a resolute supporter of this project from the off and has knitted enough scarves and socks during this long process to kit out a pharaoh for virtually any eventuality in the afterlife. Indeed, she is so well versed in the area that in Egypt our tour guide around the Valleys of the Kings and Queens consistently rubbished my pronunciation of Hatshepsut whilst uniformly and lavishly praising hers. I'm totally over this, of course, but I would still like to point out that it sounded to me like we said the *exact same thing*. In truth, Julie has been a fantastic desert guide for helping to shape the vast dunes of information that swept across my desk into meaningful routes and I thank her for all her advice and wisdom over the years.

# CONTENTS

# LIST OF ILLUSTRATIONS

# PART ONE

## Curse Stories

# 1

# King Tut and the Dead Earl

## Opening the tomb

THE IDEA OF the mummy curse always conjures up the story of the opening of the tomb of the pharaoh Tutankhamun in the winter of 1922–3 by
the archaeologist Howard Carter and his wealthy patron, George Herbert, the
Fifth Earl of Carnarvon.

Carter and Carnarvon had worked as a team of excavators in Egypt since
1907, discovering a number of minor tombs in the necropolis of Thebes and
publishing a well-regarded scholarly study of their efforts, *Five Years' Explorations at Thebes*, in 1911. In 1914, they finally acquired their long-desired concession, a legal permit to excavate, issued by the Egyptian Antiquities Service, in
the Valley of the Kings. They stepped into the concession of the remorseless
tomb-hunter Theodore Davis, a retired American lawyer who quitted the area
loudly declaring that the Valley of the Kings was an exhausted site with no new
tombs left to discover. Davis had a cavalier reputation, however, and Carter was
convinced that the tomb of Tutankhamun had not yet been found, despite
some tantalizing discoveries bearing the boy-king's royal name. War service
then interrupted their planned excavations, Carter returning to the site in 1917.

By early 1922, Carter counted six seasons of systematic searching in vain for
signs of the tomb. Their fellaheen – teams of native Egyptian labourers – had
moved an estimated 200,000 tons of rubble to no effect. Lord Carnarvon
intended to abandon the expense of the project, but was impressed by Carter's
commitment to one last season. Carter made his living in Carnarvon's employ,

and as a dealer in Egyptian antiquities. With money made in part from commission-selling Carnarvon's finds to the Metropolitan Museum in New York, Carter offered to fund this last season from his own pocket if the concession was retained. Carnarvon promptly paid for the lot. 'And then', as Carter put it, in his account of the discovery, 'hardly had we set hoe to ground in our last despairing effort than we made a discovery that far exceeded our wildest dreams.'[1] In the rubble beneath the workmen's huts that had been established to work on the tomb of Rameses VI, Carter's fellaheen struck a step and soon uncovered a stairwell of sixteen steps that led to a sealed door. Having established that this was an apparently untouched tomb, Carter immediately re-buried the find. On 6 November 1922, he telegraphed Carnarvon in England in the deferential language of the servant: 'At last have found wonderful discovery in Valley; a magnificent tomb with seals intact; re-covered same for your arrival; congratulations.'[2]

By 23 November, Lord Carnarvon was on the site with his daughter, Lady Evelyn Herbert. The steps were cleared again, and this time the door was entirely uncovered, revealing the seals of pharaoh Tutankhamun, but also evidence that the door had been breached and poorly re-sealed by tomb robbers in antiquity. This door opened onto a corridor, filled with rubble to protect the tomb, which had also been tunnelled before. In three days, Carter's workers had cleared a passage of thirty feet to a second sealed door. On 26 November, that 'day of days', Carter made a small breach in the upper left-hand corner of the door, and put a candle through the hole:

At first I could see nothing, the hot air escaping from the chamber causing the candle flame to flicker, but presently, as my eyes grew accustomed to the light, details of the room within emerged slowly from the mist, strange animals, statues, and gold – everywhere the glint of gold. For the moment – an eternity it must have seemed to the others standing by – I was struck dumb with amazement, and when Lord Carnarvon, unable to stand the suspense any longer, inquired anxiously, 'Can you see anything?' it was all I could do to get out the words, 'Yes, wonderful things.'[3]

Carter's account, written (or ghost written) only months later, convincingly conveys his disorientation at the find, referring repeatedly to 'our bewildered brains'.[4] He speaks of the 'strained expectancy ... of the treasure-seeker' only to cancel this out immediately: 'Did these thoughts actually pass through our minds at the time, or have I imagined them since? I cannot tell. It was the discovery that my memory was blank, and not the mere desire for dramatic chapter-ending, that occasioned this digression.'[5] Where memories were blank, mythologizing would soon step in.

This primal scene with a candle at the door was soon slickly modernized. Within a day, cables brought electric light off the grid serving other tombs in

**Figure 1.1** Antechamber of the Tomb of Tutankhamun (Griffith collection, University of Oxford).

the valley lit for tourists, through the corridor to the doorway of the antechamber. English and Egyptian dignitaries were conducted to view the bizarre sight of a room stuffed with ritual objects which had been disturbed and scattered by hasty tomb robbers thousands of years before. Ominous sentinels in wood and gold leaf, representations of the pharaoh, guarded another sealed door that promised more discoveries, including, they hoped, the sarcophagus of the pharaoh himself.

*The Times* carried the report of its correspondent on 30 November, at which point the discovery of the tomb became a global news story: Tutankhamun became the King Tut of headline writers. *The Times* reported on 'the most sensational Egyptological discovery of the century' and expressed amazement that there was anything left to be found in Luxor, where even the 'smallest urchin' was an antiquity hunter.[6] This appeared on the same page as the news that the new Egyptian cabinet had resigned, and in the same month that the Cairo correspondent had 'feared that public men will be openly murdered' in the unstable political situation in the capital.[7] *The Times* could thus moralize in its editorial that Tutankhamun was 'the patron of a counter-reformation', perhaps a significant symbol 'even now when the Eastern lands are trembling between war and peace'.[8]

A few days later, the paper carried the view of the Egyptologist Alan Gardiner that 'one cannot help hoping that Lord Carnarvon, who has worked for so many years in Egypt without any adequate compensation for all his efforts, will be able to bring home what is not absolutely essential for the purposes of the Cairo Museum'.[9] Concessions given by the Egyptian Antiquities Service carried the proviso that the contents of undisturbed tombs would be the entire property of the Egyptian state. Trouble loomed ahead. As Elliott Colla observes: 'It is impossible to overestimate the degree to which the discovery of King Tutankhamun's tomb changed everything about how Egyptian national elites looked at their past.'[10]

In early December, the tomb was once again reburied to allow Carter and Carnarvon to make arrangements to manage a site now the focus for Egyptians, tourists and a gathering world media. Carter had a steel door made to specifications to secure the tomb, and began collecting experts to help with the work of cataloguing and preserving the find: English archaeologists, American photographers and draughtsmen, seconded from the New York Metropolitan Museum dig nearby, expert linguists, and a chemist from the Egyptian government department for advice on preservation. Carnarvon returned to England before Christmas.

On 10 January 1923, Carnarvon finalized an exclusive reporting deal with the chairman of *The Times*, his old friend J. J. Astor. The paper paid Carnarvon £5000 and would give him 75% of fees for syndicated reports and photographs. The next day, Carnarvon spoke to a massive audience at a specially convened meeting of the Egyptian Exploration Society at Westminster Hall. *The Times* deal, catastrophically, alienated every rival newspaper as well as the Egyptian press and the nascent nationalist government. Mass circulation newspapers in England would instruct their correspondents to do everything to scupper the exclusive. A. H. Bradstreet, the special correspondent at Luxor for the *Morning Post*, first expressed disbelief at the notion of a London deal, dismissing 'an amazing rumour... of which no definite knowledge can be obtained here' that might even go as far as closing the whole Valley of the Kings. If this happened, he warned, 'it is proposed to hold protest meetings'.[11] Once the nature of the deal had been confirmed, Bradstreet expressed disbelief that the Egyptian government, officials at the Antiquities Service or the Egyptian press would countenance their reduction to bystanders given second-hand news. He openly agitated in Cairo for the exclusive to be broken.[12] Bradstreet was said to have told friends that he would 'drive C. and C. out of their minds for having sold a piece of the world's ancient history to the London *Times*.'[13] Valentine Williams, the correspondent for Reuters, pressured British officials and the Foreign Office to override the deal. Others plumped for journalistic subterfuge, trying to beat *The Times* telegraph to London. As if this wasn't enough, *The Times* noted that 'malicious' rumours against Carter and Carnarvon were beginning to circulate in Egypt: 'the mass of Egyptians are firmly convinced that Lord Carnarvon has stolen the more valuable pieces in the chambers.'[14] There were stories of aircraft landing in the desert in the dead of night to carry the hoard away.

It took seven weeks to clear the antechamber of its objects, each item laboriously documented, photographed and carried out to a nearby empty tomb which was put into service as a temporary laboratory. This took place under the intense gaze of tourist crowds and the restless journalists from the world's press. The *Illustrated London News* offered a double-page sketch of large crowds in the valley 'where the click of cameras has become as familiar as the creak of local water-wheels'.[15] Each day, the press lovingly detailed the 'Knick-Knacks of the King' as they appeared.[16] Only the *Illustrated London News* carried photographs from the tomb, some reprinted in lavish colour editions, each image usually marked with '*The Times* World Copyright'. The editor, Bruce Ingram, was personally close to both Carnarvon and Carter, and so was able to carry some of their private photographs too. Bradstreet, in comic mode, spoke of 'social success' in Egypt now being measured by the ability to secure access either to the tomb or to Howard Carter. 'Many deep schemes' were hatched in the Winter Palace Hotel, causing Carter 'overwhelming aggravation'.[17] At the beginning of February, one Cairo dealer wrote to Ernest Wallis Budge, the keeper of Egyptian and Assyrian antiquities at the British Museum, that an exhausted Carter had visited him and privately confessed 'I wish I had never found the tomb'.[18] By 17 February, the team was ready to break the seals on the burial chamber and discover if the pharaoh remained in situ. With self-conscious theatricality, they arranged two arc lamps, one either side of the door, and a wooden stage to stand on, the invited handful of dignitaries sitting in rows of chairs to witness the opening. Beyond the door, the chamber was almost entirely filled with a shrine covered in gold leaf, and shrines within shrines that protected the presumably intact sarcophagus. Edging around this treasure, they found an open store, stuffed with golden statuary and guarded by an impressive Anubis figure. Carter recalled the 'dazed, bewildered look' of the esteemed visitors invited inside.[19]

Figure 1.2 The Fifth Earl of Carnarvon (Griffith collection, University of Oxford).

Ten days later, the process of closing the tomb for the summer began; it was reburied again by 1 March. The world would have to wait for the next digging season to discover if Tutankhamun remained where he had been buried.

Days later, however, Lord Carnarvon fell ill. Resting in Aswan after the opening of the burial chamber, he had been bitten on the cheek by a mosquito, and then nicked the wound whilst shaving. He suffered a fever for a few days, rallied to health, but then collapsed again. Lady Evelyn Herbert was sufficiently alarmed to have her father moved to the Continental Savoy Hotel in Cairo. Blood poisoning was complicated by a bout of pneumonia. He hovered on the edge of death; his wife and doctor would soon be flown to his bedside; his son travelled by boat from India, where he was serving with the Seventh Hussars.

The popular press now had a story that did not require privileged access to the tomb. On 24 March, the *Daily Express* recycled a story from the New York *World*: 'Pharaoh guarded by poisons? Lord Carnarvon warned by Marie Corelli'. Corelli, a best-selling author of Christian and mystical novels since the 1890s, had written the following:

> I cannot but think that some risks are run by breaking into the last rest of a King of Egypt whose tomb is specially and solemnly guarded, and robbing him of his possessions. According to a rare book which I possess, which is not in the British Museum, entitled 'The Egyptian History of the Pyramids'... the most dire punishment follows any rash intruder into a sealed tomb. This book gives long and elaborate lists of 'treasures' buried with several of the kings, and among those are named 'divers secret poisons enclosed in boxes in such wise that they who touch them shall not know how they come to suffer'.[20]

When Wallis Budge denounced such speculations as 'bunkum' in the press, and that the cited text was actually in the British Museum library, Corelli wrote a wounded letter to the Keeper, appealing to her knowledge of 'Egyptian "mysteries"' and 'collection of rare books on this one subject'. She quoted Wallis Budge's own translation of the Egyptian Book of the Dead back to him for the source of the curse: 'I come forth by day against mine enemy'. 'Now,' she said, 'though I am not in any way supposing that Tutankhamen has "come forth" supernaturally to take vengeance on his disturbers, I am inclined to maintain that one of the numerous deadly poisons known in Ancient Egypt *may* have lurked among the objects handled by Lord Carnarvon.'[21]

*The Times*, the official record, disdained even to mention such speculations, instead delivering only the barest telegraphic reports on Carnarvon's deteriorating condition. He died on 5 April. In contrast to the short *Times* announcement, the *Daily Express* sensationally recorded that at the moment of his death the Continental Hotel had been plunged into darkness: 'This curious occurrence was interpreted by those anxiously awaiting news as an omen of evil.'[22] Even so, the *Express* correspondent sent to Cairo, the renowned H. V. Morton, tried to be reasonable:

> The queer atmosphere which clings to all things Egyptian is responsible for the wide-spread story that in opening the tomb of Tutankhamen Lord Carnarvon exposed himself to the fury of some malignant influence or that he was poisoned by materials left in the tomb thousands of years ago. When one calls to mind the number of veteran Egyptologists whose lives have been a series of tomb discoveries, those fables are refuted.[23]

The next day, however, the *Express* managed to debunk yet recirculate rumours about fears of a curse under the front-page headline 'Egyptian collectors in a panic'. 'All over the country, people are sending their treasures to the British Museum, anxious to get rid of them because of the superstition that Lord Carnarvon was killed by the "ka" or double of the soul of Tutankhamen.' The Museum had received an anonymous 'avalanche of parcels containing mummies' shrivelled hands and feet', and the authorities were 'not at all grateful for the present flood of gifts.'[24] These reports are not backed up in the correspondence files in the British Museum archive. There is one letter from H. Dallas (possibly Helen Dallas, the spiritualist author), enclosing a scarab owned by a friend 'who does not desire to retain it', but little else.[25] Indeed, an internal Museum memo expressed exasperation about the Express report: 'I happened to mention...that we not seldom had people sending us things anonymously that they considered unlucky, and this is the result.'[26]

Sternly, the Morning Post editorial declared Carnarvon 'a martyr to the cause of archaeological research, not a victim, as some credulous people would have us believe, to the melodramatic curse of a disturbed pharaoh.' Rumours about supernatural intervention allowed the paper to moralize that 'free education does not make mankind any less credulous' or that Europe in post-war disarray embraced the 'entrancing suggestion of a venomous curse.'[27]

It was too late to be reasonable: coverage had already turned rather Gothic. Sir Arthur Conan Doyle had just stepped off a steamer in New York at the start of another tour to promote spiritualism, for which he had been a leading advocate for several years. Doyle, so the Morning Post reported, 'was inclined to support to some extent the opinion that it was dangerous for Lord Carnarvon to enter Tutankhamun's tomb, owing to occult and other spiritual influences. He said: "An evil elemental may have caused Lord Carnarvon's fatal illness." '[28] The Express duly repeated this claim. The Morning Post displaced its voice of reason by reporting from Paris that the idea of a curse was 'seriously entertained' by occultists like Dr Mardrus, 'the well-known Egyptologist and traveller': 'Many present-day Parisians believe implicitly that these curses are capable of proving effective even after the lapse of thousands of years.'[29] Almost as a direct riposte, this was followed up by an article in the Express by the writer of metaphysical horror stories Algernon Blackwood, entitled 'Superstition and the Magic "Curse".' Blackwood explained that 'A curse is a violent and concentrated stream of thought of which ordinary minds are, fortunately, hardly capable.' He professed belief in this malign magical power, yet weakly reassured readers that 'to credit an Egyptian magician of several thousand years ago with sufficient thought power to kill a man to-day is to lay a heavier burden upon a "curse" than it can bear.'[30]

H. Rider Haggard, another best-selling romance writer and considerable amateur authority on Ancient Egypt with his own private collection of artefacts, publicly dismissed these stories whilst mourning the sensationalism that embroiled the august Egyptian dead in these displays of vulgar modernity. Talk of magical curses, Haggard stated, 'went to swell the rising tide of superstition which at present seemed to be overflowing the world.'[31] He had already written to *The Times* in the days before the burial chamber was opened to plead that the royal mummies be examined and photographed but then reinterred in the Great Pyramid to avoid the appalling fate of their being made 'the butt of the merry jests of tourists of the baser sort.'[32]

A decade later, Ernest Crawley acutely observed in his anthropological study of ill omens that 'the energy of a curse may spread.'[33] Only a week after Carnarvon's death, it was reported that Carter had fallen ill. *The Times* scotched rumours that it refused to print, reassuring readers that Carter was in 'good health'. Their correspondent reported that 'Mr Carter expressed to me great annoyance at the reports circulated of his illness, which caused him and his friends considerable inconvenience and expense.'[34] Carter's bad temper was a sign of his inability to cope with the frenzied attention around the discovery. Under stress, he continually made poor decisions. His intemperate responses to Egyptian 'interference' at the site, as he saw it, would lead him to close the dig and lock the gates of the tomb, causing him to be expelled from the excavation for much of the 1924 digging season because he had contravened the conditions of his government-granted concession. Any political leverage the British once had in Egypt was fast draining away.

These sensational stories soon acquired a different, more authoritative source from the Egyptologist Arthur Weigall, who had served as one of four regional Inspector Generals of Antiquities in Egypt between 1905 and 1914, and had long been a rival of Howard Carter. Weigall had been ousted from his post over rumours that he had been attempting illegal sales of artefacts, a story that Carter had heard and brought to the attention of the authorities in a confidential letter. Weigall had left Egypt and survived in the interim as a journalist, popular Egyptologist, novelist and even stage designer and song-writer. He was sent by the *Daily Mail* to cover the opening of the tomb, but like all the other reporters excluded by *The Times* deal, he had to watch in anger and frustration from outside the tomb. In his best-selling book, *Tutankhamen and Other Essays*, Weigall recalled the day of the unsealing of the burial chamber. He confessed himself awed by the 'solemn' event yet appalled by Lord Carnarvon's jocularity:

> I turned to the man next to me, and said: 'If he goes down in that spirit, I give him six weeks to live.' I do not know why I said it: it was one of those curious prophetic utterances which seem to issue, without definite intention, from the subconscious brain; but in six weeks' time, when Lord Carnarvon was on his death-bed, the man to whom I had addressed the words reminded me of them.[35]

Weigall's short essay on the tomb opening was bracketed by several pieces that teasingly evoked spooky tales of ominous Egyptian artefacts. These were offered within a structure of disavowal, at once asserting and rejecting supernatural explanations. 'I have heard the most absurd nonsense talked in Egypt by those who believe in the malevolence of the ancient dead,' Weigall stated, before immediately adding the clause 'but at the same time, I try to keep an open mind on the subject.'[36]

Weigall recalled helping Lord Carnarvon uncover the sarcophagus of a mummified cat in 1909 (Carnarvon's first success as an excavator in Egypt had indeed been to discover a cat). Weigall stored the mummified creature in his house, where a butler was stung by a scorpion and Weigall had fancied that the cat had 'turned its head to look at me; and I could see the sullen expression of feline anger gathering upon its blank visage as it did so.'[37] The cat sarcophagus later burst open, apparently of its own accord. He told the story of a statue of the god Sekhmet in Karnak that had a sinister reputation. English and American tourists had allegedly become supplicants to the statue, holding séances to which Weigall 'had to put an official stop' when he was Inspector General.[38] He spoke of a photograph in which 'a shadowy human face has come between the camera and the object which was being photographed.'[39] Spirit photography had a big revival in the wake of the Great War; indeed, just four days after Carnarvon died, the *Express* carried a discussion of Mrs Deane's famous spirit photographs of hosts of the war dead gathered above the Cenotaph on Armistice Day.[40] In other anecdotes, mummified skeletons grasped at him and a priest's tomb exuded 'an unaccountable sense of apprehension.'[41]

Weigall had also been associated with an earlier story of the vengeful Egyptian dead. In 1909, Weigall, his wife Hortense, the painter Joseph Lindon Smith and writer F. F. Ogilvie decided to stage a play about the heretic pharaoh Akhenaten in a natural amphitheatre in the Valley of the Queens. Weigall composed the script, and poured his energy into framing a ghost story for the spooky invite, which told a tale of Akhenaten's spirit returning to the valley every year on the same night for three thousand years. At their first rehearsal the cast were struck down with various illnesses (Mrs Smith with ophthalmia and delirium) and the play was abandoned. The story, thrilling with the possibility of malign supernatural intervention, had been widely circulated, reaching as far as the London press. Weigall himself wrote up the events for *Pall Mall Magazine*, where he honed his suspension of disbelief. Despite 'the most absurd nonsense talked in Egypt', he said, 'at the same time I have there become acquainted with certain facts which are far removed from simple explanation.'[42] He also delighted in spooking tourists in Luxor, writing to his wife that 'the great stunt is to take people to the cave and tell them the story of the play – it never fails to go down.'[43]

All of these tales were delivered in a book that elsewhere lambasted the native Egyptian for paralysing superstition, living 'in a world much influenced by magic, and thickly populated by spirits, demons, and djins.'[44] The persistence of pre-modern superstition in Egypt was one of Weigall's justifications for maintaining a strong European control of the country.

Weigall was sometimes regarded as the ring-leader of disgruntled journalists who sought revenge on Carter and Carnarvon by playing up stories of the Tutankhamun curse. But Weigall was not responsible for its details, or for the way the curse proliferated uncontrollably as a series of rumours. Hans-Joachim Neubauer's study of rumour begins with the observation that 'they so often evade capture that, on the whole, they constitute an invisible literature, one that is forever changing shape.'[45] A form of interpretation, neither necessarily true nor false, rumours have no origin or destination, but thrive in the very act of their circulation, prospering from denials just as much as assertions. Hearsay 'refers to other, absent narrators, to people who are not there. In the background of conversations in which this voice speaks there is a chain of anonymous speakers begun somewhere indeterminate and leading nowhere in particular. This series … gives rumours their strange authority.'[46] As Neubauer notes, too, the speed of rumours in permeating a whole society can give them a 'supernatural feel': here, the medium perfectly suits the message.[47]

Tutankhamun rumours are always already cited from somewhere else. *It was said* that on the day that Carter had laid bare the entrance to the tomb his pet canary had been devoured by a cobra, that emblem of pharaonic power. The American Egyptologist James Breasted, closely involved with the Tutankhamun dig, recalled that 'News of this spread quickly and all the natives now said, Alas, that was the king's cobra, revenging itself on the bird for having betrayed the place of the tomb.'[48] *It was said* that a clay tablet had been discovered in the antechamber of the tomb with the inscription 'Death shall come on swift wings to whoever toucheth the tomb of the Pharaoh.' Carter and Carnarvon allegedly destroyed the tablet to prevent the superstitious fellaheen from abandoning the excavation and so, one believer in the curse states, it was 'wiped from the written record of the tomb's discovery.'[49] The anthropologist Henry Field, however, remembers on his visit to the tomb that 'Death to those who enter' was in an 'inscription over the door.'[50] *It was said* that Lord Carnarvon's three-legged dog, Susie, back at Highclere Castle in England, howled mournfully and dropped dead at the precise moment of her master's death, even accounting for the two hour time difference. The Sixth Earl of Carnarvon ascribed this story to a superstitious Scottish servant, using the cliché of the credulous Celt.[51] *It was said* that when the mummy of the king was finally unwrapped, a wound on the cheek exactly matched the place where Carnarvon had been bitten by the fateful mosquito. Soon enough, when anyone loosely connected to Carnarvon or the opening of the tomb died, their deaths were folded into the dreamlike elaboration of the curse rumour.

In May 1923, the American railroad magnate and robber baron George Jay Gould, died in the south of France of pneumonia said to have been contracted on a visit to the tomb of Tutankhamun. In September 1923, Carnarvon's half-brother Aubrey Herbert, a Tory MP and expert on Turkish and Middle Eastern affairs, died after a long illness. Arthur Mace, Carter's co-worker and co-writer of the first volume of the book of the tomb's discovery, suffered a complete breakdown of health in 1924 and had to retire from Egypt after twenty years in the field. The eminent radiologist Sir Archibald Douglas Reid also died in January 1924. He was said to have aided the X-ray study of the sarcophagus of Tutankhamun (in fact he had been ill for three years with cancer, a fate of many other radiology pioneers).[52] Later in 1924, the assassination in Cairo of Sir Lee Stack, the Governor General of Anglo-Egyptian Sudan, was also incorporated into the unfolding curse. Other notable victims were said to include French Egyptologist Georges Bénédite, allegedly from a fall outside the tomb in 1926.

Close attention was paid to any association with the original excavation. In November 1929, Captain Richard Bethell, who had worked as Carnarvon's secretary and Carter's gatekeeper, was found dead at his London club in ambiguous circumstances. Three months later, Bethell's father, Lord Westbury, committed suicide by throwing himself from the window of his rooms in St James's Court in London. The Times reported that 'Captain Bethell died suddenly in his sleep and is believed to have been troubled by the legendary curse of the pharaohs which is said to fall on those associated with the excavations.'[53] Westbury's incoherent suicide note included the line: 'I really can't stand any more horrors.'[54] A Universal News Service account of the suicide claimed that 'Lord Westbury was frequently heard to mutter "the curse of the pharaohs", as though this had preyed on his mind.'[55] With an impressive sense of exponentially expanding punishment, later in the same week Lord Westbury's hearse on the way to the cemetery 'knocked down and killed Joseph Green, aged 8...Another boy was injured.'[56] Later, in 1934, New York's Metropolitan Museum had to fend off rumours that their curator of the Egyptian section, Albert Lythgoe, had a terminal illness related to his presence at the opening of Tutankhamun's tomb. When Arthur Weigall died in the same year, the Daily Express carried the headlines 'Arthur Weigall, who denied Tutankhamen's Curse, is Dead', followed the next day by the inevitable assertion: 'A Curse Killed Arthur Weigall.'[57]

Weigall's fate illustrates one of the principal laws of this literature: curses are recursive. That is, there is a tendency for those involved in disseminating curse stories, even those who actively dismiss them, to get caught in their machinations.

The kernel of the rumours around these particular deaths can at least be found in published sources. Gerald O'Farrell's impressive claim that Sigmund Freud was eventually murdered by shadowy authorities for knowing too much about the truth behind Tutankhamun is based only on 'suppressed' evidence entirely beyond verification or falsifiability. This includes the claim that Freud's first operation – supposedly for cancer – in 1923 was a deception and the first attempt in a conspiracy to kill him.[58] Other enthusiasts have continued to track the Carnarvon curse into the present day. By 1975, Philipp Vandenberg counted thirty-six victims. Barry Wynne has suggested that the death of Mohammad Ibraham, Director of Antiquities, in a car accident in 1966, followed the official denunciation of curse stories by the Egyptian government. When treasures from the tomb were displayed at the British Museum in 1972, rumours circulated that the Royal Air Force crew that transported the items from Egypt were also subject to a series of misfortunes.[59] In 2006, the free London newspaper *Metro* carried the headline 'Is Boy, 3, latest King Tut Victim?', regarding a story about the Fifth Earl of Carnarvon's home in Egypt, 'a luxury villa said to be jinxed by the Curse of Tutankhamen.'[60]

Such stories have been partly fostered by allegedly authoritative sources. George Herbert's son, the Sixth Earl, was entirely prepared to contribute to this weird fusion of history, myth and occultism surrounding the circulation of the King Tut story in the 1970s. His memoirs claim that his father was very interested in spiritualism and the occult and that he relied on two psychics for advice, Cheiro and Velma. Cheiro was the stage name of 'Count' Louis Harmon, the celebrated chiromancer. Cheiro's reminiscences described early wanderings in India and Egypt, where 'I occupied myself with ruined tombs, temples, and kindred things in that land where the children of occultism had built their pyramids.'[61] Part of Cheiro's shtick was the use of a magical female mummy hand for divinations, given to him, so he said, in Karnak by an initiate of Ancient Egyptian wisdom (he claimed the hand belonged to one of the daughters of the pharaoh Akhenaten, thus dynastically close to Akhenaten's successor, Tutankhamun). In 1922, Cheiro and his wife noted that the hand began to bleed and they were accosted by spectral visions of an imploring woman. Cheiro received an automatic message (a message assumed to be from a spirit that takes over the body of the medium, often during trance). The message ran: 'Lord Carnarvon not to enter tomb. Disobey at peril. If ignored would suffer sickness; not recover; death would claim him in Egypt.'[62]

A letter of warning to Carnarvon apparently prompted the Earl to see a second palmist. 'Velma, the Seer' published his memoirs in 1929, in which he recounted the tale that he had read Lord Carnarvon's hand just before he travelled to meet Carter in November 1922. He had foreseen 'great peril'. A second sitting soon after showed that 'spots had greatly increased in density and that the one on his Life Line was perilously near his present age.' To aid prediction, they then turned to crystal-gazing. Within the crystal, Velma saw Lord Carnarvon 'in the very storm-centre of a hurricane of occult flashes' emerging from a tomb.[63] Carnarvon is portrayed as a believer in occult influences, an active member of the London Spiritualist Alliance, fearlessly embracing the romance of it all by choosing to travel to Egypt to meet his fate. When the body of

Carnarvon was returned to Highclere Castle to be buried, the Sixth Earl tells the story that a spiritualist medium phoned with a message from his dead father: 'on no account should you ever step inside the tomb of King Tutankhamen' as 'this would mean an end to the House of Herbert.'[64]

One of the Sixth Earl's reminiscences is striking for embroiling all the central figures of the Tutankhamun story in the occult:

> I had attended at least two séances which my father had held at Highclere Castle...I had watched Helen Cunliffe-Owen put into a trance on an occasion when Howard Carter had also been present. It had been an eerie, not to say unpleasant, experience which had shaken me considerably...Suddenly she had started talking in an unknown tongue which, to everyone's astonishment, Howard Carter had pronounced as being Coptic...I remembered particularly one séance when my sister had been placed in a trance.[65]

The status of the claims of these stories is inseparable from the intensive traffic in rumour in a mass culture caught up in a frenzy of 'Tutmania'. Art deco was fused with Egyptian stylings in jewellery, furnishings and architectural detailing in one of the most intense periods of Egyptian Revival design. Supernatural thrills were sought elsewhere. Pulp horror magazines seized on mummy curses. *Weird Tales,* associated with H. P. Lovecraft's myths of ancient and implacably malign races and cosmic forces, published many mummy tales in the 1920s and 1930s. From as early as 1901, cinema had exploited trick editing and special effects to reanimate Egyptian mummies, because 'these gave form to cinema's power to rearrange time and space, as well as providing resonances with death.'[66] By 1932, Karl Freund's film *The Mummy*, an early contribution to the Universal Pictures horror cycle, echoed the bare details of the Tutankhamun find and grafted these onto an older romance template of undying (and undead) love across the centuries. The film begins with a British Museum field expedition in 1921, led by Sir Joseph Whemple, uncovering the tomb of the high priest Imhotep, where they discover his body and a casket sealed with the fearful warning: 'Death – Eternal Punishment – for anyone who opens this casket'. Breaking the seal and intoning the sacrilegious 'Scroll of Thoth' reanimates Imhotep, driving Whemple's assistant insane at what he sees in the tomb. The plot then jumps ten years and eases into the melodramatic mode of the white woman menaced by insatiable foreign desire, chillingly embodied in Boris Karloff's performance as the mesmerizing Imhotep.

The screenplay by John Balderston basically repeats the structure of his adaptation of *Dracula,* one of Universal's first horror successes the year before. Balderston had also been a London-based correspondent in the 1920s, sent by the New York *World* in 1925 to cover the final opening of Tutankhamun's sarcophagus. In November 1925, the situation had completely changed: *The*

*Times* monopoly had been broken and the Egyptian government was in complete control of information, insisting on priority. Balderston was initially the only foreign journalist in the Valley of the Kings, and was consistently threatened by guards and officials not to break reporting embargoes. Balderston chafed against 'childish edicts of secrecy', objecting that 'the Arabic press shows no interest in Tutankhamen'. Meanwhile Balderston was trying to report on 'the supreme moment of all archaeological research'.[67]

Any whiff of authenticity to mummy movies, however, was soon swept away in the accelerating cycle of sequels that Universal began to pump out in desperation from 1940 with *The Mummy's Hand*. This introduced the mute and murderous mummy Kharis, played by Lon Chaney Jr in three further sequels.[68] Meaningful contexts are lost; the curse is emptied out; the mummy becomes a shuffling dullard dishing out indiscriminate violence in a subgenre of films that even enthusiasts find maddeningly repetitive.[69] Evelyn Waugh had already complained that the Tutankhamun discovery had been 'vulgarized in the popular press' and that Carnarvon's death had meant 'the nation wallowed in superstitious depths', producing an 'irrelevant bubble of emotion and excitement'.[70]

## First interpretations

What to do with this strange confabulation of fact and fiction in the rumours that mutated around Tutankhamun? Where do these stories come from? I mean not just the fantasia of confusing, contradictory detail, but the very *idea* of the curse, for, as weary academic Egyptologists often explain, Ancient Egyptian culture actually had very little concept of the curse. In one of the most authoritative popular accounts of the mummy, Salima Ikram and Aidan Dodson brush past the curse in two paragraphs, declaring that there was no curse in Tutankhamun's tomb and that 'only two have been recorded from other tombs'.[71] Charlotte Booth lists three tombs that have formulations that might be regarded as curses on those who transgress tombs.[72] Rather narrower research has examined the ritualized rhetoric of 'Execration Texts', exploring how 'the names of the king's enemies were written on pottery bowls or platters which were then smashed into hundreds of fragments, thereby destroying the men whose names were written on them.'[73] Later research has focused on what have come to be termed 'threat formulae' in Ancient Egyptian culture. As Katarina Nordh explains, formal threat rhetoric exists, but it is nearly always paired with blessings. Where these messages occur in tomb complexes, their posthumous sender praises the visitor to a tomb if he or she honours the name of the dead; the threat is a secondary, alternative consequence if you do not honour the name. This is often presented as the cast-iron guarantee of safety for any professional Egyptologist, who of course comes to preserve the memory of the name, not destroy it, as a grave-robber might. In the logic of Ancient Egyptian commemorative practices, Egyptologists must be more likely to be considered blessed rather than cursed. Nordh further suggests that 'curse and blessing formulae seem primarily to have been an internal affair of the scribal profession' and regards specific instances as working 'like target-guided missiles...capable of homing in on only what should be homed in on, and nothing else.'[74] In other words, the idea of a catch-all curse as an instantly murderous promise written on a tomb wall or sarcophagus is a fantasy, a later cultural imposition. Superstitions attached to tombs and cemeteries are common in North African Arab culture, but in the Anglo-American world these ideas appear incredibly late, in the latter half of the nineteenth century.

Usually, the Egyptologist will go no further than issuing a blanket dismissal of such superstitions. 'There is really nothing to discuss,' Charlotte Booth firmly concludes.[75] At least until recently, Egyptology had little interest in reflecting on what kind of cultural work such rumours might do. Instead some ask, as Carter Lupton has, 'Is Egyptology cursed by the Mummy's Curse?' Despite struggling to consider horror fiction and film as cultural forms in their own right, Lupton is constantly aggrieved by cavalier disregard for Egyptological accuracy in popular culture. There is, for instance – as one might be not too surprised to discover – 'a frustrating lack of consistency regarding Egyptological issues' displayed by Hammer House of Horror's *The Mummy* (dir. Terence Fisher, 1959).[76] The remake of Universal's 1932 *The Mummy* (dir. Stephen Sommers 1999) is also 'frustratingly inaccurate', its sequel further 'widening the gap with actual Egyptology'.[77] Frank Holt has similarly asked 'Have we cursed the pharaohs?' with superstitious beliefs, suggesting that since the vulgar display of Tutmania in 1923, 'matters have only grown worse'.[78] Yet to call this 'a modern curse' does nothing to explain the persistence of these rumours. Impatient exasperation can't break into their circulation but exactly repeats the superstition – presenting us with another form of the recursive curse.

Statistical rationality appears to have no force against the devilish energy of rumour either. A perhaps only semi-serious medical 'cohort' study of Westerners who entered Tutankhamun's tomb between 1923 and 1926, published in the *British Medical Journal*, has pointed out that their average age at death was 70 and that one can find 'no significant association between exposure to the mummy's curse and survival.'[79] Such surveys were conducted within ten years of the tomb being opened. It is often observed that Howard Carter lived to 64 and died of heart disease quietly at home in London in 1939. Has this cohort study and others like it dispelled the myth of the mummy's curse? Not a chance.

Rationalists might hope that proper scientific education can correct and eliminate false beliefs. A curse might be regarded as an instance of 'magical thinking', which has been defined as 'a cognitive intuition or belief in the existence of imperceptible forces or essences'.[80] Yet recent studies have suggested that far from being associated only with children or 'primitive' people, magical thinking is pervasive, perhaps even adaptive, and certainly able to coexist with more rational cognition in the modern world. 'Magical thinking has stubbornly resisted the aggressive expansion of modern science,' Nemeroff and Rozin observe, 'and, if anything, appears to be making a major resurgence'.[81] Efforts to scientifically disenchant the mummy curse might actively encourage the romance of the curse and aid the efflorescence of rumour, which must clearly be doing a different kind of cultural work than the science of Egyptology.

Howard Carter had his own idea about what this cultural work might be. He found the frenzied attention of the press 'bewildering for us, not to say embarrassing', and reflected: 'One must suppose that at the time the discovery was made the general public was in a state of profound boredom with news of reparations, conferences and mandates.'[82] Indeed, Charles Breasted colourfully recalled that the story of Tutankhamun broke 'after a summer journalistically so dull that an English farmer's report of a gooseberry the size of a crab apple achieved the main news pages of the London metropolitan dailies.'[83] Carter's rare acknowledgement of a world beyond the Valley of the Kings ignored the turmoil of Egyptian politics but gestured at larger geopolitical shifts after the Great War, the Versailles Treaty and the formation of the League of Nations that parcelled strategic land (such as Palestine and newly minted Iraq) into territories governed by mandate. Was it the specific conjuncture of new mass communication media in the 1920s, the competitive conglomerates of 'yellow' journalism in England and America, combined with the rise of radio and cinema that ensured the sensational rumours about Tutankhamun travelled so far and so fast? Was there something about the contagion of the curse that echoed the astonishing range and social penetration of these new teletechnologies?

This suggestion is taken up by Christopher Frayling and Jasmine Day in two of the best accounts of the mummy curse. Day regards the Tutankhamun curse as an instance of media manipulation, twisting the narrative of the curse away from its earlier potential as an ethical critique, albeit in sensational terms, of the violation of tombs. The media effectively 'converted curses from warranted nemeses into merciless afflictions', the mummy becoming an indifferent menace to Westerners that can ultimately justify the 'brazen acquisition fantasy' of films like *Raiders of the Lost Ark*.[84] Yet when Day suggests that 'it is obvious that the powers-that-be neutralized the subversive power of popular culture when cinema turned the curse from a criticism of grave-robbing into a celebration of it', this offers only a crude version of a culture industry that somehow orchestrates ideological messages across media.[85] It is not entirely clear who these shady 'powers-that-be' are or how on earth they might have controlled such a frenzied and unpredictable free market of rumour and superstition. Conspiracy theory is only another form of magical thinking about hidden agencies, mirroring the mechanism of the curse itself.

Other interpretations adopt more abstract modes. As we shall see in a later chapter, the Egyptian mummy was incorporated into the Gothic romance in the course of the nineteenth century, and critical studies of this field provide rich resources for interpreting the circulation of curse narratives. Indeed, it is impossible to tell the story of Tutankhamun without noting how the press framed the story by repeatedly turning to Gothic romancers like Conan Doyle, Rider Haggard or Algernon Blackwood. Gothic monsters are typically understood to negotiate liminal states between animal and human, or East and West, or, most obviously, between life and death. The mummy, like the vampire, exemplifies Freud's reflections on the 'uncanny' object, first published in 1919, as something that hovers unsettlingly between animate and inanimate status, a dead thing that might at any moment stage a fearful return to life. Freud viewed animism as the most primitive set of beliefs, yet observed that he was writing in a post-war era of spiritualist revivalism where 'in our great cities, placards announce lectures that undertake to tell us how to get in touch with the souls of the departed'. Might the dead return or punish the living for the shortcomings of their ritual propitiations? 'Almost all of us think as savages do on this topic,' Freud concluded.[86] That the dead are tabooed and their bodies carefully contained in symbolic locations is also one of the starting points of Julia Kristeva's psychoanalytic account of abjection. Kristeva suggests that the self is consolidated by determining strict bodily and psychic boundaries. Taboos enforce repulsion at what breaches strict categories of inside and outside, clean and unclean, living and dead. Superstitions proliferate where such borders are breached. The mummy's uncanny location suggests it belongs to abjection, a transgressive thing that 'does not respect borders, positions, rules. The in-between, the ambiguous, the composite.'[87]

In a more political register, Nicholas Daly has argued that Gothic mummy fiction works as a kind of allegory that 'recounts what happens to a category of ambiguous foreign objects/bodies when they enter the British economy'.[88] Mummies that come to life in museums or private collections, or who curse the violators of their tombs are revenging their expropriation in the increasingly commercial markets for Ancient Egyptian artefacts in the nineteenth century. Marx argued that objects became commodities by a magical infusion of spectral value (transposing the idea of fetishism from anthropology to economics), so stories about animate or vengeful mummies, Daly argues, might be read in Marx's terms as a kind of popular-cultural commodity theory.

Both psychoanalytic and Marxist interpretations are incredibly suggestive but very abstracted modes of reading. Liminality is a general category that incorporates every Gothic monster, from Frankenstein's creature via the vampire and werewolf to the mummy. Count Dracula has also been read as emblematic of the circulation of capital. So have zombies.[89] The question of Egypt, and Egypt at this particular historical conjuncture, tends to be reduced to sketchy background just when specificity might be most valuable in exploring the allure of the curse.

Perhaps, then, we need to return to the central actors in the Tutankhamun story. Is there something specific about the fragile Lord Carnarvon that helps precipitate the curse narrative? His sister's memoir began by admitting: 'A story that opens like Aladdin's Cave, and ends like a Greek myth of Nemesis cannot fail to capture the imagination of all men and women who, in this workaday existence, can still be moved by tales of high endeavour and unrelenting doom.'[90] 'Workaday' euphemistically hides the immense economic and class differences that divided the Earl from the vast majority of readers of popular reports about the discovery of the tomb and its allegedly fatal consequences.

In fact, there was a great fascination with associating aristocratic dynasties with particular 'lucks' and ill omens into which Carnarvon's fate can be neatly slotted. In the 1920s and 1930s, a cluster of books recorded and analysed this tradition. Charles Beard focused on the most famous of these, the Luck of Edenhall, a chalice held by the Musgrave family, allegedly since the fourteenth century, and long claimed to be a cup left behind after a fairy celebration. One eighteenth-century ballad included the couplet: 'When this cup shall break or fall/Farewell the luck of Eden Hall.'[91] Beard limited belief in these lucks to the 'primitive and uninstructed mind' that gave 'superstitious veneration to whatever is derived from a remote or unknown origin.'[92] This was Edward Lovett's view too, as he built his collection of charms, talismans and superstitious beliefs from the London populace.[93] J. G. Lockhart offered a more extensive array of aristocratic curses and repeated folk tales in which powerful dynasties are doomed by those they dispossess. The curse was 'the ordinary way in which the weak retaliated upon the strong.'[94] The 'Cowdray Curse', for instance, was issued by a monk on the family of Sir Anthony Browne who had been gifted a monastery from Henry VIII during the dissolution. A cast of persecuted Quakers, shepherds and midwives damning their oppressors follows, leading to the famous 'Tichborne Curse' in which the family descended from Sir Roger Tichborne paid a dole to the poor for centuries to fend off a curse on the continuation of the male line should such charity end. Cessation of payment in the nineteenth century coincided, so it was said, with the famous legal 'claim' over the baronetcy that financially ruined the family. To Ernest Crawley, oaths, curses and blessings were rudimentary social forms of redress, superseded in 'the course of ethical evolution' by the law.[95] Continued beliefs were so-called 'survivals' from earlier phases of development, ritualized forms of resentment that were often associated with the poor, the primitive or the colonized.

Yet anthropological confidence that this was a dying tradition failed to notice a continuing obsession with stories of cursed objects and doomed dynasties. In 1909, *The Times* reported on the sale of the Hope Diamond to the Cartier jewellers from the collection of the ex-Sultan of Turkey, Abdul Hamid. 'Like most other famous stones,' the report noted, 'its story is largely blended with tragedy.'[96] Long believed to have been stolen from a Hindu idol in India, the huge blue-tinted diamond was bought by Louis XIV in 1668 before it passed down the royal line into the possession of Marie Antoinette. Several aristocratic ladies were said to have worn the gem as a necklace, only to lose their heads to the guillotine. It was stolen in the Revolution, but reappeared re-cut in the collection of the profligate gambler George IV in England. It was purchased from the king's heavily indebted estate by Henry Hope in 1830. His heirs fought violently over their inheritance and the remaining family fortune and art collection was gambled away by the feckless Lord Henry Hope, who inherited the diamond in 1887. He was forced to sell it in 1902, and it soon spent a year in Constantinople where 'its alleged adventures for the brief space while there seem to beggar the wildest fiction.'[97] In 1910, Pierre Cartier tempted the American newly-weds Edward and Evelyn Maclean with the romantic history of the stone. Evelyn Walsh, daughter of a fabulously wealthy prospector-turned-businessman, had just married the heir to the *Washington Post* media empire, and their combined wealth had already bought the famous 'Star of the East' diamond. Cartier failed to persuade them in Paris, but travelled to America with the Hope Diamond in 1911 and closed the deal. Richard Kurin suggests Pierre Cartier built on the breathless *Times* account to fashion an alluringly dangerous history, much of it fantastic. The association with the *Washington Post*, however, meant that 'it became instant folklore early in the era of modern mass communication.'[98] The Maclean family seemed to be impressively doomed. Evelyn was addicted to laudanum and eventually confined to a lunatic asylum in 1933, in the same year that she allegedly pawned the Hope Diamond to help raise the ransom for the kidnapped child of the aviator Charles Lindburgh. Edward Maclean's political ambitions ended in public humiliation, complicated by alcoholism. He declared the *Washington Post* bankrupt in 1932. Their son, Vinson, was killed when hit by a car in May 1919. Their daughter committed suicide in 1946.

Certain gems have been traditionally associated with ill luck. The Koh-i-Noor diamond was rumoured to have accumulated a murderous history and some feared for the British throne when it passed into English hands in 1849 as a result of a series of annexations. It was displayed at the Great Exhibition with great fanfare, before being re-cut and worn by Victoria. It seemed to have no ill effects on British power, however, although a vengeful history gathers around a fictional version of the diamond in Wilkie Collins's *The Moonstone*.[99] The Orloff Diamond was imbued with another story of theft from an Indian idol, and the fate of the Russian aristocracy and royal line was rather less rosy than that of their English cousins.

The circulation of rumours about the Hope Diamond and the Tutankhamun curse might be plausibly linked through Thorstein Veblen's reflections on the conspicuous consumption of the 'leisure class'. Veblen developed the theory that superiority of class was demonstrated through the conspicuous refusal to engage in productive work and through ostentatious expenditure on beautiful objects, the taste of the leisure class determined by 'a gratification of our sense of costliness masquerading under the name of beauty'.[100] In an era of unfettered American capitalism, the nouveau riche demonstrated unlimited wealth by consuming 'freely and of the best in food, drink, narcotics, shelter, services, ornaments, apparel, weapons and accoutrements, amusements, amulets, and idols or divinities'.[101] As an English aristocrat, George Herbert pursued other signifiers of leisurely wealth: shooting, hunting, collecting. His indulgence in fast cars (he was the third registered car owner in England), led to a near fatal accident and the medical advice that he winter abroad in Egypt for his fragile health. Whilst there, he would have taken up archaeology as another signifier of leisurely labour, not least because it involved doing little work oneself other than to direct teams of fellaheen. Meanwhile, the new intensive methods of excavation required wealth, as did any serious attempt to enter into the market in antiquities.

Intriguingly Veblen suggests that the sense of the right to this wealth of the leisure class was reinforced by a pervasive belief in *luck*. Veblen devotes a whole chapter to how superstitious beliefs in 'an inscrutable preternatural agency' pervade the leisure pursuits of sport and gambling, but also how, across all classes of society, luck helps 'to conserve... habits of mind favourable to a regime of status'.[102] But if luck signalled resignation at inequality, delight in thrilling stories about curses on the aristocratic or nouveau riche family might suggest a channel where class resentments surfaced. After all, these curse tales rippled through societies riven with labour disputes, union organization and panic about the growing power of socialist and communist political parties.

This reading focuses closely on the historical context of the 1920s. Whilst suggestive, it is limited by a rather telling fact. The curse of Tutankhamun was not the first story to circulate about Englishmen struck down by the Ancient Egyptian dead. Indeed, in many ways the Tutankhamun story followed a script that had already been prepared for it by at least two prior instances that were widely known in the late Victorian and Edwardian periods. Precisely because they circulated as rumours, these stories are poorly remembered, often returning in incoherent or fantastically elaborated fragments to bolster up the Tutankhamun case. To my surprise, no one has properly researched these stories. And yet, to my mind, the peculiar histories of the Victorian gentlemen Thomas Douglas Murray and Walter Herbert Ingram hold the key to the allure of the mummy curse. Let's try to piece together their adventures.

# 2

# Thomas Douglas Murray and 22542 (The 'Unlucky Mummy')

I T WAS TO be fifty years before the treasures of Tutankhamun were exhibited at the British Museum, when an exhibition travelled from Egypt in 1972. Yet there were always uncanny thrills to be had in the Egyptian Rooms. In 1927, the *Illustrated London News* carried a serious article on the jewels and amulets found with Tutankhamun and their relation to Egyptian theology. The same issue included an item headlined 'The "Ghost" Anyone May See at the British Museum':

> In the Egyptian Sculpture Gallery at the British Museum there stands erected vertically against the wall the black basalt coffin of Sebek-Sa, which is empty. If, however, the visitor chances to look through a glass case which contains a statue of Isis holding a figure of her son, Osiris-un-Nefer, a view may be obtained at a certain angle through the glass of Sebek-Sa's coffin, now no longer empty, but, apparently, with an 'occupant' who fits exactly the space within the coffin. Lest anyone might suspect supernatural influences, we hasten to state that this effect of the coffin being occupied is produced by the ordinary process of reflection...The 'occupant' is a reflection of another exhibit – the white stone effigy of Hes-Petan-Ast...This explains the reason for what is popularly termed the 'British Museum Ghost'.[1]

The editor, Bruce Ingram, was a serious Egyptologist yet not above encouraging play within the august museum. This fake ghost was only a temporary side effect of a display, easily resolved. The Museum had a more recalcitrant object in these rooms, however. Earlier, in 1921, two years before the death of

Carnarvon, a brief article in *The Times* on the Egyptian galleries in the British Museum noted that:

> a change has been made in the place assigned to the Lady of the College of Amen-Ra (No. 22542). This is the so-called 'unlucky mummy' about whom so many stories have circulated without any foundation. It was said by all sorts of people that anyone who interfered with her would meet with calamity, and the late Mr. Stead predicted that if any further attempt was made to move the lady it would probably result in the utter destruction of the whole room, such was the virulent nature of the princess.[2]

Rumours about the 'unlucky mummy' were clearly sustained enough to reach the pages of *The Times* and be referred to as if they were common knowledge. They could also be concretely linked in recent memory to W. T. Stead, the world-famous New Journalist, campaigning editor and spiritualist who had died in 1912.

What was the unlucky mummy? The stories that surround this artefact have been so persistent that inquirers to the British Museum are directed to an information sheet that was put together in 1995 to describe the object and fill in some of the 'vast web of mythology [that] has formed around it'.[3] Acquisition 22542 is a gessoed wooden 'mummy board', an inner coffin lid, strikingly painted with the image of an unknown woman from the 21st or 22nd dynasty, certainly from a high-ranking family within the priesthood, and thus described in early British Museum catalogues, composed by the Keeper of the Egyptian Rooms, Ernest Wallis Budge, as 'The Priestess of Amen-Ra'. It was donated to the Museum by Mrs Warwick Hunt on behalf of her brother, Arthur F. Wheeler, in 1889, along with the rest of a small private collection of Egyptian objects, including some mummified crocodiles and a human mummy hand with finger-ring still attached.

After this information on provenance, the sheet tells a loose version of the myths around its purchase in the 1860s or 1870s, gesturing vaguely at the accidents, misfortunes and deaths said to have been suffered by the Englishmen who purchased it and brought it home, as well as subsequent misfortunes associated with those who tried to photograph the lid. Unsurprisingly, the sheet follows the version told by Wallis Budge that these rumours were fanned by the publicity-hungry W. T. Stead and his friend Thomas Douglas Murray, 'an amateur Egyptologist and associate of the excavator Flinders Petrie'. The information sheet in effect recirculates late Victorian and Edwardian rumours with an air of wearied resignation at the misguided fascination they continue to exert. Yet by repeating Wallis Budge's account, which was aimed at tarring his rival Flinders Petrie with occult associations, it obscures significant details.

Thomas Douglas Murray was not a latecomer to the story but the man who purchased the mummy lid and to whom the curse was principally attached, or

Figure 2.1 The unlucky mummy (British Museum).

rather from whom the curse began its impressive path of contagion through Victorian and Edwardian London. Douglas Murray, in other words, was one of the models for the doomed Earl of Carnarvon and for the mummy's curse.

Thomas Douglas Murray was a society gentleman, well known in artistic and aristocratic circles, who died in 1911 at the seemingly very uncursed age of 70. His relationship to the unlucky mummy is a complicated tale to reconstruct because it is a story that begins with his annual journeys to Egypt in the 1860s, but comes into wider public circulation only after a famous journalist investigated the story in 1904. This journalist, Bertram Fletcher Robinson, was a dashing young reporter during the Boer War, who had then risen to the editorship of the *Daily Express* at the age of 34. He first heard the British Museum story from Ernest Wallis Budge at a soirée early in 1904. He wrote a brief note to Wallis Budge from his London club: 'I hope you remember me at Lady Sykes' the other evening. May I have a look at the Egyptian Coffin of your most interesting story?'[4] That summer, Robinson published a front page story in the *Daily Express* under the headline 'A Priestess of Death. Weird Story of an

Egyptian Coffin. Mummy's Romance.' Robinson identified 22542 as 'a problematical royal personage' in the British Museum, claiming that 'about this same coffin there hangs as terrible a story as ever an Edgar Allan Poe or a Balzac or Kipling produced from a gloomy imagination'.[5] Using initials only to preserve the anonymity of the gentlemen involved, Robinson was the first to circulate the story in public. It was picked up as far away as Atlanta in America.[6]

When Robinson died suddenly in 1907 of enteric fever at the age of 37, he was subject to the law of the recursive curse and was assumed to have been its victim. Robinson was a towering man, a celebrated Cambridge rugby blue, hunter, writer, versifier, a larger than life figure who inspired much fraternal devotion. His friend Archibald Marshall recalled in his memoirs: 'The very last time I saw him he told me a wonderful tale about a mummy which had caused the death of everybody who had had to do with it. He was collecting his material, already had enough for a sensational story and was on the track of more ... I don't know whether he ever wrote that story, but it cannot have been long after that he was dead himself.'[7] Douglas Sladen, creator of *Who's Who*, similarly recalled meeting 'poor Fletcher Robinson, who would have been one of the greatest journalists of his day if he had survived.'[8] With a casual air, Sladen remembers Robinson as 'one of the persons whose death was attributed to incurring the displeasure of the celebrated Egyptian mummy in the British Museum.' He continued (telescoping the timescale and eliding details):

> The popular account of his death is that, not believing in the malignant powers of the celebrated mummy-case in the British Museum, he determined to make a slashing attack on the belief in the columns of the *Daily Express*, and went to the museum, and sent his photographer there, to collect materials for that purpose: that he was then, although in almost perfect health, struck down mysteriously by some malady of which he died.[9]

Robinson published his piece on the unlucky mummy and also reported ghost stories from the Boer War with a studiously neutral air.[10] He also wrote several Gothic tales, detective stories and murder mysteries, including *The Trail of the Dead*.[11]

Yet Robinson's death, widely mourned by his fellow journalists, was probably the impetus for an outline of the alleged curse that appeared in *Pearson's Magazine* in 1909, the cover emblazoned with an image of 22542, and which spoke of a 'terrible story' that 'will never be written in full; but some of its chapters may be told in a few words.'[12] The essay was signed pseudonymously and again the historical actors were replaced by initials.

This report likely prompted William Stead to syndicate an article on the story, which flashed the rumour of the London mummy curse around the world. The

**Figure 2.2** Cover of *Pearson's Magazine* (University of London Library).

Correspondence files in the British Museum, for instance, carry a cutting sent by someone from the *San Francisco Examiner*, which screamed 'Ghost of Mummy Haunts the British Museum. Must Go Now.' Stead claimed to be a personal friend of the lifelong victim of the curse (the unnamed Douglas Murray), but ended with the warning tale of the journalist Robinson, who had written up the story for the *Daily Express* 'and within a few weeks he had died'.[13]

Robinson was merely the frame for the story of the Douglas Murray curse, but his death seemed to confirm that even testing the strength of the chain of rumour associated with the Priestess of Amen-Ra thrilled with risk. It helped the story that Robinson had many friends in Fleet Street (he was the nephew of the editor Sir John Robinson and close to the well-known journalist and editor Max Pemberton, and to Owen Seaman, the editor of *Punch*) and was considered a hero of the Boer War. But it *really* helped that he had became a fast friend of Arthur Conan Doyle.[14] Doyle had met Robinson in South Africa in 1900 during the Boer War. Robinson reported for the *Express*, Doyle had volunteered as a medic, and was involved in treating the disastrous outbreak of enteric fever amongst the British troops, a disease that killed 15 000 troops. Robinson and Doyle returned to England on the same boat, where the two men swapped writing plans and story outlines. Robinson, who was schooled in Newton Abbot in Devon, possibly entertained Doyle with superstitions about haunted moors. Certainly, a year later, after wet weather ruined their golfing weekend, Robinson and Doyle had agreed to collaborate on a creepy tale based on Devonian folklore about a spectral hound. Doyle visited Robinson in Devon in May and June 1901 to soak in the atmosphere, and toured the moors with Robinson's driver, Harry Baskerville. Doyle's fee was massively increased at the mere prospect that this tale might be the chance to revive the Sherlock Holmes franchise, dormant since the detective's fatal encounter with his nemesis Moriarty at the Reichenbach Falls in 1894. Robinson's writing role accordingly diminished. When *The Hound of the Baskervilles* was published, Doyle's dedication read: 'This story owes its inception to my friend, Mr Fletcher Robinson, who has helped me both in the general plot and in the local details.'[15]

It is striking that the novel hinges on an aristocratic family curse, shaped by Doyle with evidently detailed knowledge of English traditions of lucks and curses, even down to the manuscript of the legend of 'The Curse of the Baskervilles' being composed in the 1740s, exactly the time when the fabrication of such 'ancient' reliquaries was fashionable. Out on the moor, Watson succumbs to magical thinking, spooked by 'the feeling of an unseen force, a fine net drawn around us with infinite skill and delicacy'.[16] The atmospheric writing strains to evoke a liminal territory on the edge of English civilization where superstition merges into everyday experience. The allegedly rational solution to the Baskerville deaths still feeds into the formula for family curses, as Holmes solves the case through a proper understanding of heredity and threat of degeneracy within aristocratic bloodlines.

Robinson had formed the Our Society crime club with Conan Doyle, Max Pemberton and others in 1904, and so was associated with the 'club tale' tradition of weird and wonderful adventures popularized by Robert Louis Stevenson. Doyle had already published 'Lot No. 249' in one of these interlinked collections, a story about an Oxford student whose occult studies in rooms stuffed with Egyptian artefacts allow him to reanimate a mummy to enact his murderous desires.[17] Bertram Fletcher Robinson's sudden death in 1907 could thus be successfully intertwined with two curse stories, blurring romance literature and rumoured true story.

It was Doyle who recalled Robinson's fate in the immediate wake of the death of the Earl of Carnarvon. In his sensational comments in New York a day after the death, Doyle was reported as saying that:

> The death of Mr. Fletcher Robinson (formerly on the staff of the 'Daily Express') was caused by Egyptian 'elementals' guarding a female mummy, because Mr. Robinson had begun an investigation of the stories of the mummy's malevolence...I warned Mr. Robinson against concerning himself with the mummy at the British Museum. He persisted, and his death occurred. He became engrossed in the subject, and wrote several articles for the 'Daily Express'...I told him he was tempting fate by pursuing his inquiries, but he was fascinated and would not desist. Then he was overtaken by illness. The immediate cause of death was typhoid fever but that is the way in which the 'elementals' guarding the mummy might act.[18]

This was merely the fate of the messenger, a warning about passing on rumour: Bertram Fletcher Robinson was only the elaborate frame tale for the story of the unlucky mummy itself. This artefact was also recalled in the press coverage around Carnarvon. As the *Express* reported the inundation of the British Museum by artefacts from terrified collectors, the headline story explained:

> The Museum weathered a similar storm some years ago, when the story of the curse of the Priestess of Amen-Ra became public. Sufficient scare-gifts were received to fill a large show-case. A long chain of fatalities have been attributed to the curse of the Priestess. Men who have made fun of the superstition have died within the year. Another story is that a photographer took pictures of the Priestess and placed the plates in his safe. When he went to look at them some weeks later the glass had become a thin brown powder.[19]

Already, by 1923, these details are half-remembered urban myths, detached from specific names and dates to ease their circulation. Even those accounts that continued to recall Thomas Douglas Murray slightly modulated the details with every telling, aiding the elaboration of this complex dream-work of rumour. Any attempt to reconstruct the story of Thomas Douglas Murray must therefore grasp that it is a palimpsest of its tellings and also of the hints of what has *not* been written down because it is too dangerous to do so.

This is the essence of the story circulated by the *Daily Express* in 1904 and repeated by *Pearson's Magazine* and Stead in 1909. Some time in the 1860s, a party of five English friends travelled down the Nile to Thebes, where they were entertained by a lady of title (presumably Lady Duff Gordon, author of the famous *Letters from Egypt*, who lived in Luxor for seven years to pacify her tuberculosis until her death in 1869). Mr D (Douglas Murray) decided to buy a memento of the trip, and Arab treasure hunters showed him the coffin lid of the Priestess of Amen-Ra. It had a rare beauty, but 'a face that was filled with a cold malignancy of expression, unpleasant to witness'.[20] The purchase was made, but the Englishmen then decided to draw lots as to who was to have the case in England. The lottery was won by Mr W (Arthur Wheeler). What followed was 'a history marked by an uncanny series of fatalities'. 'On the return journey of the party, one of the members was shot accidentally in the arm by his servant, through a gun exploding without visible cause.'[21] Another member of the party died in poverty within a year. Mr W also 'found, on reaching Cairo, that he had lost a large part of his fortune.' Ruined, Mr W passed the case to his sister (Mrs Warwick Hunt), who displayed it in her house. In the 1880s, Madame Blavatsky, the notorious occultist and founder of the Theosophical Society, saw the lid and warned that it radiated evil intent. An attempt to photograph the mummy case resulted in the death of the photographer, but not before 'the face of a living Egyptian woman' was captured on a photographic plate. After these events, Mr D – or perhaps others – persuaded the sister to send it to the British Museum, where it was recorded as a gift in 1889. Bertram Fletcher Robinson, who had researched this story, considered the curse to end at this point: 'Perhaps it is that the priestess only used her powers against those who brought her into the light of day and who kept her as an ornament in a private room; but now standing among queens and princesses of equal rank, she no longer makes use of the malign powers which she possesses.'[22] Robinson's death from an exotic fever, however, opened a new chapter, of which the *Pearson's* account was merely the first entry.

In 1913, Ada Goodrich-Freer, a well-known writer in psychical and occult matters, published a much more detailed account of this story in the *Occult Review*. She claimed to use documents passed to her directly by Thomas Douglas Murray, who had given her the permission to tell the true history of the curse of the Priestess of Amen-Ra. She visited the Egyptian Rooms with Douglas Murray and 'found myself gazing into the eyes, sad rather than malignant, of a beautiful Egyptian countenance'.[23] Douglas Murray had died soon after their visit in 1911.

Goodrich-Freer is not exactly a reliable source. She was a practising psychic, claiming second sight from her Scottish ancestry, and was used as a 'sensitive' by the Society for Psychical Research. She co-wrote *The Haunting of Ballechin House* with the Marquess of Bute in 1899, a book whose claims were widely derided, not least for gaining what was perceived to be credulous coverage in *The Times*. The Ballechin House report inspired Shirley Jackson's Gothic masterpiece, *The Haunting of Hill House*. Goodrich-Freer had also worked with W. T. Stead, co-editing his occult journal *Borderland* (1893–7), where she signed herself 'Miss X'. Douglas Murray would certainly have known her through

W. T. Stead, and through psychical circles in London, her authority perhaps further bolstered by her published research in folklore. After 1906, as Mrs Hans Spoer, she had also spent time in Egypt.[24]

Douglas Murray's documents, as presented by Goodrich-Freer, tell of a journey down the Nile in 1868, involving a brief stay with Lady Duff Gordon and hunting in mummy pits near Dayr el Bahree and in the Valley of the Kings. The party, which included AFW (Wheeler) and Mr Y, travelled up the Nile, returning later to Thebes, where Arab traders presented them with mummy artefacts for purchase. Lots were drawn: AFW won the mummy case, Douglas Murray only a vase. Douglas Murray was, nevertheless, 'the first victim of the misfortune which the priestess brought in her train.'[25] In this version, it is Douglas Murray who loses his arm in a hunting accident, shooting snipe near the pyramids. In a process of contagion familiar from the Carnarvon story, the curse then moved quickly to Douglas Murray's associates. Of the Englishmen in the group, both a tutor and his young student die, leaving AFW with the case. Goodrich-Freer then turns to a statement drawn up by AFW's sister (Mrs Warwick Hunt). AFW, it seems, lost his fortune gambling, emigrated to America and lost his remaining money in a cotton farm that suffered first floods, then fire. 'To every one of his nearest relatives misfortune came, and the family estates had to be sacrificed.'[26] In 1869, the mummy case was warehoused in Tilbury, before the sister, who apparently moved in London's occult circles, brought it home. The Blavatsky warning reappears in this account; much more detail surrounds the attempt to photograph the case, dated to September 1887. The foreman who took the case to the photographer died, as did the photographer himself. The photograph with the spectral image (this time of a male figure) was sent to the gentleman deciphering the hieroglyphs. 'In a few days [he] went down to his place in the country and shot himself.'[27] In Goodrich-Freer's account, after the long-suffering AFW died in 1899, the case was presented to the British Museum (it was actually presented in 1889).

Unlike Robinson, Goodrich-Freer suggests that its entry into the British Museum did not neutralize the threat. 'There has been much talk of various misfortunes said to have befallen the officials of various grades in the British Museum who have come within the influence of the priestess', stories that the Museum authorities denied.[28] She spoke of a well-known society girl who taunted the priestess to do her worst, only to fall headlong down the Museum's elegant neo-Classical steps (in a later re-telling, this figure is identified as Lady Beatrice Gascoyne-Cecil, who married Baron Harlech in 1913, a politician and trustee of the British Museum).[29] Goodrich-Freer spoke, too, of Robinson, who 'died at an early age, within a year of a visit to the mummy case, which he photographed with the assistance of a well-known photographer, who also died within the year.'[30] Again, the timeline of Robinson's death, three years after his article, is compressed for dramatic effect. The last testimony comes from a friend of Douglas Murray, the author and Fellow of the Royal Geographical Society, Winifred Gordon. Her brother, Captain Bertram Dickson, a military attaché and vice-consul in Van, returned from Persia with artefacts that he showed to the Keeper of Egyptian and Assyrian Antiquities, Ernest Wallis Budge, standing near the priestess. Gordon attested to the financial ruin and accidents that subsequently haunted him. Goodrich-Freer fails to offer the rather impressive detail that Dickson was the first airman to be involved in a mid-air collision at an air show in 1910. That is pretty unlucky. Severely injured, he died in 1913, but not before persuading Winston Churchill to establish the forerunner of the Royal Air Force.[31]

Follow-up letters in the *Occult Review* confirmed the malign influence of the priestess in the Egyptian Rooms. Horace Leaf recalled visiting in 1904 with a nervous friend who 'appeared filled with horror and refused to approach it.'[32] He soon died. More impressive testimony came from another psychical 'sensitive', Elliott O'Donnell. In his splendid survey, *Haunted Houses of London*, he explains that 'I have been visiting the British Museum with the idea of obtaining impressions as to the alleged haunting of the Oriental Department.'[33] O'Donnell spent some time with the mummy Katebit, with its own reserve of ill-repute, before passing on to the mummy case of the Priestess of Amen-Ra. 'I suddenly and instinctively felt that something had passed through the glass frame containing the mummy case and had planted itself by my side.'[34] A malign elemental then attached itself to O'Donnell for two weeks, tormenting him and orientalizing London in a fevered paranoid vision:

> I was continually seeing strange dark faces – all of them Egyptian both in colouring and cast of features – peeping at me from behind curtains, or peering down at me from over balustrades, and always with the same baffling and peculiar enigmatical expression in their long and glittering eyes.[35]

Having judged at least four other objects to be occupied by species of 'indescribably, damnably beastly' elementals, O'Donnell offered his considered view that the Oriental Rooms were haunted.[36] 'I can feel the presence of other ghosts, and their name is legion, the very atmosphere is impregnated with them.'[37]

It was perhaps inevitable that the chiromancer 'Count' Louis Harmon would also claim a central role in a story he wrote up as 'The Famous Mummy Case of the British Museum.' Cheiro claimed to have warned Carnarvon not to travel to Egypt, but revealed that he had also been consulted by Thomas Douglas Murray before his fateful trip down the Nile (Harmon seems to forget that this journey took place in the 1860s, making this reading somewhat unlikely). As he read the gentleman's hand, 'an unaccountable feeling of dread and horror seemed to creep from it' – presumably because this was the hand Douglas Murray would shortly lose in his shooting accident.[38] Cheiro was assailed by visions of 'some occult force' shattering the hand, hieroglyphs and the glimpse of a lottery and an unwanted prize.[39] All of these visions would of course come true. In Cheiro's telling, the familiar tale develops some extra elaborations. There is direct testimony from Douglas Murray, unpacking the case back in London: 'As I looked into the carved face of the Priestess on the outside of the mummy case, her eyes seemed to come to life, and I saw such a look of hate in them that my very blood seemed to turn to ice.'[40] It is also claimed that Douglas Murray gave the case to an unidentified but 'well-known literary woman', whose mother dies, fiancé runs away and pets go insane. The gift firmly returned to Douglas Murray, an Egyptologist friend examines the case, and soon afterwards takes an apparently accidental overdose of chloral. In the British Museum, sinister events multiply. 'It was rumoured that some unaccountable thing happened to anyone who attempted any drawing or sketch of this remarkable-looking mummy case.' A 'well-known artist' had made four attempts, Cheiro claimed, abandoning the plan after being trampled by a horse in Great Russell Street.[41]

1926 saw the posthumous publication of the autobiography of the famous romance writer Henry Rider Haggard. He had composed these volumes in 1912, but held them back. Perhaps because 1912 was within a year of Thomas Douglas Murray's death, it prompted Haggard to digress from the discussion of his own encounters with Egypt and tell the story of the curse on the British Museum mummy case as it was told to him by his friend Ernest Wallis Budge, the Keeper of Egyptian Antiquities at the Museum. 'One day in the autumn of 1889 a gentleman was shown into Dr Budge's room in the British Museum,' Haggard explained, with a photograph of the fated mummy case. As soon as Wallis Budge had agreed to take the item, the man broke out:

> 'Thank God you have taken the damned thing! There is an evil spirit in it which appears in its eyes. It was brought home by a friend of mine who was travelling with Douglas Murray, and he lost all his money when a bank in China broke, and his daughter died. I took the board into my house. The eyes frightened my daughter into a sickness. I moved it to another room, and it threw down a china cabinet and smashed a lot of Sèvres china in it . . .' With these words he left the room and Budge saw him no more.[42]

This figure is presumably a version of the shadowy Arthur Wheeler, on whom this account provides some rare detail. (Indeed, Wheeler has remained frustratingly elusive. There was an Arthur Francis Wheeler who attended at Oxford just after Thomas Douglas Murray, matriculating in 1865 and taking his degree at Brasenose College in 1869, but I have not been able to pick up his trace.)[43]

The writer on the occult Montague Summers repeated much of this material in his re-telling of the curse of the priestess in 1946, but added further detail about the fate of photographers. The spectral image on the photographic plate occurs in a Baker Street studio, where soon afterwards 'the photographer died suddenly and in the most mysterious circumstances.'[44] Later, once installed in the British Museum, an Egyptologist commissioned the Oxford Street photographers W. A. Mansell to photograph the case. The Mansell firm certainly held one of the official contracts to photograph and document objects in the Museum collection. A junior took charge of the mummy case: 'Upon the way home in the train, he injured by some unaccountable accident his thumb, and hurt it so badly that he was unable to use the right hand for a long time. When he reached home he found that one of his children had fallen through a glass frame and was suffering from severe shock.'[45]

These anecdotes perpetuate, elaborate and legitimate the circulation of rumour, because any form of record of the Priestess by writing, drawing, or photography apparently awakes malefic intent. It is safest, it would seem, to *gossip*, because this exists below the threshold of public discourse or representation and the curse seemingly cannot trace the labyrinthine pathways of gossip to any punishable source.

Nevertheless, and despite his appearance in Haggard's account as a happy contributor to this circulation, Ernest Wallis Budge, Keeper of the Egyptian Rooms, did his best to stamp on these rumours. Part of the onerous duties of the Keeper was to respond to hundreds of queries from the public, often demanding opinions on items brought back from Egypt, or for personal introductions to the Museum collections. Every time the story of the Priestess of Amen-Ra was relayed in the press, Wallis Budge's postbag bulged with requests for his opinion. This became particularly acute in 1909. Cuttings came in from all over the world, with requests for an authoritative judgment about the Priestess of Amen-Ra. 'I do not believe in the mystery but suppose it had some origin,' one correspondent wrote from Ireland. 'I have seen you open a mummy in the museum and your book on the mummy is most interesting. You are the best authority on the subject and hope you will excuse my troubling you.'[46] Several were well meaning warnings of danger, suggesting that the priestess be returned to her resting place. There was an anxious plea from a visiting Serb, and a note on behalf of 'a group of French clerks': 'I respectfully beg to suggest in the general concern, this Mummy should be carried back to her temple in Egypt when she should never have been sent away in foreign countries. Although I am not at all superstitious, I think this would be the best way to give satisfaction.'[47]

Wallis Budge's responses to these queries are only patchily preserved (although he was an early convert to taking carbon copies of his typed letters). In March 1909, for instance, he offered a measured statement of the extent of his knowledge of the mummy case to a titled lady, explaining that 'The mummy board was brought here in 1886 by Mr Wheeler. I received it from him and wrote the label for it.' He had nothing to say about its career before arriving in the Museum: 'The alleged mishaps to the original purchaser and his family rest on the authority of Mr Douglas Murray.' He regarded the spectral image on the photograph of the case to be a fake, however, and knew of only one death of a Museum commissaire who had worked in the Egyptian Rooms. He had been aged 72, and died of a stroke. Bertram Fletcher Robinson's typhoid fever had taken, in Wallis Budge's view, a familiar course of decline.[48] By the end of the year, Wallis Budge's assistant was drafted in to write responses to queries about 22542. 'So far as I am aware,' another inquirer was told, 'there is no intention of removing it from exhibition. I ought perhaps to add that no credence is attached here to the fanciful stories told about the object.'[49]

Wallis Budge was not just bothered by personal notes, however. The London Bureau of the *Chicago Daily News* was urgently in contact, sending a telegram to 'The Chief of the Mummy Section' to ask 'Is there any glimmering of truth in the attached cutting?'[50] It must have been particularly galling to receive a query from the *Al-Muktataf* newspaper in Cairo, seeking confirmation on the circulation of superstitious beliefs in the imperial centre: 'Is there any foundation for the story of the mummy of the Egyptian priestess in the British Museum related in the "Express" on the authority of the late Fletcher Robinson?'[51] The office of the editor of *The Times* also requested clarification following Stead's publication of the curse story. 'If you would kindly let me know what credence to attach to this statement. Of course, I shall treat your answer as confidential.'[52] Reports that the British Museum had withdrawn 22542 from display prompted Wallis Budge to prepare a mimeographed point-by-point rebuttal.

> The man who helped to carry the case in met with *no* accident.
>
> The cover was photographed for Mr Fletcher Robinson by Mr Mansell, but the camera was *not* smashed and the face of Mr. Batt, the operator, was *not* cut. I was present at the time…
>
> The story of the priestess for whom the cover was made *cannot be written*, for we know nothing about it, not even her name!
>
> The statement that the cover is to be removed from the case is wholly untrue. I have not even heard the rumour, and had the authorities been meditating any such thing I, as Keeper of the Department, would naturally have heard of it.[53]

Meanwhile, for all his apparent exasperation, Wallis Budge collected an envelope of press cuttings relating to the curse in his department, marked in his handwriting 'Mummy Coffin of Priestess of Amen-Ra'. Mostly undated and unsourced, these record further elaborations of the curse. Under the headline, 'Curse of a Mummy', one cutting reports that 'superstitious persons will find secret satisfaction in the latest chapter – now to be told – of the story of misadventure and death that is associated with the curious Egyptian coffin lid.' Whilst the 'scientific professors' of the Museum 'naturally scoff', the story reported the recent suicide of an unnamed scientist who had studied the coffin. The reporter prefers to take the side of the 'Museum attendants, who avoid the priestess' corner as if it were infected with the plague.' A French article about 'La Momie Fatale' records 'la néfaste influence' of the object, with 'les yeux immenses et l'expression diabolique.' A full-page splash of the *American Examiner* from September 1909, meanwhile, is dominated by a double exposure of the coffin lid with a sexy show-girl, under the headline 'That 3000 Year Old *Hoodoo* Wins! At last the misbehaving spirit of the Egyptian Priestess of Amen-Ra has frightened the British Museum directors into hiding the mummy-case from vulgar eyes.' In this iteration of the story, the nameless woman has become Princess Hetare, daughter of Amen-Hotep III who was killed for her sacrilegious worship of Aten by the priesthood of Amen-Ra. It was they who 'decreed that trouble and woe should pursue her through all eternity'. The malignant mummy caused one man to lose an arm, but also, somehow, prompted another four shootings in a suspiciously American-sounding 'street brawl'. One of the carriers of the case to the British Museum also met with a nasty end, run over by a train and cut in half. The envelope, perhaps understandably, contains another typewritten rebuttal by Wallis Budge, this time from the 1930s, which seems to be his last statement on the matter.

In his 1920 autobiography, Wallis Budge recalled his personal dealings with Stead and Douglas Murray. They had asked for permission to hold a séance, but Wallis Budge drew the line at psychical research in the Egyptian Rooms. In the midst of a robust defence of the continued export of Ancient Egyptian artefacts and remains to England from incompetent and superstitious Arabs, Wallis Budge observed

> in passing that many distinguished psychical men have visited the mummies in the British Museum for other than archaeological purposes, and among these may be mentioned Mr. Douglas Murray and Mr. Stead. These gentlemen used to say that they could distinguish between the different 'spirit personalities' which they alleged were present in the First Egyptian Room, and declared that they were able to hold intercourse with them... They were convinced that the mummies in that room were visited nightly by the souls who had lived in them on earth, and they were anxious to obtain permission to make arrangements to pass a night in the mummy rooms, so that they might converse with the souls.[54]

Wallis Budge brushed over whether he had refused their request to invite 'several "first-class mediumistic persons"' into the museum overnight, perhaps prompting later rumours in the 1920s that an exorcism had been conducted in the Egyptian Rooms. Meanwhile, Thomas Douglas Murray's relation to 22542 (called the 'haunted mummy' by Wallis Budge) was reduced to a footnote.

Wallis Budge confirmed that Douglas Murray had bought the case later presented to the Museum by Arthur Wheeler. 'The board came to the British Museum with an evil reputation for bringing down calamity, disease and disaster on everyone connected with it.' Wallis Budge gestured vaguely at stories about the case that 'have taken such a hold on the imagination of a certain section of the public that contradiction is in vain.'[55] Wallis Budge returned to a dismissal of these tales again in 1934, declaring that 'the responsible parties' for the whole farrago of the unlucky mummy 'were Mr Douglas Murray and Mr W. T. Stead, both in their time notable figures in psychic circles'. He claimed that they attached the story to 'Mr Wheeler's mummy-case' only *after* they had visited it in the Egyptian Rooms.[56]

Yet the Correspondence files reveal that Wallis Budge knew Douglas Murray and his story very well, the two men meeting and corresponding fairly regularly between 1899 and 1910. In 1904, Wallis Budge spent an evening with Douglas Murray's private dining circle, the Ghost Club. Douglas Murray's notes include invitations to Wallis Budge to join soirées at his townhouse, as well as arrangements to introduce visitors such as the Countess de Contardone, Mrs Gerald Wellesley and Lady Hunter and the celebrated actress Mrs Patrick Campbell to the Keeper of Egyptian Antiquities, after Douglas Murray had chaperoned them to the Egyptian Rooms to view the notorious mummy case.[57] In 1900, he sent Wallis Budge the famous spirit photograph of the mummy case. 'The photo is genuine, negative and print both untouched,' he tried to persuade the Keeper.[58] Later that year, he asked Wallis Budge: 'Can you discover if there is any curse on those who moved the mummy from its resting place – with reference to the mummy of which I sent you a photo. There have been odd statements by Mme Blavatsky and others as to the penalties connected with all those who had to do with its transfer from Luxor.'[59] Wallis Budge knew that Douglas Murray was no latecomer to the story of the Priestess of Amen-Ra.

There is little evidence of much contact between W. T. Stead and Wallis Budge. Stead wrote to the Keeper in 1909, enclosing a letter of introduction written by Douglas Murray, then wintering in the Riviera. Stead respectfully announced that 'I shall be very glad to wait upon you any time that may be most convenient to you.'[60] This means that they had not met before, and the meeting was likely to confirm details of the mummy's curse that Stead was shortly to publish. There is no surviving response or record of a meeting and certainly no evidence that Stead's apparent request to commune with the Egyptian spirits overnight was granted. However, Stead knew Thomas Douglas Murray well. They both moved in the same circles of psychical and spiritualist investigators. Stead's monthly *Review of Reviews* had chosen Murray's biography of Joan of Arc as its 'Book of the Month' in September 1902, long before Stead published the article that told his friend's curse story in all its chilling detail. Of the victims of the priestess, Stead proclaimed in his article relaying the tale, 'One of these is personal friend of my own. I had a letter from him this very day.' After a dramatic pause, he added: 'It was written with his left hand.'[61]

The connection of Stead to the unlucky mummy in the British Museum was to give the priestess perhaps the greatest single exercise of her curse.

When the RMS *Titanic* sank on her maiden voyage in 1912, Stead was the most famous Englishman on the boat. The *Review of Reviews* recorded that 'in Oxford Street at midday when the loss of the *Titanic* was certain, the only name I heard mentioned by the groups on the pavement was his.'[62] The obituaries reflected whilst he was 'one of the best known personages of the day...he would probably have made an even greater political mark if he had not dabbled in spiritualism.'[63] Nevertheless, Stead came to embody a model of quiet English heroism and Christian stoicism on the *Titanic*. In the last hours of the boat he was reported as giving up his lifebelt and his place in the lifeboats, and exhorting the orchestra to a final rendition of 'Nearer My God to Thee'. Stead was serene in his confidence in the afterlife, from which, indeed, he would soon confidently begin to pronounce through many mediums around the world within hours of his death.[64]

There was intense interest in, and many contradictory reports about, Stead's last hours.[65] One of his dining companions, the lawyer Frederick Seward, reported that

> Mr. Stead talked much of spiritualism, thought transference and the occult...He told a story of a mummy case in the British Museum, which, he said, had had amazing adventures, but which punished with great calamities any person who wrote its story. He told of one person after another, who, he said, had come to grief after writing the story, and added that, although he knew it, he would never write it.[66]

Stead had perhaps forgotten that he had actually already published the story of the priestess. But he did remember the fate of Fletcher Robinson, and his emphasis on the dangers of *writing* the story once again foregrounds the role of rumour. Lower down the hierarchy of knowledge, Stead apparently thought that merely gossiping was safe. Nevertheless, this report of Stead's last conversation was to prompt the rumour that the mummy case was *itself* on board the *Titanic*. The British Museum, allegedly, had decided to be rid of the accursed object and had sold it either to a New York museum or a millionaire collector. This rumour is mentioned in passing by Goodrich-Freer, and Wallis Budge evidently knew of it, since in his last rebuttal of the rumours before his death he asserted: 'I did not sell the cover to an American. The cover never went on the *Titanic*. It never went to America...and it is still in the first room in the British Museum, bearing the number 22542.'[67]

Despite this, the mummy has become intertwined with the fate of the *Titanic* as the mythic significance of the sinking has grown. Philipp Vandenberg enthusiastically asserts the presence of a mummy belonging to a Lord Canterville on the *Titanic*. 'The mummy was encased in a wooden crate and, because of its great value, had not been placed in the hold of the *Titanic* but behind the command bridge... Did Captain Swain, too, look into those fatal radiant eyes?'[68] An addendum to the *Titanic* story has the mummy case somehow surviving the sinking and arriving in America only to cause sufficient havoc to be shipped back to England in 1914. It was in the hold of the *Empress of Ireland,* which sank in the St Lawrence River with the loss of 1029 lives. 'Deciding it best to send the mummy back to Egypt,' a recent deadpan account further elaborates, 'the millionaire then shipped it on the *Lusitania,* which was sunk by a German torpedo in 1915, taking 1198 lives with it.'[69]

These are minor losses, however, compared to the rumour that the academic Egyptologist Margaret Murray (no relation) claimed that she invented merely to exploit the credulity of a professor and practising occultist at University College London. In Margaret Murray's tale, after 22542 was rescued from the *Empress of Ireland,* 'the mummy-case was then sold by auction, was bought by a German, who presented it to the Kaiser, and it caused the war.'[70] In these last additions to the rumour network, the grasp of the priestess stretches out from the Egyptian Rooms, her wrath achieving world-historical levels. Margaret Murray claimed that she wanted to 'make a strong protest against the absurd stories of the occult practices of Egyptian objects as well as the wild tales of curses,' but it has to be said that inventing further rumours about the Priestess of Amen-Ra is a distinctly odd way of going about debunking myths. Rumours are difficult to negate, and they readily incorporate their negations. Murray's inventions simply became part of the mutating story.[71]

As early as 1938, artefact 22542 was being used as 'an excellent example of how myth is manufactured. Thousands of people are vaguely familiar with the story and implicitly believe what they have heard. Very often their accounts are almost unrecognisable, so violent are the distortions which a legend will suffer in transmission.'[72] In almost perfect illustration of this observation, it is worth quoting at length a re-telling from 1993, which exemplifies how the details of the British Museum mummy have become fused with a myriad other stories:

> There is a persistent rumour in Egypt that Hatshepsut left behind an evil curse on anyone who despoiled her grave or attempted to remove its contents from the shores of the Nile... In 1910, the British Egyptologist Douglass Murray [*sic*] is said to have been among the next to feel the curse. An American treasure hunter approached him in Cairo, offering for sale one of several portions of Hatshepsut's multilayered mummy case. The American died before he could cash Murray's check. Three days later, Murray's gun exploded, blowing off his right hand... En

route to England with the sarcophagus, he received word via wireless telegraph that two of his closest friends and two of his servants had died suddenly. Upon his arrival in England, he began to feel superstitious, and left Hatshepsut's case in the house of a girlfriend who had taken a fancy to it. The girlfriend soon came down with a mysterious wasting disease. Then her mother died suddenly. Her lawyer delivered the sarcophagus back to Murray, who promptly unloaded it on the British Museum. The British Museum already had more sarcophagi than it needed. Not so, the American Museum of Natural History in New York; so a trade was arranged for Montana dinosaur bones. Before the deal was complete, the British Museum's director of Egyptology and his photographer were dead... The curators loaded the sarcophagus into a crate and saw it lowered into the hold of a ship. And on April 10 1912, the ship sailed – Southampton to New York. Hatshepsut departed for America on the Titanic.[73]

Whilst some elements rigidly survive, the *Titanic* punch line forces Pellegrino to erase sixty years from the timeline. Thomas Douglas Murray resurfaces, at once updated and oddly merged with Frederick Douglass, the slave abolitionist. A nameless priestess won't do, either, and needs to be fused with named royalty. The tomb of the female pharaoh Hatshepsut had been discovered by Howard Carter with much publicity in 1902. The anomalous queen pharaoh was the model for menacing Queen Tera in Bram Stoker's *Jewel of the Seven Stars*, thus allowing key curse stories to resonate once more across factual and fictional discourse.

Fragments of these different sources have since been combined and recombined on internet sites in a delirium of de-sourced cut and paste text.[74] Sceptics tend to transmit a version of the story without comment, just as much as enthusiastic advocates. But no one has really thought to ask: who was Thomas Douglas Murray? How much of his story is based in fact and how much is entirely fantastic? What was it about him that made him such an exemplary conduit for curse narratives in the Edwardian period?

Thomas Douglas Murray was born in 1841, eldest son of Thomas Boyles Murray (1798–1860), prebendary of St Paul's and rector of St Dunstan's in the East. His mother, Helen Douglas, was daughter of Major General Sir William Douglas, who had commanded English troops in the Irish Rebellion of 1798. The family lived in Brunswick Square, Bloomsbury. His father wrote several church histories, was active in the Society for Promoting Christian Knowledge, was a member of the Society of Antiquaries, and also published the pamphlet poem *A Day in Crystal Palace*. He left a very modest sum to his widow, but his three sons were all to become wealthy gentlemen. Henry Boyles Murray (1843–1910) went to Marlborough before buying a commission in the 84th (York and Lancaster) Regiment of Foot in 1861. He rose to Captain, but sold his commission in 1868, after which he devoted himself to a lifetime collecting modestly in the decorative arts. He left his collection to the Victoria and Albert

Museum in 1910. Although, somewhat tragically, the expert curators of the various divisions of the V&A found this collection worthless, many of the best pieces being of poor quality or fakes, it was accepted because he also left them £50 000 to establish the 'Captain H. B. Murray Bequest'. The interest on the capital was soon used to buy valuable items from the German and Dutch Renaissance.[75] Charles Wyndham Murray (1844–1928) also went to Marlborough and entered the army as an officer in the Gloucestershire Regiment. Unlike his brother, Wyndham Murray went on to have a distinguished military career, serving during the Zulu War in South Africa in 1879 and in the occupation of Egypt in 1882, where he was wounded at the legendary battle of Tel-el-Kebir. He also spent a year in the war of nerves with the Boers and Germans in Bechuanaland in 1884, where he became friends with Cecil Rhodes and proudly assisted in the annexations that would help the formation of Rhodesia. He was promoted to Colonel but resigned his commission in 1888, and in 1892 decided to campaign for the parliamentary seat in Bath on the spur of the moment and 'without the slightest knowledge of anything connected with that pursuit'.[76] He remained the Tory MP until 1906. After nearly twenty years in the ceremonial Royal Bodyguard, he was knighted in 1917 and wrote his memoirs for strictly private family circulation in 1925.

In contrast to his brothers, the life of Thomas Douglas Murray has been relatively undocumented, yet he left traces in bewilderingly diverse aspects of Victorian London life. He was educated at St Paul's School, then at Rugby public school between 1858 and 1860, before entering Exeter College in Oxford. He received his degree in 1864. He was at Exeter College at the same time as Albert Basil Orme Wilberforce, the youngest son of Samuel Wilberforce who had famously clashed with Thomas Huxley over Darwin's theory of evolution in 1860. They became lifelong friends and Douglas Murray named Albert Wilberforce, later Chaplain to the House of Commons and author of *There is No Death*, as his executor. Douglas Murray entered Lincoln's Inn for legal training and was called to the bar in 1866, but there is no record of him ever practising as a barrister at law. Instead, he appeared to dabble in numerous artistic and gentlemanly pursuits. He married Anne Hodgson in 1868; she was formally presented to Queen Victoria at court in 1870. They had two children, Frank Wyndham Sholto Douglas Murray, who rose to the level of Captain in the army like his uncle, and Annie Mabel Murray.[77] Douglas Murray owned property in Wiltshire, but rented several addresses in the fashionable parts of London, including an imposing mansion at 34 Portland Place. He engaged in field sports, including shooting, fishing and riding hacks, for which he won prizes at the Islington Agricultural Show in 1871 and 1872. These shows were noted as one of 'the largest assemblies of the wealthy and the high-born' of the season.[78] He was first elected to the Royal Geographical Society in 1870 and re-elected in 1890 and 1894. In 1880, Douglas Murray became the Honorary Secretary for the

Frank Buckland Memorial Fund. Buckland was a surgeon who became a full-time journalist and proprietor of *Land and Water*, and was Britain's leading authority on fishing and fisheries; his extensive natural history collection was left to the South Kensington Museum. His memorial committee met frequently at Douglas Murray's house.[79]

The personal connection to Buckland gave Douglas Murray the chance to write a few signed travel notes from Egypt in the late 1860s, although many of the journal contributions were unsigned so it is difficult to know how seriously Douglas Murray dallied with journalism. He appeared to be only a gentleman amateur at writing, producing two books much later in life: a biography of the imperial adventurer Sir Samuel Baker co-written with A. Silva White in 1894 and a biography of Jeanne d'Arc in 1902, largely a translation of documents of her trial, which he presented in person to Pope Pius X at a private audience. It was later used by George Bernard Shaw as source material for *Saint Joan*.

The Douglas Murrays were great socialites: his surviving letters show close friendships with aristocrats and a penchant for chaperoning beautiful women about town and for friendship with men concerned with domestic and colonial government. In the arts world, Douglas Murray knew the painters John Millais, William Blake Richmond and James Whistler (there is a comical letter from Douglas Murray congratulating Whistler on his 'Ten O'Clock' lecture but suggesting publication, as many could not hear in the crowded hall).[80] One of Millais's protégés, the painter Louise Jopling, remembered that 'One of the houses that gave the best entertainment in the seventies and eighties was that of Mr and Mrs Douglas Murray, who lived in Portland Place. There one met everybody who was somebody – artists, musicians, actors and actresses, and all those of the beau-monde who affected artistic and Bohemian society.'[81] We have already encountered Douglas Murray's attempts to introduce the leading actress of the day, Mrs Patrick Campbell, to the mummy case. The Douglas Murrays held balls whose guests were recorded in the society pages of *The Times* or *John Bull*; even the cancellation of Mrs Douglas Murray's reception in Portland Place for the return of the national hero Henry Stanley from darkest Africa in 1890 was carried in the press.[82]

The connection to Stanley spoke to Douglas Murray's interest in travel and Empire. His attendance at lectures and meetings of the Royal Geographical Society tended towards African subjects. He was an associate of Sir William Mackinnon, wealthy owner of the British India shipping line, who formed the British East Africa Association in the 1880s in an attempt to colonize the interior of the East African coast, raising money for the effort that the British government seemed reluctant to commit. When Douglas Murray set out to navigate the world in 1890 via Italy, India, Burma, China and America, 'taking our daughter to see something of the world,' he asked Mackinnon for letters of introduction along the route.[83] At a difficult time, he suggested to Mackinnon that he could agitate on behalf of H. M. Stanley through his friendship with Sir Leslie Stephen, leading editor and literary intellectual. He knew Sir Harry Johnston, explorer and colonial governor and one of the architects of the Cape to Cairo strategy formulated by Lord Salisbury for the British Empire in Africa in the 1880s and 1890s. He was also a friend of Sir Samuel Baker, the celebrated explorer who discovered the source of the White Nile in 1865, and who then went on to carve out the province of Equatoria south of Egypt in the Sudan, all in the name of the Christian mission to suppress the slave trade. Baker was later the subject of a 'Splendid Lives' treatment to inspire boys to patriotic derring-do at the edges of Empire, and perhaps it was the lionizing of Baker that prompted Thomas Douglas Murray to travel to Egypt once he completed his studies in Oxford in 1865. Douglas Murray's memoir of the great man appeared in 1895.[84]

Another link is opened up by Douglas Murray's friendship with Henry Stanley. Stanley married Dorothy Tennant in July 1890, a ceremony that Mrs Douglas Murray and her daughter attended. Dorothy was one of the beautiful Tennant sisters, their mother a society hostess who knew Henry James, Flaubert and other leading artists of the day.[85] Dorothy Tennant's sister, Eveleen, became an accomplished society photographer (she had been photographed as a child by the photographic pioneer Julia Margaret Cameron). Eveleen married Frederic Myers, the poet and psychologist who was the driving force behind the Society of Psychical Research (SPR), which was established in 1882. The SPR was a group of earnest seekers after spiritual truth, eminent Cambridge-educated men who are often taken as emblematic figures of Victorian crisis, since they comprehended the full effects of the new findings of the biological and physical sciences on traditional faith, and were mostly pained and reluctant agnostics as a result, unable to continue with Christian belief but unwilling to give it up. Men like Myers and the respected Cambridge professor of philosophy Henry Sidgwick responded to the crisis induced by scientific naturalism by using the techniques of empirical scientific research in an attempt to 'prove' the existence of the soul or spirit, or the survival of some aspect of the personality after bodily death. Perhaps the new experimental sciences could 'explain' the supernatural effects of ghosts, visions of the dead, haunted houses or telepathy (a term Myers coined in 1882). In public, these researchers did their best to present the SPR as an august scientific institution, without predisposed belief, although many like Myers privately believed that the mediums they investigated were in contact with the spirits of the dead. The SPR included leading figures of the establishment amongst its members.[86] Many, keen to preserve their respectability and to avoid any association with the occult, kept their spiritualist beliefs very private and did not join such a public project. Myers, fervently publicizing his researches and tirelessly pushing the project of psychical research, often had his character questioned. Thomas Douglas Murray, an ardent spiritualist in later life, knew Myers but was one of those who kept very quiet about his beliefs. Even so, Douglas Murray's intimate association with leading spiritualist believers and psychical researchers surely explains how the story of the mummy curse began to circulate as a rumour in London society in the late Victorian and Edwardian period.

In 1882, the same year that the SPR was founded, a dining club was established by the spiritualist writer and medium the Reverend William Stainton Moses and the occultist Alfred Alaric Watts. It was called the Ghost Club (not to be confused with the better-known Cambridge Ghost Club that had been formed in 1862). It was started, as a brief history of the Club outlines, 'expressly so that persons who might object to any general publication of their experiences might be encouraged to relate them at the Ghost Club in strictest confidence.'[87] It was also decidedly a *club* not a society: 'We propose rigidly to confine ourselves to Clubbable men,' Stainton Moses explained.[88] There was some overlap with Masonic rules here, but although Douglas Murray was a Mason, he was not active in those circles. They met once a month for dinner, for many years at the Maison Jules restaurant in Jermyn Street or in Pagani's in Great Portland Street, before discussing their supernatural experiences over cigars. This was the rule: 'That every member shall, from his own personal knowledge, or from some accredited testimony, produce an original Ghost Story, or some psychological experience of interest or instruction, once during each year.'[89] Initially, the Club had ten members, all men (women were only admitted as guests in 1929). 'Brother Ghosts' who joined were able, with the permission of their fellow diners, to ask non-members to attend provided that they were willing to tell a good story. Thomas Douglas Murray was elected to the Brotherhood of the Ghost Club in May 1896, and became president of the Club between 1898 and 1900. He was active in the Club for over a decade and last attended in November 1910, in the last year of his life.

Membership of the Ghost Club was dominated by the middle-class elite of Christian spiritualism, rather than the plebeian, dissenting and radical version that took hold in working-class communities, particularly in the north of England.[90] Alfred Alaric Watts was married to the daughter of William and Mary Howitt, leading London spiritualists. Dr Stanhope Speer, a leading supporter of spiritualist research, host of many séances at his town house, and employer of Stainton Moses, was a founding member. Alfred Sinnett, who helped introduce theosophy and Indian mysticism to England, attended from the start. The barrister and leading spiritualist advocate Charles Massey, the lawyer who had defended the medium Henry Slade over a charge of making illicit gains by fortune-telling in a famous trial in 1876, was in regular attendance. The prominent diplomat and spiritualist convert Laurence Oliphant also joined early. The scientist Sir William Crookes became the leading light of the Club after the deaths of Stainton Moses in 1892 and Alaric Watts in 1901. In 1911, the poet and mystic William Butler Yeats was elected to replace the recently deceased Thomas Douglas Murray and attended regularly, updating his Brother Ghosts on contacts with his spirit guide Leo Africanus. The occasional guests could be impressive, and it was Douglas Murray who did his best to involve prominent society figures. He invited Sir Harry Johnston, who was elected a member in 1903. Henry Stanley was his guest in March 1903, Ernest Wallis Budge in June 1904, the eminent painter Sir William Blake Richmond in 1905 and journalist William Stead in January 1909. Sir Arthur Conan Doyle attended later, in 1923.

The first rule of the Ghost Club was never to talk about the Ghost Club. They took secrecy very seriously; a severe internal inquiry was conducted when a column in *The Observer* mentioned the Club in passing, in slightly mocking terms.[91] This was the only public breach into print of the private discussion about the supernatural promoted by the Club. There were good reasons for this circumspection. After Stainton Moses, the most prominent figure in the Club was the chemist Sir William Crookes. Crookes, a Fellow of the Royal Society and proprietor of the *Chemical News*, had amazed the scientific world by announcing in 1871 that he had scientifically measured and tested the existence of a new force in nature, which he called 'psychic force', that he believed was exercised by mediums in séances.[92] Many felt he had been duped by his test medium, the teenage girl Florence Cook. Crookes took many photographs of this medium and the spirit 'Katie King', whom Cook claimed she could manifest in full spirit body at dark séances. Crookes breathlessly reported in the spiritualist press of one séance where 'Katie never appeared to greater perfection, and for nearly two hours she walked about the room … On several occasions she took my arm when walking, and the impression conveyed to my mind that it was a living woman by my side, instead of a visitor from the other world.'[93] Crookes' apparent credulity made this one of the great scientific controversies of the age. The ridicule, and the damage to his chemical businesses, meant that Crookes soon stopped his public pronouncements on spiritualism for over twenty years, eventually climbing back to the respectable heights of the Presidency of the British Association for the Advancement of Science. The Ghost Club, of which he attended nearly every meeting for nearly twenty years, was a private outlet for his beliefs, and he was clearly enraged by a Brother Ghost blabbing to the press.

Amazingly, though, for all this secrecy, each meeting of the Club was meticulously minuted by a nominated secretary, and sixteen volumes of minutes with other materials were gifted to the British Library after the Club was wound up in 1936. To protect the reputations of surviving members, the material was embargoed for a further twenty-five years. Here, in the thousands of pages of handwritten minutes, is a detailed record of a crucial aspect of Thomas Douglas Murray's life in his later years. And there were several occasions when

Douglas Murray recounted the curse of the Priestess of Amen-Ra to his Brother Ghosts.

This means that we can compare these private accounts to the public record of Douglas Murray's association with Egypt. That connection began early, when he took the Nile tour soon after his graduation from Oxford. A brief biographical note in *Who Was Who* simply notes that Douglas Murray spent twelve winters in Egypt after 1866. This was during the height of the Belle Époque in Egypt, when French influence still dominated Cairo. The Khedive Ismail, the ruler installed by the Ottomans, glimpsed modernity at the International Exposition in Paris in 1867 and vowed to transform Egyptian society with huge and costly infrastructure projects, financed by European investors. In 1869, Empress Eugénie travelled to Egypt for the ceremonies to open the new Suez Canal, designed and built by her cousin, the visionary engineer Ferdinand de Lesseps. The cost of the entertainment was legendary – a new opera house was built (although Verdi's *Aida* was not quite ready to perform) and the Gezira Palace, constructed to receive Empress Eugénie, held lavish balls for the Europeans nightly throughout the winter season. Wealthy visitors struggled for berths in the most fashionable hotels and invitations to the celebrations. One irate traveller protested that 'it was not amusing, as there was such a mob of people, some of the roughest, the chief part of the rough element not being English, fortunately'.[94] Within six years, this bubble would burst, as Ismail defaulted on his loans. The Canal, which had cost £20 million to build, was purchased by the English for £4 million, Ismail was deposed, and the path to dual control by British and French banks, the Urabi revolt and eventual British occupation was set.[95]

Douglas Murray got to know Ferdinand de Lesseps; Wyndham Murray recalled that the engineer stayed with his brother whenever he travelled to London. This connection would have secured acquaintance with the elite of the diplomatic, military and Egyptological colony of the English and French in Egypt.

As a youthful traveller in Egypt, Douglas Murray's attitude tended decidedly more towards that of a tourist rather than an authoritative Egyptologist. This was conveyed in his series of travel notes on his journey up the Nile published in Frank Buckland's sporting weekly *Land and Water* in 1868 and 1869. Internal clues suggest that this was not the record of his first visit to Egypt, but the letters remain a relatively standard orientalist travel narrative about the discovery of the exotic East. His first dispatch compared the 'magnificence' of Thebes, 'the grandest ruins of the old Eastern world', with the 'demoralisation and misery as it now exists amongst the modern race', and described meeting 'dejected specimens of Arab life, natives despondent and broken' by corrupt misrule. Douglas Murray was open about suggesting that 'European energy and intellect' could revivify Egypt as 'the granary to the whole civilised world'.[96] This was entirely in line with the rhetoric of modernization adopted by the Western powers in Egypt. Douglas Murray's group left Cairo behind, travelling up the Nile in style, carrying a piano and a good wine cellar plus 'a few luxuries', and arriving at Thebes to a gun salute arranged by the Theban consul. They were focused on the possibilities of shooting 'many varieties of snipe, wild geese, ducks, quails and partridges', with a slim chance of 'bagging an alligator'.[97] They made the inevitable visit to Lady Duff Gordon, who was in the last year of her life and privately rather weary of her role as a tourist destination after the publication of her *Letters from Egypt*. Indeed, her letters at one point record her delight in shocking 'some European young men out shooting' with her familiarity with local Arab families, suggesting that Douglas Murray's group was rather typical.[98]

In terms of the ancient culture that surrounded them, Douglas Murray was anxious to portray the Arabs, rather than the Europeans, as the tomb raiders. As soon as they arrived in Thebes, the boat 'had been attacked by a crowd of natives, bringing various antiquities from the tombs.'[99] It was as if one stumbled across an already established economy which had always been there, rather than understanding oneself as the very *condition* of the illegal trade in antiquities, a neat piece of evasion. On Christmas day, they visited familiar points of reference – 'Belzoni's tomb', the fallen statue of Rameses, and then to the Valley of the Kings to see 'Harper's tomb'. This landscape struck Douglas Murray as 'fit scenery, sufficiently weird, silent and mysterious for the repose of Egypt's greatest dead.'[100] The four men on this part of the trip then travelled to the mummy pits 'where one may walk through rows of those dark brown Egyptians, swathed in their fine linen clothes … The vast charnel house into which we now descended was crawling with antiquities and alive with bats.' Douglas Murray shot seven of these 'perverse' creatures 'who beat their ill-omened wings in our faces.'[101] The adventurers survived the intense heat and a rock fall, and succeeded 'in tackling an Egyptian lady, who was carefully brought to light and solemnly unswathed.' The booty was a chignon and a mummified foot, which Douglas Murray claimed would be taken for a collection in England. Perhaps these were among the items presented to the British Museum by Wheeler's sister in 1889.

In this 1868–9 trip, Douglas Murray travelled as far up the Nile as Dendera, where the temples allowed him to reflect on the static and 'archaic simplicity' of Ancient Egyptian sculpture in contrast to the 'barbarous and narrow-minded prejudice' of the Islamic Arabs who destroyed or defaced what had survived.[102] He then returned to Thebes, where he called on the consul to concentrate on the matter in hand:

> As I was anxious to take back to England a good mummy, we at once proceeded
> to business, and agreed the next day to start with the consul's son to see the
> opening of a mummy case near Dayr el Bahree … However, before we left the
> consul's house, we were informed that there was something for our inspection

on the premises, and in an upstairs room was produced a very richly orna-mented mummy case with its mummy complete. This, Mustapha told us, he intended for the Prince of Wales on his visit to Thebes. Two cases enclosed the mummy, each elaborately painted and perfect in every respect...the eyes, com-posed of ivory with pupils of polished jet, gave great character and expression to the face...Raising the lid of the outer coffin, which was solid and very heavy, there appeared the more vivid colours and still finer workmanship of the second case, within which lay the body, as yet untouched...The hands and face of this inner coffin were delicately carved and painted a bright red in the likeness of a good-looking Egyptian.[103]

The rich details of this account already suggest a kind of coming into posses-sion, yet the story comes to an abrupt halt when Douglas Murray recalled the legal situation. 'Let it suffice that the mummy was perfect, and of beautiful finish, and might now have been in England but for an unfortunate rule that all antiquities, of any importance, in passing the customs, are forfeited.'[104] Unless there is an occlusion in this printed account, this is not the elusive moment of acquisition of the Priestess of Amen-Ra (which must, nevertheless, have been semi-legal at best, waved through on account of good connections). Instead, Douglas Murray was taken to a mummy pit and firmly relocated the problem-atic ethics of acquisition back with the Arabs. His guides 'extracted...an an-cient Egyptian lady of swarthy aspect and powerful aroma, whose chest the Arabs soon tore to pieces like ghouls, with fingers and nails, anxious to obtain some memento of the deceased one.'[105] A few piecemeal prizes, however, were gained from this expedition. For a figure so allegedly haunted, Douglas Murray showed very little sense of dread in picking through these 'mouldy and mil-dewed' mummies. The tour ended with a train journey from Cairo to Suez to visit the nearly completed Suez Canal, and sailing its length with 'my most kind and hospitable friend, M. de Lesseps.'[106]

Ada Goodrich-Freer used these published letters as a record of Douglas Mur-ray's fateful encounter with Egypt. She interpolates a different story in these travel notes, though, almost as if, between the lines, an occult narrative can be discerned. But these were not the notes of the journey during which Douglas Murray suffered such a life-threatening shooting accident. That had happened the year before. Douglas Murray's discretion about his misfortune in print was either gentlemanly fortitude but perhaps also something to do with embarrass-ment. A *Land and Water* editorial in 1868 had moralized on 'the respect which is due to the muzzle of a gun', and warned its readers to be careful following the fatal shooting accident of Captain Buckley.[107]

These are the only public notes written by Douglas Murray on Egypt that I have been able to find. For the Ghost Club, however, he told a rather different story. When Douglas Murray first attended, in 1894, his reputation as a man associated with supernatural vengeance was surely known by the Brother

Ghosts; sitting with them was a man bearing the physical wound that was the consequence of the curse. He avoided his own plight, however, and his requisite ghost story was about the religious painter James Tissot, whom he claimed was regularly visited by the spirit of 'his favourite model', whose identity had been confirmed by communications at a séance.[108] Once Douglas Murray was elected a full member in May 1896 (proposed by the founder, Alaric Watts), he became more forthcoming. In June, he dominated proceedings, revealing at great length the details of his séances with Ada Goodrich-Freer in which she had contacted the spirit of the explorer Sir Richard Burton.[109] Then, as an addendum, the minutes recorded:

> Bro. Murray mentioned that in 1866–7 he was up the Nile. On one occasion he had a dream which he related at breakfast. He dreamt he was in prison and was sentenced to be hanged. Expressing a preference for decapitation or being shot he was marched off to petition the governor that he might be shot. On this he awoke. On that day they went to the Pyramids, taking a gun which he had marked 'dangerous' – as it went off half-cock – and had put aside. Returning from the Pyramids, he slipped and the gun went off, shattering his right arm. He thought of his dream and commiserated with himself, as if the injured person were someone else, with such thoughts as 'What a very unfortunate thing for this young man, just as he was going into the Blues, too.' The dream had perhaps been given him as a preparation.[110]

There is no record of the reactions to this account. For the next few meetings, Douglas Murray reported on his dealings with the Preston Manor ghost in Brighton, apparently a good test of whether the famous spectre there might be laid to rest after a skeleton was discovered during building works and was given a proper burial. But Douglas Murray repeated the story of his premonitory Egyptian dream to the Ghost Club two years later, with a few more details:

> He dreamt that he was in Turkey, and was condemned to be hanged . . . The next day, while returning from a shooting expedition he accidentally shot himself in the wrist. He had however been strongly impressed by the dream, and had thought out the situation. He was therefore able to take the accident quite coolly and calmly, and he thought that this had in all probability saved his life, as he was some distance from medical aid.[111]

The focus of these accounts is strangely tangential and marked by a kind of traumatic dissociation. In another iteration of the incident to the Club, he emphasized that 'he did not think that the sufferer was himself. He was full of sympathy for the unfortunate victim, as for some one apart from himself.'[112] Douglas Murray's interest is in the premonitory dream, a favourite of psychical researchers, rather than in the dramatic content of the dream and subsequent events. Crucially, he does not appear to associate the incident with the purchase of the mummy case in Egypt; his unconscious locates the origin of the violence instead in a standard fantasy of oriental cruelty.

Nevertheless, peppered through the minutes, Douglas Murray periodically mentions his inquiries to the Egyptologists Ernest Wallis Budge and Flinders Petrie on matters relating to the 'spirit' beliefs of the Ancient Egyptians. 'The President [Douglas Murray] said that he had been told by Wallis Budge that the Ancient Egyptians believed that the statues of their ancestors facilitated communication with the departed.'[113] The next month, Douglas Murray reported: 'Wallace Budge [sic] said there was no trace in Egyptian lore of any believe [sic] that the spirit reappeared in the tomb.' When Douglas Murray was asked if the Keeper was 'unduly materialistic', he responded 'no; his tendencies were distinctly towards the occult.'[114] Later, Douglas Murray reported that 'Flinders Petrie had made careful inquiries among the Arabs as to any stories of ghostly appearances in the tomb, but without result.'[115] The context for these remarks is not always clear, but it is as if the Ghost Brotherhood were keen to hear more about their president's story.

The mention of Flinders Petrie finally prompted Douglas Murray to offer the Club his first account of the mummy case. His version reads like this:

> The President further related that when travelling in Egypt, he and his friends obtained two mummy cases, which were distributed by lot, and one of them fell to the share of A. F. W. From this time everything went wrong with him – He lost his money on the turf, then went to America, and invested in cotton land, where again he was unfortunate, and the misfortunes fell not only on himself but on every one of his near relatives, and eventually the family estates had to be sacrificed. The mummy case was eventually sent to the British Museum, and with the object of having the cartouche deciphered, a photograph was taken in the presence of A. F. W.'s sister. She asked the photographer whether he had ever found anything photographed upon the plate which had not been visible to the naked eye. He scoffed at the idea, but a few minutes after being in the dark room, he returned and pointed out the semblance of a human form, which appeared in the photograph, but was not visible on the mummy case. The photograph was sent to the gentleman who had promised to decipher it, and was returned by him a fortnight later. A few days afterwards he went down to his country house, and shot himself. The man who carried the cartouche to the photographer died a few weeks afterwards of brain fever, and the photographer himself died within two years.[116]

For Douglas Murray, all the misfortune lies with Wheeler. Indeed, just as he had dissociated himself from the accident, he often distanced himself from any link to 22542 in his letters to Wallis Budge. Urging Wallis Budge to find the time to meet Lady Hunter and Mrs Wellesley, for instance, he pleads: 'We want a talk on mummies – Tell them of the "Wheeler" mummy – whose photo came out with a human face and of the mummy whose eyes follow you about the room.'[117] When trying to arrange a date for Mrs Patrick Campbell to visit the Museum, Douglas Murray hopes Wallis Budge will show them the Egyptian curios, 'not forgetting the Blavatsky mummy case of revengeful fame.'[118] Either Douglas Murray was working unconsciously very hard to deny his association with the curse, or he genuinely did not understand himself to be its victim.

In November 1900, on spooky All Souls' Day, when the boundary between this and the other world is supposed to be at its thinnest, Brother Levander told the Club that he had seen Wallis Budge unroll a mummy at University College (an event that did take place in 1889), and had secured a piece of mummy wrapping that he had later introduced to a séance. 'The effect was startling – the medium seemed almost to take leave of her senses, and to be struggling violently against some obsession. He took away the mummy cloth and after she had recovered, she told him that the high-class Egyptian had been endeavouring to gain possession of her.'[119] In an addendum to this account, Douglas Murray updated the tale of the Wheeler curse. He recounted that he had visited the clairvoyant Mrs Montague with Miss Wheeler (perhaps Arthur Wheeler's daughter). The medium immediately grasped that they were 'in some way connected with a mummy' which has 'caused you a great deal of trouble'. The only way this could end, they were told was 'by one of you going to the King's Hall of the Great Pyramid, and there reciting the litany of the dead. Should you fail to accomplish this before the end of this year, dire disaster will overtake you both.' With a great dramatic sense, Thomas Douglas Murray, informed his fellows that it was not possible for him or Miss Wheeler to travel to Egypt in time and that 'they had decided to await events'.[120] Minutes can't convey the tone in which such accounts were delivered, and perhaps this was told with an All Souls' Eve ghost story gleam in the eye. The incident with Miss Wheeler was never mentioned again.

In 1904, Douglas Murray finally arranged, after much cajoling, for Ernest Wallis Budge to dine with the Ghost Club. The Keeper played a straight bat. He listened to Douglas Murray's re-narration of the story of the Priestess of Amen-Ra, and 'having been asked if anything had occurred since it had been placed in the British Museum, said nothing had occurred.'[121] He had encountered nothing supernatural in the Egyptian Rooms, even at night. Instead, he sidestepped the issue by relating beliefs and superstitions in Egypt. If Arabs intend to keep a mummy, he told them, 'they break off a toe or some other part, so that the spirit cannot walk about.'[122] He agreed with Sir William Blake Richmond about the appalling desecration of Ancient Egyptian sites. Then, in another sidestep, Wallis Budge fulfilled the terms of Club dinners by telling the story of the Walter Ingram mummy curse – the subject of the next chapter – in which he had played a tangential role. It did not dwell on the supernatural. Wallis Budge's lack of sympathy with the Club's shared spiritualist beliefs was not appreciated, and Douglas Murray was later forced to defend himself for inviting too many suspicious or sceptical guests. The Ghost Club was indeed turning more avowedly spiritualist, rather than open-minded on these matters; this was why Sir Harry Johnston tendered his resignation in July 1905.[123] Soon Vice-Admiral W. Usborne Moore was elected a member, a man who sent several letters to Wallis Budge demanding his opinion of a 'psychic portrait' of Cleopatra, produced by a medium in America.[124] The Club then began arranging séances before their dinner gatherings. The visiting spirits included the psychical researcher Frederic Myers and former club president Charles Massey. Douglas Murray also reported on encounters with the spirits of Colonel Burnaby and Herbert Stewart, two soldiers famously killed in Egypt in the disastrous attempt to rescue the Victorian hero General Gordon from the dastardly Muslim fanatics at the siege of Khartoum in 1885.[125]

As the rumour about the British Museum mummy curse grew in the new century, after Bertram Fletcher Robinson's *Daily Express* report in 1904, the Ghost Club now seemed to follow rather than shape its sinuous development. It was the theosophist Alfred Sinnett who informed the Brothers that 'the British Museum authorities had now boarded up the mummy case', a rumour widely reported in the press but which was quite untrue.[126] Sinnett counted eleven deaths associated with the curse, with yet more shenanigans involving hapless photographers, slightly garbled from earlier accounts. Douglas Murray was absent from this dinner, but Sinnett reminded the Club of the story, that 'Murray had not long possessed it before he lost the use of his arm.'[127] With more public circulation, Douglas Murray's already ambivalent ownership of the story got looser. 'The case originally contained the mummy of a girl, alleged to be the beloved of a black magician', Sinnett confidently elaborated. Nevertheless, rather brutally, Sinnett professed 'he could understand events happening to Murray who inadvertently caused the grave to be desecrated', but was bewildered why so many others were also affected.[128]

The last serious discussion of the mummy curse at the Ghost Club came after William Stead had been the guest diner in January 1909. Douglas Murray aided Stead at a séance with the mediums Mr and Mrs Tomson at about the same time.[129] In June of that year, Douglas Murray came to the Club to report that 'Mr W. T. Stead had asked his permission to write up this story.'[130] This may have been in deference to Club rules of confidentiality, given William Crookes' anger at leaks to the press about their dealings. In May 1909, Stead had opened 'Julia's Bureau', named after his long-term spirit contact, Julia. This project was to be a spiritualist 'switch-board' which would act as a bridge for contacts between the living and the dead.[131] Douglas Murray reported to the Club that Stead had already asked Julia's opinion of the dangers of being contaminated by the mummy curse if the story was written down. Julia's advice proved carefully ambivalent: 'What is true is that there is a certain danger attending the writing of anything about her [the priestess]. Yet on the other hand you might be able to break the spell and help her to escape from the self-created prison in which she lives.'[132] This was to prove enough for Stead, who published the tale. However, Sinnett was not impressed, believing that it was not the priestess but an 'elemental' that was the cause of the trouble, 'whose sole duty it was to damage anybody with whom it came into contact, such elemental being of low intelligence, and its actions almost mechanical.'[133] Here the shape of the shuffling mummy, taking indifferent revenge on the modern world, begins to emerge out of the chrysalis of Douglas Murray's story. Events would bolster Sinnett's sense of an exorbitant revenge. As we know, Stead published Douglas Murray's story around the world in 1909, anonymizing his friend's fate. Stead then died on the *Titanic* three years later. Although dead, he was soon back in contact with spiritualist friends. When the boat sank, however, the Club minutes only recorded 'Great regret at the death of W. T. Stead.' There was no recorded discussion of any association of Stead's death with the mummy curse.[134] Very soon, a new generation of members were dominant in the Ghost Club, and one senses from the minutes that the case of Douglas Murray rapidly dispersed into the world of general rumour. Brother Ghosts no longer had a special relationship with the Priestess of Amen-Ra.

The Ghost Club minutes provide a rare glimpse into the private, unguarded world of Victorian gentlemen. The era celebrated modernity and progress, but of course had many conservatives and counter-revolutionaries. But it is rare to find, even in the weird world of psychical research, a worldview so dictated by magical thinking as that of the Ghost Club. Yet this was not confined to the closed circle of the members: Douglas Murray and the others continually expand their anecdotal range into the heart of the establishment. Sympathetic lords and ladies, artists and diplomats are constantly used for source material. The Club hears rumours that even the august man of science Sir Richard Owen has experienced a haunting and Douglas Murray reported from the librarian of Windsor Castle on the ghostly appearance of Queen Elizabeth I, but 'that orders had been given from a high quarter to keep silent about the occurrence'.[135] Sir Henry Stanley was happy to discuss his telepathic powers in darkest Africa, 'to read the mind of the native, even in cases where he could not speak the language.' Sir Harry Johnston, a sceptic who soon resigned from the Club, entirely concurred, 'and said he had quite a reputation for it amongst the natives'.[136] This is magical thinking, but functional, adaptive, reasoned out by reasonable men who exerted considerable social and political power.

There is, however, a profound disconnection between the rich private resource of the Ghost Club minutes and the public record. The trace of Douglas Murray in public discourse conceals the cursed figure of rumour behind the respectable behaviour of a London gentleman. Many of these activities were still connected to questions of Egypt and Empire, however, suggesting a continuity and coherence to his life.

Douglas Murray's serious interest in Egyptology was evidenced in the provision in his will to set up a travelling scholarship in the Department of Egyptology at University College London. It still exists, although awarded infrequently owing to the small capital involved. This £200 gift was strictly 'payable only in the event of Mr Flinders Petrie being still connected with the said College at the time of my decease and still carrying out the excavations in Egypt therewith.'[137] Petrie, like Wallis Budge, was a poor scholar who was considered a prodigy and was given patronage by private benefactors interested in archaeology. He first travelled to Egypt to survey the pyramids in 1880 and became an archaeologist for the Egyptian Exploration Fund when it was set up by Amelia Edwards after 1882. Petrie also sketched a racial typology from Ancient Egyptian reliefs for the eugenicist Francis Galton in 1887. Amelia Edwards left a modest sum to establish a Chair in Egyptology at University College in 1892, with enough conditions to ensure that Petrie was the only candidate. From this position, Petrie trained many subsequent field archaeologists: 'He found archaeology in Egypt a treasure hunt; he left it a science.'[138] Douglas Murray's explicit attachment of the money to Petrie might suggest that he was embroiled in the professional rivalries among the institutions of the nascent science of Egyptology. The British Museum disliked the establishment of the Egyptian Exploration Fund, run as it was by enthusiastic amateurs with a commitment to searching for Biblical truths of the Exodus. But Petrie was also scandalized by Wallis Budge's brazen smuggling activities and privately referred to him as 'Bugbear'. Part of Wallis Budge's attempts to undermine Petrie was consistently to term Douglas Murray an 'associate' of Petrie, a man who had absolutely no patience with supernaturalism.[139]

Douglas Murray's interest in Empire also extended to the Far East, perhaps because the Chinese Embassy was one of his neighbours in Portland Place, although the fashion for Japonnais style was at its peak in the 1870s too. The weird exoticism of the Chinese Ambassadress visiting the Douglas Murrays was remembered by Louise Jopling. 'No mere man was allowed to look upon the face of "The Tottering Lily", as she was called. The great lady hobbled in, on the smallest feet one had ever seen...I don't think she spoke any English, but her manners were charming.'[140]

This Chinese connection prompted the Douglas Murrays to become importers and breeders of Pekingese dogs. In 1891, when they were in Canton as part of their world trip, the Consul General Sir Chaloner Alabaster presented the Douglas Murrays with a Pekingese puppy, a great rarity outside the palace grounds of the Emperor. According to Lillian Smythe, the Pekingese were meant to represent the god Fo, the protector of faith, and thus were the embodiment of the Chinese Emperor. It was therefore immensely symbolic that when English soldiers commanded by Lord Elgin notoriously looted and destroyed the Summer Palace of the Emperor of China in 1860, Queen Victoria had been presented with the first Pekingese dog to reach England – a dog that was sensitively named Lootie.[141] The Douglas Murrays undertook their own smuggling operation, which he wrote openly about for a short article in a book on the Pekingese. 'In 1896,' he explained, 'after five years' endeavour, we succeeded in getting a pair of Pekingese from the Palace. They were the well-known Ah Cum and Mimosa.'[142] Allegedly, these were 'smuggled out of the Palace in the cage of Japanese deer.'[143] This pair of dogs effectively founded the breed in England. So important was Ah Cum that when he died in 1906 the dog was stuffed and presented by Thomas Douglas Murray to the South Kensington Museum, displayed 'as the most typical specimen of the breed.'[144] There is no record of Douglas Murray's attitude to his modern act of mummification. Perhaps he undertook the taxidermy ironically, but it appeared to be purely a gesture of scientific record, preserving the father of the line. The Pekingese Club was formed in 1904 by Lady Algernon Gordon-Lennox, who had been introduced to the breed by the Douglas Murrays. The Douglas Murrays became prominent figures in this world as a result. But there was a schism in 1908 over maintaining the purity of the breed, dissenters forming the Pekin Palace Dog Association. The Douglas Murray Challenge Trophy was first awarded in 1905. It is still annually presented for best in breed.

The world of rare breeds further secured the Douglas Murrays in London society. As Harriet Ritvo has observed, the elaborate classifications by dog clubs 'metaphorically expressed the hopes and fears of fanciers about issues like social status and the need for distinctions between classes.'[145] Many breeders were aristocrats, and the Committee of the Japanese Spaniel Club included leading Conservatives alongside Mrs Douglas Murray, such as Lady de Ramsay (wife of former Tory whip in the Lords), Lord March and his sister-in-law, Lady Algernon Gordon-Lennox, whose husband had been another aristocratic hero in the Boer War.[146]

The Pekingese dog in particular became such a signifier of wealth that the American banker and art collector J. Pierpont Morgan allegedly offered £32 000 to buy one from the London breeder Mrs Ashton Cross. The sociologist Thorstein Veblen considered such artificial breeds perfect exempla of the taste of the leisure class, 'rated and graded', he said sourly, 'in aesthetic value somewhat in proportion to the degree of grotesqueness and instability of the particular fashion which the deformity takes in a given case.' They embodied value purely in their 'honorific character as items of conspicuous waste.'[147] Yet these were insecure symbols, since pedigrees only had the illusion of constancy. The Kennel Club, established to preserve standards and determine purebreds, had only been formed in 1873. After the turn of the century, the aristocrat Judith Lytton directly attacked the alleged purity of the Pekingese breed in England

(and thus, in a way, the class status of the Douglas Murrays themselves). Only a 'coarse variety' had been established in England, a 'ridiculous caricature' of the proper imperial Chinese type, and she accused the Pekin Palace Dog Association of wishing to 'reproduce living monsters'.[148]

When Thomas Douglas Murray died in 1911, his very brief *Times* obituary proclaimed that he would be remembered for two things: 'He was instrumental in establishing the first permanent bandstand in Hyde Park, and was also interested in the breeding of Pekinese spaniels in this country.'[149] Perhaps anxious to give a slightly more enduring testament to a friend, his co-writer A. Silva White wrote a letter for the following day, arguing that Douglas Murray was 'like his prototype, Samuel Baker,...an Elizabethan Englishman – a rare type these days – and his wide acquaintance among public men and leaders of thought was not without influence on questions of the day, in which he took an immense personal interest.'[150] This already recognized that his friend's preference for the exercise of private influence would leave little determinable trace in the public record.

There is a weird disjunction between these remaining traces of Thomas Douglas Murray's life and his role as a cipher in the story of the curse of the Priestess of Amen-Ra. Where he surfaces in the press or in archives and reminiscences, there is absolutely no connection between his place in society and the ominous curse that was rumoured to be associated with him. Yet Douglas Murray visibly bore the mark of the curse, having lost his arm to the vengeful priestess. People, it seems, were discreet enough not to mention it. Of his family and friends, it was only his brother who offered an account of the accident nearly sixty years after it occurred.

When at Exeter College, or immediately after he left, he went with a small party of friends to Egypt and arrived at Thebes. It was settled among his party that if any Arabs brought interesting curios for purchase they would draw lots or toss up who should take them. The first object to be brought was the top part of a mummy coffin with the portrait of the occupant painted outside – a very desirable curio with, I believe, an inscription that anybody who disturbed the mummy would come to trouble. It was the portrait of a Priestess of the god Amen-Ra, whose mummy had probably been inside when the Arabs took it. Almost immediately after it came into his possession he was shooting quail when something happened with his gun, which in those days was a hammer gun. It probably slipped off his shoulder, with the result that the charge went from the muzzle of the gun quite close into his right arm just below the shoulder. He would have bled to death on the sand but he kept his head and showed a young man who was with him how to make a tourniquet. He was taken to Cairo and had the arm amputated, which quite put an end to his military career. Afterwards the mummy case, which he would no longer keep, went to another member of the party who kept it for a time, but later died from a gunshot wound. A third member of the party had it and, though very well off at the time, everything seemed to go against him and he died in poverty. His widow sent the mummy case to the British Museum, where it still remains, but there have been stories of several troubles which have occurred.[151]

Wyndham Murray's only comment on these events was rather evasive: 'No doubt these are all curious coincidences. Still they are very mysterious and may possibly have some significance of which in our present knowledge we have not the solution.'[152] It is only one of the handful of times that his brother Thomas appears in his memoirs. Wyndham was evidently closer to his other brother, Henry, school pals and 'best of friends through life', as he mournfully confessed during his assiduous attempts to ensure that the Victoria and Albert Museum accepted Henry's bequest of nick-nacks.[153] Wyndham's account of the curse reads like someone who circulates the rumour, rather than being particularly privy to inside information about the true story. Nevertheless, when the writer on the occult Montague Summers told the story of the Priestess of Amen-Ra in his book *Witchcraft and Black Magic*, Sir Wyndham Murray had a more active role. After 'official denials and vague prevarications' by the British Museum 'Colonel Sir Wyndham Murray, KCB, was obliged to send a letter to the public press' in which he affirmed the truth of the train of accident and disaster that had followed many of those who had come into contact with his brother's artefact. Wyndham Murray, 'strongly and very rightly went on to deprecate the jarring flippancy of these denials, which, to put it in the mildest terms, were not in accordance with the facts.'[154] If true, it suggests that close family members were invested in the story of the curse too.

As to be expected when dealing with a rumour, there are many gaps and missing links in this story. There is, however, one final detail that is rather haunting. In his last will and testament, Thomas Douglas Murray does not give priority to the disbursement of his estate but instead focuses on directing his executors what to do with his corpse. He requests that his body be kept in a warm bed for thirty-six hours and that 'my body shall be kept free to the air until decomposition has distinctly and clearly made considerable progress' before a post mortem be conducted conclusively to prove death by making incisions into the 'basilic vein'. Even then, Douglas Murray requests 'that my body shall remain in the coffin with face exposed and uncovered for a space of twelve days and nights that it shall be watched day and night.' This strange request was actually in accord with Sir Benjamin Ward Richardson's 'Signs and Proofs of Death', which was attached to the will in a pamphlet. Richardson argued that waiting for putrefactive decomposition was the only sure way of distinguishing death from cataleptic trance states and other forms of suspended animation.[155] The codicil expressed a change of mind from burial to cremation, disposing of the physical remains entirely, but as a result the post mortem doctor was directed to 'sever my spinal cord completely high up in my body', presumably to ensure no pain could be felt if all other tests had failed to register that he was still living. Many Victorians were terrified of premature burial and there was an almost loving indulgence in sensational stories about these incidents. Douglas Murray was a spiritualist, but he clearly did not simply accept the welcome embrace of death as merely a passage of transition in the evolution of the life of the soul, so integral to spiritualist belief. But then we know that Douglas Murray, more than most, needed to be sure that the dead and the undead were not confused.

However, as was almost inevitable with every spiritualist researcher at the turn of the century, Douglas Murray's spirit did return at a séance. His return was reported to the Ghost Club in July 1913. Members of the Club had met with the medium Mrs Wriedt (who had famously reached Stead soon after the sinking of the *Titanic*):

> The incident of the greatest concern was the spirit return of Douglas Murray. One of the sitters spoke about going to Egypt. Murray said 'Don't bring anything back, not even a mummy case, not even a cat.' He said 'I have found my arm'; and when Bro. Yeats was introduced to him he said 'I am glad to know the gentleman who took my place.'[156]

It is striking that in Yeats' 'All Souls' Night' – the most important night of the year for the Ghost Club – the repeated phrase of the poem is 'Wound in mind's pondering/As mummies in the mummy cloth are wound.' Indeed, these are the last words of his collection *The Tower*. That poem speaks, too, 'of mummy truths to tell/Whereat the living mock.'[157] Yeats openly names the ghosts of the Irish past that visit him in this famous poem, but underneath, as ever uncatalogued and unnamed, I wonder if he was also remembering his uncanny encounter with the spirit of Thomas Douglas Murray, and recalling the story of his curse.

If the spirit of Douglas Murray at this séance still sounded anxious about Egypt, he was at least happy to transcend his wound in the life after death, becoming whole again. So Douglas Murray's afterlife was not to be a member of the shambling, ambulatory undead. Instead, it was to live on in the half-life of circulating rumour, his name largely forgotten, his accomplishments lost. It was a fate that Ancient Egyptian nobles, anxious to preserve their names for eternity, would have regarded with horror.

# 3

# Walter Herbert Ingram and the Coffin of Nesmin

T HE SECOND PRECURSOR story of a mummy's curse had a shorter public life, rumours about it evolving rapidly and disjointedly in a short period of time. It was frequently told to bolster the spooky stories surrounding the Priestess of Amen-Ra, coiled around it like ivy, but it was not much of a reference point by the time Carnarvon died. Nevertheless, the fate of Walter Herbert Ingram, who died in 1888 at the age of only 33, helps to consolidate a sense of what significant elements were needed to put a curse rumour into circulation.

Amazingly, one of the earliest records of the fate of Walter Ingram is the entire substance of the historic first exchange of letters between Rudyard Kipling and Rider Haggard, later to become close friends and allies. Kipling was in London in 1889, being feted as the latest young writer to appear from the colonial margins. To break the ice with the current holder of that celebrity, Rider Haggard, Kipling offered him a tale he had clearly heard at a London club, in his distinctive slangy tone:

Dear Mr Haggard,

Forgive a junior's impertinence but this thing was picked up the other day across some drinks and it seemed – but of course you know it.

There was first one Englishman and one mummy. They met in Egypt and the live man bought the dead, for it was a fine dead. Then the dead was unrolled and in the last layers of the cloth that malignant Egyptian had tucked away a communication service of the most awful kind to the address of any man who disturbed him. He should die horribly in the open as a beast dies at the hand of a beast and there should not be enough of him to put into a matchbox, much less a mummy case. Whereat they laughed and of course later the Englishman went to your country and became 'fey' insomuch that he was weak enough to fire a shot gun into an elephant's trunk. Then he was dealt with after the manner of elephants till he was blackcurrant jam. But the rest of the camp would have taken what remained to the sea. So they cached it with great care and put a watcher on it. And there came at night a Beast, such a Hyaena as never was and raked out that corpse and gave tongue to all the other beasts and – nothing remained, or it might have been that (as happened not long since in India) the elephant returned to find her dead and battered the corpse afresh into the earth. These things the native watcher told when the camp returned with the coffin.

Were the mummy not in it I could and would take the thing and play with it. But there is a King of Egypt already and so I bring the body to his feet – for what it is worth.

Yours sincerely, Rudyard Kipling.[1]

Kipling hints that this is already a well-known tale doing the rounds of club rooms (Ingram was a member, like Kipling, of the Reform Club). Haggard probably knew the tale from his hours spent at the Savile Club. In Haggard's autobiography, this curse story comes immediately after he narrates how Wallis Budge came into possession of Thomas Douglas Murray's mummy case. Here, Haggard names Ingram, and gives a more orderly account of the life and strange death of Walter 'Midge' Ingram, the curse falling when Ingram 'bought [the mummy] in Luxor, and was said to have carried it off without paying the native what he wanted for it.'[2] Haggard never used the tale, perhaps because he was very much closer to the soldier Walter Ingram than Kipling imagined, and perhaps also because Andrew Haggard, Rider's brother, had similarly sent a mummy called Nesmin back to London at about the same time with rather unnerving effects (as we shall see in chapter 7).

The transition from vague rumour to a substantive history came as the story of Walter Ingram passed into print. Ingram's death was widely reported: the news made the front page of the *Illustrated London News*, but this was unsurprising since his father had founded the journal. Nevertheless, Ingram's death was also sketched for the front page of the *Penny Illustrated Newspaper*.[3] The earliest published account of the curse aspect that I have found was offered by Admiral Lord Charles Beresford (1846–1919). Affectionately known as 'Charlie B', Beresford was one of the celebrities of late Victorian society. A dashing sportsman, fearless sailor, Tory minister and later naval lord who shared a mistress with the Prince of Wales, he was celebrated on picture postcards and other imperial ephemera and was a constant presence in the popular press. In 1896, the *Strand Magazine* carried an interview with Beresford about his early life and exploits. It contained an account of his desperate attempt to reach General Gordon in the famous Relief Expedition of 1885, commanding a boat on the Nile under heavy fire from Muslim rebels. The interview also had an odd interlude. Since this must be one of the earliest and most complete records of the story, it is worth quoting at length:

> Here I must digress for a moment to tell the weird, extraordinary story of the ultimate fate of Mr Herbert Ingram, Lord Charles Beresford's most brilliant and dashing volunteer... So keen was Mr Ingram's interest in the Gordon Relief Expedition, that he actually took his own steam launch out to Egypt to join the expeditionary forces. He was at Abu Kleah, Metemmah, and anywhere else where there was any hot fighting to be done. As a kind of souvenir of his adventures in Egypt and the Soudan, Mr Ingram at length bought a mummy for £50 from the English Consul at Luxor. The mummy was that of a priest of Thetis, and it bore a mysterious inscription. After obtaining, at Cairo, the necessary permits, Ingram sent the mummy home in a big case, which was opened by his brothers at the offices of the *Illustrated London News*. Over the face was a papier-mâché mask, which is now deposited in the British Museum. The last-named institution was asked to send along an expert to decipher and translate the inscription, which was long and blood-curdling. It set forth that whosoever disturbed the body of this priest should himself be deprived a decent burial; he would meet a violent death, and his mangled remains would be 'carried down by a rush of waters to the sea'...
>
> Sometime after sending the mummy home, Mr Ingram and Sir Henry Meux were elephant-shooting in Somaliland... When they sighted the elephants, Sir Henry went after a bull, and Mr Ingram turned his attention to an enormous cow. His method was to turn round in his saddle, fire a shot, and then gallop his pony on ahead, dodging the infuriated elephant among the trees. At last, looking back for another shot, he was swept out of his saddle by the drooping bough of a tree. The moment he reached the ground, the wounded elephant was upon him, goring and trampling him to death...
>
> For days the elephant would not let anyone approach the spot, but eventually Mr Ingram's remains were reverently gathered up and buried for the time being in a nullah or ravine. Never again was the body seen, for, when an expedition was afterwards dispatched to the spot, only one sock and part of a human bone were found; these pitiful relics were subsequently interred at Aden with military honours. It was found that the floods caused by heavy rains had washed away Mr Ingram's remains, thereby fulfilling the ancient prophecy, the awful threat of the priest of Thetis.[4]

Miscommunication starts early. Beresford confuses the name Walter Herbert Ingram with that of his father, Herbert, who had founded the *Illustrated London News* in 1842, the newspaper that produced a revolution in print culture in the mid-Victorian period. After a tempestuous business career, Herbert Ingram drowned with his eldest son (also called Herbert) in a boating accident on Lake Michigan in 1860. The son's body was never found, producing an uncanny echo with Walter's unrecovered body three decades later. The print vehicle of the *Illustrated London News* has already featured in these Egyptian stories, partly because the later editor, Sir Bruce Ingram, who ran the magazine continuously between 1900 and 1963, was fascinated by Egypt and remained one of Howard Carter's few close friends and supporters (and was one of the executors of Carter's will). But with Walter Ingram's death in 1888, the weekly journal became an integral part of these curse narratives. There was a doom attached to the medium as well as the message.

Local press picked up Beresford's story and recycled the account verbatim.[5] The details had been reduced and simplified when it appeared as a secondary tale in the *Pearson's Magazine* account of the Priestess of Amen-Ra in 1909. Ada Goodrich-Freer only briefly recounts the story in the *Occult Review* in order to prevent it being confused with the Douglas Murray narrative. In this version, 'one of the fellahin, employed in its removal, said to him [Ingram]: "Do you know what is going to happen to you? You will be torn to pieces and scattered like grass!"' The death in Somaliland, Goodrich-Freer reports, was confirmed by Wallis Budge as fulfilling 'a part of the ritual inscribed on the mummy-case', a vengeful rage being one of the 'by no means unusual accompaniments of Oriental emotion.'[6]

Wallis Budge was to become involved in this alleged curse story at several points; he was closer to it, in many respects, than the Priestess of Amen-Ra. When he was a dining guest of the Ghost Club in 1904, he disappointed his hosts by saying little about Thomas Douglas Murray. He did, however, tell Walter Ingram's story, who had returned from Egypt with a mummy coffin 'notwithstanding the fact that he had been warned by an Arab not to do so.'[7] Wallis Budge confirmed that he had been dispatched to the offices of the *Illustrated London News* by the then Keeper of Antiquities, Samuel Birch, to offer translation services. He told the Club that the translation was 'very interesting and that in the inscription were extracts from a book, of which there was a copy in the British Museum, containing a very unusual and special curse.' Rather than developing this rather surprising concession to curse narratives, Wallis Budge instead got lost in details of ownership. Ingram had wanted to sell to the Museum. 'The mummy was sent to the Museum and it was arranged that the purchase money should be paid out of the next government grant.' However, there was another claim on the coffin, from Lady Meux. 'Dr. Budge declined to give it up: he shortly afterwards went to Egypt and on his return found it gone.'[8] He then related how Walter Ingram had been killed elephant shooting, his remains washed away, apparently conforming to the curse. The Ghost Club minutes record no discussion following Wallis Budge's account.

Wallis Budge's early involvement in the story, and thus the potential authority he could give to the authenticity of the mummy curse, was clearly known in occult circles. In 1909, at the height of the circulation of the Thomas Douglas Murray story in the press, Wallis Budge was also contacted by Ralph Shirley, the editor of the *Occult Review*. Shirley had heard the story of the Ingram curse from Professor William Barrett, the eminent physicist and leading light of the Society for Psychical Research. Shirley enclosed details of

> ...a certain Mr Ingram, who went on a hunting expedition in Egypt and was killed there by an elephant. A short time before this he took possession of a mummy, and it appears that the inscription on the mummy case stated that the person who disturbed the mummy's resting place should be killed by wild beasts in a foreign land, and that his bones should find no resting place... I understand that the mummy to which the story alludes is, or at any rate was, in your charge, and I gather that you transcribed the inscription.[9]

In a sack of mail demanding clarification after Stead and *Pearson's Magazine* had recounted the Douglas Murray curse, this additional request only added to the sense in which Museum artefacts were being hijacked by popular superstition.

The story of Walter Ingram began to fragment early because the artefact itself was broken up and moved fairly quickly between owners. It is a matter of historical record that Walter Herbert Ingram did volunteer for the Gordon Relief Expedition of 1884–5, travelling up the Nile with the *Illustrated London News* sketch-artist Melton Prior. Their progress was reported in weekly columns throughout the winter, although Prior was the better known figure as a veteran war artist, and the journal did not emphasize the family connection. Walter Ingram did purchase a mummy and coffin in 1885 and returned it to the offices of the *Illustrated London News*. In London, the cartonnage mummy mask inside the three coffins and covering the face of the mummy was donated to the British Museum in the same year (it is number 24402 in the catalogue).

The coffin itself, however, although initially claimed by Wallis Budge, was actually presented to Lady Meux, wife of Ingram's hunting partner, Sir Henry Meux, for her private museum of Egyptian artefacts that she had gathered at one of their country homes, Theobalds Park, near Waltham Cross. Wallis Budge examined the coffin at the *Illustrated* offices, but was also paid by Lady Meux to produce a description and full translation of the hieroglyphs on the coffin of Nes-Amsu (now translated as Nesmin) for a privately printed catalogue of her collection in 1893. The hieroglyphs, as they are translated in this catalogue, contained no curse, only the titles and genealogy of Nes-Amsu and ritualized appeal to the goddess Mer-Sekhet: 'May his limbs be gathered together for him, may his body be again knit together for him.'[10]

**Figure 3.1** Cartonnage mask of Nesmin (British Museum).

During the 1890s, Lady Meux acquired two other coffins, including one of an unnamed priest of Amen-Ra.[11] Out on the edges of London, the nature of the curse rumour shifted: 'The mummy was said to place a curse on those associated with it. The curse was said to be to the effect that anybody who removed the mummy would die childless and suffer a horrible death.'[12] Walter Ingram, died at the age of 33, whilst his wife was pregnant (she gave birth to a daughter), but this version of the curse was surely retrofitted to include Lady Meux, who died childless in 1911. Lady Meux left her Egyptian collection to the British Museum, but partly because of her dubious reputation and partly because she insisted on the collection being displayed together, rather than integrated into the collections of the Museum, the gift was refused. Her executors instead auctioned the coffin, which was purchased at Sotheby's in London by

Figure 3.2 Coffin of Nesmin (Rhode Island School of Design).

agents for Randolph William Hearst for £72. This was one of the insatiable acquisitions of antiquities by the American newspaper magnate and was probably stored in his warehouses rather than reaching his Californian mansion, his bizarre mock medieval cathedral that he built on the hills above the Pacific Ocean at San Simeon. When Hearst's media empire approached bankruptcy and collapse in 1939, the Coffin of Nesmin was sold by Sotheby's, and acquired by the Rhode Island School of Design, where it still resides, apparently now free of any evil reputation.[13]

With each successive move, the curse seemed to fall away from the artefact, yet in its wake rumour ran riot. In his unreliable reminiscences about visiting Tutankhamun's tomb, for instance, Henry Field shifted the accompanying Ingram story sideways:

There is a story about Sir Bruce Ingram, long-time editor of the *Illustrated London News*, who was given a mummy's hand as a paperweight. The wrist was still bound with a copper bracelet set with a scarab. The hieroglyphs on the scarab, translated, proved to be, 'Cursed be he who moves my body. To him shall come fire, water and pestilence.' Several months later the editor's beautiful country house burned to the ground. It was rebuilt and a flood promptly swept through its ground floors. Sir Bruce did not wait for pestilence. He sent the mummy's hand back to the Valley of Kings.[14]

None of this was true, yet something of this sensational story still persists in the display of Egyptian artefacts in the 'Ripley's Believe it or Not' museum chain. Since 1968, Ripley's has displayed the mummified hand of an Egyptian princess, allegedly purchased by Walter Ingram. The accompanying cartoon explains:

> WALTER INGRAM of London, England, brought back from Egypt in 1884 the mummified hand of an ancient Egyptian princess, which was found to be clutching a gold plaque inscribed:
>
> Whoever takes me away to a foreign counry will die a violent death and his bones will never be found!
>
> 4 years later Ingram was trampled to death by a rogue elephant near Berbera, Somaliland, and his remains were buried in the dry bed of a river but an expedition sent to recover his body found a flood had washed it away.

Ripley Entertainment Incorporated is amiably honest about placing sensation before accuracy in its displays. When I asked about the provenance of this mummy artefact, Edward Meyer, Vice-President of Exhibits and Artefacts, explained that 'we do not have this particular mummified hand, although we do have several mummy hands in our collection that when we display, we typically reference this story.'[15]

By this point, the story of Walter Ingram has been scrambled and long detached from the original artefact. Even access to the Ingram family papers only allowed Isabel Bailey latterly to produce yet another variation on the fate of Walter Ingram, who in Egypt 'for some reason or other, unwound the wrappings of a mummy. Having done this, he found inside the poor remains an inscription to the effect that whoever did what Mr. Ingram had just done "would die a violent death within three months and his body would be scattered to the winds of heaven."'[16] The Ingram family memory, at least, does not appear to carry the burden of this curse with much attention.

Rather remarkably, though, a fund of family lore has survived through Walter Ingram's daughter. Walter Ingram's wife, Ethelinda 'Fay' Ingram, pregnant at the time of his death, gave birth to Walterina, who in turn had four children, ensuring the line continued. Walter Ingram's great-granddaughter, Anne Bricknell, still holds a few evocative fragments of this rather awe-inspiring ancestor. The material traces are odd and unnerving: the fatal bullet that Walter misfired at the elephant, mounted on a plinth; a metal plaque to a lost object, inscribed with the legend 'Looted at Undini by Walter Ingram, July

1879'; miniatures of his campaign medals from the Zulu War and for battles in Egypt at Abu Klea and Metemmah (the medals themselves have been auctioned); an oil portrait of Walter as a child; and a hefty photographic album marked 'Walter Ingram, Walton on Thames' that is pasted with news cuttings and photographs. Other mementos have been sold: a small bust of Walter Ingram as a child has gone, and there is only an auction list of a handful of Egyptian antiquities, including an ushabti in the shape of the goddess Bast, sold years ago. The bullet is the most haunting of these traces, presumably autopsied from the elephant that killed Ingram and then presented to the family, a violent and disturbing memorial in lieu of a body.

Walter Ingram had married Ethelinda 'Fay' Hemming, youngest of five daughters of a wealthy industrialist who owned a country house in Worcester and a large townhouse in Grosvenor Place. The family were hunters and shooters; Fay remembered in a memoir that her eldest sister was 'a good shot' and that 'her husband was as brave as herself, for neither of them knew what fear was.'[17] The memoir by Fay's niece includes an unsourced cutting, with yet another modulation of the tale:

> There is a remarkable story connected with Walter Ingram and his life in Egypt. It has to do with a mummy in the British Museum, which was supposed to exert some baneful influence, or may have been guarded by some evil-disposed 'elemental', for every one who came into contact with it met with misfortune. This was the mummy of a queen Walter Ingram had bought while hunting in Somaliland. Inscribed upon its breast were the words: 'May the person who unwraps me die rapidly, and may his bones lie unburied.'[18]

Although Ingram's death within a year of their marriage was a 'terrible shock', Mrs Ingram is portrayed as one of those 'outstanding characters' who survive trauma with great pluck. Even though her husband had been killed hunting, 'Shooting was certainly her favourite sport, but the love of a horse was deep within her heart. She was a splendid whip.'[19]

Fay's daughter was christened Walterina. Bearing the name of the 'cursed' father, she did perhaps inevitably suspect that the family destiny might be shaped by the alleged curse. As it happens, she had some reason to be nervous. Her father and grandfather had drowned. Her sister Maudie inherited the Hemming estate and married Colonel Cheape. Of their children, one daughter drowned in an accident on the Isle of Mull in 1896. Another daughter was drowned in 1914 in the famous sinking of the *Empress of Ireland*, a catastrophe almost as large as the *Titanic*. Of their sons, Captain Leslie Cheape was killed in Katia in Egypt, whilst the heir to the estate, Colonel Hugh Gray-Cheape, was drowned in the sinking of *Leasowes Castle* as he was bringing his regiment back from Egypt. Biblical curses tend to extend from fathers to sons 'even unto the third and fourth generation'. Walter Ingram had no sons, but both grandsons, Edward Walter Kennard and Malcolm Ingram Kennard died young. Lieutenant-Commander Edward Kennard of the Royal Navy was killed in action by an enemy mine on the Rangoon River in 1945. He was exactly the same age as his grandfather, and his body was similarly not recovered (as a surviving letter from his commanding officer attests). Anne Bricknell, Walter Ingram's great-grand-daughter, was sufficiently exercised by the thought of the family curse that she sent a Valentine's Day card to the British Museum in a wonderfully ambiguous act of propitiation. She does not believe in curses, but it seemed worth trying. It appeared to work: her three sons prosper, and one of them, Ingram's great-great-grandson, has survived two army deployments to Afghanistan.

Aside from these family traces, the Ingram curse confirms a number of per-sistent features about these late Victorian and Edwardian tales. As in the Eng-lish tradition of lucks and curses, it is a dynastic narrative concerning ambiguous inheritance. Indeed the Coffin of Nesmin gets rather impressively entangled in three further family histories. The *Illustrated London News* remained an Ingram-owned and -edited newspaper for over a century. Herbert Ingram had founded the weekly with money earned from a quack medicine, Parr's Life Pills, a folk remedy with an elaborately fabricated folk history. The profits from the news-paper allowed Herbert Ingram to regain the 'lost' family seat of the Ingrams, Swineshead Abbey in Lincolnshire. Social position with aristocratic preten-sions re-secured, Herbert Ingram was nevertheless involved in both public and private scandals in the 1850s before drowning with his eldest son in 1860. The death of his youngest son in Somalia in such violent circumstances provided the perfect conditions for the flowering of a family curse. Since Sir Bruce Ingram was the famous editor of the *Illustrated London News* and an enthusias-tic recorder of the last golden age of tomb discoveries in the Valley of the Kings, his incorporation into the rumour was inevitable.

The passage of the coffin to Lady Meux and then Randolph William Hearst tied it to two of the richest and most conspicuous consumers of their times.

Valerie Susan, Lady Meux, was an extraordinary figure. Susan Langdon was of uncertain parentage, and had worked in the music halls in London, possibly as something more than just a 'hostess'. She was the mistress of Captain Reece, and in dubious employ at the Casino de Venise in Holborn when she met the young heir to the Meux brewing fortune, Sir Henry Bruce Meux. Their rapid marriage in 1878 under common licence suggested blackmail to some (the 'bounce' of entrapping a wealthy man into marriage with the threat of expos-ing a sexual liaison was a common blackmailing trick). Women in polite soci-ety refused to visit or receive her, to her bitter resentment, although she was risqué company for respectable men who evidently responded to her 'legen-dary sensuality'.[20] The Meux family itself never acknowledged her existence,

Figure 3.3 James Whistler, 'Arrangement in Black' (Honolulu Academy of Arts).

despite its own problems with respectability. Sir Henry's father was declared insane and had a lingering death from syphilis, whilst his mother was a severe alcoholic who was controlled by minders in Paris from engaging in embarrassing public behaviour.[21] Control of the brewing fortune had been regularly and scandalously contested in the courts through the course of the nineteenth century. It did not help that Sir Henry Meux had already purchased a country house, 41 Park Lane as a townhouse, and at least £10 000 worth of diamonds for his low-born wife by 1881. It helped even less that she was painted ostentatiously wearing these diamonds by James Whistler. 'Arrangement in Black' was Whistler's first commissioned portrait after being bankrupted by his pyrrhic victory in the libel trial against John Ruskin; he was a ridiculed avantgardist, barely respectable.

Her frank stare, painted face and diamond parure and necklace did little but increase Lady Meux's dubious reputation. Whistler painted her again in 1882, in 'Harmony in Pink and Grey', which was shown at the fashionable Grosvenor Gallery. Further planned portraits were abandoned in mutual exasperation (Meux sent maids to sit in her stead, then later threatened to employ another painter to 'finish' Whistler's impressionistic works). Lady Meux later wrote to Whistler that 'I suppose we are both a little *eccentric* and *not* loved by *all* the world, personally I am glad of it as I should prefer a little hate.'[22]

Following the eventual death of Sir Henry's father in 1883, the couple moved to the family seat at Theobalds Park, where Lady Meux constructed her Egyptian museum. Walter Ingram must have been a lifelong friend of Sir Henry Meux: they were at Eton and then Trinity College in Cambridge as exact contemporaries, and Ingram even joined them on their honeymoon yacht in Egypt in 1879 for a spot of hunting with the groom. When Ingram was killed in Berbera, in alleged fulfilment of the curse, he was with Sir Henry. The coffin that Ingram had presented to Lady Meux accordingly 'rose in celebrity'.[23]

There was already a tinge of occultism about Lady Meux in the 1880s: one obituary recalled that 'she was to be seen at the meetings of the Theosophical Society in St John's Wood in the early days when Mme. Blavatsky still lived.'[24] Some of the spookiness of Egyptian collections might have rubbed off on her too. For a few years, she was very close to Wallis Budge. He worked at Theobalds Park on two editions of the catalogue. She knew him familiarly enough to confess in a brief note that 'my nerves are getting worse' and fondly recalled days with Wallis Budge's wife Dora with affection.[25] She not only employed Wallis Budge to give authority to her private collection, but even lent the couple money to assist in the purchase of a house. Lady Meux also helped with Wallis Budge's legal costs when the Keeper was sued for slander in the early 1890s. However, their relationship soured. Wallis Budge hinted to the Ghost Club that Lady Meux had only acquired the Coffin of Nesmin legalistically, with a pencil-written note by Walter Ingram to the effect that he wished to gift her the object. Later, they would exchange bitter letters about money owed. In 1906, Wallis Budge sent her an account for 6927 hours of translation work, costed at 8.5 pence an hour. Lady Meux professed herself 'much surprised to receive an account from him for translating mss which she published for his benefit alone. Lady Meux would like to remind Dr Budge ... that all the books she has published were done so for Dr Budge's benefit, as she took no personal interest in

Figure 3.4 James Whistler, 'Harmony in Pink and Grey' (Frick Collection).

them.'[26] Wallis Budge preserved batches of her letters and drafts of his wounded responses, perhaps fearing further legal trouble.

The Meux marriage was not happy. The couple had no children. Sir Henry Meux died of complications related to alcoholism in 1900, leaving all of his money to his wife. Lady Meux turned to horse racing, training a Derby winner in 1901, but was also feared to be running through the Meux fortune at some speed. She did leave a vast estate when she died in 1910, but in an act of revenge on the Meux family that had snubbed her, she left most of it to Admiral Sir Hedworth Lambton, providing he changed his name to Meux.[27] Admiral Meux, as he rapidly became, unsentimentally auctioned off her collections in a sale that lasted eight days.[28] In a will full of controversy, Lady Meux also instructed that several early Christian manuscripts from the British looting of Maqdala in Ethiopia, which she had acquired at auction, be returned to Emperor Manilek. The Emperor had admired them on a visit for the coronation of Edward VII in 1902. This clause was overturned on a technicality (it was a promise given only to Manilek, who had since died) and the manuscripts remained in England, to continuing Ethiopian outrage.[29] Sir Hedworth too died childless in 1929. Theobalds Park was sold, and the Meux brewing brand came to an end in 1964.

Although the Coffin of Nesmin was never closely associated with Randoph William Hearst, the story of the Hearst family might also loosely lend itself to a reading of misfortunes shaped by a curse. Hearst hardly died childless (he had five sons), but his political ambitions for the presidency were dashed in 1904 and much of his fortune was lost in the Great Depression. He struggled with alcoholism for years. He lost control of his newspaper holdings in 1937, with debts of $125 million, and was only rescued from bankruptcy by his mistress, the film star Marion Davies. He was understood to be the model for Orson Welles' *Citizen Kane*, which sketched the majestic rise and fall of a media mogul. Family scandal recurred forty years later when his granddaughter, Patty Hearst, was kidnapped by the Symbionese Liberation Army (SLA) in 1974 and held to ransom. She notoriously joined her captors' cause, criticized her father's response to the kidnap demands, and assisted in bank robberies to fund the revolutionary activities of the SLA.

The stories of the Hemming daughters and the Ingram, Meux and Hearst families reinforce a sense that conspicuous consumption by the leisure class in this era brings with it a symbolic commentary of lucks and curses in circuits of rumour and gossip. In that sense, much more so than in the Douglas Murray story, the Ingram curse reinforces the aristocratic doom that fell on Lord Carnarvon. In these stories, the supernatural supplement to the traffic in ancient objects might be regarded as a displaced form of class resentment. By the late nineteenth century, a global market meant that the Egyptian artefact was a fetish both in the anthropological sense of being a magical object and in Marx's related sense of a commodity that conceals its true conditions of production and circulation. It is lucky but also cursed, of course, to inherit preposterous wealth. The cursed Egyptian object is the displaced marker, the fetish that at once reveals and conceals this nugget of popular wisdom.

Yet no rumour would flourish if it carried just a single interpretation. Like dreams, these curse stories condense and over-determine multiple and even

Figure 3.5 Walter Ingram with campaign medals (Anne Bricknell).

contradictory meanings. Walter Herbert Ingram, although the son of a successful businessman, who had been to Eton and Cambridge, was not a particularly
wealthy man (his estate was valued at £1405 on his death).[30] But Ingram's part
in the story begins to suggest a different kind of emphasis. It is significant that
after Carnarvon and Douglas Murray, this is the third tale of a shooting man
and the third to be embroiled very directly in the colonial history of Egypt.

Ingram's career as a gentleman-adventurer and soldier included a sojourn
in South Africa and decoration for his role in the Zulu War of 1879. The Anglo-
Zulu War did not exactly cover the British army in glory. After several years of

British demands for concessions from the highly organized tribal society and military hierarchy of the Zulus, Lord Chelmsford confidently marched into Zululand to dismantle what was portrayed as a primitive, militaristic tyranny that was an enemy of federation and social progress in southern Africa. The British forces, though, were shockingly overrun and defeated within days of arrival at Isandlwana. The next day, a small force under Lieutenant John Chard garrisoned at the mission station Rorke's Drift held off a Zulu attack, an act of defiance amidst the catastrophe that resulted in a stand that was mythologized in England and the award of eleven Victoria Crosses. Chelmsford's humiliating defeat prompted a campaign driven by a desire to exact revenge, with extra troops sent to destroy not just the Zulu army, but the whole military culture of their civilization. The *Illustrated London News* followed this campaign exhaustively, using dispatches from Walter Ingram and relaying Melton Prior's drawings that fixed in images the fate of the plucky English forces against dark savages. Melton Prior visited the battlefield at Isandlwana a few months after the battle: 'I have not witnessed a scene more horrible,' he said. 'Here I saw not the bodies, but the skeletons, of men whom I had known in life and health, some of whom I had known well, mixed up with the skeletons of oxen and horses.'[31]

Walter Ingram's involvement in this war included a role as one of Dunn's Scouts, an intelligence team led by John Dunn, a dubious soldier-adventurer, a man with 'a fondness for wild adventures', who had lived with the Zulus for over thirty years as a state councillor to the king (accruing forty-eight wives in the process) before betraying their confidence and helping ensure British military victory over King Cetswayo's forces.[32] As his badge of ownership 'Looted at Undini by Walter Ingram, July 1879' attests, Ingram was present at the Battle of Undini (now known as Ulundi), his medal listing him as serving with Baker's Horse. Ulundi was the deciding battle of the war, when Lord Chelmsford, disobeying orders, proceeded to attack the Zulu forces largely to save his own reputation before the new commander Garnet Wolseley had reached the front. Armed this time with Gatling guns, the British massacred advancing Zulu warriors in their hundreds. 'The Zulus, firing wildly, pressed forward in their usual loose order, and sought to close with the British troops, but the steady and well-sustained fire of the infantry, supported by the Gatlings and artillery, rendered this impossible.'[33] After being softened up with thirty minutes of sustained fire, the retreating Zulu warriors were picked off one by one by the advancing cavalry. It was estimated that six hundred Zulus were killed by the cavalry. Chelmsford then ordered the looting and razing of Cetswayo's Royal Kraal. 'Ulundi was fired at 11.40 a.m., and the adjacent kraals shortly afterwards ... Every military kraal in the valley that had not previously been destroyed was in flames; and not a sign of the Zulu army was to be perceived.'[34] One wonders what object Walter Ingram took as his memento of this act of revenge.

Ingram then returned to England and purchased a lieutenancy in the 1st County of London Yeomanry, Middlesex Hussars. However, in the national fervour that erupted during the summer of 1884 to rescue the besieged General Gordon in Khartoum, Ingram joined the Relief Expedition literally under his own steam – hiring a private launch to travel up the Nile to catch up with and join the British military forces massing in southern Egypt. General Gordon had been sent into the Sudan to orchestrate the strategic retreat of British garrisons as an Islamic religious and military uprising surged across northern Sudan under a self-declared redeemer, the Mahdi. Gordon was a great hero of the British public, although his political and military masters found him erratic and resistant to orders. Gordon preferred to develop his strategy from Bible study, prayer and his own intuitions. He came to fame in the wars in China, bringing Christianity to the heathens, where he used a baton to 'conduct' his troops in battle. It was Gordon's fellow Christian crusader, W. T. Stead, at the height of his political influence during his editorship of the *Pall Mall Gazette*, who argued loudly for Gordon to be given command of forces in Sudan, and then equally loudly for Gordon's relief when he was besieged. Gordon's evangelical belief in the Christian liberation that came with British colonialism in fact made him entirely unsuited to conducting a retreat from an Islamic uprising, a religion he associated with slavery, and it was his own procrastination in Khartoum that led to him being surrounded and besieged. The *Illustrated London News*, along with Stead and many other patriotic newspapers, was instrumental in painting Gordon as 'the child of romance', whose adventures had been 'more wonderful than [any] to be found in the wildest Oriental romance.'[35] It was the strength of public opinion that eventually persuaded a reluctant Prime Minister Gladstone, after months of delay, to send a force under the command of Sir Garnet Wolseley to rescue Gordon from the Islamic forces massed around Khartoum. The Relief was to prove another unhappy chapter in the history of the British army.

The *Illustrated London News* sketch-artist Melton Prior recalled arriving at Shepheard's Hotel in Cairo in September 1884, where he 'received a telegram from Walter Ingram ... asking me to wait for him as he was coming to join me.'[36] They started together down the Nile, but their tiny first boat sank. The second was powered by coal, scarce in a war economy, which had been personally provided by Ferdinand de Lesseps, the builder of the Suez Canal. Prior left Ingram to chug along the Nile, whilst he went ahead by train. They joined up again at Wadi Halfa, and Prior sketched the laboured attempts to raise the boat through the rapids of the Second Nile Cataract. During this difficult passage, the boat capsized and Ingram saved the engineer of the launch, H. J. Mitchell, from drowning and was consequently awarded a bronze medal by the Royal Humane Society.[37] Ingram and Prior eventually joined the main body of the British forces massed at Korti, and marched with the Desert Column commanded by

Sir Herbert Stewart. Ingram had fallen in with a small Naval Brigade contingent, no more than fifty men, led by Charles Beresford, who pulled a heavy Gardner gun behind his white horse.

After an exhausting desert march intended to surprise the Mahdist forces, the British forces were attacked by a large Arab army at Abu Klea on the 17 January 1885. This battle was where Walter Ingram first came to the attention of Lord Charles Beresford for his cool-headed actions when the defensive square was breached by repeated waves of attacks and the Gardner machine gun jammed. With enemy forces inside the square, the British lost nearly two hundred men. The dead included Colonel Frederick Burnaby, one of the most celebrated dashing officers, adventurers and travel writers of the era, painted in a wonderfully louche pose by James Tissot (a friend of Douglas Murray). His death in part made the breaking of the square at Abu Klea a symbol of British sacrifice and heroism against overwhelming odds; there was national mourning at the news of his death.

For later Victorians, the square formation was a potent emblem of imperial duty, as Luisa Villa suggests, representing 'a thin screen against barbarous forces attacking it on all sides.'[38] The desperate struggle at Abu Klea was recounted in innumerable boys' books. It is depicted in G. A. Henty's *The Dash for Khartoum*, where 'to the survivors of those corps who had formed the rear face of the square, the scene they had gone through seemed a wild and confused dream.'[39] The scene in which Walter Ingram played his part was also commemorated in the central stanza of one of the most famous imperialist poems of the era, Henry Newbolt's 'Vitai Lampada.'

> The sand of the desert is sodden red, –
> Red with the wreck of a square that broke; –
> The Gatling's jammed and the Colonel's dead,
> And the regiment blind with dust and smoke.
> The river of death has brimmed his banks,
> And England's far, and Honour a name,
> But the voice of a schoolboy rallies the ranks:
> 'Play up! play up! and play the game!'[40]

Ingram did his own bit to add to this mythology at the time. He wrote a letter to the *Morning Post*, describing himself modestly as merely 'an onlooker and civilian' at Abu Klea, where 'nine out of ten firmly believed it was to be their "last march"' before the attack, yet which came on open ground allowing the British sustained volleys of fire. It was all very sporting, Ingram emphasized: 'Arabs were seen tending and carrying off their wounded. Not a shot was fired by the British soldier, although it was quite probable that these very Arabs would in another ten minutes be again charging down upon us.'[41]

Count Gleichen, who fought in the battle as a lieutenant and was wounded, recalled 'niggers dancing about on the hills' and then, after the retreat, 'dead Arabs in hundreds strewed the ground, mostly with a fiendish expression still on their faces.'[42] Passing the battlefields later, Gleichen saw bodies 'still lying about the country, all in a mummified condition, and smelling horribly. The air was so dry that they would not decay properly, but simply dried up in the hot sun and stank.'[43]

At Metemmah, where there was another famous battle with Mahdi forces, the commander of the Desert Column Herbert Stewart was badly wounded, dying several days later. With Burnaby dead, command of the Column went to Sir Charles Wilson, who had no previous field experience, and was to become the scapegoat for the Relief's failures.[44]

On the Nile at Metemmah, the plan had been for Beresford's Naval Brigade to take two fortified steamers upriver to Khartoum. Beresford, however, had succumbed to illness and could barely stand and all of his officers had been killed. In his memoirs, Charles Wilson recalled:

> Beresford...asked me to appoint Mr Ingram, of the 'Duke of Cambridge's Hussars', to the Naval Brigade, as he had no officers and could not go about himself. To this I was glad to give my consent, and made him acting lieutenant on the spot. Ingram had come up the river as the correspondent of some small newspaper, making this an excuse for getting to the front...He was a keen soldier, and fought in the front rank as a volunteer in the squares at Abu Klea and Metemmeh...Many of us had noticed his gallantry, and his quiet determined manner, so that it was a real pleasure to be able to give him some definite position within the force.[45]

Writting in 1885, Wilson added that 'I hope it may be the means of getting him a commission: men of his stamp are invaluable at critical moments.'[46] Here was a man in the Burnaby mode and Walter Ingram was appointed as Acting Lieutenant. With Beresford ill, Wilson took command of the boats and set off for Khartoum. The steamers, no larger than penny ferries on the Thames, set off with only fifty men of the Sussex Regiment on board, together with a crew of Egyptians, Turks, Bashi-Bazouks and Sudanese soldiers. Fatally for his reputation, though, Wilson hesitated several days before heading for Khartoum with these steamers, investigating rumours of Mahdist columns in the area. On the journey upriver, Wilson's flotilla was constantly harried by gunfire from Mahdi forces, often from well-fortified gun emplacements, and they continually ran aground on rocks and sandbanks. Each accident proved a lengthy delay. It was only when they got within sight of Khartoum on 28 January 1885, the city glittering in the distance, that they received the news that Gordon had been slaughtered just two days before. The Brigade's responsibility was now to return through the victorious Mahdist forces on the Nile and convey this catastrophic news to the commander of the Gordon Relief.

The steamers barely made it through the gunfire. 'We all had narrow escapes', Wilson recalled.[47] The boats ran aground again, and they were forced to land on Mernat Island and build a defensive zeriba, none of them really expecting to live. Relief boats then came up, with Beresford in command to effect a rescue of these men. On the *Safieh*, Walter Ingram manned the Gardner gun that had been hastily bolted to the deck on railway sleepers. Protected by some boiler plate, and under fire for many hours from the Wad Habeshi fort, Ingram acted 'admirably', according to Beresford, firing the Gardner gun relentlessly into the fort.[48] Prior confirmed that Beresford 'spoke highly of the zealous part taken in this last exploit by his new lieutenant.'[49] Beresford, rather self-servingly, believed that the *Safieh*'s act of bravery, thirty men holding off three thousand Dervishes, decisively affected the situation in the Sudan, shattering the confidence of the Mahdist revolt. But their heroic attempt was a rearguard action, the first act in the British retreat from Sudan. When the news reached England of Gordon's death, there was national mourning, but also a rage at Gladstone for his fatal delays: the GOM, the Grand Old Man, became the MOG, Murderer of Gordon.

When Ingram returned to England, he gave a public lecture entitled 'To the Rescue of Gordon (illustrated by dissolving views)' in London.[50] He seemed to write no more about it, however. But there was another memento: the mummy of Nesmin.

What would it mean to purchase a mummy and coffin as a memento in this context? Perhaps Walter Ingram had some of the enthusiasm for Ancient Egypt that would be shown by his nephew, Bruce Ingram. But it was just as likely that he shared the view of the military commander of the Gordon Relief, Garnet Wolseley: 'When I am told that such or such a monolith was erected by Rameses the Third of the Eighteenth Dynasty, it is gibberish to me; it recalls nothing I take any interest in or care to investigate.'[51] The mummy was a trophy, shared with a hunting buddy and displayed with other hunting spoils in the country mansion. It thus enters a different economy of signs. 'The association of the big game hunter with the march of empire was literal as well as metonymic', Harriet Ritvo suggests.[52] What the trophy expressed was 'the force and power that supported and validated the routinized day-to-day domination of the empire.'[53] There was little big game in Egypt, as Douglas Murray had attested in his notes for *Land and Water*. Perhaps bagging a mummy replaced the elephants and rhinos of more southerly climes, and reasserted a confidence in English domination of Egypt and the Sudan, shaken after Gordon's death. Equally, the vengeance of the mummy might have had less to do with powers imputed to the Ancient Egyptians and much more with the contemporary geopolitics of North African resistance to British imperialism.

Hunters were celebrated figures and their memoirs were popular books. Frederick Selous, a famous South African hunter and imperialist adventurer who helped secure the territory that became Rhodesia, lectured to large audiences in London in the 1890s. James Sutherland published his *Adventures of an Elephant Hunter*, proudly claiming the world record for his bag of 447 male elephants in the memoir of 'a life of wild, exhilarating excitement…far removed from the restricting influences of a complex civilisation.'[54] Ingram was not of this order, yet his death was reported in sporting magazines.[55] In fact, one of the more detailed descriptions of his death appeared in Sir Samuel Baker's hunting memoirs:

> We have recently seen a distressing example in the death of the lamented Mr. Ingram in Somaliland; who, although well mounted, was overtaken by an injured wild elephant and killed. This was a female, and it appears that Mr. Ingram, having followed her on horseback, had fired repeatedly with a rifle only .450. The animal charged, and owing to the impediments of the ground, the horse could not escape, and Mr. Ingram was swept off the saddle and impaled upon the elephant's tusks.[56]

Ingram, although mourned by Baker as 'one of the most daring and excellent men, who was an excellent representative of the type which is embraced in the proud word "Englishman"', was in fact used as a warning about the fashion for small calibre guns and hollow bullets.[57] Big game needed big guns – but not too big, as that would be unsporting. Stories of deaths or narrow escapes from cunning or malign creatures, though, legitimated the slaughter: it was a civilizing mission, rendering savage lands amenable to human control. Chasing a cow might have been poor show (female game was already beginning to be protected), but Baker's account of Ingram's death made it clear the elephant was injured and dangerous. In any case, Baker shared the common view that 'the African elephant is more savage, and…is not so dependable as the Asiatic.'[58] Even so, by the time another hunter in Somaliland published his account only ten years later, he found no elephants: 'They have all been killed or driven far to the west.'[59]

Some accounts of Ingram's death were at pains to point out that he had been disadvantaged by a typical act of generosity, in lending his usual gun to a fellow hunter and being left only with a .450 bore. But he was hunting in very dangerous terrain. The hunter Frank L. James had published his account of the first entry by white men into the interior of Somaliland, beyond the port of Berbera, calmly listing the numbers of traders and explorers who had been killed by the 'semi-civilised Somal' in recent years: 'To be killed was the fate of nearly every white man who ventured into the country.'[60] Indeed, just like Ingram, Frank James was killed by a wounded elephant whilst hunting in West Africa in 1890. Guy Dawnay, another soldier veteran of the Egyptian wars and a well-known

Conservative politician, had also been killed hunting elephant in the area in 1889. All three, Ingram, James and Dawnay, were part of a close-knit community of big-game hunters that included Douglas Murray's idol, Sir Samuel Baker. Indeed, one man, E. Lort-Phillips, was present in the hunting parties when each man was killed.

Ingram's death was therefore already symbolically over-determined by these hunting exploits even before the superstructure of the curse attached to the story told about his death. More obviously, though, the Ingram curse is clearly related to a difficult passage in British military history, when setbacks in the African colonies, north and south, began to reveal the limits of military command structures which had been left to ossify into privilege and preferment. Ingram's bit parts in the Anglo-Zulu War and Gordon Relief connect him to critical moments of humiliation, weaknesses in command only reformed after the catastrophic failures at the start of the Second Boer War in 1899. And it was not just Ingram's curse that offered a displaced account of these failures. Thomas Douglas Murray was evidently haunted by the war in Egypt too. His self-inflicted gun wound prevented a military career, but his brother was to fight in the successful military action against the Urabi uprising in Egypt in 1882. Yet Thomas Douglas Murray had many personal contacts with people disastrously caught up in the Mahdist uprising and the failed Gordon Relief. Douglas Murray's great imperial hero, Sir Samuel Baker, had a younger brother, General Valentine Baker, who was in charge of the Egyptian police in the 1880s. He had headed an Egyptian column that had been crushed at El Teb by a Mahdist force and lost the strategic port of Suakim, cutting General Gordon off from the sea. Douglas Murray's fellow Ghost Club member Sir Alfred E. Turner was a Major General who had also joined the Gordon Relief. He recalled arriving in Cairo and looking on the face of the mummy of the 'great Rameses': 'It was with a strange feeling of awe that I looked upon the mummy in its glass case.'[61] Turner refused to let Sir Charles Wilson take the full blame for the failure to rescue Gordon. 'It is more than doubtful, however, whether the arrival of Sir Charles Wilson with the steamers and his tiny escort of twenty men of the Sussex Regiment would have made any difference, and probably they would have shared Gordon's fate.'[62] Remember, too, that Douglas Murray's séance table was visited by the fallen heroes of the Gordon Relief. He told the Ghost Club that he had been visited by the spirit of Fred Burnaby, the Colonel killed by a lance wound to the neck at Abu Klea, and by Sir Herbert Stewart, who died a lingering death from a bullet in the groin a few days later at Metemmah.[63]

The curse of the mummy unfolded by the fates of Thomas Douglas Murray and Walter Herbert Ingram is like a rebus or conceptual knot that binds together many diverse strands of late Victorian and Edwardian culture. They prepare in advance the bizarre reception of Tutankhamun's tomb and the Earl of Carnarvon's death many years later. If we replace the automatic dismissal of a silly superstition with a dogged persistence in pulling at every strand these rumours offer, the curse can operate as a means to unravel a whole cultural ethos.

Yet these last three chapters, which closely follow the contours of the rumours as they surfaced in print culture, don't by any means exhaust the full significance of curse stories. The stories in themselves can't explain why the genre emerges – why at all, why in the Gothic mode, and why so late in the West's encounter with Egypt. One of the earliest fictional accounts of an Egyptian curse seems to have appeared in America in 1869, surprisingly written by Louisa May Alcott in sensation mode.[64] The American relationship to Egypt produced a different set of dark rumours, some deriving from the story that Egyptian rags from mummies which had been imported to make paper just before the Civil War resulted in a cholera outbreak in Maine.[65]

What remains so puzzling and enigmatic is the wholesale transformation during the course of the nineteenth century of feelings of awe, sublimity and wonder at the surviving traces of Ancient Egyptian culture to a sense of threat and menace. In the early nineteenth century, London crowds flocked to see artefacts and entertainments associated with an ancient world fully opened up by Napoleon's 1798 invasion. Seti's tomb was reconstructed to triumphant public acclaim in the Egyptian Hall in Piccadilly by Giovanni Belzoni in 1821. London revelled in the creation of these exotic, orientalized spaces, in theatres, dioramas and panoramas. Cemeteries, tombs and public architecture indulged in a craze for neo-Pharaonic designs, to the extent that the Gothic revivalist Augustus Pugin mocked these forms in his *Apology for the Revival of Christian Architecture* in 1843. Mummy unwrappings were society events, conducted without a hint of transgression or doom. Men like Thomas Pettigrew, who published his *History of Egyptian Mummies* in 1834, became famous for their theatrical skills at unwrapping. Pettigrew unwrapped mummies at the Royal Institution and the Mechanics Institute, and chiselled open a particularly recalcitrant body in front of six hundred people at Exeter Hall on the Strand in 1837.[66] Local scientific institutes organized events centred on the unwrapping of mummies gifted by wealthy benefactors for the education of the public. Indeed, the fashion for unwrappings in the 1830s and 1840s produced an associated rash of one-act plays about awoken mummies, played as broad farce, without a hint of tragedy. Awakened mummies in Jane Loudon's *The Mummy!* (1827) or Edgar Allan Poe's 'Some Words with a Mummy' (1850) were mouthpieces for satirical commentary on contemporary mores, rather than ambulatory trajectories of vengeance.

What happened? In these wider contexts, the curse story is merely a symptom of a curdling in the English cultural imagination about Egypt. Indeed, if we track these larger transformations, my sense is that the curse could be re-situated to become a prism through which we can perceive large shifts in Victorian society.

This is the bold claim I now want to pursue over the next five chapters. These will detail the shifting conception of Egypt in the English imagination through the spaces of London, literature, and various discourses of the supernatural. Each offers its own cultural commentary on the colonial relation that the curse eventually came to re-cast in the latter part of the nineteenth century.

# PART TWO

## Contexts

# 4

# Egypt in London I:
# Immersive-Exotic Spaces

O N ST GEORGE's Day, 1924, the British Empire Exhibition at Wembley was opened by George V. With fifty-six participating colonies and dominions, laid out on a grid of streets named by Rudyard Kipling, the Prince of Wales declared the site 'a complete and vivid representation of all your Empire'. It provided, the King agreed in a speech broadcast by new-fangled wireless around the world, 'a vivid model of the architecture, art and industry of all the races which come under the British Flag'.[1] Twenty-seven million people passed through this temporary site in its two summer seasons, dominated by the Olympic Stadium and by the British palaces of industry, engineering and arts. The colonial spaces, carefully sized and distributed according to their economic and ideological importance, offered a mix of education and sensation, from the large-scale reconstructions of an Indian Moghul palace and a walled West African city, to the smaller delights of a life-size Prince of Wales sitting on his horse sculpted in Canadian butter or Jaffa oranges from Palestine, a territory which had just come under British mandate in 1922.

Adjacent to the main complex, physically and ideologically, was an amusement park, reached by crossing a reconstruction of Old London Bridge, just next to the Burmese pagoda. It was in this forty acre amusement park, just over a year after the sensational discovery of Tutankhamun's tomb, that millions of visitors to Wembley paid a shilling and three pence to descend a replica of those sixteen famous steps into a full-scale reproduction of the tomb. It was housed in a building designed by the architectural designer William Aumonier to evoke the stark rock face of the Valley of the Kings. You approached the entrance protected by a low stone wall, welcomed by men wearing Egyptian fezes, before descending into a complex of walkways with views onto all the tomb chambers. The contents of the tomb had been reconstructed by a team of artisans in workshops off the Tottenham Court Road, under the guidance of the Egyptologist and stage designer Arthur Weigall. The centrepieces of the display were the golden couches and the golden throne and it was said that over £1000 worth of gold leaf had been used in the recreations of the objects.[2]

Howard Carter had been rather typically convulsed with rage at the news of this vulgar amusement. This was surely because he had himself been barred by the Egyptian authorities from the actual tomb, and operations at the site had been shut down. 'It seems as though the model of the tomb in the British Empire Exhibition grounds at Wembley must do duty for the real one as a place of pilgrimage for visitors', the *Illustrated London News* opined.[3] Hearing very late of the Wembley simulacrum, Carter issued a writ to try to prevent the show going ahead only two days before the opening on the grounds that the fakes must have been reproduced from copyrighted photographs taken at the site by Harry Burton. Wembley Entertainments could easily demonstrate that the objects had been photographed by many journalists as they exited the tomb, and the writ was withdrawn.[4] The fake tomb became one of the most successful attractions in the park. Within days of opening, resumed work at the real tomb lifted the lid of Tutankhamun's sarcophagus to reveal the body within.[5]

This fake tomb, 'doing duty for the real one', as the *Illustrated London News* put it, was an inevitably conflicted space. The memorial brochure for the exhibit implicitly evoked a royal and imperial parallel with the present day, calling Tutankhamun 'a King of Egypt, one who was famous in his day, inasmuch as he ruled over not one but two kingdoms.'[6] The tomb emphasized the wealth and power of Empire embodied in the artefacts, just as the British Empire Exhibition itself intended. Yet the reconstruction of the tomb had to be situated outside the official imperial site, because Egypt had never been a colony or dominion and in 1924 was at the beginning of indigenous, nationalist and anti-colonial rule. The tomb therefore does not feature anywhere in the official guidebook to the Exhibition. Located outside the educative purpose of the Empire Exhibition, the tomb became an amusement, situated right next to the Safety Racer, a double-track mountain railway switchback ride. This, presumably, caught Carter's ire too: he was wanting not simply to control rights, but also to prevent the fatal slippage of Egyptological knowledge out of the framework of science and political power and into the maw of mass commercial entertainment.

And what, exactly, did the crowds enter the tomb to experience? It was the discovery of the age, of course, yet beyond the reach of all but a privileged few to encounter directly. Perhaps the tomb did, after all, function within the purpose of these international and imperial exhibitions to inspire awe, bringing the far-flung home, and domesticating the spectacle of the exotic through tourism without travel. These exhibitions offered 'an emotional mapping', Alexander Geppert suggests in one study of imperial exhibitions, 'the subjective creation of an imaginative topography' that helped bind the visiting crowds to the service of British power.[7]

Yet surely the draw of the tomb was also to experience the frisson of a fatal story. The Fifth Earl of Carnarvon had crossed this threshold and died six weeks later. Who could resist the funfair dare-devilry of restaging this transgression? The sixpenny memorial brochure to the tomb included a poem by C. E. Briggs called 'The Seeker', which set the tone in its opening lines:

> If thoughts of necromancers, prophets are but true,
> With ghastly fear and dread they would our hearts imbue.
> For once the seeker sought, and having found, there came
> The figure of revenge, and then no more than name
> Was left to grace the earth as though it were due.

This addressed Tutankhamun as a 'seeker' of secret mystical knowledge, his early death commanded by the 'Ominous, forbidding' Ra. The objects in the tomb, described and recreated within the exhibit and once again within the poem, seem to contain the possibility of concealing the truth of this awful secret. The poem ends with a warning that indirectly references the fate of Carnarvon but presumably sweeps the visitor into its murderous logic too:

> Then the elementals in solemn conclave took
> A vow so terrible that e'en the temple shook,
> Tho' be it centuries have passed, that he shall die
> Who desecrates the place where King and treasures lie.
> So is told the tale in an old Egyptian book.[8]

Although the last line typically relativizes the belief in vengeance by placing it in the realm of Egyptian superstition and rumour, it would have been unlikely that any other exhibit in the British Empire Exhibition got near so delightedly threatening to kill its visitors, or was so financially successful in doing so.

One hundred and three years earlier, in 1821, another London crowd flocked to a reconstruction of a royal Egyptian tomb. Yet the recreation of two rooms of the tomb of Seti I at the Egyptian Hall in Piccadilly did not appear to trade at all on the frisson of fear or transgression, visitors instead reporting on the exhibition as a space of social congregation and distraction rather than dread. This chapter explores the history of the exotic Egyptian spaces that were constructed in London between these two tombs, considering whether we can find part of an answer to the rise of curse narratives in the way the meaning of these strange insertions of foreign spaces into the urban fabric changed over the course of a century.

The category of social space, Henri Lefebvre argued, is never empty or neutral but continually and actively produced. Space therefore 'may be said to embrace a multitude of intersections' whose tensions can be teased out not just by a history of space but a history of the representations of space.'⁹ Although Lefebvre sought means to crack open the glaze of abstracted Western urban space, he was prone to generalizations about non-Western space because, as he rather disarmingly put it, he was 'lacking adequate knowledge of the Orient'.¹⁰ Yet to pay proper attention to these spaces is to reveal a lost conflicted history of London as a city built on a matrix of imperial relations.

Across the next two chapters, I want to pursue the phantom presence of Egypt in London. This first chapter traces a line from the Egyptian Hall in 1821, through the immersions in foreign worlds promised by dioramas, panoramas and theatrical extravaganzas, and in the fantastical displays of Egyptian or more nebulously 'Eastern' spaces that proliferated in London's new West End. These entertainments offered Egypt as a sublime and marvellous space, rather than one of fear and trembling. The following chapter, on Egypt as it appeared in the temporary international exhibition sites that emerged after the Egyptian Court was built for the Crystal Palace in 1854 and in official sites like the British Museum, tells a very different story. For now, I want to convey the sense that Victorian and Edwardian London was not a homogeneous space, but riddled with pockets of these odd exotic zones that dynamically connected the population of the centre to the periphery. These domestic contact zones seismically registered geopolitical movements as global networks of trade and power shifted through the century. In other words, they track how the meaning of Egypt changed over time.

## The Egyptian Hall, Belzoni's tomb and 'Mummy' Pettigrew

The first wave of Egyptomania is commonly held to have hit England in the wake of the French surrender of Egypt in 1801. Part of the ransom to release the ragged remains of the French army from starvation and disease was the transfer of ancient objects collected by Napoleon's savants to British ownership. Yet these had less impact in London – where they were stored in temporary sheds – than the translation of Dominique-Vivant Denon's heavily illustrated *Travels in Upper and Lower Egypt During the Campaigns of General Bonaparte in that Country*, which appeared in 1803. The etchings of melancholy ruins complied with rhetorics of the sublime and the conventional sentiment *sic transit gloria mundi*, so pass the glories of the world. In contrast, the Egyptian Revival in architecture and design, if such a thing existed, was an oddly self-cancelling

Figure 4.1 Thomas Hope's Egyptian room, 1807 (University of London Library).

thing.[11] In the eighteenth century, Egyptianate flourishes had been part of the florid language of Giovanni Piranesi's rococo designs. Piranesi's flights of fantasy culminated in an entire Egyptian café interior, completed in Rome in 1768. The first room in London constructed on rigorously Egyptian lines was in fact built by the wealthy Dutch industrialist Thomas Hope in his house in Duchess Street in 1804. An avid collector of classical artefacts, Hope built Greek, Roman and Egyptian rooms as complete environments, to which members of the Royal Academy were invited to take ticketed tours, all with the aim of improving English taste in design.

In his influential guide, *Household Furniture and Interior Decoration*, Hope's commentary on the Egyptian room explained that he had mixed a small number of actual antiquities, which he wanted to keep separate from his Greek collection, with decorative elements merely inspired by Egypt. The friezes were taken from papyri and the ceiling from the interior of a mummy case, effectively turning the room into a coffin. The plate above clearly shows a mummy on display in a glass case in the centre of the room, although Hope made no comment on it. Nor, apparently, did any of his visitors.

For all this careful effort, the whole purpose of Hope's Egyptian room was intended as a strongly negative lesson for tastemakers. Since Hope's comments effectively dictated the exclusion of Egypt from tasteful design for the rest of the century it is worth quoting at length:

Let me however avail myself of the description of this room, to urge young art-ists never to adopt, except from motives more weighty than a mere aim at novelty, the Egyptian style of ornament. The hieroglyphic figures, so universally employed by the Egyptians, can afford us little pleasure on account of their meaning, since this is seldom intelligible: they can afford us still less gratifica-tion on account of their outline, since this is never agreeable; at least in as far as regards these smaller details, which alone are susceptible of being introduced in our confined spaces. Real Egyptian monuments, built of the hardest materi-als, cut out in the most prodigious blocks, even when they please not the eye, through the elegance of their shapes, still amaze the intellect through the immensity of their size, and the indestructibility of their nature. Modern imita-tions of these wonders of antiquity, composed of lath and plaster, of calico and of paper, offer no one attribute of solidity or grandeur to compensate for their want of elegance and grace, and can only excite ridicule and contempt.[12]

Egypt is the negative that helps secure the dominance of Grecian neoclassical design. Grandeur is site-specific and untranslatable. The influence of Egypt through Denon's *Voyage*, which was reliant on the Napoleonic invasion of Egypt, might also be politically suspect in England.[13] Egypt in London will therefore always be regarded as out of place, vulgar and merely faddish. It would never form part of the language of government or public architecture, which remained either Italianate or Gothic.[14] Hope fully anticipates the later denigra-tion of popular forms of Egyptian styles built in 'lath and plaster' – what J. S. Curl has called the 'commercial picturesque'.[15]

Nevertheless, the irony of Hope's project was that his negation was conducted through the creation of positive objects and designs. These were soon dissemi-nated in mass-produced copies by the designer George Smith and others with-out recourse to Hope's framing discourse of good taste. Already the British victory in Egypt had inspired an Egyptian Hall at Goodwood House (c.1803–6), then at Stowe (1805), then an Egyptian Hall extension at Craven Cottage in Fulham, 'being an exact copy from one of the plates in Denon's *Travels in Egypt*.[16] Wedgwood potteries had been issuing Egyptian-inspired designs since the 1790s, the Lyceum Theatre staged *Ægyptiana* with its vast exotic scenography to great acclaim in the wake of Nelson's victory at the Battle of the Nile in 1799, and cheap Egyptianate furniture became popular after Hope's designs were copied. This flurry of the Regency exotic prompted Robert Southey's famous com-plaint, in the midst of an attack on 'Fashionables', that 'everything must now be Egyptian: the ladies wear crocodile ornaments, and you sit upon a sphinx in a room hung around with mummies, and with the long black lean-armed long-nosed hieroglyphical men, who are enough to make the children afraid to go to bed'. Southey also complained about the fashion for Egyptian lettering on shop boards, which 'as the Egyptian had no letters, you will doubtless conceive must be curious'.[17] He was probably thinking of the Egyptianate façade of the *Courier*

Figure 4.2 The Egyptian Hall, Piccadilly (London Metropolitan Archives).

newspaper in the Strand. Sir John Soane, in lectures on art and architecture, had attacked Egyptian style for its 'tiresome monotony', Ackermann's *Repository of Arts* following suit by denouncing 'the barbarous Egyptian style' in its 1809 annual. These denunciations all came three years before London got its first full-scale neo-Pharaonic building.[18]

William Bullock was a compulsive collector of exotic materials, who had first opened a display in Liverpool in 1800 to show objects related to Captain Cook's South Sea adventures. In 1809, he opened a cabinet of curiosities at 22 Piccadilly. It was such a success that he acquired the vacant plot at 170–1 Piccadilly in 1811. This was the heart of aristocratic and gentlemanly London, a short walk from the Royal Academy. For the building of his new 'London Museum', Bullock hired the architect Peter Frederick Robinson, who had worked on the orientalist fantasy of the Brighton Pavilion. Robinson built a standard exhibition hall, but with an elaborate Egyptian façade, modelled, very loosely, after the temple at Dendera (as pictured in Denon's *Travels*). Robinson created the illusion of an Egyptian pylon shape with apparently tapering walls topped by a curved 'cavetto' cornice. The reliefs, made before hieroglyphs had been decoded, were purely decorative. The upper floor window cornices carried the imperial Pharaonic mark. The step corbel designs of the windows onto the street borrowed more from Piranesi fireplaces than any Egyptian temple, but the very notion of windows in an Egyptian monument didn't make strict sense. Nor was there much logic to the clearly Grecian statues of Isis and Osiris that stood above the main entrance, the eye carried up to them from the columns topped with lotus-bud capitals that framed the entrance. This concoction was opened in April 1812 as the grandly named 'London Museum and Pantherion.' It became a popular London institution as the Egyptian Hall for a century.

Bullock's collection burgeoned to over thirty thousand items in the 1810s, as he coined profits with a sequence of hugely successful exhibitions. He sold the collection and the Museum in 1819 in a disastrous attempt to fund a silver-mining project in Mexico. After a mixed career as a variety hall, presenting, amongst others, the diminutive General Tom Thumb, the Egyptian Hall was eventually taken over in 1873 by the stage magician and anti-spiritualist campaigner John Neville Maskelyne, becoming in its last thirty years London's 'Home of Mystery'. Macqueen-Pope reminisced that the place had a decided air of 'mystic strangeness' about it in its last years, the neighbouring display window of the taxidermists Rowland Ward thrilling visiting children even before they entered the building.[19] The Hall was demolished in 1905.[20]

The building never entered the respectable pantheon of London architecture. Leigh Hunt's dismissal of it in 1861 still echoed Hope:

> much praise cannot be given to the building called the Egyptian Hall. Egyptian architecture will do nowhere but in Egypt. There, its cold and gloomy ponderosity ('weight' is too pretty a word) befits the hot, burning atmosphere and shifting sands. But in such a climate as this, it is nothing but an uncouth anomaly. The absurdity, however, renders it a good advertisement. There is no missing its great lumpish face as you go along. It gives a blow to the mind, like a heavy practical joke.[21]

Bullock surely did think of the façade in functional, advertising terms rather than formal, aesthetic ones. But he had more invested in the effect of the interior on his visitors. On opening, the Egyptian Hall contained two display rooms, a great hall and his Pantherion, a diorama of a tropical forest that contained a taxidermied array of 'the whole of the known Quadrupeds' distributed around an Indian hut. As if this were not enough, this spectacle was entered by way of a 'basaltic cavern' that was modelled on Fingal's Cave in Ireland. The whole effect, the Museum *Companion* explained, was 'assisted by an appropriate panorama effect of distance, which makes the illusion produced so strong, that the surprised visitor finds himself suddenly transported from a crowded metropolis to the depth of an Indian forest'.[22]

This experience of displacement from everyday London, the visitor disoriented by a transitional passage before being enveloped in a totally other exotic environment, was one of the central urban pleasures of the nineteenth century. One was moved *there*, paradoxically, by being immersed in an entirely enclosed space *here*. The margin was brought to the centre not by opening up to it but by folding it into the heart of the metropolis, the other becoming the secret sharer of the same. The greater the immersive illusion, the better the sensorium was tricked, and there was a technological arms race by entertainment entrepreneurs throughout the century to maximize this reality-effect, ending up, of course, with the cinematograph (adopted quickly into the variety shows in the last years of the Egyptian Hall). Spatial dislocation could be further reinforced by temporal transports into historic or prehistoric worlds: spatial immersion, in other words, could also effect the illusion of time travel. This was bodily not spiritual transport, entertainment not transcendence. And yet what the Victorians chose to immerse themselves in is highly significant.

Bullock's early shows retained the wild mix typical of cabinets of curiosities, involving animal specimens, suits of armour, 'a small collection of shoes of different nations' and 'remains of a mammoth, mummies, etc.'[23] The cellars of the Egyptian Hall ended up like a lumber room of the Victorian exotic unconscious. Albert Smith remembered in the 1850s sifting through 'the accumulated rubbish of Laplanders, Egyptian mummies, overland emigrants to California, Holy Land Bedouins, electro-biologists and Ojibbeways'.[24] Yet in 1821, the new owners of the Egyptian Hall hit on a show that united the building's form with its exhibition of Egyptian antiquities, creating a cohesive immersive environment that was the sensation of the season. This was Belzoni's recreation of the tomb of 'Psammis, son of Necho'.

The extraordinary Giovanni Battista Belzoni had spent several years in London working as 'The Great Belzoni', a circus strongman, seen at Sadler's Wells by both William Wordsworth and Thomas De Quincey.[25] In 1815, he travelled to Egypt after it had been opened to foreigners by the Pasha Muhummad Ali.[26] Belzoni hoped to make his fortune with a hydraulic invention to modernize irrigation in the Nile delta. When this failed, he was hired by the British consul Henry Salt to use his expertise in hydraulics to solve the problem of transporting the vast statue of Young Memnon (Rameses II) from the west bank of the Nile at Luxor to England. Between 1816 and 1819, Belzoni undertook three expeditions in which, despite persistent French attempts to block his efforts, he had incredible results. Young Memnon (inspiration for Shelley's 'Ozymandias' sonnet) had defeated Napoleon's technicians, who had tried dynamiting it to move the colossus. 'I found it,' Belzoni recalled, 'face upwards, and apparently smiling at me, at the thought of being transported to England.'[27] He orchestrated hundreds of Egyptian peasants to move the statue of Memnon over a kilometre to the Nile banks for transport by boat. He then travelled up the Nile as far as Philae, where he took impressions of the Temple and staked a claim on a fallen obelisk for later transport. On his second journey, Belzoni hired workers to remove tons of sand to re-open the vast temple at Abu Simbel, in the hope of finding treasure. On his return to Luxor, Belzoni discovered four royal tombs in the Valley of the Kings, including the most extensive and elaborate tomb in the complex, that of Psammis (Seti I), complete with its magnificent alabaster sarcophagus. With the artist Alessandro Ricci, Belzoni spent many months in the tomb sketching transcriptions of the hieroglyphs and wall paintings, also taking mouldings. On the second journey, Belzoni accumulated an impressive number of objects for Salt which were later purchased, rather reluctantly and at reduced price, by the British Museum. The Museum (having just paid £35 000 to Lord Elgin for the Parthenon marbles) refused to pay for Seti's sarcophagus, which was purchased instead by Sir John Soane for £2000. In Giza, Belzoni solved the mystery of how to enter the pyramid of Khephren. It was simple really: he blew a large hole in the side using dynamite. The empty burial chamber still bears the enormous signature of Belzoni on its wall, his mark of conquest. On Belzoni's third journey, the French consul Drovetti effectively blocked him from access to most major sites, so he struck off into the desert and rediscovered the ancient town of Berenice. His final act, which enraged Drovetti and effectively secured Belzoni's banishment from Egypt, was to help move the obelisk from Philae up to Cairo for transportation to England for the collector William Bankes. The royal cartouches on the obelisk were to prove important in finally translating Egyptian hieroglyphic script in the 1820s.

Belzoni returned to London in 1820, where he scrawled down his *Narrative* in somewhat eccentric English in a matter of months. Although the book unhappily railed at conspirators and defamers of his reputation, the sensational narrative made him the literary lion of the season. *The Times* hailed Belzoni as making 'the most striking and extensive discoveries for which Europe has ever been indebted to the skill and labour of any one individual.'[28] However, the financial recompense for his labours in the service of Henry Salt had been left somewhat unclear. Credit did not accrue to him, but to his gentleman employer, and Belzoni continued to be anxious and touchy about his status, especially as he was resolutely ignored by the British Museum. A strongman could not be a serious dealer in antiquities.[29] The exhibition at the Egyptian Hall, situated just around the corner from his publisher John Murray, was his way of profiting from his labours in the desert.

In 1819, the new owners of the Egyptian Hall had hired the architect J. B. Papworth to Egyptianize the great hall, to unify the interior and exterior design. Belzoni's show, which opened in April 1821 after lengthy preparation, completed the illusion by recreating full-scale simulacra of two of the most striking chambers of the thirteen in Seti's tomb complex, the pillared entrance hall and the 'Room of Beauties'. These were selected, the catalogue stated, 'the one for its great beauty, and the other for the instructive character of its emblematical representations.'[30] After entering through a steep and dark staircase, the requisite transitional space for audience immersion, the visitor found walls lined with exact reproductions of reliefs taken from the sketches and moulds that Belzoni made in situ. Within this space were fourteen display cases of Egyptian curiosities, including ornaments, idols, the toe of a colossal figure, a mummified ape, and two human mummies, one still wrapped, 'remarkable for the singular position, and binding of the arms', and one 'opened in England a short time ago'.[31] Upstairs was a large-scale model of the whole tomb, and models of Belzoni's other triumphs: Philae, Abu Simbel and the second pyramid at Giza. Continuing the theme of magnitude of age, of size, of labour, there was also a twenty-three foot long unrolled papyrus. Belzoni hoped to add the sarcophagus of Seti I to the display when it arrived in England by boat in August 1821, but his hopes were dashed by Henry Salt and Sir John Soane, the latter making it the centrepiece of his own candlelit entertainments at his home in Lincoln's Inn.[32]

The show was a great success for a year, before shutting in April 1822. Some of the curiosities were put up for auction, some being purchased by the British Museum, but many ended up in private collections (one of the statues of Sekhmet that Belzoni had taken from Karnak is still cemented above the lintel of Sotheby's auction house in New Bond Street). Soon afterwards, Belzoni set off for the Niger River in the wake of the celebrated explorer Mungo Park. Reports of his death first surfaced in May 1824, only to be confirmed by eyewitnesses six months later. In 1825, Belzoni's financially distressed wife, Sarah, restaged the tomb exhibition at hired rooms at 28 Leicester Square. These larger rooms, *The Times* reported, 'contrived to give a more comprehensive and imposing idea' than the original show in the Egyptian Hall.[33] Despite this puff, Sarah Belzoni was soon in difficulties and by November she was forced to sell the contents of the exhibition. Her supporters at *The Times* railed against the refusal of the British Museum to 'allot one spacious chamber for the physical memorials of Belzoni's unprecedented labours'.[34]

For Gillen D'Arcy Wood, Belzoni's tomb inaugurates the logic of the simulacra, the world of the 'real' copy, in nineteenth-century entertainments. These spectacular displays sought 'novelty and the shock effect of visual similitude', but in doing so were discredited as vulgar by a predominant Romantic aesthetic that valued the creative imagination over verisimilitude.[35] There was nothing to *complete* here; you only had to *surrender*. Although Belzoni's tomb was not a simulacrum, but a highly compressed and 'edited' version of the real tomb, whose true extent could be viewed in the model upstairs, it clearly traded on the pleasures of immersion and its attendant effects of temporal and spatial displacement.

The emotional experience of this fake tomb on its visitors is harder to glean. Susan Pearce implies that it was the lowly pleasures of the Gothic that dominated audience responses: 'the exhibition of the Egyptian tomb signified more than a positivist assertion of accessibility of the past: its focus was on death presented as mysterious, fascinating and spectacular, and its meaning offered a gothic experience of horror.'[36] This is what one might expect; after all, the

Gothic trades in dungeons, dusty graveyard remains and shocking encounters with corpses. But this is a retrospective imposition on responses to Belzoni's tomb, which seemed to hold no shiver of fear. In a contemporary print, the rooms of the exhibition are a place of congenial urban lounging and social circulation. Lady Blessington's discussion of 'The Tomb' remarked that 'here persons of all rank meet, and jostle each other with impunity', although the actual extent of social mixing was limited by the high entry fee.[37] She watched groups of schoolboys 'amusing themselves by discovering likenesses to each other, in the monstrous deities displayed on the walls', and mocked a group of fashionable ladies who were disappointed by the educational virtues of the exhibition, perhaps having hoped to look at a 'set of Egyptian frights'.[38] For Lady Blessington, the exhibition was a 'chastening lesson' in the ignorance of supposedly civilized nations, not a sensational horror show.[39] The tone of Edward Upham's response was contemptuous of the 'primeval apostasy' of the Egyptians from Christian monotheism, but he was clearly fascinated to see an unwrapped mummy in a public display rather than on those 'rare opportunities afforded by the cabinets of the great collectors'.[40] This extraordinary preservation suggested that Ancient Egypt 'had possessed herself of the most valuable secrets of nature'.[41] Awe was tinged with a sense of secret knowledge, then, but there was no terror in this account either.

It is striking that even when Belzoni is among the mummy pits in his *Narrative*, he hardly ever resorts to a contemporaneous language of the Gothic. There is a memorable passage about his stay among the villagers of Qrna, who lived in the tombs cut out of the cliff faces. 'But what a place of rest!' Belzoni exclaimed, 'surrounded by bodies, by heaps of mummies in all directions; which, previous to my being accustomed to the sight, impressed me with horror.'[42] Clambering through cramped spaces stuffed with mummified remains unable to rest unless sitting on corpses, Belzoni assures the reader that they do not smell, but the dust was 'rather unpleasant to swallow'.[43] Toying with the abject in this jocular tone, it is nevertheless clear that the mummies themselves carry little import: Belzoni is in the pits 'to rob the Egyptians of their papyri', the true source of value. Belzoni happily feeds mummies and their wooden cases to camp fires at night, finding that he is 'indifferent about them at last, and would have slept in a mummy pit as readily as out of it'.[44] There is no dread because this sort of superstition is insistently placed in the foolish Egyptian natives. Even a bey, one of the local leaders, is portrayed as a 'slave to superstition', and Pasha Ali himself is depicted as a credulous Arab, fearful of electricity.[45] Belzoni's modernity (implicitly shared by the reader) is marked by standing above this childish magical thinking. This sceptical distance seemed to be repeated in commentary on the London tomb too.

Early nineteenth-century attitudes to the matter of mummies can be illustrated through a different kind of London social space, in the brief craze for mummy unwrappings in the 1830s. The mummy that the catalogue to the Belzoni exhibition described as 'opened in England a short time ago' was unwrapped by the surgeon and antiquarian Thomas Pettigrew. He was one of the founding members of both the Royal College of Surgeons and the British Archaeological Association. Pettigrew's fascination with Egyptian mummies made him London's leading expert in this new field in the 1830s. Dr Pettigrew became famous for his public unrolling of mummies, which were situated somewhere between scientific demonstrations and public entertainments. They offer another kind of public space for an encounter with Ancient Egypt in early Victorian London which this time focused entirely on embalmed bodies.

After offering Belzoni his medical assistance for the exhibition, the young prodigy Pettigrew clearly became fascinated by Egyptian mummies. He copied poetry and prose inspired by Egypt into his commonplace book in the 1820s, and then in April 1833 used his position at Charing Cross Hospital to give a public lecture on embalming followed by a practical demonstration unrolling a mummy. Pettigrew's career as a surgeon had clearly advanced enough for him to be able to afford to purchase at Sotheby's for £23 a mummy from the estate of the Consul-General to Egypt, John Barker.[46] This was not the first example of a 'scientific' mummy unrolling in England; there had been a mummy examined at the Royal Society in 1763 and some researches at the British Museum in the 1790s. In the wake of both the Egyptian campaigns and Champollion's cracking of the hieroglyphic code, interest intensified. Augustus Granville read a scientific paper on his examination of a mummy to the Royal Society in 1825. In 1828 the Leeds Philosophical and Literary Society had staged an unrolling of Natsef-Amun, in a complete sarcophagus that had been acquired by the dealer Giuseppe Passalacqua in Trieste before apparently passing through the hands of both Henry Salt and William Bullock.[47] Pettigrew's lecture at Charing Cross was notable enough to be repeated in London with two more mummies. Pettigrew then received an invitation to unroll another one at the prestigious Royal Institution in July 1833. Michael Faraday, a close associate of Pettigrew, had turned scientific public lectures at the Royal Institution into magical spectacles with new forces of electricity and magnetism, and these became extremely fashionable occasions. Tickets to Pettigrew's demonstrations were much sought after. Whilst Faraday was a brilliant showman, Pettigrew's demonstration proved a little more laboured, yet it was still a society event.

The evening began with Pettigrew's standard lecture on Egyptian embalming techniques, derived largely unchanged from Herodotus. This discourse, delivered over the sarcophagus, nurtured anticipation for the coming spectacle (sometimes, Pettigrew theatrically placed hangings, painted with hieroglyphs, around the stage to increase the immersive effect). At the Royal Institution, Pettigrew was assisted by John Davidson, who reported that they unrolled at least two hundred yards of bandages before the bituminous state of the rags made them inseparable from the body. A stone scarabaeus was woven into the cloth and they uncovered a lapis lazuli necklace along the way. Prevented from a full unwrapping, they worked on the head instead, pulling out nine yards of cloth and resin from the skull. Pettigrew's findings were limited: 'If, therefore, I have thrown no new light upon this interesting subject; I have, at least, the satisfaction of adding my humble testimony to the correctness of Herodotus.'[48] Another unrolling at the Royal Institution by Pettigrew a few years later took over three hours to complete.[49]

In the following year, Pettigrew staged another demonstration before a packed audience at the Royal College of Surgeons of a mummy that had been purchased from Henry Salt. He was assisted this time by Richard Owen, who was to become one of the most eminent palaeontologists of the Victorian era. The tone of *The Lancet*, in its first years as the medics' professional journal, was at once jocular ('It has been buried twice – once in Egypt and once in Lincoln's Inn Fields') and dismissive ('this exploration…afforded a good exemplification of the old adage "Much cry and little wool" ').[50] In the same year, Pettigrew published his *History of Egyptian Mummies*, which he claimed to be the first study of its kind in English, so securing his expertise. In the West mummies were first encountered as *mumia*, a rare medicine exported from Egypt to treat wounds. Being a surgeon, Pettigrew focused on this history, and professed no interest in Ancient Egyptian architecture or culture, declaring it 'defective in spirit' and 'deficient in taste'.[51]

Pettigrew was evidently part of a generation of reformers who wished to professionalize medicine and raise the lowly social status of the surgeon. This was the era of new professional societies, not just for medicine (the British Medical Association was founded in 1832), but for science in general (the British Association for the Advancement of Science first met in 1831 and the word 'scientist', which failed to catch on, was coined in 1834). The new medical establishment in London had just undertaken an exercise of authority by ejecting John Elliotson from his professorship for his use of mesmeric treatments in the wards of University College Hospital. Such 'magical' beliefs were being thoroughly marginalized.[52] As part of this reformist movement, Pettigrew, in another book on superstitions, traced 'magical' treatments back to their origins, which were oriental in the case of talismans and amulets. He expressed satisfaction that 'modern researches in the healing art' had advanced beyond 'the errors of our ancestors'.[53] Mummy unwrapping was therefore embedded in a reformist and rationalist model of scientific investigation, a literal unravelling of the natural object before the supposedly disinterested gaze.

Pettigrew was particularly interested in using the skulls of his mummies to 'prove' by craniometric analysis that Ancient Egyptians had not been African but Caucasian in origin.[54] This remained a constant Victorian focus for mummy unwrappings. As Robert Young has detailed, Ancient Egyptian skulls became a key token in debates on the origins of 'Negroes' between factions of anthropologists during the American Civil War.[55] Even as late as the public unravelling of a mummy by Wallis Budge in 1889 at University College, the main conclusion of a rather uninteresting exercise was that Egyptian mummies were not 'Negroes'.[56] It is therefore unsurprising that there is no hint of dread or anxiety in Pettigrew's thoroughly materialist exploration of ancient remains.

For all the rhetoric of disinterested investigation, there was a kind of delight in the brute mechanics of opening up these recalcitrant bodies. Unrolling was also a sport. In 1837, Pettigrew successfully unrolled a mummy at the end of a lecture course on embalming at Exeter Hall, off the Strand. It was such a success that a month later he returned to unwrap 'Mr Athanasi's splendid mummy, from Memphis'.[57] This proved more difficult. One journalist recorded that 'the mummy was, in fact, almost embodied in this substance, and it became a work of absolute labour to Mr Pettigrew and his assistants, by dint of cutting, hammering, and chopping, with very strong tools, to remove the impediments which intervened between them and the objects they were seeking to expose.'[58] An audience watched Pettigrew wrestle with this corpse for three hours before he confessed defeat. It did not impress some reviewers: a reporter for the *Figaro in London* declared that 'Pettigrew positively glories in the unclean process, and pulls about the encrusted carcase with a fervour of purpose which may be scientific, but which is nonetheless nasty in the extreme.'[59] This report would surely have suggested that Pettigrew was cursed, if such an idea had been available.

These demonstrations occurred before the strict demarcation of scientific experiment into closed laboratories. Studies of early nineteenth-century scientific education suggest that it took place in hybrid social spaces, in coffee houses, general lecture halls, rooms above pubs, and commercial ventures like the Adelaide Gallery, 'Blending Instruction with Amusement' on Regent Street.[60] George Birkbeck's Mechanics' Institute (where Pettigrew also unrolled a mummy) was designed to improve the scientific knowledge of London's artisans. The charter for the Royal Panopticon of Science and Art in Leicester Square, one of the largest of these ventures, declared as its aims 'To exhibit and illustrate, in popular form, discoveries in science and art...[and] to instruct, by courses of lectures, to be demonstrated and illustrated by instruments, apparatus, and other appliances, all branches of science, literature, and the fine and useful arts.'[61] Pettigrew's papers show direct evidence of this mixed social space for scientific demonstration. He made mummies the centrepiece of scientific *conversazioni* that he held at his grand house on Savile Row. He could also move lower down the social scale: one card is an invitation from Johann Spurzheim, one of the pioneers of phrenology, to attend the dissection of a brain 'tomorrow morning at ten o'clock precisely at the Moon and Anchor, Strand'.[62] This location did not necessarily make the science conducted marginal, although it was socially distinct from the upper circles of the Royal Society.

One of the liveliest disputes in urban scientific culture at the time concerned electrical theories of life. Luigi Galvani's famous experiments with the electrical simulation of nerves had been demonstrated on the corpses of executed criminals in London before fascinated audiences – the kind of gruesome detail that fed directly into Mary Shelley's 1818 novel, *Frankenstein*. The theory was associated with atheism and political radicalism because it replaced theology with electrical biology. The dispute increased when it was reported in 1836 that the gentleman experimenter and radical Andrew Crosse had spontaneously generated life from galvanic batteries.[63] It might be possible to read Pettigrew's exploration of ancient mummification practices within the same matrix of concerns, as the new men of science extended their domain to essential but always controversial questions of life and death. In other words, the fashion for unrolling mummies in the early 1830s was part of a complex moment of scientific professionalization and authority.

Pettigrew and his mummies moved from the respectable scientific terrain of the Royal Institution in 1833 to the commercial world of Exeter Hall in 1837. He also later repeated this experiment in paid lecture series leading to a final unrolling on Jersey. Perhaps this was because his social status was not always entirely secure. Although a surgeon to the aristocracy (he vaccinated the daughter of the Duke of Kent, later to become Queen Victoria) and a leading light in the formation of several scientific societies, there were sometimes questions over his professional behaviour. There was a quarrel with the Duke of Sussex, whose library he had catalogued, and a murky dispute over an alleged bribe at Charing Cross Hospital, which caused him to leave his post there in 1835. Pettigrew had a reputation as a quarrelsome schemer among the emergent scientific community. Although Pettigrew retreated somewhat from public life after the problems at Charing Cross, he still demonstrated unrollings. Gabriel Moshenska estimates that Pettigrew probably unwrapped over forty mummies in his career.

In 1852, Pettigrew conducted his weirdest commission, which was to adhere strictly to Ancient Egyptian techniques when embalming the body of the 10th Duke of Hamilton. Hamilton had spent several years building a vast mausoleum on his Scottish estate, in Roman rather than Egyptian style, which *The Times* reported as 'the most costly and magnificent temple for the reception of the dead in the world – always excepting the pyramids'.[64] It stood over one hundred and twenty feet high. The Duke was mummified and then placed in an ancient sarcophagus that he had purchased personally in Egypt thirty years before, although the interior cavity had to be chiselled out a bit more to fit his modern frame. The ostentation of Hamilton's funerary rites was his only achievement, according to *The Times*: 'he has not left anything by which he will be remembered.'[65]

**Figure 4.3** Pugin's mock design for an Egyptian-style cemetery (*Apology for the Revival of Christian Architecture in England*. University of London Library).

Since all Ancient Egypt seemed to represent to early Victorians was a dead culture and a culture of the dead, the association of Egyptian revival designs with cemeteries became a common one. In the great reforms of London's over-stuffed burial grounds in the 1830s, newly established cemeteries borrowed heavily from Egypt. Abney Park cemetery in Stoke Newington opened in 1839, and adopted Egyptianate elements into its entrance gates, in part to announce that it was an ecumenical graveyard. These notions offended the church architect Augustus Pugin, who was at the forefront of the Gothic Revival. He mocked the intermixing of styles adopted by the new Cemetery Companies prompted by the discoveries of Belzoni on the banks of the Nile, sketching his own debased stereotype of the design.[66]

Whilst Highgate Cemetery was broadly conceived in a Gothic mode, the company developing the site did build a number of exotic zones for burial, including the famous Egyptian Avenue, a catacomb entered through a gate of lotus-bud columns that housed sixteen family sepulchres. They were not a great success and took decades to fill.

The architect Thomas Willson was responsible for the most impressive proposal of the era, suggesting that a huge pyramid be constructed on the site of Primrose Hill, larger than St Paul's Cathedral, which would act as a mausoleum that could house up to five million bodies and thus solve London necropolitan overcrowding at a stroke. Stock was sold in the Pyramid General Cemetery

**Figure 4.4** Entrance to the Egyptian Avenue, Highgate Cemetery (Roger Luckhurst).

Company, but the plans did not come to fruition.[67] In these designs, Victorians actually seemed alert to the august respect for the dead in Ancient Egyptian culture, in contrast to the shameful disregard for modern bodies evidenced in the repeated scandals that prompted a Royal Commission on burial practices in 1842.

Belzoni's exhibition was only indirectly responsible for 'Mummy' Pettigrew's displays and the fashion for neo-Pharaonic funerary architecture. One might believe that immersion in the tomb of Seti I was a deathly experience, a form of ghastly premature burial. But the exhibition in fact ran in parallel with a whole array of immersive entertainments that were about stimulating the sensorium rather than smothering it. Egypt would play a major role in these entertainments too.

## The exotic panorama and the theatrical extravaganza

The quintessential immersive entertainment of the first half of the nineteenth century was the panorama. The first version was patented by Robert Barker, who opened the first in London on the Haymarket in 1789 before raising by subscription enough money to construct the first purpose-built panorama rotunda on the corner of Leicester Square in 1793. This became famous as Burford's panorama when it was taken over by the Burford family and stood on the site until 1861.[68] The panorama was a vast painted scene that was wrapped 360 degrees around the inside of a circular building, and was viewed from a raised platform in the centre. It was designed to provide the illusion of a seamless view, the painted scene rendered apparently infinite by disguising the top and bottom edges and diffusing the light source so that light appeared to come *through* the image. The view offered was technically 'impossible' because it had to synthesize all points and depths of view into a single painted scene. Typically, visitors' experience of immersion began in passing through long passageways that led under the structure, before they were elevated to the central viewing platform, which utterly transported them from the reality outside. Indeed, London's first mechanical elevator was designed to transport people up to the platform of the Colosseum, the vast rotunda, larger than the dome of St Paul's cathedral, that opened in Regent's Park in 1829. Designers were forever seeking new ways to maximize the *trompe l'œil* effect, one stating: 'It is by removing from the eye all elements of *comparison* that we succeed in tricking it to the point where it hesitates between nature and art.'[69] Subsequent designs finessed this illusion in various ways – for instance, by adding 'real' elements like shrubs and trees, which were planted among rocks built out at the bottom of painted scenes. Some gave depth by adding layers to the painted image, and then by lighting certain windows or doors in the scene with candles and lanterns. This tends to explain why so many of these entertainments burnt down. Later additions developed the illusion of being at sea, for example, by fitting out the platform in the form of a ship's deck and using hydraulic devices to incorporate the sense of pitching and rolling on waves.

Dioramas added movement to the image. These extensions of the panorama were first patented by Louis Daguerre in Paris in 1821 and soon came to England, one being built in Regent's Park and another, billed as the Poecilorama, showing at the Egyptian Hall in 1828.[70] Dioramas could move whole audiences across the scene by rotating the amphitheatre, or conversely by arranging for the painting to pass by the viewer on rollers to give, as in one case, a compressed experience of a sea voyage around the world. Designers, though, had to choose between the reality-effects of a space that was all-encompassing but static, and a less immersive dynamic scene that moved, that unfolded like a story-board in time.

Although these entertainments received some praise from painters, their pursuit of simulation and reality-effects typically situate them as lowly forms of entertainment in the aesthetic hierarchy. William Wordsworth's 'Residence in London', the seventh book of *The Prelude*, refers to those 'mimic sights that ape/The absolute presence of reality', only to consider them the work of the 'mechanic Artist', 'imitations fondly made in plain/Confession of man's weakness and his loves.'[71] They were therefore in the same category as Belzoni's tomb, blocking the powers of imaginative faculty by forcing it to surrender to overwhelming simulation.

What did these panoramas display? What seems odd at first is that they often presented a version of the very city in which they were situated. So the Colosseum in Regent's Park opened in 1829 with a famous panorama of London, painted by Thomas Hornor, as seen from the novel angle of the roof of St Paul's cathedral, the view taking in the whole of the city to an imaginary horizon some twenty miles beyond the city limits. To some, this suggests that the panorama was a means of mastering urban space as London exploded beyond the bounds of any single person's comprehension. The 'Eidometropolis' display, on show near Blackfriars Bridge in 1802, was named for this very attempt to present an *idea* of the city.[72] The simulacrum was actually better than the chaos of direct experience. As one commentator remarked, 'he who has seen the London panorama [first] is able to find his way through London.'[73] These panoramas were also successful when they displayed battle scenes from contemporary wars, Robert Altick suggesting that they became 'newsreels of the Napoleonic era', rushing to translate recent battles into vast canvases for domestic patriotic audiences.[74] A particularly successful show in Leicester Square in 1799 put the viewer in the middle of the Battle of Aboukir, for instance, the triumphant defeat of Napoleon by British naval forces led by Admiral Nelson off the coast of Egypt the year before. The Battle of Waterloo was another defining moment, although panoramas were also consistently used to understand defeat, as in the staging of the catastrophic engagements in the Crimea. In France, where the trend for panoramas continued much later into the century, the National Panorama repeatedly re-presented the French defeat by Prussia in 1871. These shows perhaps aimed to engineer a national public as an imagined community built on heroic sacrifice.

A third trend in panorama shows was immersion in exotic lands. Wordsworth's description of London's panoramas immediately follows a bewildering experience of the streets, awash with uncontainable exoticism, 'all specimens of man', 'Moors/Malays, Lascars, the Tartar and Chinese,/And Negro Ladies in white muslin gowns.'[75] The panorama is a space of leisure, a safely delineated interior, even if these shows also 'boast of foreign Realms'.[76] Notably, however, Wordsworth preferred the panoramas of Rome or the Falls of Tivoli, where the press of exotic peoples was removed. He immersed himself in simulations of empty cities and landscapes. Yet as the technology of the panorama advanced, the display of the exotic was increasingly tied to messy human encounters with others in the international scene. In 1829, for instance, sympathy for Greece against the Ottoman oppressors made the panorama of the capital of the Ottoman Empire a great success at Burford's Panorama. In the 1840s and 1850s,

Figure 4.5 Sketch of David Roberts's panorama of Cairo (London Metropolitan Archives).

scenes from Hong Kong, Nanking, the Himalayas, Contstantinople and the Crimea followed conflicts in the Opium Wars, the Afghan War and the Crimean War. Transport and communication technologies compressed space and time, and the panorama curled like a tickertape record of conflicts telegraphed from distant lands around the walls of London interiors.

Political immediacy was not the only motive for displays of the immersive-exotic. Manufacturing sublime spectacles was still at the core of entertainment, and so classical ruins remained popular, allowing for conventionalized moral expressions of *sic transit gloria mundi*. After the artist Frederick Catherwood returned from his journey to the Holy Land in 1834, Burford hired him to paint scenes, including the city of Jerusalem. Egyptian ruins also featured heavily, Catherwood painting the Temple of Karnak for Burford in 1835. The ruins of Nineveh and Babylon were also popular following Austen Layard's discoveries in the 1850s. The artist David Roberts, already famous for his gigantic paintings of Egyptian scenes, such as *The Departure of the Israelites from Egypt* (shown in the British Diorama on Oxford Street in 1829), eventually travelled extensively in Egypt from 1838 to 1840. In 1847, David Roberts, designed a panorama of modern Cairo for Burford's panorama, the pyramids reduced to distant specks on the horizon and focusing instead on the famous mosques of the city. The *Illustrated London News* noted that Egypt was 'becoming the point of contact between Europe and Asia' with the opening of the overland route through Egypt in the 1840s, which reduced the transport time between England and India and made it increasingly pivotal to the strategy of British imperialism.

To up the ante, the Egyptian Hall opened a moving panorama of the Nile in July 1849, in which visitors travelled down the Nile to the Second

Cataract, along the west bank, before returning to Cairo following the east bank, scenes partly painted by the respected artist of Egyptian themes Joseph Bonomi.[77]

Painters associated with exotic subjects, incidentally, were also adept at turning their London studios into immersive spaces. The most famous of these was Frederick Leighton's Arab Hall in his home in Holland Park, completed in the 1870s. In the studio of the orientalist painter Carl Haag in Haverstock Hill, the artist created elaborate fake Islamic tableaux in his rooms to continue painting the Cairo scenes he had observed in the 1850s. 'Entering the room,' one journalist commented, 'the visitor is at once impressed with the idea that it is scarcely possible that he can be in an English home, in our great metropolis, so instantaneous is the change to that of rich, but not oppressively sumptuous, Eastern existence.' This was indeed 'Cairo in London'.[78]

Interpretations of the panorama tend to read it as a technology of 'absolute dominance' through representation, an embodiment of the imperial gaze that renders everything equivalent, rather like Jeremy Bentham's parallel invention, the panoptic prison.[79] In the fixed image, time is abolished and the exotic other is removed from history, rendered safe for domestic contemplation. In Timothy Mitchell's account, the panorama is the first stage in what he terms the 'world-as-exhibition', a pictorial framing of the Orient that also disciplined and controlled it.[80] With a slightly different inflection, Walter Benjamin, in his *Arcades* project, uses the experience of immersion within the panorama as exemplifying the totalizing dream world of modern capitalism, a disoriented daydream of consumption which closes off any possibility of imagining alternatives. 'The arcades and *intérieurs*, the exhibition halls and panoramas' are, Benjamin suggests, 'residues of a dreamworld' from which we must awaken.[81]

It would be hard not to read these commercial entertainments in this way, but it is also difficult to ascribe a single cognitive or ideological function to complex sensorial experiences. Viewers might well have experienced a feeling of mastery, but time after time visitors reported a sense of disorientation and vertigo when they first encountered these entertainments, complaining of dizziness or seasickness or fainting fits, a result of the 'impossible' and vertiginous perspectives and a sense of being overwhelmed by an edgeless image. 'There is something unaccountably perplexing to the sense and reason in this sight', one visitor complained in 1832.[82] Any claim of mastery in the panorama was in a dialectic with being disabled and overrun, a full surrender of the senses rather than a smooth operation of panoptic power. Exotic scenes would have redoubled this feeling of disorientation, and some of the pleasure of this experience was surely also about encountering recalcitrant rather than entirely malleable otherness.

This relates elements of the journey into the panorama to the sensations sought in the phantasmagoria, the magic lantern projections pioneered by Étienne-Gaspard Robertson in Paris from 1789. Robertson projected Gothic

Figure 4.6 George Wyld's 'Great Globe' in Leicester Square (London Metropolitan Archives).

and ghoulish visions, ghostly creatures looming and swirling around his terrified audiences. Surrender to terror was a common response, one report of a phantasmagoric display in London in 1825 recording 'the hysterical scream of a few ladies' flashing through the crowd, which produced an 'indiscriminate rush' for the exits.[83] Marina Warner has expertly traced the contributions of these technologies to a new language of subjective interiority, but places the imaginative capacities of the phantasmagoria in direct contrast to the realism of the panorama. Perhaps, though, immersion in exotic landscapes and ruins produced its own species of disorientation and subjective disorder. It is striking nevertheless that Egyptian landscapes, as with Belzoni's tomb, largely avoided Gothic tropes of horror.

By 1850 these panoramas, these little slivers of exotic otherworldliness, had infiltrated much of the West End of London. Leicester Square was one of the epicentres of this explosion. Indeed, there were so many panoramic displays within reach of the square that Dickens satirized this in a piece for *Household Worlds*, sending an elderly fragile gentleman Mr Booley on a perilous, hair-raising voyage around the world, eventually revealed as being experienced entirely through panoramas a short walk from his home. Mr Booley visits the slaves and native Americans of the Mississippi, the Maoris of New Zealand, and the wastes of the Arctic. In Egypt, he travels down the Nile from Alexandria to the Temple of Abu Simbel, 'among temples, palaces, pyramids, colossal statues, crocodiles, tombs, obelisks, mummies, sand and ruin; he proceeded, like an opium-eater in a might dream.'[84] It is not one of Thomas De Quincey's terrifying nightmares, however: Egypt in London is an urban amble.

The panorama was only one way of experiencing urban immersion in the exotic East. Some grasp of the density of these experiences can be gained by stepping beyond Burford's rotunda on the corner of Leicester Square and looking about. In 1851, George Wyld's model of the world, which enfolded the entire globe inside a London rotunda, was built in the centre of the square, a parallel to the Great Exhibition. Wyld added a Turkish and Oriental Museum, 'illustrative,' one guide says 'of life in Turkey, Armenia and Albania, with life-like models of the interiors of palaces, harems, bazaars, offices of state, and courts of justice, with priests, soldiers and janissaries.'[85] It also contained a waxwork typology of Eastern races, teaching audiences the difference between Bashi-Bazouks, Constantinople Jews, dancing Dervishes and Greek villagers.[86]

Meanwhile, in 1852, on the other side of Leicester Square, the Royal Panopticon of Science and Art was proposed as a new institution 'to exhibit and illustrate, in popular form, discoveries in science and art'.[87] At the core of the building was a vast rotunda intended as a lecture and display space. The design for the façade of the building, unveiled in the *Illustrated London News* in 1852, revealed a startling imitation of the Saracenic style. The text explained that this 'finished specimen' was of a style 'which has as yet no perfect exemplification in the metropolis':

> The splendid remains at Cairo have afforded much that is now reproduced; and it is from an actual Daguerrotype of one of the mosques that the model of the dome has been taken, whose intrinsic beauty in this instance affords an ample apology for the strict adherence of the architect to the magnificent original.[88]

When finally completed in 1854, the Royal Panopticon appeared with a much reduced dome, although all the other Islamic details, including the minarets, remained. Now it was possible to walk out of the Burford or Wyld panoramas into a London space where the exotic had bled into the architectural fabric of the city. When the Panopticon failed as an educative venture, the building was remodelled in the 1860s by Frederick Strange, and it became the famous Alhambra theatre, perhaps the most elaborate mock-Islamic architectural design ever constructed in London. The theatre was built twice; after burning down, the building that reopened in 1882 further accentuated its Eastern promise.[89] Macqueen-Pope nostalgically recalled that 'on a summer night, when you approached the Alhambra from the West, across the square...and saw the crescent moon ride in the sky between the Eastern cupolas which shone dull

Figure 4.7 Proposed design of the Royal Panopticon, 1852 (London Metropolitan Archives).

gold in its silver light, you doubted very much if East and West did not meet, after all. If they did, it was at the Alhambra.'[90]

If this immersion was not enough, you could venture into the Turkish baths next to the Alhambra, visit the German bierkeller in the Café de l'Europe or drink Turkish coffee in Frascati's, served by 'a dark-faced individual in full Turkish attire'.[91] The vast Trocadero Restaurant in nearby Piccadilly, taken over by the Lyons tea firm in 1894, was also decked out in full orientalist style, with Moroccan, Indian and Turkish influences. Leicester Square was intoxicatingly Eastern. Along the Strand, which Macqueen-Pope called the High Street of

Figure 4.8 The Alhambra, Leicester Square (London Metropolitan Archives).

Bohemia, theatres vied to compete with the Alhambra style. The façade of the Tivoli Music Hall mixed up Plantagenet windows, French Empire pilasters and Romanesque arcading, whilst inside the restaurants offered private dining rooms decked out in Japanese or Arabian styles. The closer you got to the centre of the imperial metropolis, the more it seemed to disperse into a set of exotic spaces. It was not the borders that were hybrid, but the epicentre.

After the popular entertainment of the panorama, the most immersive experience available to Victorians and Edwardians was undoubtedly the theatre. The exotic East featured here too, in many different registers. The Alhambra was famous for its exotic ballets, and Victorian and Edwardian London was periodically convulsed by erotic fevers generated by theatrical extravaganzas spread by lascivious fantasies of the East. Arthur Symons constructed his decadent aesthetics around his absorbed spectatorship of these ballets in Leicester Square.[92] When Maud Allen danced the Dance of the Seven Veils barefoot and bare-legged at the Palace Theatre in 1904 'in most exotically scanty oriental attire' it caused a sensation.[93] When Nijinsky danced in the intensely erotic and violent piece *Sheherazade* at the Opera House in 1911, the intellectuals of Bloomsbury were similarly overwhelmed. In contrast, the reality-effect of contemporary Egypt was pursued on stage most obsessively by the actor-manager Augustus Harris at the Drury Lane Theatre, in darker tones.

When a young Harris was appointed to run the vast Drury Lane Theatre in 1879, this unofficial national theatre was in severe financial trouble and had been dark for several months. Harris responded with a series of extraordinary theatrical extravaganzas that used modern technology to create what Edward Ziter calls 'unified environments', tableaux that used scenography, a built-out stage with angled wings, costumes, music and hundreds of extras to fold the audience completely into the scene.[94] Full-sized boats would depart from docks, with huge crowds waving from the deck. The Thames would flow across stage. Desert camps with real camels and horses appeared. Full-scale battles, with large artillery, would swarm across the stage. The sets were overwhelming, the actors virtually lost in the complex choreography of machinery.

After his first success in the 1880 season, with a modestly ambitious epic called *The World*, Harris responded to the New Imperialism fostered by Sir John Seeley and other ideologues and staged a series of imperial extravaganzas. Given the geopolitics of the early 1880s, many of these focused on Egypt. Harris's 'built-out East' aimed 'to place the spectator in the exotic terrain, to provide a readable view from the ground without sacrificing the claims of mastery, implicit in geography's view from above.'[95] His plays were standard melodramas, in which white women were menaced by dastardly Arabs and redeemed by dashing Englishmen. In *Human Nature* (1881), a soldier's stained reputation is saved by heroic sacrifice against fanatical Arab forces, denounced as 'a gigantic wave of inhumanity, sweeping all before it, and leaving but horrors in its course.'[96] In *Freedom* (1883), Harris recreated the Egyptian uprising and the British military engagement with the Mahdi rebels and the eventual British occupation of Cairo. In *Khartoum!* staged only six weeks after General Gordon's death, Harris responded to the outpourings of national grief by restaging the military battles of the relief column and breathtakingly rewriting history by saving Gordon from his violent death. Scenes in this compensatory fantasy included the departure of the troop ship, the Mahdi's desert camp, a Cairo bazaar, a cataract on the Nile, the Battle of Abu Klea, and an 'Oriental ballet' interlude.[97] A major success, this show spilt beyond the edges of the auditorium. Harris purchased Gordon Relief memorabilia, such as a piece of carpet from Gordon's residence and the revolver of John Cameron, the *Standard* reporter killed in battle. He displayed them off the Saloon, in a simulacrum of the prison cell that held Ahmad Urabi, the Egyptian army officer who had first organized the revolt against the British. Harris worked every trick to ensure that the distancing effect of the proscenium stage was breached, the East rushing in to envelop the audience.

The Drury Lane spectaculars were never accepted as high art. More respectable audiences would probably have received their conception of Egypt via stagings of *Antony and Cleopatra*, such as Lillie Langtry's performance at the Princess Theatre in 1890, where the production was as 'authentically "Egyptian"' as possible, including 'such "archaeological" touches as a mummy case'.[98] Yet even as Harris's theatrical entertainments took a darker view of Egypt after decades of gossamer *Arabian Nights* fantasies, Drury Lane was not in the business of communicating terror or doomed encounters with an accursed colonial inheritance. Melodrama allows the cunning Arabs to plot, but the reassertion of English power and pluck is never in question. Harris's plays are 'exuberantly jingoistic', happily aiming to work as cultural armatures of imperial ideology.[99] But the sensorial overload and feeling of surrender to immersive experience might well have complicated any straightforward didactic hopes for these plays.

## Bazaars, West End shopping and exotic consumption

Exotic immersion in Egyptian or generically Middle Eastern spaces in Victorian London was nearly always a commercial entertainment experience. As we've seen, the brash allure of this architecture was set against the sober classical or Gothic styles favoured by government offices or state-funded museums. As the West End grew into a distinct urban destination for entertainment or shopping for all classes from the 1850s, an intrinsic link between consumerism and the oriental and exotic was explicitly developed. This was more than just a semiotic association.

Émile Zola's novel, *Au bonheur des dames* (1883) was based on his detailed research at Paris's famous department store, Le Bon Marché, which had opened in 1852. Zola is obsessively focused on how women shoppers become 'fascinated, intoxicated' by the experience of shopping in these brand-new department stores, repeatedly depicting scenes of disorientation, loss of self and near orgasmic delight.[100] This pleasure is offset by detailing the economic realities of the armies of shop-girls who work inside this 'terrible machine'. The seduction begins with the entry to the shop, which the owner, Mouret, 'transformed into an oriental saloon. From the very threshold it was a marvel, a surprise, which enchanted all of them.'[101] Mouret's purchase of whole markets of carpets from the Levant creates an entirely enclosed world:

> This sumptuous pacha's tent was furnished with divans and armchairs, made with camel sacks, some ornamented with many-coloured lozenges, others with primitive roses. Turkey, Arabia, and the Indies were all there. They had emptied the palaces, plundered the mosques and bazaars ... Visions of the East floated beneath the luxury of this barbarous art, amid the strong odour which the old wools had retained of the country of vermin and of the rising sun.[102]

What has been memorably described as 'the exotic-chaotic decorative style' in department stores was intended to divorce the shopper from any external perspective, creating a strictly capitalist logic of immersion in dream worlds of consumption.[103] Zola's critique of this 'harem-like decoration' locates the tinge of corruption in the stench of the East that is the base note underlying this Western consumer heaven.

The Oriental Rooms of Le Bon Marché had a major impact on the way that the department store was introduced to London in the 1870s. William Whiteley built up his store in Bayswater from small beginnings, before building a massive 'Universal Provider' store in the 1870s on Westbourne Grove. The area was already commonly known as 'Asia Minor' for its allegedly exotic, Eastern population, and George Augustus Sala's report of a visit to the store from 1875 described the shop as harem-like, a place to enter 'the sweet waters of Asia'.[104] In 1885, Whiteley's devoted specific rooms to 'Manufactures of Eastern Nations', from India and China to Turkey, Egypt, Syria and Morocco. Debenham and Freebody's in Wigmore Street also had an Oriental Department. These were responses to the exotic allure of consumption associated with the more exclusive Liberty's in East India House on Regent Street, which had been at the forefront of the craze for Japonnais and Chinoiserie in the 1870s. Liberty's opened an Eastern Bazaar and their 1898 catalogue promised another experience of being carried away:

> Wandering amidst the labyrinth of stalls, each with its own peculiar class of wares, the atmosphere redolent of Eastern perfumes, one can hardly imagine that we are in a Regent Street establishment, but that we have suddenly been transported on the wings of a genii to far distant Eastern Climes. All the Nations of the Orient seem to be represented in this wondrous place.[105]

A similar Eastern exoticism was used by Gordon Selfridge when he opened his Oxford Street store in 1909. Selfridge promoted the store as an American rationalization of insular English culture, and did so by celebrating cosmopolitanism through commerce. In 1911, the store was caught up in the craze for eastern dress prompted by the Ballets Russes performances of *Sheherazade* starring Nijinsky at the Royal Opera House. Turkish culottes and harem pantaloons became fashionable; the store staged oriental-themed nights in its top-floor ballrooms.[106] Rudi Laermans observes generally that in the department store 'commodities were frequently staged … within Oriental decorations. *The Thousand and One Nights*, in particular, served as a nearly inexhaustible source of inspiration.'[107]

No wonder, then, that Virginia Woolf's reflections on Oxford Street observed that the vulgar ambition to display signs of opulence was marked in the preposterous architecture: 'they stretch stone fantastically; crush together in one wild confusion the styles of Greece, Egypt, Italy, America and boldly attempt an air of lavishness.'[108]

In fact, Le Bon Marché was not the innovator in this association of commerce and the Orient. The Persian term 'bazaar' entered common English usage in the very early nineteenth century, the *Oxford English Dictionary* citing Southey's description of Exeter Change on the Strand as 'a sort of street under-cover … with a row of shops on either hand'. The nascent idea of the department store emerged from these imitations of Eastern markets. The first London bazaar was built in Soho Square in 1816 and was a great success. It was soon followed by the Grand Oriental Bazaar on the Strand, famous for its toyshops. The Queen's Bazaar on Oxford Street, built in 1828, shows how shopping fused with other entertainments. The *Mirror of Literature* recorded that it stocked '*bijouterie* and nicnacs, the *nouveautés* de Paris and Spitalfields, Canton in China and Leather Lane in Holborn, toycarts for children and fleecy hosiery for old folks, puff and pastry and the last new song, inkstand, taper lights, pen wipers, perfumed sealing wax, French hair paper, curling wheels and all the fair ammunition of love and madness.'[109] The building also contained waxworks, models of the city of Alexandria, and the 'British Diorama', which, alongside classic scenes from England such as Tintern Abbey, also showed David Roberts's gigantic paintings of Egyptian scenes, *The Temple of Apollinopolis* and the *Departure of the Israelites from Egypt*. These overlapping entertainments reinforced the sense that commercialized experiences of being transported were often coded as oriental.

Why was this so? Some commentators at the time proposed that these new shops appealed to the feelings of 'luxury' and 'boundless command' that gave women shoppers 'a sense of power approaching in its depth and intensity to the consciousness of omnipotence which is supposed to be the peculiar possession of an Oriental potentate.'[110] Perhaps because the self-gratification of consumption seemed fundamentally opposed to the Protestant work ethic, consumer experience was recoded as nebulously 'Eastern', recasting this new kind of consumption as inherently exotic. Men could then worry about the 'mystical feminine meaning' of idle shopping.[111] The department store, as in Zola's novel, was imagined as a harem, that fantastic space 'of *generalized perversion* and of the *absolute limitlessness of pleasure'*.[112]

But shops were not a female-only space: women were being manipulated by cynical entrepreneurs, mesmerized or carried away by shopping just as hypnotists were portrayed as dangerous foreign men with nefarious designs on virtuous English women.[113] A lot of commentary on nineteenth-century dreamworlds of consumption pursues a thesis of immersive spaces as places of 'numbed hypnosis', where oriental figures are negatively coded.[114] Yet again, though, this feels as if it reduces complex and conflicted experience, which regards consumer pleasure as an inherent ideological mystification. Mica Nava's reading of cosmopolitanism, in contrast, suggests that orientalism in the commercial domain was different from bureaucratic or 'scientific' knowledges of the East. In the department store the Eastern other has to entice rather than horrify, promise intimacy and allure rather than asserting hierarchy and difference. Even the most commercial forms of this cosmopolitan allure retain an ambiguity, the possibility that occidental women might desire in a fantastical Orient a different kind of existence.

This kind of ambiguous commercial exoticism filtered into the corners of everyday life. With the Egyptian cigarette, so heavily advertised in London at the turn of the century, one might say that one reached the apotheosis of the immersive experience of commercial exoticism, letting the East enter the lungs and permeate the bloodstream of the Western body. The Ottoman and Russian habit of smoking tobacco in rolled paper had been introduced among English soldiers during the Crimean War. After the occupation of Egypt in 1882, Egyptian production of tobacco for export was intensified, becoming a major cash crop.[115] Brands of 'luxury' Egyptian cigarettes flooded the English and American markets. Long before Camel introduced a blend of tobacco with an iconic Egyptian branding in 1913, it was possible to smoke 'Egyptian Deities' or local, hand-rolled cigarettes that were named after British imperial figures like Lord Rosebery or Lord Cromer. The Alexandria Cigarette Company, which sold the Luxor brand, established offices in New Broad Street in the City. Many companies used collectable cigarette cards to depict Egyptian gods, artefacts or generic oriental scenes.

British consumers of Egyptian luxury cigarettes presumably connected to associations of sensuous intoxication, the slothful pleasures of the harem, which was commonly depicted in a haze of hookah smoke (and its suggestion that shared smoking was integral to an abandoned, orgiastic world).[116] This was distinct from Yellow Peril panics about the loss of self to the opium pipe in London's East End Chinese opium dens, a panic that intensified in the 1890s but reached its zenith with the overdose of the young music hall starlet Billie Carleton in 1918, a death blamed on the dope-dealers of Chinese Limehouse.[117] In contrast, the Egyptian cigarette was smoked to escape the drear West for a moment, rather than abandon oneself entirely to the East. In Kate Chopin's ambiguous short story, 'An Egyptian Cigarette', first published in 1900, the narrator is given a mysterious box of unmarked cigarettes presented in Cairo 'by a species of fakir'. The woman takes 'one long inspiration of the Egyptian cigarette' and its 'subtle, disturbing current passed through my whole body'.[118] She is plunged into a visionary experience that may be a memory, a fantasy, or a transport to another soul, an access to desperate, delicious desire amidst desert dunes, where 'the weight of centuries seemed to suffocate my soul'. Recovering, she crushes the rest of the packet, having tasted possibilities she prefers to contain.[119] The story exactly rehearses the ambiguities of cosmopolitan consumption for women analysed by Mica Nava.

This tantalizing tobacco promise evidently worked for commercial sales. In November 1928, Carreras, famous for their Black Cat cigarettes, opened the huge neo-Pharaonic factory at Mornington Crescent, just north of Euston in London. Derided at the time, in keeping with all reactions to Egyptian architecture in London, it was restored in 1996 to its original, gleaming fake white splendour. The designs were modelled after the Temple of Bubastis, the cat-headed god, and two black cat sculptures flanked the impressive doorway. At the opening ceremony, the road was covered with sand and selections from Verdi's opera *Aida* were performed on the steps.[120] The harsh economics of imperial import and export calculations was hidden behind the flash of this exotic Art Deco façade.

In these commercial immersive-exotic spaces, we are often a very long way from an ominous or threatening Egypt. Egyptian associations were multiple and contradictory, and the new phase of commodification in Victorian England clearly relied on the East to evoke notions of luxury and pleasure rather than terror or fear. Yet Karl Marx called the commodity a 'social hieroglyph', as if it were an enigmatic Egyptian object, for a reason.[121] The commodity contains many contradictory forces. The next chapter turns to the place of Egypt in the 'official' spaces of international exhibitions, public ceremonial spaces, and museums. These tried to appeal to the educated and disinterested gaze of connoisseurship, but were always intertwined with the commercial worlds that exploded around them. Nevertheless, it is in these spaces that we can begin to detect a different tone resonating about Egypt in London.

# 5

# Egypt in London II:
# The Exhibitionary Universe

E DWARD FREEMAN'S *History of Architecture*, published in 1849, argued that the Ancient Egyptians might have been the first to develop systematic architecture but it was still marked by 'rudeness and imperfection'.[1] In his chapter on the later development of Arabian architecture, he conceded that the buildings of the Islamic East 'delighted in astonishing the eye' and were 'rich, wonderful, calculated to enchant at first sight', yet immediately warned that the Eastern style 'will not bear critical examination'. This architecture came from a sterile culture which had not developed for a millennium, and the most spectacular examples of 'Saracenic fancy' only revealed that 'the work was uncontrolled by any law of taste or consistency'. 'Their splendour,' he concluded, 'is mere barbaric magnificence superadded to fantastic and inconsistent forms.'[2] John Ruskin also warned about the 'undisciplined enchantment' of Eastern architecture in *The Stones of Venice*.[3] A short while later, at the time of the Indian Mutiny, he declared the Alhambra style 'detestable', fit only for ivory palaces of 'cruelty, cowardice, idolatry, bestiality'.[4] Yet these were not the only judgments of the exotic East: my last chapter suggested that the linkage of the Orient with opulence, luxury and excess made the Islamic style a significant vehicle for the explosion of commodity culture in Victorian London. The West End happily transformed itself into an Eastern fantasia in defiance of sanctioned taste.

It might be reasonable to expect 'official' architecture to have a stronger investment in the English style, and indeed public buildings adopted either neoclassical or Gothic modes, firmly rooted in notions of the racial north.[5] This sober style was also exported to the colonies as a lesson in English solidity.

Yet only two years after Freeman's pronouncements, the Great Exhibition opened in Hyde Park. Inside Joseph Paxton's glass and iron construction, built by subscription under royal patronage, this space embraced a global network of products, cultures and styles. The very iron struts of the Crystal Palace carried bright, primary colour patterns that were borrowed directly from Islamic architecture. The iron fretwork in the railings around along the upper galleries also used Moorish patterning. Much condemned in the press before the opening, the use of colour was soon considered a triumph of innovative design. 'Islamic ornament and colour,' Edward Ziter has suggested, 'were the raw materials from which Britain constructed its monument to surplus.'[6] Thomas Douglas Murray's father, the Reverend Thomas Boyles Murray, was prompted to versify on 'such orient visions' in his pamphlet-length poem, *A Day in the Crystal Palace*:

> Twas well for language, from exhaustless springs
> Of Eastern imagery, to fill the breast
> With gardens, palaces, and sparkling things
> Creations fair of Araby the blest.[7]

The internal designs were made by Owen Jones, who had spent years studying the Moorish architecture of the Alhambra complex in southern Spain and had travelled in Egypt, sketching ancient monuments, between 1829 and 1834. In contrast to the condemnation of sterile Eastern design, Jones believed that Islamic polychromy and patterning were a pious expression of religious fervour and was an advocate of incorporating these elements to revive English design. His success with the Crystal Palace led to commissions to design the interiors of St James's Concert Hall, off Piccadilly, and Osler's magical glass shop in Oxford Street.[8]

Half of the space within the nineteen acres of the Crystal Palace was given over to displays of products from Britain and its colonial possessions. These included an Indian elephant (a stuffed one hastily borrowed from a regional museum), the famed and possibly cursed Koh-i-Noor diamond, Canadian timber and furs, and a Tunisian Court of fabrics and textiles. The rest of the space presented foreign goods, from America, Russia and colonial rivals. The small Ottoman display was dominated by Turkish goods, with only about five hundred samples of raw materials and modern manufactures from its Egyptian dependency, mainly textiles, silverwork and leather.[9] Although Egypt and Turkey were given a relatively prominent place on the corner of the transept near the Crystal Fountain, this was a meagre display. This all changed when Paxton's building reopened in 1854, massively extended, as a private concern on Sydenham Hill.

Owen Jones was responsible, with Joseph Bonomi, another artist-traveller who had spent over ten years in Egypt, for designing one of the great sensations of Crystal Palace in Sydenham: the Egyptian Court. The new Palace contained several historical courts, designed to offer a miniature guide to the art and architecture of the ancient civilizations of Egypt, Greece, Rome and the newly rediscovered Assyrian cities of Nineveh and Babylon. The entrance to the Egyptian Court was approached by an avenue of eight lions, cast from the British Museum 'Prudhoe' lions (sculptures Lord Prudhoe had brought back from the Sudan in 1828). The façade reproduced friezes of the Egyptians at war at the height of their empire in the nineteenth dynasty, and spelt out the Queen's own hieroglyphic cartouche as 'ruler of the waves, the royal daughter, Victoria.' The interior of the court was divided into seven areas, including reproductions of the tomb of Beni Hassan, friezes and wall paintings, a hall of columns and a museum with items copied from treasures in Cairo. Ruins were magically restored to their pristine colours and forms, reproduced in lath and plaster. The aim was immersion: 'The moment the visitor entered the Court they were effectively transported across space and back in time to Egypt', blurring the line of 'reality and fantasy.'[10]

The *pièce de resistance* was in the inner courtyard, which was dominated by large-scale models of the twin statues of Rameses from the temple at Abu Simbel, who glowered down at visitors in vibrant colours from an impressive height through the palm trees. The space was designed to show, in opposition to Freeman or Ruskin, 'the exquisite beauty, refinement and grandeur of Egyptian art.'[11] This recreation of Ancient Egyptian monuments was backed by the most authoritative scholars of the time. The Crystal Palace Company issued the pamphlet *The Egyptians in the Time of the Pharaohs* by Sir John Gardner Wilkinson with an introduction to hieroglyphics by Samuel Birch of the Oriental Department of the British Museum. The Egyptian Court was the most spectacular rendition of Egypt in London in the mid-Victorian period (it was destroyed in the Palace fire of 1866).

The morphing of the official Great Exhibition into the commercial venture of the Crystal Palace shows how difficult it is to separate out public and private buildings or their ideological purposes in this era. Nevertheless, this chapter attempts to cluster together Egyptianized spaces in London that had a different temper from the largely commercial or entertainment aspects of panoramas, dioramas, bazaars, theatres or department stores. The massive international fairs that followed from the Great Exhibition were of course primarily trade fairs. But they were underwritten by public subscription and carried an ideological freight beyond the celebration of free trade and spectacles of production and consumption. The space of the fair was also meant to be an instructional zone, educating the millions of visitors in certain national and international narratives of identity and belonging. As the century went on, these lessons were progressively inflected through questions of Empire and the relationship of the colonial margins to the centre. The rhetoric of free trade and universal

**Figure 5.1** The Crystal Palace, North Transept, Abu Simbel figures (National Monuments Record).

brotherhood at the Great Exhibition of 1851 was displaced by harsher racial divisions and typologies at the London International in 1862, the Colonial and Indian Exhibition in 1886 or the nearly annual shows at Earl's Court from the 1890s.

In these immersive environments, sublime effects or the encounter with cultural difference were intended as more than delightful distractions: they were meant to create itineraries that would, as it were, walk new imperial citizens into being. This was also supposed to be the aim, in a rather more sedate manner, of the new museums in the metropolis that were opened to the general public through the course of the nineteenth century. In these environments, artefacts, reproductions of exotic spaces or living spectacles of foreign cultures from Africa, Asia or the Middle East, were used to teach explicit lessons about the superiority of Western modernity, and to display how European enlightenment was transforming supposedly backward parts of the world.

This view of the instrumental purpose of the exhibitionary universe of the nineteenth century relies on an influential argument in recent museum theory. Tony Bennett's *The Birth of the Museum* argues that these institutions were 'machines for progress' that directed the masses through displays organized in developmental narratives, moving from the primitive to the advanced, savage to civilized, East to West.[12] The universal survey museum, like the British Museum or the Louvre, aimed to turn unruly masses into modern, rational citizens by conducting them on an evolutionary trajectory: 'By performing the ritual of walking through the museum, the visitor is prompted to enact and thereby to internalise the values and beliefs written into the architectural script.'[13] This was often the stated aim of many museum reformers and exhibition guides. It was Augustus Henry Lane-Fox (later General Pitt-Rivers) who tied what he called the 'principle of continuity' in the historical development of a particular artefact like a boomerang or spear to evolutionary principles, and aimed to embody this in his museum displays, so that a museum tour would educate the visitor by enacting the process of development from the simple to the sophisticated before their eyes. This was derived from Herbert Spencer's trajectory of social evolution from the simple to the complex rather than Darwin's biological theory. Lane-Fox tried out this idea in one of the first exhibitions at the Bethnal Green Museum in 1874, set up with the explicit aim of educating the artisanal work force of the East End. He had grander plans for an ideal evolutionary museum, built on concentric circles of progressive human development to push home the lesson that 'Nature makes no jumps' but developed in a gradualist, evolutionary way.[14] Such a museum would scientifically refute ideas of social revolution espoused by radicals. Museum organization educated the visitor in the principles of gradual social evolution, but also aligned the viewer with a sense of Western racial supremacy. The English viewer was meant to understand that the displays of the cultural, technological or ethnographic development from the simple to the complex culminated with *him*: the Englishman as evolutionary apotheosis. 'A museum,' David Murray said in 1904, 'is the easiest means of self-instruction. It is one of the surest means of producing enlightenment and of raising the people above the depressing influence of dull and common-place surroundings.'[15]

Egypt has been made an exemplar of this functionalist view of museums and exhibitions in an important analysis by Timothy Mitchell. In the Paris

Exhibition of 1889, the 'Rue de Caire' recreated a whole chunk of a winding Cairo street, complete with real tumbledown architecture, with real camels and their drivers, real belly-dancers and real haggling bazaar owners, cunning Arabs imported into the exhibition site to play up to the stereotype of wanting to defraud you of every last centime. The reality of these elements was extremely questionable, of course (any swarthy complexion would do to play a 'native'), but framed inside the exhibition these spaces carried greater claims to authenticity than the orientalist fancies of London's theatres and shops. The success of this exhibit, or more accurately the exotic dancers that featured in it, ensured that the Cairo street was a staple of many subsequent international exhibitions. For Mitchell, these spaces render the 'world as exhibition', a pictorial representation from which the viewer stands back and objectifies Egypt. The simulacra became more real than Egypt itself: when the writer Gérard de Nerval finally travelled to Egypt he was disappointed and bewildered and preferred the library of the French Institute built by Napoleon to the teeming streets of Cairo. He wrote to Théophile Gautier, 'I really wanted to set the scene for you here ... but it is only in Paris that one finds cafés so Oriental.'[16] In this instance 'the Orient refused to present itself like an exhibit', Mitchell argues, and so the actuality of Egypt 'appeared simply orderless and without meaning'.[17] Nerval's experience was repeated over and over again, embodying Edward Said's view of orientalism as a '*textual* attitude': 'It seems a common human failing to prefer the schematic authority of a text to the disorientations of direct encounters.'[18]

This model suggests that the Egyptian Orient is a construction of the exhibitionary universe, of world's fairs and museums that organized its vanished past, exposed its debased present and idealized its colonial future. As in the previous chapter, I want to put some pressure on this account. In fact, Egypt held an odd and anomalous position in many world's fairs and particularly in British colonial exhibitions, where the technical status of Egypt left it outside the central displays of dominions of the Crown and hovering on the margins of many exhibition grounds. Similarly, museums struggled to incorporate Egyptian antiquities into their displays. When they did, these objects did not necessarily settle into narratives that rehearsed the development of art and civilization. It is in the museums, it seems, that mummies stubbornly resisted the transition from sacred remains into scientific artefacts. Visitors, equally, refused to be educated in the proper manner about them and instead invested them with rumours and superstitions, leaving curators to resent the persistence of primitive magical thinking within their institutions rather than celebrating their role in the forward march of Western rationality. Indeed, I want to suggest that an important part of the genesis of the curse of the mummy resides in the space where the museum fails to dictate the reactions of its audience to the objects it transports to the imperial metropolis.

# Egypt at the world's fairs

The Great Exhibition, staged in London's Hyde Park in the summer of 1851, was the apotheosis of the British assertion of its home-grown model of industrial capitalism. It aimed to rededicate the nation to this model, particularly among the working classes who had staged Chartist marches in the same park just three years earlier. Many local trade organizations orchestrated mass travel for factory workers to the Palace. Walter Benjamin argued that the world exhibitions 'were training schools in which the masses, barred from consuming, learned empathy with exchange value. "Look at everything; touch nothing."'[19] The innovative international focus of the Exhibition was ascribed to the genius of Prince Albert and the Exhibition was carried on a wave of peace and cooperation rhetoric. But this internationalism was also driven by fervent ideologues of free trade who wished to abolish protectionism around the world, the better to bind global trade to the British economic model. An early embodiment of Victorian globalization, the one hundred thousand commodities displayed by fourteen thousand exhibitors were meant to render visible the comprehensive geographical extent of the industrial revolution. As *The Times* anticipated two months before the opening: 'There the orderly arrangement of every contribution and the subordination of each part and object to the idea of one great and systematic display' would ensure that 'the Crystal Palace will at once become a perfect epitome of the world's industry.'[20]

This cornucopia of stuff was organized into four main categories – raw materials, machinery, manufactures and fine arts – notionally intended to follow the path of the production process from origins to glamorous end products, thus explaining the invisible mysteries of industrialism to its consumers. Apart from the opulent Indian Court, designed by the East India Company from East India House in London, the British possessions were mainly presented as distant places that supplied the raw materials to the British workshops of the world. Maps and charts, alongside George Wyld's rotunda model of the world that opened in Leicester Square in 1851, aided the attempt to represent the integration of core and periphery. But there was no better education for this end than simply promenading through the Crystal Palace itself, mastering the world in an afternoon.

Visitors too were as much on exhibition, with a great deal of anticipation (and some fears) about the influx of foreigners into London for the show. William Thackeray's poem on the opening proclaimed 'within its shining streets/A multitude of nations meets:/A countless throng/I see beneath the crystal bow/And Gaul and German, Russ and Turk,/Each with his native handwork/And busy tongue.'[21] Strict rhyme and metre neatly contained this Babel, whilst Henry Mayhew and George Cruikshank's *1851* emphasized the racial chaos prompted by the Exhibition in an exhaustive listing of Esquimaux, Hottentots, Truefits, Cingalese and Maripoosans converging on London.[22] Elsewhere, the exotic and cruel Chinese were satirized in Henry Sutherland Edwards's *An Authentic Account of the Chinese Commission Sent to Report on the Great Exhibition* and the visiting black dignitaries of the imaginary 'Cannibal Islands' featured prominently in Thomas Onwhyn's *Mr and Mrs Brown's Visit to London to see the Great Exhibition of All Nations, How they were Astonished at its Wonders, Inconvenienced by the Crowds, and Frightened out of their Wits, by the Foreigners.* In one cartoon at the refreshments room, three cannibals look expectant at the prospect of being served Mr and Mrs Brown's son, whilst Chinamen and Turks look on. As Jeffrey Auerbach observes, the obsessive racialization of the representation of the crowds of the Exhibition, despite the comparatively small numbers of actual foreign visitors, was another way of defining Britishness through registering and demarcating racial difference.[23] By cataloguing people as well as things, the Great Exhibition laid out economic and social relationships in an easily navigable grid. 'Exhibitions offered the empire and nation as total, participatory pictures' in which everyone and everything 'could be envisioned, illustrated and imagined according to common ethnographic terms and visual modes'.[24]

This may have been the abstract ideal for the Great Exhibition, but the actual experience of being immersed in the crowds within the glasshouse was often one of distaste, bewilderment or confusion. In *The World and its Workshops*, James Ward confessed to a 'state of mental helplessness' on his visit, whilst Thomas Carlyle's dissenting opinion was a telling metaphor of the Exhibition as 'one inane tornado'.[25] The problem started with the four main divisions of objects, which were subdivided by the commissioner Henry Cole into a further thirty categories. These prompted a host of anomalies and definitional problems, queries about placement being resolved locally and somewhat arbitrarily. Logical organization was obstructed by the need to place heavy industrial technologies on the ground floor, leaving smaller and lighter materials for the galleries. Sequence was interrupted by decorative courts, such as the Medieval Court designed by the ardent Gothic revivalist A. W. N. Pugin. Pugin's court was controversial due to its prominent Christian cross; although it was not a crucifix, it became a target for anti-Catholic sentiment and he was requested to lower its position. Pugin's advocacy of medieval artisanal work against soulless modern factory production also appeared to argue against the whole industrialist ethos of the Exhibition itself. All of these elements, aside from the overwhelming volume of stuff on this site, suggest to Jeffrey Auerbach that there was a large gap between the educative ideal and the 'vague and muddled' experience of an actual visit to the Exhibition: 'There was no way to walk the exhibits in the order in which they were meant to be seen.'[26]

A similar complaint about incoherent organization was made about the Crystal Palace at Sydenham. Here Egypt was transformed from a backwater of industrial productivity, barely registering at the Great Exhibition, to the subject of one of the key historical courts through which visitors were conducted on their immersive promenade through the history of civilization. However, it was difficult to undertake this tour in proper sequence, as one guidebook commented:

> It is to be regretted, that in arranging the works of art and interest which abound in the building, greater attention was not paid to some order of succession, whether in point of time or style, so that the visitor, passing by regular gradation and by progressive steps, might the more easily retain those valuable lessons which may be obtained from almost every department.[27]

The *Routledge Guide* therefore undertook to furnish a plan for visitors that would actively direct them through the developmental sequence, starting with 'ancient and medieval art' before 'proceeding gradually onward, to arrive at the productions of art and industry of the present time'.[28] This itinerary started with the Egyptian Court, which began with 'pure and simple' forms of 'exquisite taste', the architecture and religion in perfect harmony, before offering a lesson on 'the simultaneous degeneracy of man and art': 'This great land is now the deadest of all lands: its palaces and temples are the habitation of sore-eyed Arabs, who light their fires with the gilded coffins of dead princes'.[29] The *Guide* then followed the Grecian, Roman and Alhambran Courts, but carped that the Assyrian Court was placed out of order, and was fanciful rather than historical. The only advantage was to see Nineveh without 'the attacks of the Turcoman and the Kurd, thievish Arabs, or lying guides'.[30] Even so, the developmental lesson was disrupted by the demands of spectacle and entertainment.

The eminent French historian Hippolyte Taine was harsh, seeing little educative virtue in the commercial enterprise of the Palace at Sydenham. His dyspeptic comments described it as 'a monstrous pile' containing an 'agglomeration of incongruous curiosities' which put him in mind of corrupt imperial Rome. The Caesars at least had original Grecian treasures; in Sydenham there were only plaster casts and 'monsters made of cardboard'.[31]

Defeat by the spectacle of the mathematical sublime at these exhibitions was accompanied by a delighted feeling of confusion which came at the expense of any instructive virtues. Confusion was certainly a common observation of exhibition visitors. George Augustus Sala, who had started as a journalist working for Dickens in 1851, was later sent to the Paris Exhibition of 1878 to cover its entire summer season. After fourteen weeks, he declared: 'My mind has become a kind of chaos, in which catalogues, descriptions of processes, photographs of exhibits, restaurateur's bills, lottery tickets, lists of Grand Prizemen and Gold Medallists, cabmen's numbers, and shopkeepers' cards, all more or less connected with the Exhibition, are mingled in inextricable confusion.'[32] The thesis of the 'world as exhibition' argues that the visitor was presented with an ordered and disciplined picture which he or she could survey, or learn to survey. Immersion in the exhibition site did not always seem to realize this plan.

Still, the idea of seasonal exhibitionary universes, microcosms of the world built in temporary wonderlands, raced across the world after 1851. Paris followed in 1855, and so did Madras with its Industrial Exhibition. There were shows in Berlin, Chicago and New York, and also in Jeypore, Adelaide and Melbourne. As the imperial scramble for territory intensified towards the end of the century, exhibitions in England, France and America 'institutionalized' a style that was noted for what Paul Greenhalgh has called its 'baroque excesses.'[33] Each sought to outbid the others, to be larger, taller, louder, and once the 1867 Exposition Universelle in Paris introduced the idea of individual national pavilions for each participating country, the architectural excesses reached a whole new level. Outside the cycle of international expos, London began to host annual summer spectaculars at Earl's Court on internationalist and imperialist themes. The theatrical impresario who organized these shows was Imre Kiralfy who built the White City showground in west London in 1907, a 140-acre site of simple white stucco buildings that could be annually transformed with wood and plaster façades into whatever exotic fantasia was required. It was modelled on the White City built for the Chicago World's Columbian Exposition of 1893. Kiralfy indulged the oriental style, and White City staged some of the most elaborate orientalist displays of the Edwardian era.[34]

The presence and meaning of Ancient Egypt or the immersive-exotic charms of replicas of spaces from modern Arabian Cairo at these exhibitions shifted with the geopolitics of European diplomacy and assertions of imperial power. Egypt was ostensibly an Ottoman possession until 1881, but the increasing freedom granted to its Khedives, who opened up to European investment under Muhammad Ali's policy after 1811, meant that France and England were constantly vying for informal influence in Egyptian court circles. France was in the ascendancy at mid-century, which is why it was Paris not London that transformed the representation of Egypt at the Exposition Universelle in 1867. Indeed, Paris would consistently give Egypt more significance and centrality in these shows, even after the British occupation in 1882.

Paris 1867 was designed to outdo the London exhibitions of 1851 and 1862 in size, cost and popularity, being a monument to the ambitions of Louis Bonaparte. Central palaces of industry and commerce proclaimed the French version of universalism and free trade, but these were surrounded by national pavilions. This started a trend for architectural competition among exhibiting nations that would push subsequent exhibitions to ever greater extravagance. They were also increasingly populated by 'natives', and *Bradshaw's Handbook* promised the visitor Persians, Hindoos and Esquimaux, 'in short the whole human family...seen at home, and in their traditional attire'.[35] The cluster of Egyptian buildings was considered a great success. There were several pavilions in the complex. There was a neo-Pharaonic replica of the temple of Philae, complete with avenue of sphinxes, designed by Claude Mariette, the French director of the Museum of Antiquities in Cairo. It contained 'mummies, arms, tools, musical instruments, etc.'[36] There was also a *salamlik*, or great hall, modelled in the shape of a Greek cross, rich with elaborate Islamic tiling and ornament, and a *wikala*, a bazaar built around a courtyard. In the middle of the courtyard was a statue of Jean-François Champollion, the French savant who had 'solved' the enigma of hieroglyphic script, thus rendering Egypt finally fully transparent to Europeans. An Egyptian *dahabiyya* boat was berthed nearby, turning this stretch of the Seine into a facsimile of the Nile.[37] Crucially, there was another neo-Pharaonic structure called the Isthme de Suez, which showed models, plans and panoramas for the Suez Canal, then under construction under the command of the French engineer Ferdinand de Lesseps, cousin to the French Empress Eugénie. The Ottoman quarter with mosque, bathhouse and 'typical' Turkish house was adjacent, along with the Morocco and Tunis displays. The passage from Cairo to Istanbul was a single, crooked street, an elegiac fantasy for a Cairo already 'lost' to development. On visiting this site in 1867, Hippolyte Gautier proclaimed: 'The entire Orient is before you; do not look for machines here, or for the practical inventions of the human mind; you are in the domain of the contemplative life: the agreeable precedes the utilitarian.'[38] The space of the exhibition site directed these contrasts between industrious West and its Eastern other.

At the heart of this simulacrum, strangely, was the Khedive of Egypt, Ismail himself, who was invited to Paris and set up court inside the Exhibition to receive visiting delegations. A back-handed compliment, this only demonstrated Egyptian dependency on the European core, played out in miniature in the Exhibition grounds. The *Bradshaw Guide* described this as the 'kiosk' of the Viceroy, situated just behind the Egyptian café. Ismail was transfixed by Parisian modernity (and, so it was said, by Empress Eugénie). The centre of Cairo was to be partially remodelled along the lines of Baron Haussmann's transformation of Paris, with slum clearance and wide, radiating boulevards. Ismail's aim was to build the Suez Canal in order to revolutionize Egypt's place in world trade. For the opening of the Suez Canal in 1869 in Egypt, Ismail reproduced some of the crazy excesses of the 1867 international exhibition, building in Cairo an Italian opera house and the Gerzira Palace in full Alhambra style (but designed by German architects) especially to receive Empress Eugénie. The *belle époque* temporarily migrated to Egypt, as Europe's royalty, aristocracy and wealthy industrialist classes vied to be seen at the nightly balls. The extravagance of the opening ceremonies, on top of the rickety financing of the Suez Canal project, were symptoms that Egypt's modernization was built on unsustainable European credit. Soon, French and English banks took control, Ismail was deposed and the English government purchased the Suez Canal in 1874 for a fraction of the price of its construction. Punitive taxation of the Egyptians was imposed to finance repayment. These were preludes to rebellion, British military engagement with Egyptian forces at Tel-el-Kebir and the occupation of Cairo by September 1882.

Even with British occupation, London exhibitions in the 1880s did not incorporate Egypt in any major way into their displays, obviously because Egypt had not been officially annexed to the British Empire. At the Colonial and Indian Exhibition of 1886, held in grounds between the South Kensington Museum and the Royal Albert Hall, the hierarchy was clear: India was the jewel, represented by the reconstruction of an Indian palace approached through a symbolic 'Jeypore Gateway' that transported you, so *The Times* said, 'into the stately splendour of that unchanging antique land of the East'.[39] Adjacent was a museum, organized by province, and an India and Ceylon tea room. The *Official Guide* noted that the Secretary of State for India and the Indian government had donated nearly £30 000 to the cost of the exhibition.[40] Consequently, the Colonial Hall was draped in Punjabi chintzes, like an oriental tent, and natural history dioramas staged elephant and tiger attacks and showed 'Indian Jungle Life'. This was followed by displays from the white colonies of Canada, Australia, New Zealand and South Africa. In smaller areas, on the northern periphery of the grounds, were goods from Ceylon, Mauritius, Hong Kong, Borneo and the West Indies. Official records of the exhibition were tedious actuarial accounts of the flow of raw materials – coal, ore, gems, tea, cocoa, sugar, gums, oils and fats – from the margin to the centre.[41] At the end of the central avenue, a giant relief map of the world instructed visitors on the extent of British colonial possessions. 'Ethological Sub-Courts' educated visitors in the gradations of racial difference by displaying 'life-like models, appropriately costumed, of armed men and women of the wilder tribes'.[42] Another immersive environment was the 'Old London Street', 'a quaint and picturesque thoroughfare' that took visitors on an accelerated passage through time from medieval London, via overhanging Elizabethan houses, to reconstructions of the homes of Oliver Cromwell and Dick Whittington.[43] This had been left over from the International Health Exhibition of 1884; entertaining perhaps, but intended to be instructive as to civilization's steady improvement on questions of hygiene and home. At the Colonial and Indian Exhibition there was no space for the sublime ruins of Ancient Egypt or much romance of the East; the only trace in the *Guide* is an advertisement for Luxor cigarettes. Egypt was an economic and political problem to be 'solved' and hope rested in increasing the exports of cotton and tobacco.

In contrast, the Parisian evocation of this fanciful terrain seemed to accelerate the more their power drained away. In 1889, the Paris Expo was famous for its marvels of modernity: Gustave Eiffel's iron-lattice gateway to the exhibition site on the Champs de Mars, and Thomas Alva Edison's pavilion of electric light. The spirit of Jules Verne dominated the imaginary realm of the exhibition. Western orientation towards the future was sharply defined against the primitive stasis of the East. More than ever, the machines were juxtaposed with villages of Sengalese, Congolese or Dahomeyans, a world, the *Pall Mall Gazette* reported, of 'aboriginal savages' recently discovered in the depths of Africa and in the process of being civilized.[44] This was at the height of the 'native village' concept, living dioramas mixing prurience and instruction in progressive colonization in equal measure.[45]

The innovation of 1889 was to introduce a funfair adjacent to the 'official' site, a zone of unbridled entertainment and profit unencumbered by any weighty educative purpose. Increasingly, Egypt would appear in these zones, shifting into pure entertainment. There was no official Ottoman display that year, the Turks staying away, meaning that the construction of the Orient was left to others. The sensation of the 1889 Exposition was the 'Rue de Caire', the Cairo Road, made up of twenty-five buildings designed by Ferdinand de Lesseps, and populated by camels, drivers, market traders and, most entrancingly, belly-dancers. The Rue de Caire was intended to compress every Egyptian epoch into one stretch of street, and was built by the businessmen Delort de Gléon with rubble transported from Cairo (he recorded this street in his book *L'architecture arabe des Khalifes d'Egypte à l'Exposition Universelle de Paris en 1889* with twenty-eight photographic plates).[46] De Gléon claimed that 'the Rue de Caire on the Champs de Mars was more authentic than the streets of Cairo itself, because...it was impossible to find an untouched old street in Cairo'.[47] This gave the simulacrum claims to a noble memorial purpose, but it was the lascivious possibilities that drew the crowds and justified its location in the funfair. The Cairo street was transposed to the Chicago World's Fair in 1893, when it reached its largest extent, with over a thousand 'natives' employed to populate a street that ran from an imitation of the temple at Karnak to cafés promising belly-dancers in back rooms. At this size, Greenhalgh comments, 'the Rue de Caire seemed to escape all intended categories and become an independent force in itself'.[48] When it returned to Paris for the 1900 Exposition, it became the site where Decadents dared to speak the desires excised from official catalogues or illustrated guidebooks. The impressively dissolute Jean Lorrain claimed that within the bounds of the Exposition Paris was now 'the city of the Orient, Paris conquered by the Levant.' He confessed:

> At the Cairo Café where we are seated in front of steaming cups, a delicate, frail Egyptian girl, barely fourteen years old, with a finely modelled face of light amber, smiles at us with all her enamel teeth and her large, green eyes; she is sheathed in reddish-brown silk which makes her look like a gleaming serpent.[49]

Men desired exotic girls and women, and women desired exotic men. At the Ceylon tea house the women panted after the exotic *garçons* and one of the Sinhalese waiters was pointed out to Lorrain as 'one who has lost count of his conquests'.[50] It was in these exotic cafés, too, that Oscar Wilde spent some dreamy afternoons in the last months of his life in exile, as Robert Ross recalled.[51]

In London, articulating this economy of desire would not have been allowed to reach the level of utterance. At the Greater Britain Exhibition at Earl's Court in 1899 there was a Cairo street, although the plans submitted for the building works called it 'Cyprus Street' until very late in the day.[52] This contained an Arabian café and school, a mosque and minaret and an open bazaar, and was symbolically located over a Moorishly decorated bridge over the Midland Railway and next to the switchback railway in the entertainment park. It was mentioned only in passing by a jaded *Times* reporter, who termed the whole exhibition 'very much the same as usual'.[53] The main show had mustered only five official colonial exhibitors. It also contained a British Science Pavilion that gave anthropological backing to the colonial project in Africa, and a Hall of Religions that provided a narrative of evolutionary development from savage to civilized theology. Most of the public interest was in the 'Savage South Africa' pageant, a separate commercial venture at the Empress Theatre next door. The twice-daily show, featuring nearly two hundred Matabele, Basutos and Kaffirs, legitimated the dubious annexations by Cecil Rhodes in southern Africa, staging battles from the Matabele War of 1893 and, like the Drury Lane extravaganzas, focused on the heroic self-sacrifice of British soldiers. There was already some distaste over the transport of native populations 'to be stared at and to take their chance of being demoralised in such strange and unedifying surroundings',[54] a view that would cause the African village to be closed down in the first season of the 1924 British Empire Exhibition and eventually end native village displays by 1939.

More attention was paid to the Franco-British Exhibition of 1908 because it was the first major event at the new White City complex in west London and the first bi-national show, wreathed with the rhetoric of *entente cordiale* between old rivals after some tricky colonial flashpoints in the 1890s. The 1908 Olympics was held in London as part of the international exhibition, and Shepherd's Bush tube station was built to transport the expected crowds. The Franco-British Exhibition included Imre Kiralfy's most extravagant orientalist displays: 'perhaps no more grandiose Islamic experience [was] ever contrived for the inhabitants of London'.[55] It centred on the flashy Court of Honour, 'a very pleasant treatment of a Hindoo idea', ornate Indian buildings and domes situated around a boating pool with a cascading fountain lit by thousands of electric lights at night to create 'a brilliant Oriental fantasy'.[56] It was, one architectural reviewer acidly observed, 'the kind of Indian architecture one associates with

Earl's Court,' where 'every possible feature is surmounted by a dome or cupola.'[57] This was 'impressionist architecture', 'neither real nor thorough', the exhibition site giving Kiralfy 'the chance to model in plaster the fantasies which he dare not attempt in stone.'[58] Emphasizing the continued importance of India to the British conception of Empire, money was invested in constructing a separate large Indian Pavilion: 'They say that it cost the India Office fifty thousand pounds just to collect the exhibits shown here. It was money well spent. The work in hand was to show the people at home the life and work of a country hugely mysterious, hugely unknown.'[59]

Representations of the Middle East were reserved for the French Algerian Palace and a separate Palace of the Colonies. Located here was an oriental bazaar, where one commentator scornfully observed that 'inside were Arabs, Turks, Germans, English, and even a few French, speaking an outrageous polyglot gibberish.' These crowds ignored 'the instructive objects scattered among this trash', drawn instead to 'glass trinkets' like 'savages'.[60] Educative purpose was clearly losing out to the frenzy of immersive consumption. This is underlined by a host of planning permissions for the pavilion of the Imperial Ottoman Tobacco Regie and smaller kiosks for Abdulla, Makajik and Ardath tobacco concessions.[61]

Egypt, as might now be expected, was pushed into the funfair to vie with the scenic railway and the 'Flip-Flap' ride (the thrill of the season). Under the towering track of the helter-skelter, one photograph reveals a showman outside the Egyptian columns and sphinxes of the Pharaoh's Daughter exhibit. This was a large theatre that could seat seven hundred, and the building was constructed in full mock Ancient Egyptian pylon style. The show, the *Illustrated Review* tantalizingly reveals, 'was an illusion, which presented the spectacle of that lady slowly changing from her mummy state to warm life, and slowly returning to the tomb again'.[62] The stage also required 'a concrete tank sunk below the level of the auditorium and a considerable quantity of water is required for the performances'.[63] Nearly 350 000 visitors paid for entry to this exhibit.[64] There were some health and safety concerns that the Pharaoh's Daughter had been built too close to the rifle range, although the only accidental deaths at the Franco-British Exhibition came from a balloon fire in the Aerodrome.

These details seem to suggest a very different kind of entertainment from either the august reconstructions of Ancient Egypt at Sydenham or the commercial or erotic distractions of a Cairo street. A gentle fantasy of reanimation of a delectable Ancient Egyptian female mummy was a commonplace in French literature (such as Gautier's *The Romance of a Mummy*, first translated in 1863), but the Pharaoh's Daughter also appeared five years after Bram Stoker's *Jewel of the Seven Stars*, with its apocalyptic consequences of an attempt at reanimating an Egyptian queen. Rumours of the curses linked to Thomas Douglas Murray and Walter Ingram were already circulating in print. Perhaps the pitch for the

Pharaoh's Daughter contained the delightful promise of curses, just as the full-scale recreation of Tutankhamun's tomb at the British Empire Exhibition in Wembley in 1924 might have done. Any frisson of fear was surely dissipated by the noise and energy of the funfair around them, however. The Egypt in London provided by the international exhibitions was not, it seems, the vehicle for the transmission of the mummy's curse. The museums, however, were a different prospect.

## The British Museum in the empire of shadows

Most of the sites in this topology of Egyptian London were intrinsically ephemeral, temporary shows or passing entertainments. Their often low cultural status and their sins against predominant architectural taste almost guaranteed either their complete disappearance or a second life dispersed in half-forgotten fragments. Amidst this urban flotsam, the Egyptian Rooms in the British Museum became an anchor for authoritative knowledge and representation of Ancient Egypt. Still the most popular rooms in London's most popular tourist attraction, the emergence and expansion of the Egyptian Rooms throughout the nineteenth century placed Egypt as a crux in the national narrative that the Museum told about the progress of civilization, the exercise of cultural power and the growth of Empire. A centre of sober scholarship and enlightened modernity, the Egyptian Rooms also gradually entered the cultural imagination as a very spooky place indeed, full of unruly or dangerous things, one of London's most haunted houses. This contradiction needs teasing out, to find at the root the uncanny mummy-thing, the sacred remains that could never be quite contained as museum artefacts, biologically or anthropologically reduced to exemplifications of pre-modern beliefs. Instead, the mummy remains a curio, which, precisely because of its location in the Museum, begins to leak strange and vengeful stories.

The British Museum was founded in 1753, the national repository for a nation being newly remoulded. It was constructed around the purchase (by lottery funding) of Sir Hans Sloane's private collection, which had been on display by appointment at his mansion in Cheyne Walk in Chelsea since 1742. London's first genuinely *public* museum, Don Saltero's Coffee House, also in Cheyne Walk, was the shadow of Sloane's collection, being assembled by Sloane's servant James Salter out of his master's discards and duplicates. The new national museum was set up in Montagu House, situated in seven acres of land that backed onto open fields in Great Russell Street. Although Sloane had accumulated over 80 000 antiquarian and natural history items, his collection contained only 150 small objects that could be described as Egyptian. The new museum acquired its first sarcophagus and mummy in 1756, when Colonel

William Lethieullier left his private collection of antiquities collected from his travels in Egypt in the 1720s to the nation. His nephew, Pitt Lethieullier, contributed a second mummy at the same time, but in keeping with the taste for Graeco-Roman classicism, any growth of the Egyptian collection was not pursued. Even so, David Wilson reports that early visitors to Montagu House 'were most struck by the Egyptian antiquities' and that 'one of the mummies even seems to have been displayed in a case that could be rotated by turning a handle.'[65]

The Museum's Egyptian collection reached a critical mass with the large treasurehouse of loot that Napoleon had acquired after his invasion of Egypt in 1798, and which was traded with England by Napoleon's defeated generals in return for the free passage of French soldiers. The booty, shipped back to England in 1802, contained the Rosetta Stone, whose importance as a key to translating hieroglyphic script was already recognized so that it was sent directly to the Society of Antiquaries. The rest of the material presented serious problems to a cramped Museum already overflowing even its planned extensions. This pile of Egyptian stuff was therefore stored in temporary shelters in the grounds of Montagu House. The first dedicated museum space for this material, the Egyptian Sculpture Gallery, was opened in June 1808, and was part of a major extension and redesign of the Museum based around the gift of Charles Townley's collection of Roman sculptures that he had been displaying in a house in Park Lane until his death. Townley's focus on Graeco-Roman statuary as the pinnacle of art ensured that the Egyptian pieces were coolly received. The *Gentleman's Magazine* praised the 'elegant Greek and Roman sculptures', but complained that they were mixed up with 'uncouth' Egyptian figures and ugly stone coffins.[66] This hierarchy of art reconfirmed the purpose of Thomas Hope's recently opened Egyptian room in his Duchess Street townhouse: the supersession of the primitive and the march of art towards Greek civilized perfection. This was reinforced by the arrival in the British Museum of the Parthenon marbles controversially acquired by Lord Elgin, and their display in a special room finally built off the Townley Gallery in 1817. The hierarchy would be further reinforced by Robert Smirke's neoclassical Grecian design for the building that replaced Montagu House, a design proposed in the 1820s but only completed in 1852. The neoclassical building, complete with its pedimental frieze over the front steps 'The Progress of Civilisation' sculpted by Sir Richard Westmacott, would place Egyptian and other 'prehistoric' materials in a strictly developmental narrative.

The Egyptian Rooms gained their first true wonder with the arrival of the head of the Younger Memnon (Rameses II) in 1819, the result, as has already been outlined, of Giovanni Belzoni's strongman efforts in Luxor as the agent of the British Consul General in Cairo, Henry Salt. Belzoni was forced to recreate Seti's tomb in the Egyptian Hall in Piccadilly because the Trustees of the

Museum refused to take him seriously as a dealer in ancient objects. Salt, too, had difficulties selling his large accumulations of Ancient Egyptian materials to a Museum on a squeezed budget. There was a scandal about Salt's semi-public valuation of his first collection, which he was forced to sell to the British Museum in 1823 at a much reduced price. Salt sold Seti's magnificent alabaster sarcophagus to Sir John Soane instead, and affronted at his treatment by the Trustees his next accumulation was sold to the Louvre for a much larger fee. The Museum picked off some choice pieces from Salt's third accumulation at an auction at Sotheby's in the 1830s. Henry Salt was symptomatic of a new dispensation, in which agents in the field worked to accumulate material in a semi-official capacity before negotiating transfer to their national collections. Some agents worked for profit, others elevated their compulsion to collect by gifting their acquisitions to national collections. In the 1830s, partly in rivalry with the collections in Paris and Berlin, the British Museum went through an intensive phase of acquisition, picking up the collection of Joseph Sams (1833), James Burton (1836) and Giovanni d'Anastasi (1839). When Egypt became part of the extended Grand Tour in the 1830s, amateur collectors also began gifting their finds to the Museum. Forgotten figures like the Reverend Greville Chester, who wintered in Egypt and the Levant for much of his adult life, became trusted agents for the British Museum, the Ashmolean in Oxford and the London collection of the Palestine Exploration Fund. Chester picked up bargains from native dealers and from work in the field and got them to England by openly bribing officials when necessary. One-off gifts or small clusters of Egyptian souvenirs from wealthy travellers would include the mummy case of the Priestess of Amen-Ra that had belonged to Thomas Douglas Murray and the cartonnage mask of Nesmin shipped back by Walter Herbert Ingram. As the export of ancient objects became subject to increasing controls, the somewhat opaque provenance of these gifts could be used to put distance between the metropolitan collection and questionable methods of acquisition. Through such agents, these museums became 'centres of calculation', with an ever-growing network of contacts passing back information and materials from the periphery to the core, 'networks built to mobilise, accumulate and recombine the world' around the power of the imperial metropolis.[67]

It was the appointment of Samuel Birch as an assistant in the Department of Antiquities in 1836 that transformed the British Museum into a proper centre for Egyptology (a term first used in English only in 1859). Birch joined a department that covered the entire ancient world, coins, the Orient and the medieval cultures. When possible, he focused on publishing his translations of Egyptian papyri and Assyrian cuneiform tablets. It was only in 1866, after further division and specialization of Museum departments that Birch became Keeper of Oriental Antiquities and was able to concentrate solely on Egypt. He was a classic Victorian armchair scholar: he worked in the Museum until his death in

1885 but never travelled to Egypt or Assyria, corresponding instead with agents, poring over the materials that were being sent back to the centre, whilst producing the translations of Books of the Dead, hieroglyphic dictionaries and grammars that taught enthusiasts how to read the lie of the Ancient Egyptian land.[68] Importantly, Birch took up Edmund Oldfield's proposal to reorganize the objects in the Egyptian Room into chronological order during a major reorganization of the Museum in the 1850s, arranging statuary and mummy remains according to Manethos' dynastic king lists, but also conforming to the emergent museological consensus to display things developmentally, within the universalizing framework of the progress of civilization. In 1880, with the building of the South Kensington Museum, the natural history collections were moved out of the British Museum, opening up further space for the display of antiquities. Prints from this mid-Victorian era show contemplative visitors in the light and airy, sedate and ordered Egyptian Rooms, undertaking the perambulations that would walk them into rational citizenship. So it was hoped, anyway.

Yet for most of his career, Birch was the only Museum appointment in the field, a low-paid scholar in a black silk chimney-pot hat, 'quite the worst in the Museum', the brim full of ancient dust, slaving away in a tiny office full of 'weird sounds' from the heating pipes.[69] For decades, Birch personally arranged the displays, composed each explanatory label, and catalogued the Egyptian holdings of the Museum in ninety-eight handwritten volumes. His office was a drop-in centre for students, rival scholars, travellers, amateur collectors with curious finds, oddballs with mad Biblical history theories seeking material proof in the Museum collection, and the dealers who lived and worked in the streets around the Museum. As the trade in antiquities grew, Birch was increasingly called upon to judge whether artefacts were authentic or forged. A single man could not cope with the amount of materials pouring in from excavations and dealers in materials from Egypt and Assyria. In 1883, at the personal intervention of William Gladstone, Ernest Wallis Budge was appointed as Birch's first proper Assistant Keeper. Birch died in 1885, and in the reorganization that followed his successor was given the new title of Keeper of Egyptian and Assyrian Antiquities.

Birch's student, Ernest Wallis Budge, was a poor scholar, of questionable parentage and decidedly not a gentleman. His linguistic skills in Hebrew and Syriac while still a schoolboy came to the attention of Birch, who let him study in his rooms at the Museum when he was too young to use the Reading Room. Along with Wallis Budge's employer W. H. Smith, Gladstone financially supported his degree in Semitic languages at Cambridge (where he was the only candidate in 1882). Trained to be an expert in Assyrian, Wallis Budge had to undertake a crash course in Egyptian hieroglyphics when appointed. He became a controversial figure, hated by rival factions within the Museum and beyond for his underhand methods in the field.[70] Birch's successor as Keeper of the Egyptian Rooms, Peter Le Page Renouf, despised Wallis Budge and tried to block his progress, with little success. The factionalism was so extreme that Wallis Budge was sued for slander over claims that he had discovered pilfering from Museum digs by the field agent of the eminent Assyriologist Austen Henry Layard. Wallis Budge built up a defence fund, partly with money from Lady Meux, but lost the case. Damages were minimal, however, and he retained his Museum post and succeeded to the role of Keeper in 1894.

His first trip to Egypt was in 1886, where he was asked to advise on the personal excavations of General Grenfell, then Commander of the Frontier Force, in newly discovered tombs at Aswan. Wallis Budge arrived in the precarious military and diplomatic situation of the early years of the British occupation. He had a budget of £100 for the purchase of antiquities for the British Museum, but on his arrival in Cairo he was commanded by the British Consul General Sir Evelyn Baring in a severe personal interview to desist from any trading that would destabilize diplomatic relations with Egyptian or French officials. This view was reinforced by the diplomat Sir John Gorst, who was 'wholly opposed to the export of antiquities'.[71]

Wallis Budge was openly contemptuous of such a stance, and embarked on a career that was breathtaking in its hungry acquisition and disregard of the legal niceties supposedly enforced by the Egyptian Antiquities Service. Wallis Budge saw no reason why the British national collection should suffer, whilst the French, Germans and the private collectors exploited a corrupt system. The laws on antiquities were, to Wallis Budge, simply 'absurd'.[72] Wallis Budge ignored Baring and began accumulating box-loads of material to send back to England, trained in subterfuge by experienced collector and smuggler the Reverend Greville Chester. Despite constant surveillance and interference by agents of the French Director of Antiquities, Eugene Grébaut, Wallis Budge managed to accumulate tewnty-four boxes of material and a total of 1482 items for the British Museum. As a side project, Wallis Budge also collected eight hundred ancient skulls from mummy pits in Aswan for Alexander Macalister, Professor of Anatomy and Zoology at Cambridge. As ancient artefacts, export was banned, but when they were reclassified as 'bone manure' Wallis Budge was able to transport them legally. At the end of his trip, he could rely on military contacts made in Aswan to outfox both Evelyn Baring and the French Director of Antiquities, and ensure his loot was not impounded in Alexandria.

On later trips, Wallis Budge added personal missions to his itinerary. In 1895, he carried £1000 to acquire materials for his friends Henry and Lady Meux for their private collection in Theobalds Park, as long as the Principal Librarian of the British Museum deemed them surplus to the national collection. He continued to rely on the help of highly placed military officers to assist his smuggling operations. General Kitchener always helped, whilst Colonel Maxwell censored press telegrams that revealed Wallis Budge's movements.[73] 'I am so watched,' he wrote back to the British Museum, 'that I am afraid to risk the smallest thing being found in my possession on my way out of the country.'[74] He travelled by military transports to avoid being searched. His surviving letters are often coy about committing to paper any detail of his transactions with his contacts ('I went to see a certain native' or 'I went to the desert near the pyramids and met a man' – two occasions when he returned with purchase of papyri).[75] However, Wallis Budge later recalled how he foiled the outcry over his purchase of a valuable papyrus by cutting it into small sections, hiding it between photographs in an album wrapped in gaudy paper, dodging the Antiquities Service by travelling fourth class to Suez before taking a mail boat out of the country.[76] 'He despoiled the ancient East without a scruple to pile up treasures for the national collections,' one friend indulgently reminisced. 'It pleased him to be called a "robber" in the interests of his country.'[77]

The archaeologist William Flinders Petrie, who was set to make archaeological fieldwork a scrupulous forensic science in a long career that began in Egypt in 1880, was horrified by the cavalier spirit of the man he privately nicknamed Bugbear.[78] When questions were asked in the House of Commons about 'rumours' and 'grave doubts' over Wallis Budge's methods in 1892, the eminent politician Arthur Balfour warned off any further discussion, arguing that 'the utility of any action Mr Budge may take in the future will be considerably impaired, to the great detriment of the Museum and of public learning if his conduct were discussed.'[79] With this kind of official sanction Wallis Budge could ignore legal questions and professional developments in archaeological practice. He eventually retired in 1924, lamenting the decline of the Egyptian adventure.

Wallis Budge's underhand methods resulted in an extraordinary tripling of the size of the Egyptian collection at the British Museum. In those forty years, he also witnessed the strange supernaturalizing of the Egyptian Rooms, with the circulation of rumours about the unlucky mummy and stories of uncanny disturbances and strange accidents. These were all later trumped by the frenzy of speculation about cursed artefacts following the death of Lord Carnarvon. In April 1923, in Wallis Budge's last year of service, the newspapers excitedly reported that the British Museum had been inundated with 'parcels containing mummies' shrivelled hands and feet' from private collectors now terrified of being cursed.[80] Wallis Budge always publicly deplored these stories as a professional Egyptologist and his surviving records in the archive show his spirited rebuttals to individual correspondents and journalists, as we have seen.

Yet Wallis Budge must also have regarded curse stories as a strategic means of keeping the British Museum's Egyptian Rooms at the centre of London's cultural world. He published popular books on Egyptian religious beliefs, on the Book of the Dead, mummies and Egyptian magic at a remorseless rate. He was centre stage for the unwrapping of the mummy Bak-Ran at

University College in 1889.[81] He suffered Thomas Douglas Murray's list of eminent visitors to the cursed Priestess of Amen-Ra and attended the Ghost Club in 1904. Edith Nesbit dedicated her popular children's tale *The Story of the Amulet* to Wallis Budge for his assistance in imagining a magical device that can summon the Queen of Sheba whose magic sent animated artefacts dancing down the neoclassical front steps of the Museum. 'He was a marvellous storyteller', Victoria Markham remembered, recalling dinner parties at his home in Bloomsbury Street, tucked into the maze of side streets next to the British Museum. 'Like Scheherazade, he could keep a company at dinner spellbound till dawn with tales of his experiences both East and West. They would range from adventures on Nile and Tigris to the most thrilling of ghost stories.'[82]

The long period of Wallis Budge's reign over the Egyptian antiquities in the late Victorian and Edwardian period is one of the cruxes in the pursuit of the sources for rumours of curse stories circulating in London. He was intimately involved in the tall tales attached to both Thomas Douglas Murray and Walter Herbert Ingram. But it is not a question of saying that Wallis Budge was *responsible* for these stories; rather that Wallis Budge intensified something that was ingrained in the logic of displaying ancient remains in the modern museum.

I have already sketched out an influential argument that regards the Victorian creation of the national collection or universal survey museum as an instrumental pedagogical device. The museum is a modern technology because it converts the private, aristocratic 'cabinet of curiosities', designed on secret harmonies, into public democratic institutions ordered on transparent taxonomies and aesthetic or scientific sequencing. The national collection confirms the privileged place of the European democratic state in the development of civilizations, nations and empires. The museum disciplines unruly mobs into educated citizens (although in 1780 and again in 1848 troops were stationed in the British Museum grounds to hold off rioters and revolutionaries). Built in the heart of the major European capitals, national collections became, according Barbara Black, a 'monitored and controlled' model of the city, an idealized version of what lay beyond the gates.[83] Enlightenment reigned in these rooms, producing a regulated order: 'We learn to read and see alike in the museum, which, as a setter of standards, heralds the advent of a standardised existence.'[84]

But the Museum was never quite experienced like this. The collection was always expanding faster than its underpaid keepers or cramped rooms could manage. Things were stuffed in storage, unregarded, uncatalogued, lost, sometimes left to rot. For all the accumulation, the developmental logic was frustrated by gaps in the archive and the limits of display space. Government Select Committee investigations into the state of the National Repository tell a story of almost permanent crisis. Important gifts were refused due to lack of space.[85] The Principal Librarian informed the Select Committee that 'visitors are bewildered and confused by the extent and variety of the collections' and that 'objects are too crowded together, and they are very often mixed in a manner that they ought not to be', with many important items barely visible in crepuscular basements.[86] Keepers often fought bitterly against extending opening to the wider public. For decades, entry to the Museum was made by personal application for restricted numbers of tickets to particular collections. 'As an educational museum,' Pitt-Rivers thundered in 1891, 'it is simply bewildering.'[87] Thirty years later, from a very different, Modernist perspective, Paul Valéry regarded the universal survey museum as 'a domain of incoherence. This juxtaposition of dead visions has something insane about it, with each thing jealously competing for the glance that will give it life.'[88]

This animistic idea that the accumulation of dead things in the museum might yet contain a secret life deserves some reflection. For Victorian ethnographers and anthropologists, animism was a symptom of the 'lower psychology' of savages. The most primitive form of religious belief was that souls might remain after death by moving into inanimate objects.[89] Developmental theories of evolution suggested such beliefs were always superseded by a more sophisticated theology, and, later, by a scientific understanding of causation. Yet, as Edward Tylor observed in his conclusion to *Primitive Culture*, 'there seems no human thought so primitive as to have lost its bearing on our own thought, nor so ancient as to have broken its connection with our own life.'[90] Modern, Victorian rationality could always be undercut by what Tylor called 'survivals' from lower stages of thought. That the British Museum became the location for cultural fantasies about reanimation implies that its enlightened, educative role was often subverted by these 'survivals' of magical thinking. Rumours about cursed objects might exasperate curators, but they are evidence that the disciplinary role of the Museum never functioned perfectly or at all uniformly. Indeed, this is closer to what the Postmodern anthropologist James Clifford suggests, that we need to recall artefacts' 'lost status as fetishes': 'This tactic... would accord to things in collections the power to fixate, rather than simply the capacity to edify or inform.'[91] And mummies became sites for these fixations because they were survivals in the modern Museum of older 'magical' forms of collecting associated with cabinets of curiosities.

Before the arrival of the public museum in the eighteenth century, the aristocratic cabinet brought together wonders, objects of extreme rarity and value that were 'marked at the outermost limits of the natural', ranging through jewels and precious metals to sacred relics, exotic amulets and evidence of chimeras that only existed otherwise in myth or rumour: griffin claws and unicorn horns.[92] The cabinet was a secret concentration of princely power, a hoard of wealth but also of occult forces, an apparatus for the exercise of sympathetic magic. The objects in a cabinet were condensations that became intermediaries to invisible worlds, whether of distant exotic lands or realms beyond the ken of ordinary folk.[93] Any decent cabinet of medieval or Renaissance curiosities required either a mummy or a sample of *mumia*, the powdered essence of mummy that was held to have powerful curative effects on wounds. Aristocrats often carried it in pouches for easy access. 'True Mummie is taken from the monuments and stony chambers of the anciently dead in Egypt,' the surgeon Ambrose Parey wrote in 1634, though already warning about the industry of fake manufacture of *mumia* for gullible Christians from 'the mangled and pu-tride particles of the carcases of the basest people of Egypt.'[94] In the early sev-enteenth century, Walter Cope took the unusual step of displaying his cabinet of exotic curiosities in London, which included Virginian fireflies, Chinese porcelain, African amulets and an Egyptian mummy.[95] Robert Hubert of London collected a mummy that he recorded in his *Catalogue of Many Natural Rarities* in 1665. And in 1681, the Royal Society cabinet was disparagingly re-ferred to as 'a ware-house of Aegyptian Mummies, Old Musty Skeletons, and other Antiquated Trumpery.'[96]

The occult or magical force of the cabinet might have decayed into more secular sensations and curiosities in a general process of disenchantment, but this process was never uniform and indeed encouraged a 'wistful counter-Enlightenment' that longed to retain wonder and weirdness.[97] The British Museum could never control how its displays might be read. Wallis Budge recalled that Samuel Birch was constantly harangued by the eccentric auto-didact Daniel Smith who believed he had found the common alphabet beneath all ancient languages, cracking a code that meant he was able to interpret every text in the museum. 'When not engaged in harrying the officials, he sat in the Egyptian Gallery, over one of the hot-air gratings, and meditated upon the wilful ignorance and blindness of the officials and the magnitude of his great discovery.'[98] The delusional Smith was fictionalized by Walter Besant as Daniel Fagg in *All Sorts and Conditions of Men* (1882), plotting his revenge on the Keeper of the Egyptian Rooms and telling anyone who will listen of the ex-traordinary secret that the British Museum contains in ignorance: the tablets of the commandments given to Moses. 'They don't know what they've got...I know where they are kept; nobody else knows. It is in a dark corner; they are each about two feet high; and there's a hole in the dark corner of each for Moses's thumb to hold them by.'[99]

Meanwhile, anti-Catholic agitators accused the Museum of promoting superstitious and pagan idolatry, whilst adepts of the Egyptian Hermetic tradi-tion – theosophists, scholars of occult traditions and magicians of the Golden Dawn – pored over arcanae in the Reading Room, hunting for secret know-ledges that might tap into the lost energies of Egyptian magic.[100] The postbag was full of helpful correspondents who had Masonic theories about Ancient Egypt, or had done psychic readings of particular artefacts, or, as in the case of Ellen Chadwick Merry, claimed direct descent from the Egyptian pharaohs and who demanded that 'our tombs, our bones of our ancestors, and our claims to these sacred relics must be respected'.[101] At the high points of rumours circulating about the unlucky mummy or the curse of Tutankhamun, spiritualists, occultists and ghost-hunters took the psychic temperature of the Egyptian Rooms. Elliott O'Donnell, the psychic investigator, declared the Rooms thoroughly haunted by malevolent spirits and elementals: 'their name is legion, the very atmosphere is impregnated with them'.[102] Even the mainstream press indulged in jokey haunting stories, as in the *Illustrated London News*'s guide to producing a ghost by using the reflections in display cases to superimpose a spectral occupant on the empty tomb of Sebek-Sa.[103]

Jonah Seigel has observed: 'Even in the most well-lit gallery each component part on display as much as the ensemble those parts constitute is shadowed by ghosts of promise or disappointment... Unasked for gifts, trophies of plunder, voids suggested by the presence of objects always in surfeit though never quite sufficient – *all* museums are haunted in some measure'.[104] The museum dreams of itself as total and complete, with mastery over its items and their interpretations, but there is always a ghostly supplement that it cannot contain. 'The structure of the archive,' as the philosopher Jacques Derrida once pronounced, 'is *spectral*'.[105]

If these counter-Enlightened interpretations remained stubbornly persistent into the late Victorian age, it may have been not only because the scientific displays of the British Museum were competing with all the sensational exotic entertainments of the imperial metropolis, but also because the city was still riddled with small, private collections of Egyptian artefacts, continuations of the tradition of cabinets of curiosities accrued as symbols of private wealth and power. Nearby, the Soane Museum hosted evening candlelit soirées around Seti's alabaster tomb in what Soane called his 'Egyptian Crypt'.[106] For Soane, a Mason, these occasions might well have had occult designs, being recreations of Eleusinian mysteries. Across Lincoln's Inn, the small collection of the Royal College of Surgeons, formed from the private collection of John Hunter, contained several mummies, displayed along with other medical monstrosities. In 1886, Lord Brassey purchased the ornate Indian room that had been built for the Colonial and Indian Exhibition of 1886 and had it reconstructed as his smoking room in his mansion at 24 Park Lane. The room was opened, by appointment, as a museum of exotic Eastern artefacts, between 1889 and 1918. Henry Wellcome amassed a vast collection of medical material, including Egyptian papyri and funerary artefacts that were publicly displayed in his museum that opened on the Euston Road from 1932. To the north-west of London, Lady Meux's private collection of Egyptian antiquities at Theobalds Park had a cursed mummy and intimate links to Wallis Budge at the British Museum. John Lee's private collection of Egyptian antiquities had been catalogued in the 1850s at Hartwell House (complete with Egyptianate follies in the grounds) to the west of London. In Southwark, the Cuming family collected a hundred thousand objects, including hundreds of objects from Egypt, which were displayed in their home, later the Cuming Museum, known as the 'British Museum in Miniature'. To the south, Frederick Horniman, from the Indian tea merchant family, built up an enormous private collection of exotic materials from his travels. Near to the Crystal Palace at Sydenham, the Horniman Museum was opened to the public in 1890. He added to his Eastern collections after two journeys in 1894 and 1896, the latter including a fortnight in Egypt. After these journeys, Horniman opened his New Oriental Saloon, which contained a display of five mummies. Emphasizing the old-fashioned nature of this collection, Horniman was even involved with a public mummy unwrapping at the Dulwich Scientific and Literary Association in February 1897. To add to the frisson, this was another priestess of Amen-Ra, a mummy named Peta-Amen-Neb-Nest-Tain. At the end of the demonstration, visitors were each given a small square of the mummy cloth. When the Horniman collection was presented to the people of London on Frederick Horniman's death in 1901, one of the first professional fieldwork anthropologists, A. C. Haddon, was called in to assess Horniman's collection. 'The day has passed when we can consider a collection of "curios" as a museum', Haddon reported acidly.[107] Perhaps Haddon knew that one of the former curators at the Horniman was Samuel Mathers, a man steeped in occult lore and a self-proclaimed magician who co-founded the Hermetic Order of the Golden Dawn (a man we will return to in chapter 8). Later, just before World War II, another small private collection of some two thousand antiquities went into exile in London with its Jewish owner. Sigmund Freud had been an obsessive visitor to Viennese dealers in antiquities who openly sold unprovenanced objects; his collection now forms part of the Freud Museum.[108] This is merely a partial list of London 'cabinets': it is self-evident that the model of the enlightened British Museum hardly superseded the existence of cabinets and their exotic wonders. The Museum was surrounded by renewed versions of it.

Indeed, this logic of the uncanny doubling of the Museum was played out very precisely in London topography. The more the authority of the British Museum grew, the more institutions of marginal knowledge clustered around the edges of the Museum site in Bloomsbury. The Spiritual Institute, founded by James Burns in 1863, was located just round the corner from the Museum in Southampton Row, and became one of the major centres for spiritualist séances and publications in London. The Swedenborg Society (followers of the Swedish mystic Emanuel Swedenborg) took rooms in Bloomsbury Street in 1870, before moving to a large hall in Bloomsbury Square in 1925. In his townhouse in Russell Square, within a stone's throw of the back entrance to the Museum, Edward Cox undertook research into séances in the 1870s and claimed to prove empirically the existence of 'psychic force'. The British National Association of

Spiritualists took offices in Great Russell Street, opposite the Museum, in 1878. It was in these rooms that the Society for Psychical Research was founded in 1882. This shadowing effect seemed to demonstrate that the Museum's mission to bring scientific enlightenment was also always supplemented by an odd reserve of supernaturalism, seeking legitimacy by proximity to the new scientific authority.[109]

And it is also perhaps obvious why the mummy becomes a focus for this supplemental logic *within* the walls of the British Museum. Mummies are human remains not inert objects. They are liminal, suspended between stages of existence. As Wallis Budge reminded his readers, 'Believers in Osiris never regarded mummies as wholly dead objects.'[110] The mummy is the quintessential uncanny object that prompts magical thinking about dead things that might come back to life. Mary Bouquet and Nuno Porto have argued that if museum displays of mummies frame sacred rituals as anthropological belief systems, neutralizing ancient awe and dread, it may be that scientific explanations only produce their own form of 'curatorial magic' which works by conjuring secular wonder to 're-enchant the resulting materials'.[111] Perhaps, though, the history of Egyptian displays in cabinets and museums more compellingly suggests that this uneasy liminality is due to a more fundamental factor: that the mummy never quite successfully reached the status of a museum artefact.

The materials dug out of the ground of Egypt become artefacts only within the frame of the museum. The mummy might have been a sacred vessel, an ancestor, disturbing or irrelevant remains of a lost culture overwritten several times across the centuries, slow-burning fuel for desert fires, a source of disease or homoeopathic cure, an item of local barter or international trade, war booty, colonial loot or a personal souvenir before it became a museum artefact. Elliott Colla's discussion of the archaeology of Egypt reminds us that artefaction is a process or journey rather than a thing: 'Egyptology's object, the artefact, came into being somewhere between Egypt and London.'[112] Artefacts are not uncovered but engineered by scientific capture, description and taxonomy, raw materials are decanted into inscription systems that establish a new order of things. If this is a careful process of remembering, the process of creating artefacts – artefaction – is also a strategic forgetting, most often of the questionable process of acquisition in fraught colonial contexts. If many objects in the British Museum Egyptian collection had begun their passage towards the artefact as souvenirs of private collectors, these items seem, unusually, to retain the trace of that personal acquisition. Susan Stewart suggests that the souvenir is imbued with private meanings, nostalgia and reverie, making it difficult to interpret: 'There is always the possibility that reverie's signification will go out of control here, that the object itself will take charge, awakening some dormant capacity for destruction.'[113] The shape of a curse narrative is coiled within this haunting description. Thus, it is important to follow Elliott Colla's view that 'it is most precise to define the artefact not in terms of its intrinsic qualities, but rather by way of tensions and contradictions which permeate it and link it to intense political, social and cultural conflicts.'[114]

The mummy in the museum is only an artefact in this thoroughly riven sense. Their often tortuous pathways to the Egyptian Rooms might be forgotten in the neutral labels on the display cases, but the supplemental excess of rumour and superstition around a certain number of Egyptian artefacts builds a sort of monument to their prior history as unruly objects. The half-remembered details of Thomas Douglas Murray's biography cling to item 22542, halting the process of artefaction. It is exactly the disjuncture between objects and their framing that makes the British Museum a privileged location for curse narratives: the museum context cannot prevent other histories and counter-narratives breaking through the smooth sheen of artefaction. In fact, we might say that mummies remain *things*, things that resist any stable categorization between subject and object and which remain stubbornly resistant to theory. As Bill Brown puts it, 'Things lie beyond the grid of intelligibility the way mere things lie outside the grid of museal exhibition, outside the order of objects.'[115] They are things that are *stuck*, real pieces of an ancient culture, yet now out of place, unhoused or uncanny, arrested somewhere between object and artefact. In this liminal state, they are able to gather all manner of contradictory significances that exceed any neutral scientific description as museal artefacts.

Curse narratives, then, do not seem to accrue to the fantasia of Egyptian courts or neo-Pharaonic architecture or the lath and plaster oriental palaces of the international fares. Not even, it seems, do full-scale re-creations of Tutankhamun's tomb at Wembley in 1924, produce a whiff of danger. Curses seem to require a chunk of the real thing: solid, material and disturbingly out of place.

A test case for this theory would be Cleopatra's Needle. Of all the Egyptianate and oriental architecture erected in London in the nineteenth century, this was the one actual Ancient Egyptian structure to be brought to the imperial centre. The obelisk came from Heliopolis and was dedicated to Tuthmoses III in around 1450 BCE. It was gifted to Britain by Mehmet Ali in 1819, but only finally erected on the newly built Victoria Embankment along the Thames in 1878. It was brought to compete with the Egyptian obelisks in the rival imperial cities of Paris (who set up their obelisk in the Place de la Concorde in 1836) and New York (in 1861). 'Every empire worthy of its name – from ancient Rome to the United States – has sought an Egyptian obelisk to place in the centre of a ceremonial space.'[116] The misnamed, misappropriated obelisk had an unlucky history of transfer to England. George IV expressed no interest in paying for the obelisk to be moved to England. The cost was deemed too expensive for the Great Exhibition in 1851, and the Sydenham Palace Company also failed to bring it to England in 1853. It was lost to the desert sands, then rediscovered by the soldier Sir James Alexander. His campaign to bring the obelisk to England was backed with £10 000 by Erasmus Wilson. When the project to deliver the monument to England finally began to take shape, one enthusiast commented 'England is about to welcome the mightiest antiquarian stranger which has ever…"set up his rest" amidst us.'[117] Three weeks after leaving Egypt, the boat designed to transport it hit a squall in the Bay of Biscay and the Maltese sailors were alleged 'to have thrown overboard the ancient relics and human remains found beneath the obelisk, in an attempt to appease "supernatural forces".'[118] Nevertheless, in the resulting storm, six sailors were drowned and the reputation of Captain Carter was ruined. The obelisk, set adrift from tow ropes, was declared salvage. Even though it was rediscovered afloat very quickly, the costs of salvage and other legal payments doubled the cost of the whole exercise to £20 000.[119]

The obelisk was eventually erected on Joseph Bazalgette's new Victoria Embankment at the end of September 1878, the ancient monument crowning this modern urban development. There was no official ceremony, and *The Times* hoped lukewarmly that by some 'contrivances' of the Board of Works, 'the obelisk will lose its present appearance of instability'.[120] Yet it always seems to have had a melancholy atmosphere in situ in London, perhaps an echo of a long tradition that obelisks are magical or occult objects.[121] By the Needle is where, in Oscar Wilde's tale 'Lord Arthur Savile's Crime' (1887), the lord tips his mystic palm-reader into the Thames, so fulfilling his destiny to commit murder. The Needle is also where Forrester meets his Egyptian nemesis in Richard Marsh's Gothic novel *Pharos the Egyptian*. By 1936, in the lowlife novel *The Gilt Kid* by James Curtis, Cleopatra's Needle is a place that promises mysterious oriental encounters, but never delivers: 'In books, where the hero, who is an impoverished, improvident, but viceless member of the English ruling caste is sitting on an Embankment seat near Cleopatra's Needle – and it's always there that he's sitting… a sinister figure will sidle up to him in the darkness and, in broken English, will offer him a whole lot of dough. But there will be a string tied to that flock of rent.' He will only end up 'enmeshed in the toils of an unscrupulous gang of foreigners'.[122] Since being hit by bombs thrown from zeppelins in the Great War, Cleopatra's Needle has become part of an odd memorial complex, decked out with a plaque to the sailors lost in its transport and surrounded by monuments to the war dead. It is a site said to be haunted by several 'suicide phantoms', male or female figures who hurl themselves from the parapet into the Thames below without a splash on foggy nights, the stories perhaps a distorted version of Cleopatra's own end.[123] The Needle ought to stake the undead into final rest, but the obelisk is itself the uncanny thing, presiding over the wrong river now, dense with the over-written histories of Egyptian, Greek, Roman, Turkish, French and British imperialism.

But it is the walls of the museum that really act as an echo-box for this uncanny supplement to things that refuse to bed down as artefacts. The museum folds space and time, rendering the distant near, the ancient modern and the chaos of the field into ordered patterns of linear progress. If the mummy stubbornly remains a thing, it reflects a nagging ethical doubt about the display of human bodies as museum artefacts. The growth of agreements about the restitution of human remains has now formalized these ethical concerns into codes of practice for museum display or for the restitution of bodies.[124]

But if the British Museum in particular has been one of the privileged locales to think about this ethical concern in a displaced way through stubs of myth and rumour about mummy curses, it may be because the Museum houses one of the very founding objects of these kinds of curse narratives: the Elgin Marbles. It is significant that the Museum's most controversial acquisition of friezes and metopes from the Parthenon in Athens has stubbornly refused to shake off the name of the man who acquired them. Thomas Bruce, the Seventh Earl of Elgin, was sent on a diplomatic mission to Constantinople in 1799. The Turks favoured the English following the French invasion of Egypt. Part of the reward on the surrender of the French in Egypt in 1801 was to issue Elgin with a firman to remove fallen sculptures and bits of friezes from the Parthenon in Athens (long abused by Goths, Crusaders, Turks and Venetian forces who used it as a gun-powder store that blew up and severely damaged the structure in 1687). Elgin was driven, he always claimed, by a hope that the original Greek sculptures would improve English taste and save them from total loss as the Parthenon was subject to petty plunder and thievery long encouraged by the Ottoman occupiers. Between October 1801 and April 1802, Elgin's agents extended their understanding of the agreement, until they were sawing off elements of the friezes and metopes from the standing building. In a race against time from the interference of Turks and the French, soon back in favour in Constantinople, Elgin's agents sent nearly a hundred cases of materials back to England. When they were first eventually displayed in London in 1807, in a shed built at the back of a townhouse on the corner of Piccadilly and Park Lane hired by Elgin for the purpose, some tried to dismiss their importance, but most visitors, including many artists, were thunderstruck. The Elgin Marbles were 'revered,' Ian Jenkins reports, 'with near religious awe'.[125] The artist Benjamin Robert Haydon proclaimed that 'I felt as if a divine truth had blazed inwardly upon my mind and I knew that they would at last rouse the art of Europe from its slumber in the darkness.'[126] Haydon's enthusiasm would lead to John Keats's sonnets on the marbles, his confession of 'dizzy pain' before them.[127] They were eventually bought from Lord Elgin by the government in 1816, and moved to a temporary gallery in the British Museum in 1817, before a permanent gallery was completed in 1831. The move from private collection to public display was not brilliantly handled. Bits and pieces of the Parthenon material were left behind in Piccadilly, and some were found in the garden rockery of Marylebone Park as late as 1842. The Greek state first asked for the return of the marbles in 1833 (when it was newly independent), and has repeatedly done so ever since.

This brief outline barely touches the unlucky history of the Earl of Elgin that began to destroy his previously illustrious career almost as soon as he had loaded the Parthenon hoard onto British ships. He left Constantinople in 1803, but in Paris was detained and imprisoned by the old enemy for over three years. The agreement over his release effectively ended his diplomatic career. He returned to London to discover his wife refusing conjugal rights and conducting a public affair. Elgin was already facially disfigured by syphilis – he lost his nose to the pox – and his eldest son had been born epileptic and imbecilic from the hereditary effects of syphilis. Elgin sued for divorce in two court cases in 1807 and 1808, the lurid details reprinted in scandal sheets. He lost his seat in the House of Lords (as one of a representative number of Scottish lords), ending his political career. By 1810, the cost of the removal of the Parthenon marbles was beginning to pressure him financially. He estimated the cost of his selfless rescue of these treasures was £39 000, including an expensive salvage exercise to recover some cases from a shipwreck, and the vast cost of hiring a Piccadilly mansion to display them. Humiliatingly, the government refused to purchase them. Desperate, he issued a further petition to parliament to purchase the marbles in 1816, now estimating his costs at £74 000. The government agreed to buy the marbles for £35 000 only, and £18 000 of this was removed to pay off debts, and creditors took the rest. Elgin had lost vast sums. 'At long last,' his biographer William St Clair observes, 'Elgin was free of the fateful marbles which had hung around his neck for ten years and had been the ruin of his life.'[128]

Elgin was firmly fixed into a curse narrative, though, because he became the satirical butt of Lord Byron's ire about the political situation of Greece. In Byron's first publicly published poem, *English Bards and Scotch Reviewers* (1807), there was already a passing comment on Lords Aberdeen and Elgin, who 'make their grand saloons a general mart/For all the mutilated blocks of art'.[129] A scurrilous couplet about Elgin doing the rounds of London at the time could also have been composed by Byron: 'Noseless himself he brings here noseless blocks/To show what time has done and what the pox.'[130] But the attacks were amplified once Byron had visited Athens in 1810, a trip which converted him to ardent philhellenism, supporting Greek independence against the Ottoman yoke. Appalled at the stories of the sacking of the Parthenon by Elgin's agents, Byron had seen in the harbour at Piraeus some of Elgin's crates still waiting to be shipped back to England. In *Childe Harold's Pilgrimage*, the poem that made Byron a celebrity in 1812, the second canto begins with an open attack on Lord Elgin and this 'modern Pict's ignoble boast,/To rive what Goth, and Turk, and Time hath spar'd.'[131] It is then declared:

> Dull is the eye that will not weep to see
> Thy walls defac'd, thy mouldering shrines remov'd

> By British hands, which it had best behov'd
> To guard those relics ne'er to be restor'd.
> Curst be the hour when from their isle they rov'd,
> And once again thy hapless bosom gor'd,
> And snatched thy shrinking Gods to northern climes abhorr'd.[132]

Byron's extensive annotations accused Elgin of 'having ruined Athens': 'I know no motive which can excuse, no name which can designate, the perpetrators of this dastardly devastaton.'[133] This attack in one of the literary sensations of the era fell, as William St Clair observes, 'on a man who was already almost broken by his misfortunes'[134]

That 'curst' might be read as a casual rhetorical device, were it not that Byron composed a long poem, 'The Curse of Minerva' in the same year, a work deemed so exorbitant in its attack on Elgin that it was only circulated in eight privately printed copies in 1812, and not published under Byron's name until 1831. In 'The Curse of Minerva', the ancient protectress of Athens lashes out at Elgin's desecration of the Parthenon, for doing damage worse than any Goth or Turk marauder had yet achieved. Minerva decrees:

> First on the head of him who did this deed
> My curse shall light, on him and all his seed:
> Without one spark of intellectual fire,
> Be all the sons as senseless as the sire.[135]

Here, the curse classically falls on the inheritors, Byron making a cruel reference to Elgin's imbecilic eldest son (who would die aged forty, after a life of epileptic seizures and mental incapacity). His surviving son, James, the Eighth Earl of Elgin, would become notorious in 1860 for leading the looting and destruction of the Chinese Emperor's Summer Palace. But the logic of contagion common to curses soon extends the range of family inheritance. Elgin, 'loath'd in life', will discover that 'vengeance [will] follow far beyond the tomb'.[136] Elgin's acts have in fact cursed Britain entire, and Minerva's wrath is soon directed at the British imperial project, pointing to a recent rebellion of native troops in Madras as a sign of imminent collapse:

> Ganges' swarthy race
> Shall shake your tyrant empire to its base.
> Lo, there Rebellion rears her ghastly head,
> And glares the Nemesis of native dead.[137]

The poem ends with an apocalyptic vision of flames reflected in 'the startl'd Thames', London torched by fires lit 'from Tagus to the Rhine': 'Now should they burst on thy devoted coast/Go, ask thy bosom who deserves them most.'[138]

In a very influential way, Byron's rhetoric directly connects the acquisition of antiquities to the exercise of imperial power, whilst giving imaginative flight to the idea that these trafficked things themselves might bring curses down on those who carry them away, the retribution escalating exponentially. It might have been hoped that the discourse of ideal Greek aesthetics in the frame of the galleries of the British Museum would achieve the disinterested abstraction of the marbles from their difficult history of acquisition, but the subsequent controversies have shown that the marbles never quite escaped from the unlucky fate of the Earl of Elgin, proving an immense burden to the Museum authorities. I think that Byron's notions of Nemesis and curse, so important in *Childe Harold's Pilgrimage* and 'The Curse of Minerva', are one of the displaced points of origin for mummy curses too. Liminal museum objects, stuck between souvenir and artefact, are things to which spooky and vengeful narratives accrue, whether marbles or mummified corpses.

Literature animates these museum stories, because literary narrative is one of the privileged discourses that provide imaginative coherence to objects, often at a tangent to, or in open defiance of, the processes of scientific artefaction. The 'cognitive space' of the museum, Sheldon Annis suggests, is cut across by the 'dream space' of association, fantasy and drift brought by the visitor.[139] That it was Byron who helped generate museum curse stories should not perhaps surprise. As Caroline Franklin has noted, 'Byron's family inheritance predisposed him to a fascination with the Gothic.'[140] His wicked wastrel forebears left the ancestral home a ruin. Newstead Abbey was a direct inspiration to those progenitors of Gothic romance, Horace Walpole and Ann Radcliffe. Byron chased by scandal out of England, reflected long on inherited curses brought down on ancient houses. So if the Egyptian Rooms of the British Museum were one of the core spaces in which the mummy curse began to flower in nineteenth century London, it was also because the Museum rooms were animated by the Gothic imagination, a genre that broods on the rights and wrongs of inheritance. Let's now turn to some of the phases of Gothic literature to investigate their role in the rise of the belief in the curse of the mummy.

# 6

# The Curse Tale and the Egyptian Gothic

GOTHIC ROMANCE IS the secret sharer of the modern, rational and sup-posedly secular Western world. Almost as soon as Enlightenment think-ers and reformers declared war on superstition, priest-craft and ancient tyranny, a hybrid literature emerged in the 1760s that spoke in disjointed nightmare nar-ratives about the return of old forces and arbitrary terrors. The genre was an exotic flower of the freshly minted bourgeois public sphere of print, speaking the fears of its new readers in ways so exorbitant that the genre routinely attracted contempt and condemnation. The Gothic pulsed with paranoid per-secutory complexes in the Revolutionary times of the 1780s and 1790s, and seethed with renewed energy in the anxious decades of the late Victorian era. For all its fantastical weirdness, the genre always remains materially tied to the political contexts of its production.

Although of course very varied, what the Gothic romance often turns on is the question of inheritance, of what can be rightfully and wrongfully owned. It is a literature that broods on legacy, on what can be passed on. In what is com-monly accepted as the first Gothic novel, Horace Walpole's *The Castle of Otranto* (1764), the supernatural visions and terrifying intrusions from another dimen-sion commence because Manfred has murdered the rightful heir of Otranto and illegitimately seeks to establish his own line. An awful supernatural neme-sis is assembled that bursts the bounds of the castle and brings death to the usurper. Proper legal succession ensures the return of the natural order. After Darwin, inheritance developed heavier biological resonances, and the Gothic explored the residual taint in the blood that might allow the savage or the animal to leap out of the civilized body, simian Hyde from eminent Dr Jekyll. The terror of regression down the evolutionary chain inspired most of the monsters slouching through the late Victorian Gothic revival.

Because of this obsession with inheritance, the genre often turns on family curses, exploring with gruesome delectation the Old Testament promise of a jealous God to visit 'the iniquity of the fathers upon the children unto the third and fourth generation' (Exodus 20:5). Chris Baldick has argued that the shorter Gothic tale (as opposed to the labyrinthine Gothic novel) is organized around the notion of the family curse, due to the compression it can exercise, citing Edgar Allen Poe's 'The Fall of the House of Usher' as the exemplary tale, one which ends with the simultaneous collapse of both the physical house and the last member of the dynasty who lives out his final decadent days there. Inordinate punishment is typical in the Gothic tale: 'nemesis is a blaster of whole houses rather than individual miscreants.'[1] It is significant that the rise of the Gothic romance coincides with the craze in the middle of the eighteenth century to construct elaborate fables about the genealogies of aristocratic families, featuring the 'lucks' and 'curses' that survive down the generations. On the very first page of *The Castle of Otranto*, Manfred is oppressed by the 'dread of seeing accomplished an ancient prophecy' and we know that this enigmatic curse will be fulfilled and will seal his doom.[2] An anonymous tale like 'The Curse', published in 1832 and typical of macabre magazine fiction of the time, reads exactly like the supposedly 'true' stories of doomed aristocratic houses such as the 'Cowdray Curse' or the 'Tichborne Curse', which I examined earlier as possible models for Tutankhamun's curse on the Earl of Carnarvon. The tale of 'The Curse', with its promise of an unjustly executed man that 'Yet three generations, and the proud house of Rath will cease to be, and fearful will the curse fall', sounds exactly like one of the curses brought down by the weak and unjustly oppressed on aristocrats in supposedly 'true' stories of damned houses.[3]

Another way that the Gothic thinks about familial legacy is through the mysterious objects and private collections that embody inherited wealth. Indeed, for all its interest in the spectral and the supernatural, the Gothic is often conjured up from strikingly material starting points. Again, Horace Walpole inaugurates this tendency in the Gothic. *Otranto* was written in his Strawberry Hill retreat, his fanciful Gothic castle that he built on the English domestic scale by the River Thames beyond Richmond. An antiquarian and obsessive collector, Walpole designed elaborate settings for his 'Curiosities' and 'Singularities', delighting in telling visitors their dark and peculiar histories. These artefactual narratives, often dedicated to creating close associations with ancient aristocratic houses, also appeared in successive editions of his *Description of the Villa of Mr Horace Walpole*, which inventoried the ever-expanding collection. Real objects bleed into *The Castle of Otranto*, so that the portrait of Henry Cary, which Walpole placed in his Long Gallery, was claimed to be the inspiration for the spectral portrait that sighs and wanders dejectedly from the frame in a particularly delirious episode of the novel. One critic has observed that Walpole effectively constituted the novel as 'a series of calculated excurses that surrounded Strawberry Hill and the objects it housed'.[4] The Gothic leaks out from objects as a curious supplement, full of occulted commentary on the meanings of ownership and acquisition.

Mid-eighteenth century taste did not, as I established earlier, stretch to the designs or material objects of Ancient Egypt: Walpole did not collect in this area. But within a few short years, William Beckford's Gothic farrago *Vathek* (1785) displayed a new orientalized twist to the fantasies that might be curled around the private collection. Beckford, on reaching his majority, inherited the vast wealth that his father and grandfather had built from their sugar plantations in the West Indies. After a notoriously sumptuous birthday celebration, Beckford indulged his friends the following Christmas by decking out the house he had inherited as if for 'some gorgeous oriental pageant'. Beckford later recalled:

> The solid Egyptian Hall looked as if hewn out of a living rock – the line of apartments and apparently endless passages extending from it on either side were all vaulted – an interminable staircase, which when you looked down it – appeared as deep as the well in the pyramid – and when you looked up – was lost in vapour... The glowing haze investing every object, the mystic look, the vastness, the intricacy of this vaulted labyrinth occasioned so bewildering an effect that it became impossible for any one to define – at the moment – where he stood.[5]

It was this immersive, orgiastic, Eastern dream that Beckford turned into narrative for his romance *Vathek*, the tale of a cruel and wilful caliph embracing the charms of Satan and defiant blasphemy, only to end in the Hall of Eblis, condemned to the eternal flames of the Islamic hell. The antiquarian tendency for the curious and exotic is manifested in the elaborate footnotes that offer allegedly scholarly authority for the delirious excesses of the orientalist narrative. Vathek is encouraged to his exorbitant crimes by his evil mother, whose black magic powers include a penchant for 'retiring to caverns: my taste for dead bodies, and everything like a mummy is decided'.[6] The romance first appeared in French – exactly the right language for naughty oriental fantasies – and then in a pirated English edition just as Beckford was beginning his years of exile following rumours of his predilection for what *Vathek* called the 'palpitating' hearts of 'delicate boys'. The romance also included a passion for building God-defying towers, something that Beckford would himself indulge at Fonthill, the vast Gothic abbey he constructed once he had pulled down his father's house.

The towers at Fonthill repeatedly collapsed and the inordinate expense of constant building, together with purchases for his private library and his ceaseless acquisition of objects, eventually forced Beckford to sell up. The public auction in 1822 was a rival spectacle to Belzoni's tomb of Seti I at the Egyptian Hall, attracting thousands of visitors, although many dismissed Fonthill as a heap of vulgar trinkets and ostentatious display tainted with suspect Eastern tastes.[7] Just like Walpole, then, Beckford's architectural folly and his Gothic fiction folded into each other, fantasy blurring the boundaries of imaginary and real spaces. Beckford's life, his vast wealth frittered away by an exotic collecting compulsion, further Gothicizes the whole ensemble.

Given this convergence of doomed inheritance and curious or menacing objects, it is unsurprising that there is a specific Egyptian strand to later versions of the Gothic. Hundreds of Egyptian tales began to pour into magazines in the latter half of the nineteenth century, featuring amulets, pharaonic rings with strange powers, menacing, ageless visitors from the East to Western museums, and mummies behaving in unruly ways in private collections or public rooms. The explosion of print culture supported this anonymous stream of Egyptian curse tales, and many still-remembered Gothic writers contributed to the genre, including Algernon Blackwood, Rider Haggard, Richard Marsh, Sax Rohmer and Bram Stoker.

The classic late Victorian story might well be Arthur Conan Doyle's 'Lot No. 249', first published in 1894, the tale of an Oxford student called Bellingham who is swarthy and suspiciously good at Arabic and the ancient languages of the East and whose college room is 'a museum rather than a study. Walls and ceiling were thickly covered with a thousand strange relics from Egypt and the East.' At the centre of Bellingham's rooms crammed with Egyptian objects and papyri is a mummy, 'a horrid, black, withered thing, like a charred head on a gnarled bush, [that] was lying half out of the case, with its clawlike hand and bony forearm resting upon the table.'[8] To the solid Anglo-Saxon protagonist, the mummy is a repulsive object 'lifeless and inert, but it seemed to Smith as he gazed that there still lingered a lurid spark of vitality, some faint sign of consciousness in the little eyes which lurked in the depths of the hollow sockets.'[9] The abject relic is nameless, merely a purchased lot, and the narrative has no interest in sketching out a history of the mummy, since it merely serves as a demonic vehicle. Bellingham's expertise in the lost lore of Ancient Egypt, his increasingly disordered mental state, and a series of apparent accidents and near fatal attacks in college by a half-glimpsed ape-like thing lead Smith to suspect the impossible, that Bellingham has reanimated the mummy with magical rites. In a confrontation, Smith warns him: 'You'll find that your filthy Egyptian tricks won't answer in England.'[10] The narrative culminates in Smith's night walk, terrified by what he believes is a pursuit by the feral mummy close on his heels, sent as Bellingham's malign and murderous agent. Although his rational, sceptical friends refuse to accept Smith's account, they help Smith to force Bellingham to burn the accursed thing.

Conan Doyle's tone was slightly different in another of his Egyptian tales, 'The Ring of Thoth' (1890), set at night in the Egyptian rooms of the Louvre, when a dry London professor of Egyptology accidentally locked in overnight observes a magical ritual that leaves an Egyptian cursed with immortality finally and blissfully dead in the arms of his unwrapped mummy beloved. Yet, as Richard Freeman and others have observed, 'Lot No. 249' fixed the frame for the inexorable, undiscriminating and murderous mummy of horror cinema.[11] Universal studio's *The Mummy* (1932), scripted by John Balderston, who had reported on the opening of Tutankhamun's sarcophagus in 1925, begins with a curse on those who disturb the dead's repose, which prompts mysterious disturbances at night in the halls of the museum, and the threat of the uncanny repetition in the modern day of rites that are thousands of years old. But Conan Doyle was less of an influence on Karloff's subtle study of melancholic Imhotep and more on the empty, vengeful Karis of the poorer and more mechanical sequels, *The Mummy's Hand, The Mummy's Tomb, The Mummy's Curse.*

In fact, Conan Doyle's tales only serve to underline the rapid hardening of tropes associating Egypt with deathliness and vengeance in the late Victorian Gothic revival. Conan Doyle was unengaged by Egypt, travelling there only once, in 1896, in search of a winter climate for his first wife, who suffered from tuberculosis. He hated the heat, and despised the lazy and degenerate Arabs, arrested in their medieval beliefs. He later wrote, just after the opening of the tomb of Tutankhamun, that he considered the finds proved merely that Ancient Egyptian culture was 'contemptible' and 'emasculated'.[12] Egypt brought out Conan Doyle's staunch imperialism: he felt that the British occupation since 1882 had achieved more than millennia of pharaonic power or centuries of Ottoman rule and he spoke glowingly of the Empire builders who lounged in Cairo's Turf Club – Lord Cromer, the sardar of the army Herbert Kitchener, the director of military intelligence Reginald Wingate, or the irrigation engineer Sir William Garstin. Conan Doyle only bucked up at the prospect of fighting at the Sudanese border with the forces of the Mahdist Islamic uprising, men he considered to be merciless fanatics. He signed up as a war reporter for the *Westminster Gazette* and travelled south, only to be told by Kitchener that war was months if not years away and he was back in Cairo within a month.[13] He nevertheless fantasized about beating all of wily Fleet Street's old war reporters to bring the news of the outbreak of war in his story 'The Three Correspondents'. The only other result of his trip to Egypt was his novella *The Tragedy of the Korosko* (1898), in which a group of European and American tourists visiting ancient sites along the Nile are kidnapped by ruthless Sudanese rebels and Muslim fanatics in the trackless desert. In *Korosko*, Egypt beyond the thin strip of the Nile is a wilderness, a 'weird, dead country', dotted only with 'grotesque graves' of 'vanished races and submerged civilisations'.[14] The protagonist, a retired army colonel, has no interest in grasping ancient history, and sees only ruins and rubble. The story boils with dark imaginings about the cruelty of the Sudanese and their threat to white women, inflamed by propagandist tracts like *Ten Years in the Mahdi's Camp*, the sensational story of the kidnapped missionary Father Ohrwalder who eventually escaped and published his account in 1892. Whilst condemning oriental cruelty, Conan Doyle lovingly details the extermination of this vicious band by the heroic Camel Corps of the Egyptian army, with the chilling conclusion 'The nineteenth century had been revenged upon the seventh.'[15] *The Tragedy of the Korosko* was published in the year that Kitchener was finally given leave to advance into the Sudan, destroying the last stand of the Mahdist forces at the Battle of Omdurman with overwhelming force, massacring twenty thousand men and executing the wounded in the wake of the battle. It was widely regarded as final vengeance on the native political movement that had begun with the uprising in Alexandria in 1882, besieged Khartoum in 1885 and murdered the English hero General Gordon.

This cluster of Conan Doyle tales, moving between Gothic and other romance modes, amply demonstrates that we consistently need to think about the disordered fantasia of the Egyptian Gothic very much alongside the concrete political realities of the era. Stories about vengeful objects in private collections and public museums use a dreamlike logic to condense and displace and even invert grander geopolitical acts of imperial revenge. Gothic fiction about Ancient Egyptian artefacts generates allegories of the contemporary imperial situation in Egypt.

Yet, put into the full context of the fictional encounter with Egypt in English literature in the nineteenth century, two things also become clear. First, yet again, is the striking sense of the *lateness* of the merger between the Gothic's obsession with cursed inheritance and stories of curses attached to Ancient Egyptian objects. Pyramids and tombs provide some of the architecture of the first waves of the Gothic, but the first mummy curses appear only in the late 1860s and are fully consolidated only in the 1880s and 1890s. Conan Doyle's 'Lot No. 249' is in fact the *first* mummy depicted as the agent of a malign magician, very late in the century. Second, even within the confines of Gothic writing, it soon becomes apparent that there is a great variety of approaches to the matter of Egypt in the genre. Some critics regard what has been termed the 'Imperial Gothic' as a reductive and rather blunt ideological weapon for legitimating colonial power, and Conan Doyle's Egyptian-themed fiction might reinforce that view.[16] But fear, vengeance and persecutory paranoia are only at one end of the emotional spectrum of the Egyptian Gothic, which also includes fascination, awe, allure, desire and even religious transcendence. This instability, this rapid switching between emotional states, is typical of the

Gothic, the genre 'always verging on turning, on giving way to the opposing strategy'.[17] We need to respect this complex interplay of intensities. In what follows, then, I will outline the rise and peak of generic mummy curse tales and the development of what might be called the 'Museum Gothic' before complicating the picture with a sustained analysis of the fiction of Algernon Blackwood and (in the following chapter) Rider Haggard, two Gothic writers for whom Egypt became a profoundly over-determined figure for conflicted emotional states.

## Learning to curse

The claims for the date of the first literary mummy curse tale are contested. There are several nominations for Louisa May Alcott's lurid chiller, 'Lost in a Pyramid', published in 1869, although this emerged from a nest of similar tales such as 'The Mummy's Soul' (1862) and 'After Three Thousand Years' (1868) that began to stream through the popular magazines in the era of Sensation Fiction.[18] Jane Loudon's *The Mummy!* (1827) – an eccentric piece of Regency proto-science fiction inspired in part by Belzoni's display in London in 1821 – has also been 'rediscovered' as the forgotten origin of the genre.[19] This uncertainty about origins is probably because the theme brings together elements that had been developing in the fascination with the dark Orient in Enlightenment and Romantic writing for over a century but which only crystallized around Egypt after Napoleon's invasion in 1798. *Vathek*, already at the end of a long eighteenth-century tradition inspired by the translation of *The Arabian Nights*, indulges in glorious blasphemy by displacement into the Orient.[20] Beckford's vision of perversity, cruelty and mummy magic in subterranean caverns fed directly into the Romantic imagination. Robert Southey acknowledged the influence of Beckford on his elaborate orientalist epic poems, *Thalaba the Destroyer* (1801) and *The Curse of Kehama* (1810). These envision an exotic East with tyrannical potentates using black magic to conjure malign spirits to issue exorbitant curses on innocent and virtuous victims. 'And thou shall seek Death/To release thee, in vain', intones Book II of *Kehama*, 'And the curse be on thee,/For ever and ever.'[21] Southey's Orient was a textual and syncretic patchwork, a mêlée of scholarly and fantastical sources used with gay abandon. Supported by a vast industry of scholarly footnotes, they nevertheless created a generic Eastern phantasm. The poems were composed as Southey's views on the Empire shifted towards a conservative defence of the virtuous influence of Christian Britain on the paralysing superstitions and despotic governance of the East, particularly as the East India Company extended its territorial power.[22] It took Lord Byron, as the last chapter explored, precisely to invert the structure of the curse and voice it through ransacked treasures, bringing down a curse on the head of Lord Elgin for the looting of the Parthenon in 'The Curse of Minerva'. This use of pathetic fallacy is a key turning point, rendering the curse a modern product of the very encounter between the West and the East.

Thomas De Quincey also has some claim to darken the iconography of Ancient Egypt specifically with malefic intent. There is a crucial passage in the *Confessions of an English Opium-Eater* (1821), which details his persecutory nightmares under the heading 'The Pains of Opium.' De Quincey's guilt at presenting a passing Malay an enormous quantity of opium as a gift results in subsequent visionary torments of China, Asia and India, places where the sublimity of the age of cultures, empires and the teeming quantity of peoples threatens him with annihilation. In a further elaboration, De Quincey

> soon brought Egypt and all her gods under the same law...I came suddenly upon Isis and Osiris: I had done a deed, they said, which the ibis and the crocodile trembled at. I was buried, for a thousand years, in stone coffins, with mummies and sphynxes, in narrow chambers at the heart of eternal pyramids. I was kissed, with cancerous kisses, by crocodiles; and laid, confounded with all unutterable slimy things, amongst reeds and Nilotic mud.[23]

This mixing up of undifferentiated Eastern cultures was typical of the fevered orientalist imagination, although De Quincey's terrors were complicated by his addiction to that quintessentially Eastern drug, opium, an emblem of that abjected other coursing through his very veins. Egypt provides another heathen mythology, at once offering punishment and confinement but with, at the same time, a hint of corrupting pleasures that loosens the boundaries of the self into slime and mud.

Yet elsewhere, in his later essay 'The System of the Heavens' (1846), about the new photographs of the Orion Nebula taken by the Earl of Rosse, De Quincey recalled his ecstatic first sight of the colossal statue of the Younger Memnon (Rameses II) that had been dragged to the Nile by Belzoni, shipped to Britain by his patron Henry Salt and purchased by the British Museum. 'It struck me,' De Quincey said, 'as simply the sublimest sight which in this sight-seeing world I had seen', a model of peace, eternity and diffusive love, 'an emanation from some mystery of endless dawn'.[24] In a slippage typical of De Quincey's mazy and digressive style, though, this benign icon soon mutates into its terrifying opposite, as De Quincey fancies that he sees in the shapes revealed by the nebula photographs a vision of a monstrous Assyrian head looming in the skies above: 'Brutalities unspeakable sit upon the upper lip...But the lower lip...oh, what a convolute of cruelty and revenge is *there*! Cruelty! – to whom? Revenge! – for what? Pause not to ask; but look upwards to other mysteries.'[25] In John Barrell's reading, these texts reveal a psychopathology that emerges alongside Empire,

De Quincey 'terrorised by the fear of an unending and interlinked chain of infections from the East'.[26] He tries to manage his anxieties by projecting them into Eastern figures that are then cast down, but the logic of paranoia means that they only return to persecute with ever greater (indeed, astronomical) power. To De Quincey the Orient becomes 'the place of a malign, a luxuriant or virulent productivity, a breeding-ground of images of the inhuman'.[27] These fanciful terrors are important literary milestones, but they do not yet set the dominant tone for the imaginative engagement with Egypt.

The transport and display of Egyptian materials in England after the return of Napoleonic spoils from 1802 and particularly after Belzoni's display at the Egyptian Hall in 1820 and 1821, began to extract Egypt from a generalized exotic Orient and give it more specificity. The cultural result was not initially laden with doom or threat, however, as I have consistently tried to show. It is odd, for instance, to invoke Jane Loudon's *The Mummy!* as a curse text at all, since this is not ultimately the function of the reanimated pharaoh Cheops in the novel. It certainly introduces the mummy with all the Gothic trappings, borrowed mainly from Mary Shelley's *Frankenstein*, in the scene where Edric and his advisor, the German experimentalist Dr Entwerfen, use galvanism to learn the secrets of the grave. In the 'sepulchral light' of the burial chamber of the Great Pyramid, the 'unspeakable horror' of the experiment is successfully conducted.[28] In the chaos of the lightning storm that is also conjured up, Cheops is inadvertently transported to London, where a struggle over succession involves the court in interminable intrigues. His first words in London are: 'Curses on the wretches! – May Typhon's everlasting vengeance pursue them, and may their hearts wither, gnawed by the never-dying snake!' and he is met with a 'shudder of disgust' wherever he goes, a walking transgression of the natural law.[29] His role is then reduced to fitful spectral appearances as a compelling advisor to plotters at court, acting like an undead Iago. The plotters, however, often find reasons to curse his advice and Cheops is a much cursed creature. Loudon seems to position Cheops as a typical model of Eastern despotism, with a potential to corrupt benign British monarchical power. But this is a misrecognition, engineered by Loudon by exploiting readerly expectations of Gothic conventions. Cheops is ultimately revealed as a Christian moralist, who has worked to foil the plot on the English throne and who also lectures Edric never to transgress natural law again. The penitent Cheops provides an orthodox lecture on the dangers of ruling by the passions and then returns to eternal slumber. Loudon's novel is thus a conservative satire on disastrous kingship in the Regency: it has come to pass that a prehistoric pharaoh has more virtue than a corrupt English court.

Where Loudon exerts an influence, then, is on the satirical function of the reanimated mummy. Echoing the craze for public unwrappings of mummies spread by Thomas Pettigrew in the 1830s, Edgar Allan Poe's mummy awakes in high dudgeon after being stripped and electrified by a group of earnest scientists in a typical exploratory unwrapping in a museum. The mummy Allamistakeo's instant contempt for the complacency of learning in the nineteenth century knows no bounds. The august company prove unable to match his advanced state of knowledge in the life sciences: 'I perceive you are yet in the infancy of Galvanism, and cannot accomplish with it what was a common thing among us in the old days.'[30] A succession of great modern triumphs – architecture, railways, pantaloons – are dismissed with such venom that the wounded narcissism of the men of science means that they can't bear to continue the conversation. The real Egyptologist and famed unwrapper of mummies George Gliddon is particularly treated with contempt.[31] Yet Poe's sketch ends with an acknowledgement by the narrator that the mummy has spoken an unforgiving truth from his impossible place outside modernity: 'The truth is, I am heartily sick of this life and of the nineteenth century in general … I shall just step over to Ponnonner's and get embalmed for a couple of hundred years.'[32]

The satirical device of this simple inversion lasted many decades. One of Grant Allen's earliest pieces of fiction, 'My New Year's Eve Among the Mummies' (1880) reworks Poe's tale. The Victorian visitor to Egypt happens upon a new entry passage into a pyramid at night, only to find an Egyptian royal retinue in the chamber, who are reanimated for one night every thousand years. High learning and royal blood cause the pharaoh to dismiss the visitor as an ignorant barbarian, but the eventual offer to join their eternal company proves sufficiently tempting given the allure of Princess Hatasou. The narrator prepares to submit to the proper magical rites of embalming, only to lose consciousness and wake up firmly back in Shepheard's Hotel in modern Cairo. He has at least been divested of the attentions of his fiancée and her mother in his lengthy delirious illness. His experience is dismissed by his scientific friends, who persuade him not to ruin his reputation by delivering an account to the Society of Antiquaries in London. The narrative thus purports to have been written and deposited in the library of the British Museum in the hope of finding eventual proof at the next millennial reanimation inside the pyramid in 2887.[33]

Allen's throwaway tale merges satire with another Egyptian trope that develops early in the wake of the Napoleonic invasion: the mummy romance. The dreamy state in which the narrator encounters the gorgeous Hatasou loosens the Reality Principle that polices desire for the exotic other and holds out the prospect of an ecstatic if deathly union. The chance is whipped away by reawakening, and taboo is avoided whilst that proleptic state of delicious desire for the exotic Egyptian woman is preserved. Although the mummy romance can carry the threat of transgression, this is an anti-curse plot: it is precisely about the promise of the other, even if it is endlessly deferred. This story arc, repeated throughout Western fictions of Egypt in the nineteenth century, was fixed in place by Théophile Gautier's fiction 'The Mummy's Foot', published in 1840. In this short yet influential piece, the narrator enters an old curiosity shop in Paris and amidst the Malay knives, Mexican fetishes and Hindu idols is persuaded by the Jewish owner to purchase, as a morbid joke, an embalmed mummy foot to use as a paperweight. The foot had belonged to Princess Hermonthis, a pharaoh's daughter, and was 'slender and delicate, and terminated by perfectly formed nails, pure and transparent as agates'.[34] Hovering between sleeping and dreaming, the narrator senses that the foot resists passive ownership as a curio. 'Instead of remaining quiet – as behoved a foot which had been embalmed for four thousand years – it commenced to act in a nervous manner'.[35] Soon the princess hops into view and the narrator gifts her with the return of her foot. In reward, she transports him to Egypt, to the hidden burial chamber of the pharaohs, where in return for the foot he punningly asks her father for her hand. The nineteenth-century narrator is considered shoddily composed for surviving eternity compared to the robust state of Egyptian preservation. He is rudely awoken by his servant before this scene can play out.

Gautier elaborated the romance plot into a more complex full-scale novel in *The Romance of a Mummy* (1863), in which an English aristocrat is led to an untouched pharaonic tomb by an Arab dealer in antiquities. The tomb contains a perfectly preserved female mummy, which they unwrap to her delectable naked form, and a papyrus whose translation forms the bulk of the text, an account of a forbidden love between Tahoser, daughter of the pharaoh Petamounoph, and the Jewish boy Poeri. Just as Lord Evadale feels 'a sort of religious horror' for breaching the untouched tomb, so the embedded papyrus redoubles the thematic of transgressive racial desire, recording a pivotal moment when the pharaoh is defeated by the Jewish magus Moschi (Moses), and his daughter dallies with converting to this new God Jehovah, out of love for a Jew.[36]

'The Mummy's Foot' could not work more perfectly to condense into a fetishized curio the conflicting desires that animate mummy romances. Freud spoke explicitly about the foot as a sexual and magic fetish, something charged with pleasure precisely to ward off the fear and anxiety of a more menacing truth.[37] This ambivalence is marked in another tale by Gautier, his contribution to the literature of the decadent and monstrous Cleopatra, the last in the line of the pharaohs, whose satiation of her lust is rendered even more exquisite by the poisoning of her young lovers.[38] But there is also an allegory hinted at by Gautier about the unruliness of ancient things that resist their reduction to commodified artefacts in the markets and museums of the West.[39] The stripping of the mummy makes it a 'sexually charged entity' of course, but this tearing away of veils carries with it the rapine economics of imperialism too.[40]

Gautier obsessively racializes the erotics of difference, emphasizing Hermonthis' 'Egyptian type of perfect beauty', nearly Greek but for the 'slightly African fullness of her lips'.[41] In the matter of Egypt, at least, this erotic charge is more overt in French than Anglo-American literature. Flaubert's travel notes from his journey down the Nile in 1849, for instance, are largely dismissive of the ancient ruins and dealers' houses stuffed with 'mummies stripped of their bandages standing in the corner'. The monuments produce no sense of awe, only reflections on 'the number of bourgeois stares they have received'.[42] Instead, Flaubert obsessively details his sexual encounters with Egyptian prostitutes, his insatiable desire fired by racial and cultural difference. French fascination with the native woman was always openly sexualized, as Malek Alloula's book on pornographic postcards of posed women from colonial Algeria, *The Colonial Harem*, attests. Flaubert's long-suppressed notes read like the unconscious of the tame mummy romances of Anglo-American fiction that veil and suspend their desire.

The later in the century the text, the more hemmed in by threat these romances become. In Theo Douglas's *Iras:A Mystery* (1896), for instance, an Egyptologist recovers a perfectly preserved 'virgin daughter of the priest of Khames', who, an attendant hieroglyphic script explains, had been buried alive in a mesmeric state, rather than being embalmed, by her vengeful father. Her tomb is in a concealed chamber with an inscription 'invoking a curse so terrible' that the fellaheen attempt to rebury 'this bundle of malefic influence'.[43] Smuggled up the Nile on a boat that meets 'the very quintessence of bad fortune' (under conditions that dimly echo aspects of the Thomas Douglas Murray story), the mummy makes it out of Egypt and to Britain.[44] The Egyptologist, menaced by malign spectral visions of a menacing Egyptian figure, nevertheless unwraps and awakens the mummy in Edinburgh. He marries this exotic vision, but the question of sexual relations with a three thousand year old woman is cancelled by her rapid fading away, 'growing more ethereal under the advancing Shadow', with 'something of the air of a woman in decline', until she effectively vanishes from the modern world.[45]

In contrast to this fey tale, typical of many similar such English stories at the fin de siècle, the Moulin Rouge in Paris witnessed a riot in 1907 over a mime performance, *Rêve d'Égypte*, in which the writer and then music-hall performer Colette played a mummy unwrapped on stage by her lesbian lover, the Marquise de Mornay. The scene was simple: 'The mummy comes back to life in a jewelled bra, slowly and seductively unwinds her transparent wrappings, and at the climax of the dance, passionately embraces the archaeologist'.[46] Staged with Colette's cuckolded husband in the audience, totally complicit in a scenario that he had partly scripted, it is safe to say that the French seemed happy to swap ambivalent subtexts for openly perverse sexual play within the conventions of the mummy romance.

These different satirical and sexual energies nearly always cut across and complicate the tone of the Egyptian Gothic. It is rare to find tales that seek a single pitch of horror around a deadly curse, but those that do, come after the

1860s. Louisa May Alcott's brief and nasty shocker, 'Lost in a Pyramid, or the Mummy's Curse', published anonymously in 1869, is significant for repositioning Egypt from the sublime to sensational horror. The first half of the story is a shivery anecdote, told by Forsyth to his betrothed, of the time he was lost inside the pyramid of Cheops with the Egyptologist Professor Niles. The men are forced to burn mummy cases to attract attention. Nerves unstrung by their predicament, they resort to burning the body of a mummy, but only after they have unwrapped the female form, rescuing from her 'shrivelled hands' a gold box that contains seeds. Too late, Niles deciphers an inscription that 'the mummy we had so ungallantly burned was that of a famous sorceress who bequeathed her curse to whoever should disturb her rest.' Forsyth (who has no foresight), confesses to 'a vein of superstition' and 'I sometimes wonder if I am to share the curse.'[47] In the second part of the tale, Forsyth discovers on his marriage day that his bride has grown one of the seeds. The same morning, he receives news that Niles has been sapped of life and poisoned by his own experiment with the vicious flower that blooms from the mummy seeds: 'he died in great agony, raving of mummies, pyramids, serpents, and some fatal curse which had fallen upon him.' Forsyth looks upon the face of his new wife, only to find it 'drawn and pallid, as if with some wasting malady' and 'the curse that had bided its time for ages was fulfilled at last.'[48]

What prompts this vengeful turn in the 1860s? In 1857, a short story in *Putnam's Monthly Magazine* imagines a celebratory 'carnival of the dead' in the British Museum, with Egyptian sarcophagi filled with punch around which the female mummies happily dance.[49] Ten years later, Alcott's mummy sorceress clasps deathly vengeance in its bony hand and the museum at midnight induces only terror.

Alcott clearly paid close attention to Egyptian matters, trading on current discussions about whether the 'mummy wheat' frequently buried in Egyptian tombs to provide for a fertile afterlife could still be germinated thousands of years later. (Ernest Wallis Budge, whose papers at the British Museum contain a packet of mummy seeds sent to him by a correspondent, would later become an exercised debunker of this myth.) This germinal question is hardly spooky enough to produce a shift in Gothic tone, however. Perhaps Alcott was simply 'preaching to the nerves', knowing that Egyptian scenes might provide the physiological shocks sought for with the arrival of Sensation Fiction in the 1860s.[50] The explanation might be more motivated than this, though. The American Civil War placed America in a new relation with Egypt. Not only did racial anthropology point to new evidence from Ancient Egyptian skulls about the development of races, the Civil War disrupted the economy of cotton production in the south. This prompted some imports of Egyptian cotton and rags, which in turn produced rumours that the bulk material included polluted mummy rags, used to make paper, which caused an outbreak of cholera in a factory in Maine in 1863.[51] Trade routes are also pathways that generate transits of story and superstition.

Ailise Bulfin has argued that, in English fiction, the Egypt of the imagination began to darken in the 1860s as the construction of the Suez Canal by the French engineer Ferdinand de Lesseps for the Egyptian government approached completion in 1869. The canal dramatically cut the distance between Europe and the Indian subcontinent, but French or Egyptian control would have potentially split Great Britain from the Indian Empire. The dramatic geopolitical change wrought by the canal was why Disraeli fought for a controlling share in the canal company (achieved in 1875, after Egyptian finances collapsed). The value of the canal was ultimately why the British occupied Egypt in 1882, the moment when the intrigue of Egypt as an informal 'sphere of influence' transformed Egypt into a place with potentially murderous possibilities for Europeans. Egyptian occupation proved to be the fulcrum of British foreign policy for decades. Already by 1895, some leading politicians such as John Morley were of the view that 'the occupation of Egypt poisoned our foreign policy and lay at the root of all the difficulties which concerned us in the world.'[52] The canal was of course to prove the graveyard of the British Empire after the botched invasion of the newly nationalised Canal Zone in 1956.

After the uprising and the 1882 occupation, coinciding with an explosion of new popular magazines and journals in England, Egypt became a premier location for the Imperial Gothic. The form refigured the structural violence of the colonial encounter in tales of insidious natives, long-buried curses, haunted museums and mysterious, vengeful objects. This was complicated by the overlaid centuries of colonial occupation endured by Egypt: what the British had inherited from the untold centuries leaked out in disfigured allegory from the very stones. For the reiteration and modulation of this post-occupation curse narrative, let's take four of the most significant contributions to this genre: Guy Boothby's *Pharos the Egyptian* (1899), Sax Rohmer's *Tales of Secret Egypt* (1918), Richard Marsh's *The Beetle* (1899), and Bram Stoker's *The Jewel of Seven Stars* (1903).

## Plagues, scarabs and the nuclear option: The golden age of Egyptian curse stories

Boothby was a prolific Anglo-Australian pulp writer, best known for his creation of the dastardly super-criminal Dr Nikola. The writer visited Egypt in the winter of 1897, in the months before the final victory over the Sudanese Islamic uprising at Omdurman. He had contributed to the mummy romance form with his short story, 'A Professor of Egyptology' in 1894, featuring a scholar in Cairo with an 'extraordinary intuitive knowledge...concerning the localities of tombs', who proves to be a restless ancient soul agonizing over millennia for a lost love.[53] Instead, *Pharos the Egyptian* finds a powerful new reserve of malignancy. The novel is framed as a confession by a respected painter, Forrester, who has chosen banishment from his home country for his part in bringing a catastrophe upon England. Forrester was at work on a history painting of pharaoh Merenptah, when he encountered at night a menacing Arab by the Thames at Cleopatra's Needle, a figure who seemed to be coaxing a man to commit suicide at that melancholy place. Pharos evidently has potent mesmeric powers and produces in Forrester 'a great shudder, accompanied by an indescribable feeling of nausea'.[54] Pharos seems to be an Eastern impresario, presenting a beautiful yet damaged female violinist Valere to society audiences in London. She is a damned soul he clearly holds in his hypnotic power. When Pharos discovers that Forrester is the surviving son of an eminent Egyptologist, and has inherited his father's objects, including the mummy and finely decorated coffin of Ptahmes, chief of the king's magicians, Pharos unleashes an extraordinary curse upon him:

> 'Thy father, was it, wretched man...who stole this body?...If that be so, then may the punishment decreed against those guilty of the sin of sacrilege be visited on thee and thine for evermore...By Osiris, a time of punishment is coming.'[55]

The coffin stolen, Forrester tracks Pharos and Valere to Naples, Pompeii and then down the Nile to Luxor, the object reversing the usual trajectory of ancient remains, in effect removing the layers of deadening artefaction and returning to a live thing again. In Luxor, subject to the power of Pharos (of course the modern incarnation of the sorcerer Ptahmes), Forrester experiences a sequence of visions that open up the hidden history of his father's collection. Ptahmes was defeated by the Jewish sorcerer Moses and condemned to death by the pharaoh in an unconsecrated tomb. The revenge is at once familial, then, but also stands in for the wrath of the old pantheon of Egyptian gods overthrown by Christendom.

The punishment is indeed impressive. Forrester escapes from Egypt, where an outbreak of plague threatens him and Valere. They stay just ahead of the disease and reach London. Here, in a lengthy satirical passage, Ptahmes leads Forrester on a tour of a corrupt and decadent London, from the members of the Antiquarian Club and the Houses of Parliament, via the Occidental Music Hall and the slums of Seven Dials. Too late, Forrester understands that he has been conducted on this tour only to infect every level of society, for his punishment has been to act as the vector of disease, the asymptomatic Patient Zero of a plague that will turn London, and Europe beyond, into a necropolis. There are some memorable scenes of a London emptied of its people, Forrester stumbling along alone like Shelley's Last Man. The curse is another inversion of the punishments of the Old Testament God; here Egypt brings plague down on the houses of its implacable enemy.

The exorbitance of the curse on Forrester suggests an inversion and amplification of the massacres of the Battle of Omdurman, where the Maxim gun helped Kitchener inflict a ninety per cent casualty rate on the Sudanese army, killing twenty thousand and wounding another twenty-two thousand in less than a day's engagement. The vicious reprisals taken on the Sudanese, which coloured Kitchener's subsequent reputation, here stage a supernatural return.[56] In many respects, *Pharos the Egyptian* fulfils a narrative formula in the late Victorian Gothic that Stephen Arata has identified as 'reverse colonisation'. In this repeated fantasy, best embodied in Count Dracula's carefully planned arrival in England (scenes from which Boothby openly borrows), colonial paranoia breeds an inverse invasion, but one condensed into a singular terrifying creature: 'In the marauding, invasive Other, British culture sees its own imperial practices mirrored back in monstrous forms.'[57] Boothby also uses another motif that saturates the late Victorian Gothic: the mesmeric foreigner. The relationship of Pharos to Valere – the woman's will entirely subjugated to the hypnotic power of the magician – repeats that of the Eastern European Jew Svengali over the singer Trilby in George du Maurier's popular hit, *Trilby* (1894). *Trilby* was an international sensation on publication, picking up on the wonders of hypnosis and trance, but also trading on what were considered its profound dangers.[58] Odd effects of *rapport* had for a century been tied up with spooky supernatural narratives and sexual corruption, and were part of the furniture of Gothic writing.[59] Could the curse be a product of hypnotic suggestion, a nocebo reaction in the weak-willed? Many doctors warned that indulging in hypnosis sapped the will and left people (especially constitutionally weaker women) open to malign influences and sexual terrorism. This fed into even wider conservative accounts that connected weak will to racial degeneracy. Ancient Egyptian magic, dispensed through the occult power of the sorcerer's eye, put Egyptian fictions at the centre of the oneiric late Victorian Gothic.

The Edwardian author Sax Rohmer (pen-name of Arthur Henry Ward) is commonly associated with virulent 'yellow peril' racism, through his creation of the indefatigable enemy of the British Empire, the criminal genius Dr Fu-Manchu. Started in 1911, as the Manchu dynasty was being replaced by a Chinese Republic that wished to throw off foreign influence, these serial melodramas see Fu-Manchu stalking through London with a motley band of dastardly Asiatics at his beck and call. The oriental evil genius merges Eastern traits: he has the cunning of the Chinese, but also 'mummy-like shoulders', an odd shuffling gait, and a face 'identical with that of Seti I, the mighty pharaoh.'[60]

Fu-Manchu's powers seem to shade into the mesmeric and occult, talents that also have an Egyptian shade, since Rohmer elsewhere regarded all sorcery 'as a legacy from Ancient Egypt'.[61] The Fu-Manchu stories rose in fame and popularity as moral panics about 'Chinese' Limehouse in the London docks surged during World War I, another important facet of the exoticization of London at the time.[62] Fu-Manchu's plans for the overthrow of the British Empire are always just about deferred by the derring-do duo of Nayland Smith and Dr Petrie (the name an echo of the first Edwards Professor of Egyptology at University College, Flinders Petrie), at least until the next episode. Fu-Manchu's insistent return, an inevitable result of the serial form, rather undermines confidence that Britain can ever be secure from its mortal enemies, however.

Rohmer rarely rises above reiterative racism, exploiting an undifferentiated and toxic orientalism. He hit on the Far East after starting in the Middle East. The first ever story he published was 'The Mysterious Mummy' in 1903. He then began writing an Ancient Egyptian epic called *Zalithea*, which he later claimed was aided by a dream that gave him clairvoyant access to Ancient Egypt and which ended with a spectral visitation.[63] Later, in 1918, he published two books with distinctly Egyptian settings. *The Brood of the Witch-Queen* conforms to type, taking the basic plot of Conan Doyle's 'Lot No. 249', but ramping up the hysteria. At Oxford, Antony Ferrara becomes an expert in Ancient Egypt, a 'queer chap' whose rooms are 'a kind of nightmare museum. There was an unwrapped mummy there, the mummy of a woman – I can't possibly describe it. He had pictures too – photographs. I shan't try to tell you what they represented.'[64] This ellipsis seems to hide some unholy interest in young girls, although Ferrara is also repeatedly condemned as an 'evilly effeminate thing' too.[65] Later, in Piccadilly, his bachelor rooms are filled with mummies and Egyptian trinkets in a 'setting of Eastern voluptuousness'.[66] 'Egypt is in London, indeed', as one bewildered Englishman later remarks.[67] Our plucky British hero, Cairns, will fight Ferrara, partly for the soul of Myra Duquesne, 'a radiant vision in white', but ultimately for his own life. Cairns is soon beset by hypnotic attacks and monstrous hallucinations of unspeakable things crawling in the shadows which (his Egyptologist father tells him) he must battle with a stern will. In Cairo, Cairns suffers further visions that reveal Ferrara to be an adept of a hidden cult of a queen of such 'sinful loveliness' and 'splendid wickedness' that her 'name, after her mysterious death, had been erased from all her monuments'.[68] This interstitial pharaoh queen, we are told, 'was not an Egyptian but an Asiatic'.[69] The dastardly Ferrara, it seems, has found her hidden burial chamber in a pyramid accessed through a mosque (thus merging the threats of ancient and modern Egypt), and now lies there entranced, 'absorbing evil force from the sarcophagus of the Witch-Queen'. The last revelation views Ferrara as the inevitable incarnation of the high priest of this sacrilegious cult, that 'today in this modern London, a wizard of Ancient Egypt, armed with the lost lore of that magical land, walks amongst us!'[70] Cairns succeeds only by turning the black magic back on its conjurer, Ferrara destroyed by his own evil elementals. Ferrara is nothing other than an abject bundle of Eastern menace: he invokes no curses because he is the very embodiment of the malign curse directed at the colonial centre.

By 1918, this was standard pulp fare, soon to find a home in magazines like *Weird Tales*, where cults of half-man half-cat abominations worship the Egyptian god Bubastis in subterranean caverns – under Cornwall this time.[71] But Rohmer's other book of that year, *Tales of Secret Egypt*, has more nuance to it. In these interlinked stories, the English agent in Cairo, Kernaby, is an unscrupulous trader in antiquities and conducts espionage for a company in England. He is not the clean-cut uncomplicated colonial agent of melodrama, but a man using underhand methods to scratch a living trading trinkets and information. Within the Cairene world of gossip and rumour, Kernaby fences with the shadowy Abû Tabâh, a man with 'strange hypnotic eyes' and an uncanny knowledge of the city's secrets.[72] Abû Tabâh is an imam, a conjuror, perhaps a magician but also an intellectual and secular man of science. What lifts these tales above the unreflective racism is that the engagement between East and West is more dynamic than usual. Abû Tabâh is an unpredictable figure, who will sometimes beat Kernaby to the prize with his greater guile, but will also on occasion save his rival from a fatally cursed artefact. In 'The Death-Ring of Sneferu', Abû Tabâh warns Kernaby that he should be careful of any ancient object bearing a specific hieroglyph, the symbol of Set, god of destruction. Almost immediately, one of Kernaby's informers tells him of discoveries in the Pyramid of Meydum where the fellaheen refuse to continue work, frightened by the powerful spirits that they believe linger there. Kernaby scents treasure but is fully aware that 'the smuggling of relics out of Egypt is a punishable offence', and so proceeds to the pyramid in the dead of night.[73] Abû Tabâh anticipates his every move, but he is only doing this to protect his rival from the fatal power of the ring. They both discover that another English agent has stolen the fatal ring. He is found dead in his hotel, the ring on his swollen finger: 'He had been dead for at least two hours, and by the token of certain hideous glandular swellings, I knew that he had met his end by the bite of an Egyptian viper.'[74] Many of the stories revolve around powerful and enigmatic objects circulating in Cairo bazaars. Rohmer returned to this territory of unruly objects with his psychic detective Moris Klaw, a racially ambiguous 'humble explorer of the etheric borderland' living in liminal Limehouse in London, several of whose cases revolve around menacing Egyptian artefacts, such as a stolen fragment of potsherd that contains 'occult knowledge' from a temple dedicated to Anubis.[75] Klaw solves crimes by reading the psychic imprint of crime scenes, sleeping overnight in museum rooms and burgled apartments.

Whilst Rohmer lashes on helpings of weird and uncanny atmospheres, *Tales of Secret Egypt* also leans towards forms of the 'explained supernatural', as in the case of 'The Whispering Mummy', or actively satirizes the dangers of romanticizing the Orient. In 'Lure of Souls', the narrator is visiting Egypt for the first time, sees the world through the pages of Kipling or the *Arabian Nights*, and thus utterly misrecognizes what he sees: 'it's a rotten story, from a romantic point of view.'[76] A similar misrecognition occurs in the story 'Harûn Pasha', where an English visitor to Cairo, reading the streets through the eyes of Edmond Dulac's illustrations to the *Arabian Nights*, seems to have stumbled upon the hidden garden and palace of a mythical Pasha, which he declares 'a sort of fairyland'. The cruel and monstrous Pasha, it transpires, is an Englishman merely impersonating the role, mockingly demonstrating the theory that the East is really a construction of the fantasies of the West. It is mildly alarming to discover that it is Sax Rohmer who is able to share something of Edward Said's central lesson that orientalism is fundamentally a 'textual attitude', the East a discursive construction of a Western library of pre-prepared representations and actions.[77]

Perhaps the most hysterical contribution to the Egyptian Gothic was Richard Marsh's *The Beetle*. Marsh (pen-name of Richard Bernard Heldman) was a hack writer and journalist who published over seventy books. But *The Beetle* struck a chord, being serialized first in Harmsworth's popular magazine *Answers* before going into fifteen editions before the Great War.[78] It is the story of an insidious intrusion of a monstrous Egyptian being into London, a 'Nameless Thing' that relentlessly pursues the most promising politician of his generation. Paul Lessingham has this exorbitant curse placed on him, in suitably disordered English: 'yet, behold, the sap and the juice of my vengeance is in this, in that though he shall be very sure that the days that are, are as the days of his death, yet shall he know that THE DEATH, THE GREAT DEATH, is coming – coming – and shall be on him – when I will!'[79] *The Beetle* borrows its structure from Wilkie Collins, using four overlapping narrators to provide first-person testimony on events. What they witness is unclear, in part because all of the main actors are subject to intense mesmeric control by this Eastern menace, but mainly because whatever this Egyptian is keeps slipping away from any secure classification. The slippage between the accounts and the ellipses in the narrative intensifies the horrific effect.

In the first part, Robert Holt is a desperate unemployed clerk who stoops to breaking into what appears to be an abandoned suburban house west of Kensington, only to find himself locked in the mesmeric beam of a creature lying on an Eastern divan. At night, Holt hears the slithers of abject things: spiders, crawling insects, rats' feet. When he sees his gaoler, Holt 'could not at once decide if it was a man or a woman. Indeed at first I doubted if it was anything human.'[80] The face is dominated by an insectoid proboscis and glowing eyes; the skin is an ageless 'saffron yellow'. The creature unmans Holt instantly and he is hypnotically enslaved to conduct crimes, directed at undermining Lessingham, the object of the creature's revenge. Holt also witnesses – or hallucinates – something profoundly traumatic: the transformation of this man-woman-thing into a gigantic beetle. Holt's ultimate fate is to be found dead in a Limehouse slum, sucked dry of vital juices, 'the skin drawn tightly over his cheek bones – the bones themselves staring through': he is, in effect, mummified.[81] The second part, narrated by Sydney Atherton, gives more of a sight of the Egyptian, because Atherton is a man of science and powerful will, and is thus able to resist the mesmeric spell ('his was one of those morbid organisations which are oftener found, thank goodness, in the east than in the west').[82] Atherton cannot decide on the creature's gender and is unable to fix this creature racially, either: 'He was hardly an Arab, he was not a fellah...His lips were thick and shapeless, – and...this seemed to suggest that in his veins there ran more than a streak of negro blood.'[83] At least when this uncanny visitor transforms itself into a beetle, the taxonomies of entomology can help Atherton secure this impossible event: 'It appeared to be a beetle...Beyond doubt it was a lamellicorn, one of the *Copridae*. With the one exception of its monstrous size, there were the characteristics in plain view; – the convex body, the large head, the projecting clypeus.'[84] Atherton hints that he has read rumours of a semi-mythical magical ritual, 'The apotheosis of the beetle', and although this is one of the unexplained ellipses in the novel it is suggestive of the Ancient Egyptian worship of the scarab beetle as a master of eternal life. The third and shortest section is narrated by the spirited and independent Marjorie Lindon, betrothed to Lessingham and thus a prime target of the Egyptian's revenge. Her kidnap, invoking a standard device of the white woman in peril of oriental defilement, ends the section and introduces us to the final narrator, Augustus Champnell, the confidential agent employed by Lessingham to track the creature down. It is in Champnell's private office that we hear Lessingham's extraordinary confession, that during a youthful visit to Cairo, in which he indulged (we are to presume) in the brothels of the city, he was drugged and kidnapped by a secret cult that forced him into degrading sexual acts and witnessed in an underground temple the sacrifice of white women to the goddess Isis. He escaped but the trauma still affects him: we have seen Lessingham unmanned merely by hearing the word 'beetle' pronounced. He, too, has witnessed the apotheosis. The novel ends with a chase across London, the human-beetle-thing trying to smuggle Marjorie out of England, presumably to sacrifice her. The abrupt end comes in a train crash north of King's Cross. The only trace of the creature in the matchboxed carriages are unholy stains on the woodwork, which various experts cannot determine as human, cat or lizard blood.

For Marsh, Egypt is a site of an intense phobic reaction – to such an extent that *The Beetle* has been claimed as a generic merger of Gothic and 'medico-scientific accounts' of 'chronic fear and spatial phobia'.[85] If *The Beetle* has been rescued from the shadow of Stoker's *Dracula* (which it initially out-sold), it is because it is an object lesson in how the Gothic engineers the mon-ster with a 'remarkably mobile, permeable, and infinitely interpretable body'.[86] It is as if the allegorical weight borne by Egypt cannot be fixed down, and the vehicle of the metaphor itself becomes distended, forced into a forever unfin-ished flickering between forms. The Thing is abhuman, 'continually in danger of becoming not-itself, becoming other'.[87] This makes it difficult to determine final meanings. The novel encourages psychosexual readings of course, the sexual dread that drips through the text reinforced by Marsh's awareness that hypnotic rapport was denounced by some as a dangerous erotic entanglement, over-loaded by oriental stereotypes of the mesmeric foreigner. *The Beetle* also de-mands to be located with historical precision, Bulfin noting that the secret location of the cult of Isis was uncovered and destroyed by British troops ad-vancing on the Sudan. But the book also mutates beyond Egypt per se: Marsh only ever exploits Egypt as a superficial locus of phobic racism, and within a year or so 'the beetle' was transformed into *The Goddess: A Demon*, where the avenging force emerges from the horrific miasma of the Indian subcontinent.[88]

In contrast, Marsh's contemporary Bram Stoker had a much more specific relationship to Egypt and its antiquities. Stoker grew up among the Dublin Protestant elite, where he was a neighbour and protégé of Sir William Wilde (Oscar's father), who had travelled in Egypt and owned an extensive collection of ancient artefacts, including a mummy. In his travelogue, William Wilde recalled visiting Saqqara, where 'for miles it is literally strewn over with the sacking of the tombs – remains of human bones . . . ; quantities of linen, pieces of broken mummy cases, and bits of blue crockery ware.' He rescued a mummy case from a recent sacking by a French visitor, cast aside with 'the different broken parts of the body'. Later, sitting by a fire fed by wooden coffins and the contents of 'mummy-pots', Wilde inverted the usual ascription of fear to the Arab peasants: 'It is remarkable how the superstitions and prejudices of coun-tries and people vary. How few English of the lower orders would like to inhabit tombs, surrounded by the mouldering remains of human bodies, as the Arabs of Sackara do.'[89] Stoker's interest was evidently fired by such anecdotes: his library contained a number of works by Flinders Petrie and Wallis Budge, including the latter's translation of the Book of the Dead and his *Egyptian Magic*. Bram Stoker's contribution to the Egyptian Gothic, *The Jewel of Seven Stars*, was also knowledgeably built on Howard Carter's discovery of the tomb of Queen Hatshepsut in 1902. She was the female regent in the eighteenth dynasty who had thrust the male heir to the throne aside and ruled under the sign of masculine kingship for twenty-two years. Her ward, Tuthmoses III, suc-ceeded her and later ordered her cartouche destroyed, and so her name disap-peared from history for many centuries. Reconstructing this intermittently erased figure was the work of nineteenth-century Egyptologists. Famously, Hatshepsut's sarcophagus was empty, the whereabouts of the royal mummy an enigma. Stoker's novel was therefore confabulated from the mysterious gaps in this elliptical and transgressive historical record.[90]

The novel begins in the wake of an attack on the famous Egyptologist, Abel Trelawney, who has fallen into a cataleptic trance, surrounded by the ancient antiquities in his study. The narrator, Malcom Ross, is overwhelmed by the clutter and mummy-stench of this private collection:

> There were so many ancient relics that unconsciously one was taken back to strange lands and strange times. There were so many mummies or mummy objects ... that one was unable to forget the past ... The multitudinous presence of the dead and the past took such hold on me that I caught myself looking around fearfully as though some strange personality or influence was present.[91]

This is the plot of the novel in capsule form. Trelawney has obsessively devoted his life to recovering the lost mummy Queen Tera at the expense of his wife, who died in childbirth, and his daughter Margaret, whose personality will be increasingly subsumed by Tera's spirit double as the plot advances. What Margaret inherits (the name Tera encrypted in her own) lies somewhere between a psychical imprint and a biological regression. Trelawney had first found the severed mummy hand of Tera, with its freakish seven fingers, uncannily preserved. He later tracks down the mummy of the queen in the Valley of the Sorcerer, ignoring the superstitious fellaheen and the curse carved above her tomb by those who buried her: 'Hither the Gods come not at any summons ... Go not nigh, lest their vengeance wither you away.'[92] A lifetime of study of magical texts has persuaded him he can resurrect the queen with the lost sciences of the ancients. He reconstructs the tomb in the caverns beneath his Cornish home, and proceeds to unwrap the queen's body within the required magical apparatus. This unwrapping, a band of men gathered around the voluptuous yet monstrous body of an undead woman, repeats the punitive scenario of staking the vampire Lucy Westenra in *Dracula*. Unlike *Dracula* which ends in victory for our heroic brotherhood of good Christian men, *The Jewel of Seven Stars* has a memorably apocalyptic end, since the energies they are messing with prove to be rays of 'dark matter', shortly to be known as radioactivity. The 'magical' alignment of the apparatus demanded by the ancient texts builds a kind of magical nuclear device. Stoker always used the vanishing points in very contemporary sciences to open up supernatural possibilities. Queen Tera's body disappears and her violators are left for dead.

This denouement completes a logic of inversion that constitutes the arc of the novel: Queen Tera will move from lifeless artefact to renewed spirit, whilst the clueless moderns will be progressively suspended in trance, psychically swallowed by the past, and then petrified into inanimate objects around the sarcophagus.[93] No wonder the reissue in 1912 assiduously buried this ending under the rubble of a major revision which used the conventional marriage plot: the experiment fails, the noxious influences disperse, and Ross happily marries Margaret. It remains unclear if Stoker was responsible for these revisions in the last year of his life.

Stoker's tale uses no shuffling mummies, trailing cerements of the grave. The Egyptian influence remains insidious, permeating modern bodies invisibly, from a twilight zone where infection, psychical suggestion, the exertion of magical will and radioactive particles coexist in the vanishing point between science and the occult. We have moved from the histrionic accusations of Pharos to a steady and silent permeation of a domestic space with unknowable Egyptian influences, in a plot in which the poles of margin and centre are reversed by a creeping pervasion.

## The Museum Gothic

Stoker's sense of permeation of the domestic world creates, I would suggest, a more general curse-effect that contributes a distinct tone to the Edwardian Gothic. M. R. James, not one to stoop to vulgar Gothic devices, published a brief piece late in his career called 'The Malice of Inanimate Objects', which begins with observations on those 'dreadful days, on which we have had to acknowledge with gloomy resignation that our world has turned against us. I do not mean the human world of our relations and friends . . . No, it is the world of things that do not speak or work or hold congresses and conferences. It includes such beings as the collar stud, the ink stand, the fire, the razor, and, as age increases, the extra step on the staircase.'[94] The comfort and security of stuff, the binding of identity through the accumulation of objects, comes with a glimmer of a superstitious thought that these things might slip from commodity fetishes back into roles as genuine magical fetishes, gaining a secondary agency and escaping their inanimate fixity to fling themselves furiously in the faces of their complacent owners. In James's tales, collectable mezzotints become animated, re-staging violence, and even crumpled bedclothes menace smug rationalists.[95] It is an antiquarian sensibility because these tales dramatize in obdurate histories how things refuse to become possessions of private collectors or artefacts in public museums. This group of tales need not feature actual curses but are suffused with the anticipatory dread that stretches between the issuing and deliverance of a curse. Since they feature collections so heavily, we might also conceive of a 'Museum Gothic' that grows out of this strand.

In the stories we have already examined, it is the private collection that is the most unnerving location. In an era when the discourse about the educative virtues of the public museum were widely trumpeted, the private collector, hoarding objects for morbid or obsessional ends, becomes a subject of mistrust. The Oxford students like Conan Doyle's Bellingham or Rohmer's Ferrara are inherently tainted in their blood perhaps, but even the noble aims of a scientist like Trelawney are coloured by his mania for possessing objects and mastering secret knowledge. Collecting becomes a sign of mania and a route of potential contamination. One of the best stories in this regard is one of the cases of the psychic detective Flaxman Low, serial stories written by Kate and Hesketh Prichard in the 1890s. In 'The Story of Baelbrow', an ancestral English home, deep in the East Anglian countryside, is the site of a haunting that seems to emanate from their curio museum. It transpires that an 'elemental psychic germ' that has occupied the house since it was built on an ancient barrow has at last found the means for physical animation when an Egyptian mummy is added to the collection.[96] Low reflects that the traditional English ghost, an emanation of 'vague sounds and shadows', almost a comforting possession of an old house, a confirmation of its dynastic identity, has been infected by a malignant foreign force.[97] The laying of such a spirit demands an unprecedented physical violence as the mummy lurches through the house: 'With a curse he raised the revolver and shot into the grinning face again and again with a deliberate vindictiveness. Finally he rammed the thing down into the box, and, clubbing the weapon, smashed the head into fragments with a vicious energy that coloured the whole horrible scene with a suggestion of murder done.'[98] Sometimes there is no subtext; the text here openly expresses phobic colonial violence.

What about public museums? In some accounts of the Thomas Douglas Murray curse, it is implied that the donation of the mummy case to the British Museum was done to calm the enraged ka or malign elemental attached to the case, since in the Egyptian Rooms she would join the august company of kings and queens and be framed in the sacral museum world, removed from the insulting status of a privately circulated commodity. The emergence of the Museum Gothic, however, suggests that the halls of the universal survey museum produce their own occult supplement. 'All museums are haunted in some measure,' Jonah Siegel has stated. 'To gather together prized material in the hope that the Muses will thereby be encouraged to manifest themselves – that is the magic or necromancy promised by the institution.'[99] The British Museum generates its own distinct brand of necromancy, perhaps because the Reading Room that stood at its core became an emblem not only of the Enlightenment but also of occult knowledge, secreted amongst the pages of this total archive. In this era, various adepts of lost magic lore, theosophists, spiritualists, magicians of the Golden Dawn, and seekers of Hermetic truths stretching back to the Ancient Egyptians, studied avidly in the Reading Room, from earnest seekers like W. B. Yeats and A. E. Waite to the theatrical Beast himself, the self-declared Antichrist, Aleister Crowley. In fiction, it comes as no surprise that it is in the Reading Room that a Satanic figure might pass on a murderous curse written on a request slip, as occurs in one of M. R. James's most famous stories, 'Casting the Runes'. The demonic Karswell's ability to kill his enemies with curses inscribed in ancient runes is identified with the antiquarianism of the archive itself.[100] In another story by the odd Gothic writer and antiquarian Sabine Baring-Gould, the Reading Room is imagined as being populated by 'Merewigs', undead creatures who have died, but with insufficient knowledge to proceed to the next stage of development and so must continue their study indefinitely (in my experience many of the undead seem to have survived the move to the new British Library building).[101] A brief journalistic piece on the Reading Room at about the same time took fright at this 'Labyrinth of Literature', where 'weird men and weird women wander'. It was a place where 'one can be as cosy as a mummy in an airtight sarcophagus', continuing the association of the archive with the undead.[102]

This shadowing of the orderly world of the British Museum even filters into the comic modes of children's fiction. In Edith Nesbit's *The Story of the Amulet* the magical conjuration of the Queen of Babylon causes chaos at the Museum when she demands her people's possessions back and the animated objects float out of the galleries and down the neoclassical steps of the Museum. A long list of artefacts are unshackled from their labels, 'great slabs of carved stone, bricks, helmets, tools, weapons, fetters, wine jars, bowls, bottles, vases, jugs, saucers, seals'.[103] '"Theosophy, I suppose?" asks a jaded journalist passing by, before penning the headline: 'Impertinent Miracle at the British Museum.'[104] Nesbit dedicated the story to Wallis Budge, who helped her fashion the story and even gave her an amulet, although he seems to have stopped short of the affair for which she had hoped.[105] Nesbit's socialist, anti-imperial politics jut through the comic moments of her story, her critique merely a different point on the emotional scale from the histrionics of the Gothic. Indeed, Nesbit's tale was part of a cluster of fictions about disruptive magical amulets at the turn of the century, and in her study of them Jude Hill evocatively suggests that we could 'consider the glass cases as a form of lens, magnifying the potential power of the amulets inside . . . thus countering curatorial intentions to remove any sense of enchantment.'[106]

Yet just to underline how mobile these modulations of the Egyptian Gothic are, the last substantial figure we need to treat here forces us to step outside the walls of the museum and plunge into the Egyptian desert for an entirely different set of emotional effects.

## Algernon Blackwood: Egypt introjected

Algernon Blackwood's metaphysical horror was an instant commercial success from his first collection of tales, *The Empty House*, in 1906, and he became an unlikely celebrity, central, along with M. R. James, to the Golden Age of the Edwardian ghost story. Blackwood came to writing late, after spending periods of his youth in the depths of the Moravian forest and the wilds of Canada, developing a passionate nature philosophy. This was shot through with his eclectic occult interests, including early membership of the Theosophical Society in 1891, research with the Haunted House Committee of the Society for Psychical Research, and serious magical study in the Hermetic Order of the Golden Dawn, into whose Outer Circle he was initiated in 1900 by W. B. Yeats.[107] By the time he fully committed to writing fiction, his esoteric concerns had formed into a trademark drama of solitary men confronted by cosmic agencies that press invisibly through the natural world from some other dimension, often with malign intent. Weird fiction, as formalized by H. P. Lovecraft, aimed to produce 'a certain atmosphere of breathless and unexplainable dread of outer, unknown forces' and he claimed Blackwood to be 'the one absolute and unquestioned master of weird atmosphere.'[108] It is an oddly materialist mode of the Gothic, rarely ranging beyond the secondary, physical traces of these supernal energies in our mundane world. It is a form of broken-down sublime, a mode that 'allows swillage of that awe and horror from "beyond" back into the everyday – into angles, bushes, the touch of strange limbs, noises, etc.'[109]

Blackwood's early series of tales featuring the psychic detective, Dr John Silence, included one story that relied on the conventions of the Egyptian Gothic. Silence investigates cases of malignant haunting, framing his explanations in the language of psychical intrusion, ethereal vibration or magical attack. In 'The Nemesis of Fire', Silence is called to the country home of Colonel Wragge, where arson and violence seem to be centred on a prehistoric burial site in ancient woodland on the ancestral lands. What they track, as the incidents escalate, is a 'fire-elemental', perhaps mastered and directed maliciously by a black magician. There are hints, too, of connection to the Colonel's military career in the colonies, including India. The final revelations concern the secreted Ancient Egyptian mummy hidden by Wragge's brother in the grounds, its powers poorly contained by inexpertly executed protective hexes, the mummy enacting its rage at being disturbed through the agency of the fire elemental. Silence completes the ritual to exorcise the demon, but Wragge's sister has succumbed to temptation and stolen a scarabaeus from the mummy wrappings; as a consequence of her transgression she is found dead, her face choked and blackened.[110] This is a conventional mummy tale, with many derivative elements and echoes, particularly from the Flaxman Low 'Baelbrow' case. However, Blackwood's vision of Egypt and its place in his cosmic imaginary was transformed by the visits he took to Egypt in successive winters between 1912 and 1914.

Blackwood travelled to Helouan, fifteen miles from Cairo, an oasis with a view of the pyramids and the location of a former Khedival palace. His friend

Baron Knoop had purchased the palace and re-established it as a health spa, largely for tubercular Russians. Blackwood had formed an intense, platonic attachment to Knoop's wife, Maya Stuart-King (a muse also for the poet Rainer Maria Rilke), which amplified his responses to the Egyptian landscape. In the unlikely pages of *Country Life*, Blackwood opined that the 'spell of Egypt' was now vulgarized by tourism and picture postcards, 'And the monstrosity of it paralyses the mind'.[111] Nevertheless, playing on his reputation for psychic sensitivity, Blackwood discerned something else below the brash surface, something 'nameless' and 'curiously elusive'. His persistent metaphor is of something in Egypt that sinks into the depths of being, sly and unregarded, but which then resurfaces: 'from caverned leagues of subterranean gloom there issues a roar of voices, thunderous yet muffled, that seem to utter the hieroglyphs of a forgotten tongue'.[112] These unbidden recurrences mean that Egypt 'rushes up' at you, months or years later, in the midst of London, and 'from the pavement or the theatre stall and London, dim-lit England, the whole of modern life indeed, are reduced sharply to a miniature of trifling ugliness that seems the unreality'.[113] London is obliterated by Egypt's incalculable sublime, its 'shadowy magic' or 'enchantment that lulls the senses', an uprush that defeats the reason. This sublime teeters on the edges of terror, particularly amidst the horrific silence of the Valley of the Kings and 'the slow approach to the secret hiding-place where the mummy...lies ghastly now beneath the glitter of an electric light'.[114] Once inside you, Blackwood suggests, Egypt pervades.

Blackwood's evocative journalistic piece outlines the blueprint of his Egyptian fiction. He wrote a handful of Gothic squibs, featuring the transmigration of souls between London and Cairo in 'Egyptian Sorcery', and uncanny deaths in the Egyptian desert in 'By Water' or by psychic possession of the old gods in 'The Wings of Horus'.[115] But his serious fictional engagement with Egypt began with 'Sand', published in 1912. From the beginning, 'Sand' engages with Egypt by openly displacing the question of culture, modern or ancient, for the solitary encounter with landscape. Felix Henriot, hemmed in by grey London fogs, finds escape in Egypt, thus:

> Egypt had ever held his spirit in thrall, though as yet he tried in vain to touch the great buried soul of her. The excavators, the Egyptologists, the archaeologists most of all, plastered her grey ancient face with labels like hotel advertisements on travellers' portmanteaux. They told where she had come from last, but nothing of what she dreamed and thought and loved. The heart of Egypt lay beneath the sand, and the trifling robbery of little details that poked forth from tombs and temples brought no true revelation of her stupendous spiritual splendour.[116]

The spur of Henriot's psychical engagement digs beneath digging, then, to enter a mental condition that is 'utterly sand-haunted'.[117] The story builds a hypnotic rhythm of these metaphors, less of excavation than of slow burial under remorseless waves of sand. His desert experiment hovers between excavation and obliteration. Eventually, Henriot finds like-minded spirits at the hotel, an odd couple of aunt and nephew that haunt only the deserts too. Lady Statham frames their search in occult terms, a quest for the inaugural High Powers of the earth, vanished with Atlantis, whose fugitive presence they can invoke only through reviving ancient magical rites in the desert. Rumours of bad juju surround Lady Statham and Richard Vance, stories that 'belonged to the type one hears at every dinner in Egypt – stories of the vengeance mummies seemed to take'.[118] They surely also echo the sex magic rituals undertaken in the Algerian desert by Aleister Crowley, the magus and self-proclaimed Antichrist, in 1910, subject of much scandal and rumour at the time.[119] Henriot is eventually recruited, not as participant of their culminating magical rite, but to witness it from a crag above, to grasp the shape of the vast Powers they will conjure out of sand. Entering a last act where Blackwood abolishes the boundary between the literal and the metaphoric, the conjuration is at once an external, physical thing and an internal, primordial recovery from the 'centres of memory stirred from an age-long sleep'.[120] The attempt to glimpse behind the veil is, inevitably, disastrous: Lady Statham is obliterated in the sand-storm.

'Sand' was the product of Blackwood's first wintering at Helouan in 1912; he returned the next year and composed the novella 'A Descent into Egypt'. Where Henriot was merely a witness to the fatal invocation of primordial forces, the character George Isley is a direct participant in what amounts to an immersion and then psychic obliteration by Egypt. The story is narrated by a woman who bears witness to this vanishing act, who experiences her own winnowing but ultimately clings on to modernity. Isley, who considers himself unfit for modern sensibilities, has become an archaeologist, yet as always in Blackwood, he is digging beneath the shallow and mechanical excavations that surround him: 'The real Egypt lies underground in darkness.'[121] Isley holds himself above both the painstaking scientific recovery of the past and the shabby shivers of tourist rumour, remaining 'unmoved by the commonplace mysterious; he told no mummy stories, nor ever hinted at the supernatural quality that leaps to the mind of the majority.'[122] Other Egyptologists have been sapped by the deserts, broken down physically or become mentally unhinged. Isley's research is a kind of elite sensitivity, an empathetic feeling into, that leaves him increasingly exhausted: 'You live it. You feel old Egypt and disclose her,' he is told. Isley agrees, but he is aware that because it is 'difficult to realise ... in the end a mental torpor akin to stupefaction creeps into your brain' and you must simply surrender.[123]

The narrative gradually reveals the experiments in Ancient Egyptian ritual that Isley and his associate Moleson are conducting in the Valley of the Kings, an invocation that seems to summon up the ancient world of the pharaohs.

This is not magic, Moleson insists, 'it is merely scientific – undiscovered or forgotten knowledge.'[124] Progressively, Isley and Moleson become vacant people,
emptied out, psychically mummified by their obsession; in the end, they have
no selves left, and the female narrator too has been winnowed from modernity,
saved by her merely 'temperamental sympathy' with Egypt rather than gripped
by obsession.[125] The story toys with conventional revenge narratives, voicing
the threat in explicit terms: 'Egypt, which since time began has suffered rob-
bery with violence at the hands of all the world, now takes her vengeance,
choosing her individual prey. Her time has come. Behind a modern mask she
lies in wait.'[126] Blackwood, however, inverts these expectations: these are not
tales of hate and physical death but of love and the yearning for a metaphysical
transcendence into a form of eternal life, for which ancient Egyptian perma-
nence is a symbol.

The last version of this narrative, *The Wave: An Egyptian Aftermath* (1916), is
the closest to Realist conventions, being a rather mundane account of a love
triangle amongst a social elite that eventually drifts to Egypt for the winter
season. It is a story that transparently re-stages the entanglement of Blackwood
with Maya Stuart-King and Baron Knoop. It has an insistent undertow of dread
and occult determinism, however, starting with a portrait of the protagonist
Tom's early psychic life, oppressed by a repeated dream of obliteration by a wave.
It acquires an Egyptian tinge from his father's study, who is a nerve specialist and
a very early disciple of Freud (when psychoanalysis was still associated with the
occult).[127] The room is stuffed, as was Freud's consulting room, with antiquities,
bead necklaces from Memphis, amulets, bits of mummy and papyrus. The last
contains a fragment of a story of a triangle between a general, his wife and a
youth (a version of Potiphar's wife and Joseph in the Biblical account). The
youth's drowning beneath the waves Tom feels doomed somehow to repeat.

Blackwood typically studs his prose with dense patterns of metaphors of
waves rising, cresting and crashing in seas, deserts, through the nerves and in
ethereal vibrations. Tom travels to Egypt late in the book, but is instantly at
home, knowing that it will 'mesmerise his soul', 'the exhilaration and the terror'
of the place overwhelming him at once.[128] Uncanny feelings of familiarity continually crash over him as they venture up the Nile. The freedom Egypt gives, it
seems, lies in its radical discontinuity from the modern world, that 'Egypt has
left the world; Egypt is dead; there is no link with present things.'[129] Yet this
leaves Tom unmoored when Ancient Egypt continually returns to him, like 'a
stupendous Ghost'.[130] Ultimately, Blackwood resists the doomed repetition of
the Gothic genre, insisting instead that the love story will repeat with modulation – like a wave pattern – each successive reincarnation of the foundational
story, learning something new in its endless return.

What is clear from these tales is that Blackwood has little or no interest in the
specificity of Egypt, ancient or modern. Instead, the landscape and topography

of ruins provide a set of archaeological metaphors for descent into the layered personality. There is a colonial framing to this, of course: Africa has often been read as modelling either savage or unsullied 'primitive' forms of Western conceptions of selfhood in the fiction of the turn of the century.[131] Freud, too, repeatedly used the metaphor of archaeological excavation for the process of psychoanalytic interpretation from as early as 1896. He equated the analyst with 'an explorer [who] arrives in a little-known region where his interest is aroused by an expanse of ruins, with remains of walls, fragments of columns, and tablets of self-effaced and unreadable inscriptions', who then works to 'uncover what is buried'.[132] Freud's most sustained parallels with archaeology are in his study of Jensen's story 'Gradiva', about a neurotic and delusional archaeologist in Pompeii, where burial yet preservation and return to the surface suggest to Freud an exemplary model for repression. One might say, then, that Blackwood *introjects* Egypt into the ego, making it an intensive figure of subjective phantasy.[133]

Yet although Blackwood read Freud, the closer psychological model was that of the 'subliminal consciousness', developed by the pioneer of dynamic psychology (and leading member of the Society for Psychical Research), F. W. H. Myers. Myers held that 'each of us is in reality an abiding psychical entity far more extensive than he knows', all manner of powers existing below the threshold of the ordinary conscious mind. 'Our supraliminal consciousness is but a floating island upon the "abysmal deep" of the total individuality beneath it,' he asserted.[134] There, the spectrum of consciousness extended to all manner of 'supernormal' abilities, including telepathy, second sight, and ultimately contact with the 'world-soul'. Blackwood's characters (particularly Dr Silence) continually use the distinct vocabulary coined by Myers, a whole theory once praised by the Surrealist André Breton as 'Gothic psychology'.[135]

In Blackwood, the Egyptian Gothic finds one of its most elaborate modulations. He plays with the conventions of vengeful mummy fiction, but quickly to dismiss them as vulgar. Similarly, he explores the erotics of the mummy romance, only to elevate this into a far more mystical realm of timeless repetition and reincarnation. Finally for Blackwood, Egypt is an abstract figuration of ruins that point beyond themselves to the primordial and enduring structure of subjectivity itself.

This survey of the evolving versions of the Egyptian Gothic shows that they were undoubtedly central to the consolidation of the curse narrative, but rarely in the reduced form handed down as murderous revenge. The magazines and cheap editions in which these narratives of Egypt surged through late Victorian and Edwardian popular culture share similar spaces to rumour and gossip. All of these forms thrived in the gaps in the emerging science of Egyptology, providing a thrilling sense of hesitation between truth and superstition. The Gothic provides a set of narratives and conventions that harp on the curse of inheritance, the sins of the fathers and the limits of enlightened rationalism at the limits of the colonial frontier. At the height of the New Imperialism, the Gothic allowed for fatally ambiguous accounts about the pivotal place of Egypt in this aggressive new project.

Even so, my account of this literature is shaped around a hole. Possibly the most complicated engagement with Egypt in the literature of the time was also the most popular author of the late Victorian revival. Rider Haggard, the 'King of Egypt' as he was hailed by Rudyard Kipling, deserves a chapter of his own.

# 7

# Rider Haggard Among the Mummies

I N EARLY 1923, as the day of the opening of the tomb of Tutankhamun approached, Sir Henry Rider Haggard, the world-famous writer of colonial adventures and keen private collector of Egyptian antiquities, complained loudly about the sensationalism that surrounded the events in the Valley of the Kings. Although he had initially approached the editor of *The Times* with the hope of being appointed a correspondent to cover the opening, he was soon writing letters with the proposal that the body of the boy king should either be left in situ or be reburied in the Great Pyramid with other mummies from the royal cache then on display in the Cairo Museum. It would save the august dead from being 'the butt of merry jests of tourists of the baser sort.'[1] A few days later, in the *Sunday Express* under the headline 'Desecrating the Dead – a Protest', Haggard speculated about the king in the breached tomb: 'Would not he curse those who had done to him what, according to his ideas, was so great an injury or insult, or, perhaps, if he had become too charitable to curse, would he not grieve over it?'[2]

Once the Earl of Carnarvon died in April, however, Haggard abandoned the language of the curse and decried a world steeped in such credulous beliefs. In the weeks before Carnarvon's death, Haggard had already written in his diary dismissing 'the superstitions in the East, and perhaps elsewhere' for believing that Tutankhamun had struck down Lord Carnarvon with illness. 'If any accident were to happen to Mr. Carter,' he added, 'I believe that Tut's wrappings would remain intact.'[3] Following the death, he was disgusted at newspaper approaches for his opinion on the Curse of King Tut. *The New York World* had wired him for his opinion 'as to "the efficacy of magical curses against bespoilers placed around ancient mummies," ' a query he had left unanswered: 'How a paper can expect a man like myself, to make a public fool of himself, expressing opinions on such a matter, passes my comprehension,' he complained.[4] To Haggard, it only confirmed something that had been said by one of his closest friends: 'Rudyard [Kipling] asked me on Tuesday if I had noticed how every sort of superstition was becoming rampant in this country, which, I think he said, always presaged the downfall of great civilisations. It is perfectly true, the papers are full of such things.'[5] Haggard's public speech on Old Egypt two days after Carnarvon's death was reported in the *Daily Telegraph* under the heading 'Protest Against Superstition'.[6]

Yet this was the writer who, just at the start of his writing career in 1886, still working as a lawyer in Temple, had received an Egyptian mummy which his brother Andrew, then a lieutenant-colonel in the Egyptian army, had looted from the mummy pits of Akhmim in Egypt. The mummy was a fine example of late Ptolemaic funerary practices, placed in a black wooden coffin but with an extraordinary golden cartonnage mask. Now identified as Nesmin (and in Liverpool's World Museum collection), this mummy was sent to Rider Haggard's digs in Gunterstone Road, Hammersmith, and rested in the same study where he wrote *She* in four weeks. 'That stuccoed, suburban residence was a queer birthplace for Ayesha, the immortal,' he reflected on a nostalgic visit in 1917. He then added in a clipped and enigmatic sentence which ostentatiously withheld any explanation: 'In that room, also I had the experience with the mummy, which is now in the Norfolk Museum at Norwich.'[7]

Haggard's biographer Tom Pocock expands on this comment with a vague and unsourced story, pitched as family legend:

> His brother Andrew ... had shipped an embalmed, encased mummy to him in West Kensington. On arrival, it was placed upright in his study, where on this particular night he was working late. Next morning, it is said, an agitated Haggard announced that the mummy must leave the house immediately and not remain there for another night; indeed, it must be sent at once to the Museum in Norwich Castle. He would give no reason for his sudden decision but, so it was said, that morning the study was in disarray and grey with mummy dust ...[8]

Warren Dawson's short report on the mummy in 1929, knowing nothing of this odd history, explained that 'The wrappings of this mummy have never been disturbed, and consequently no examination of the body is possible,' so Haggard did not appear to have any designs on unwrapping this ambiguous gift.[9] In fact, Andrew Haggard did leave record of this mummy in his Egyptian memoirs, which located the unnerving effect of Nesmin with a rather different emphasis:

**Figure 7.1** Nesmin, the mummy briefly owned by Rider Haggard (National Museums of Liverpool).

We passed Ekhmim, celebrated for its mummies, where, by the bye, I myself at a subsequent period became the happy possessor of a mummy which was popularly supposed to be that of Potiphar's wife. Anyhow, she now reposes quietly in Norwich Museum. Potiphar's wife or not, she was quite a lady, and never created any disturbance except once, when she was distinctly heard one night by the wife and servants walking about the house of an eminent novelist, a near relation of my own, who has told the world plenty about mummies.[10]

By the time Andrew Haggard wrote his jaunty memoir on his time in the Egyptian army, he must have surely reflected on the similarity of his adventures in the mummy trade with that of his fellow officer, Walter Ingram. Ingram had also shipped his own mummy back to his family in London at about the same time, shortly after the end of the failure of the Gordon Relief Expedition. The Ingram and Haggard mummies were both, it turns out, called Nesmin.

Although this meant only that the mummified ancients had belonged to the cult of Min, an early incarnation of the god Amon, it is another slightly spooky parallel.

Did Rider Haggard know or believe that he had housed 'Potiphar's wife' in his London home? Was it this enigmatic encounter with a mummy in his own rooms that prompted Haggard's objections to the desecration of Egyptian tombs? And yet if he was so distressed, why did he build such a large collection of Egyptian and other artefacts, substantial enough to be given scholarly catalogue and assessment in the *Journal of Egyptian Archaeology*?[11] Why did he always wear a pharaonic ring taken from the finger of a royal mummy, and another one usually knotted in his tie? Was this why he was so well versed in the cursed lives of Thomas Douglas Murray and Walter Ingram? Did the events in Gunterstone Road remain coiled at the heart of Haggard's weird romances, the reason why Haggard 'told the world plenty about mummies'?

In February 1886, Haggard wrote *She* at 'white heat' and delivered it to his agent A. P. Watt with the opinion that it would be the one text for which he would be remembered.[12] This is the first sight of Haggard's immortal white queen, Ayesha, buried in the heart of black Africa:

> Before I had made up my mind...the curtain was drawn, and a tall figure stood before us. I say a figure, for not only the body, but also the face was wrapped up in soft white, gauzy material in such a way as at first sight to remind me most forcibly of a corpse in its grave-clothes. And yet I do not know why it should have given me that idea, seeing that the wrappings were so thin that one could easily see the gleam of the pink flesh beneath them...Anyhow, I felt more frightened than ever at this ghost-like apparition, and my hair began to rise upon my head as the feeling crept over me that I was in the presence of something that was not canny. I could, however, clearly distinguish that the swathed mummy-like form before me was that of a tall and lovely woman, instinct with beauty in every part, and also with a certain snake-like grace which I had never seen anything to equal before.[13]

The scene hovers between the now-familiar formulae of the mummy romance, centred on the revivified beauty, and the mummy Gothic, which will bring curses in the wake of transgression. This is only the beginning of our plucky English adventurer's exquisite oscillation between prickling terror and stiffening desire for *She-Who-Must-Be-Obeyed*. In the next chapter, she unveils before Leo and Holly, the 'corpse-like wrappings' falling to the ground to reveal 'a garb of clinging white' that shows her body's 'perfect and imperial shape'. Holly at least retains enough self-possession to realize 'the sublimity was a dark one – the glory was not all of heaven'.[14] Ayesha will lead them into uncanny catacombs where thousands of perfectly preserved dead have been embalmed with a skill surpassing the jejune attempts of the Ancient Egyptians. She will extravagantly curse her enemies and kill a female rival with her evil eye, who gets 'blasted into death by some mysterious electric agency or overwhelming will-force'.[15] She will perform weird rituals lit by the fire fuelled by mummies put to the torch and promise, in passing, to overthrow Queen Victoria and 'assume absolute rule over the British domains, and probably over the whole earth'.[16] Eventually, she steps again into the column of fire that has preserved her for two thousand years, only to suffer a terrible regression, transformed from a naked beauty that leaves Holly speechless to shrivel up into a 'badly-preserved Egyptian mummy', then a 'baboon', and finally a wrinkled, foetal thing 'no larger than a big monkey'.[17]

It is impossible to overestimate the thrilling effect of this weird romance on late nineteenth-century readers. *She*, published in 1887, surpassed even Haggard's first hit, *King Solomon's Mines*, which had been the sensation of 1885. *She* sold twenty-five thousand copies in a matter of weeks and became a global phenomenon. These books made enough money for Haggard to travel to Egypt for the first time in 1887, finally following his soldiering brothers Andrew and Arthur, both of whom spent many years posted there. The first thing he did in Cairo was to visit the Boulak Museum to be given a personal tour of the royal mummies by the German director, Emile Brugsch. 'Poor kings! who dreamed not of the glass cases of the Cairo Museum and the jibes of tourists who find the awful majesty of their withered brows a matter for jest and smiles!'[18] Haggard instead used his journey to soak in the atmosphere for his attempt to revivify the greatest African queen of all in *Cleopatra*, a romance he published in 1889.

Haggard's romances hammered home the same plot over and over again. To contemporaries, their success came in spite of their mangled artistry, and demanded explanation. For Haggard's cultural champion, the critic and anthropologist Andrew Lang, Haggard's romances cast off the effete over-analysis of naturalism and tunnelled directly into the virile energy of primal narrative: 'Not for nothing did Nature leave us all savages under our white skins.'[19] Sigmund Freud, meanwhile, confessed his dreams borrowed bits and pieces of the symbolic landscapes of Haggard's romances, whilst Carl Jung's theory of anima, the female archetype hardwired into the race memory, was formulated by repeated reference to Haggard's Ayesha.[20] The very artlessness of his tales seemed to be a guarantee that they struck at something structural or foundational. As C. S. Lewis put it, 'What keeps us reading in spite of all these defects is of course the story itself, the myth. Haggard is the text-book case of the mythopoeic gift pure and simple.'[21]

Haggard's work has been patronized or dismissed for decades as childish vehicles for the transmission of the ideology of British imperialism. More recently, his role as a very young man in southern Africa, working far beyond the frontier as a colonial official involved in the first British annexation of the Transvaal, which helped to precipitate the Zulu War of 1879 and the subsequent Boer Wars, has been explored for the tensions that it produces in his writing.[22]

The romances are suffused with a melancholia or colonial tristesse that was the paradoxical product of an era of massive territorial expansion, a partial recognition of the huge destruction wrought by carrying the torch of civilization into 'darkest' Africa. But whilst southern Africa was the crucible of Haggard's development, an essential part of this matrix was the imaginative role that Egypt played in Haggard's personal life, in his private collection of curios, in his religious and philosophical views, and across the whole span of his writing career. Egypt was there from his very first novel, a halting and cumbersome attempt at writing domestic realism.

In *Dawn*, which Haggard paid to publish in 1884, the interminable domestic wrenchings over love and marriage are disturbed when Mildred Carr reveals that beneath her home on Madeira she has carved out of the rock a cavern in which to display the Egyptian antiquities that she has inherited from her husband. The astonished protagonist, who knew 'the only things she loved were beetles and mummies', certainly above any living man, walks the gentle gradient down into Mildred's own special Hall of the Dead.[23] Six sphinxes line the corridor, in homage to the temple at Karnak. The entrance is guarded by Osiris and the walls accurately reproduce Egyptian funerary murals. 'And all around, under this solemn guardianship, each upon a polished slab of marble, and enclosed in a case of thick glass, lay the corpses of the Egyptian dead, swathed in numberless wrappings.'[24] It is as if Haggard was already carving out the space of undead romance underneath the cheerless surfaces of a realism he would shortly renounce. By 1889, Kipling had already crowned Haggard 'the King of Egypt'. [25] Haggard's obsession with the mummified dead would shortly dominate the pivotal scenes of his romances, and influence the trajectories that Egypt would take in the late Victorian and Edwardian imaginary.

## Rider Haggard's encounters with Egypt

Haggard's childhood was spent in rural Norfolk. The eighth of ten children, and the sixth son of an autocratic country squire, Henry Rider was early on deemed 'a dunderhead' by his father, and was the only son not to be sent to public school or university.[26]

This 'imaginative' child, suffering a broken succession of schools and tutors constantly deemed inadequate by his father, must have got some of his education from visits to the local stately home, Didlington Hall. William Tyssen Amherst had, since assuming the family estate at Didlington in 1855, built up one the greatest private book collections in England. He was also passionate about Egypt. He had purchased the entire Egyptian collections of Dr John Lee and the Reverend Rudolph Lieder in the 1860s, over seven hundred significant items, then travelled extensively in Egypt himself, adding further pieces.[27] The collection included the mummy of Amenhotep I and also the earliest mummy to be collected and displayed as a mummy in England in the 1730s. A later listing included five other human mummies, including an Ethiopian mummy with 'a very striking face and glass eyes'.[28] By the 1880s, Amherst had added the Large Museum to the Hall, a single-storey building over ninety feet long, which housed one of the most important English collections of papyri and monumental sculptures from Ancient Egypt. On the terrace outside were several colossal figures of the goddess Bast in black granite.

Aside from Haggard's dreamy youth, the collection of Didlington Hall inspired several leading Egyptologists. Howard Carter was a local boy, from the village of Swaffham, and had visited the collection as a child, when his father, an artist, was employed by the family. He recalled that Didlington's Egyptian objects 'aroused my longing for that country'.[29] Carter would later meet the young Percy Newberry at Didlington Hall in 1891, and his first work for the Egyptian Exploration Fund came through Amherst and Newberry. After Carter took up a post as inspector in the Antiquities Service in Egypt, he guided his friend Rider Haggard around several significant sites and he was able to help William Amherst's eldest daughter, May (Lady William Cecil), to become a significant archaeologist in her own right. The thirty-two Tombs of the Nobles near Aswan, which she excavated in 1901 and 1904, are still sometimes known as the Cecil Tombs and she wrote several books on Egypt. She took back many items to Norfolk from her digging concession. Local historians still catch at wisps of memory of being taken to see 'Lady Amherst's Mummy' at Didlington Hall.[30]

Haggard was a neighbour and later fellow collector and Norfolk landowner, a conservative who was heavily invested in the ancestral role of the farming squire for the continuity of rural traditions. He would, therefore, have followed the destruction of Didlington Hall with utter dismay. Reliant on land rents, William Amherst was defrauded by his lawyer and had to sell much of his book collection in 1906. He died, so it was said, a broken man in 1909. Lady William Cecil held on to the Egyptian collection until her death in 1919, but the family then sold it entire in 1921. Lots included several mummies, mummy cases and coffin fragments.[31] Such a precipitate collapse of an aristocratic house, particularly in the 1920s, inevitably became caught up in curse narratives. Haggard did complain about the fate of 'empty East Anglian mansions' in a letter to *The Times* in June 1923. The dilapidated Didlington Hall was razed to the ground after military use in World War II: it constitutes one of the most significant of England's lost country houses.

Other early experiences were also crucial for Haggard. At the age of 17, he was sent to London to cram for entry exams for the Foreign Office. A weak student, he was soon distracted since he had arrived in the capital at the height of a resurgence of spiritualism, with the development of dark séances and full-scale materializations of visiting spirits. Haggard joined the spirit circle of Lady Paulet, who held aristocratic gatherings at her house in Hanover Square. The circle involved the notorious medium Mrs Guppy, a very physical medium, rather famous for allegedly being 'astrally' transported several miles across London only to land heavily on the table of a séance in Lamb's Conduit Street.[32] Haggard later stated, in typically elliptical mode, that 'Undoubtedly very strange things happened at these séances which I will not describe.'[33] He did, however, reveal that he had 'conversed with and touched' two spirit girls, whose 'flesh seemed to be firm but cold.'[34] Within a year he had stopped any attendance, and warned his readers off meddling in such matters. Spiritualism was 'to be discouraged' for 'the nerves and imagination play strange tricks.'[35] He took the position that the revealed content of séances was likely to be true, even if the mechanism of communication was hedged in by fraud and suggestion. He claimed that he never attended another séance, although he contributed to the 'science' of psychical research with a very public discussion of a telepathic dream communication he believed he had received (from his dying dog) in 1904.[36] Of his closest friends, Andrew Lang became president of the Society for Psychical Research, and Kipling's sister Alice was a widely respected medium.

Part of the Paulet circle included Lady Caithness. Marie Caithness was an eclectic occultist, interested in spiritualism, Kabbalistic magic, theosophy, comparative religion and the Hermetic tradition of lost wisdom stretching back to Egypt. She was an active medium in London, occasionally giving voice to the spirit of Mary Queen of Scots. She proclaimed a new spiritual age had begun in 1882. She explored all of these avenues whilst maintaining her Catholic faith. Like many other syncretic mystics of the time, she merged the Egyptian Isis with the Christian Virgin Mary. She published on her researches extensively, and in Paris was the first president of the Société Théosophique d'Orient et d'Occident. She split from the original Theosophical Society because of her ardent belief in reincarnation, which Madame Blavatsky, the founder, initially rejected.[37]

Steeped at an early age in this heady brew, Haggard would also become a fervent believer in reincarnation, something he considered entirely consistent with his orthodox Christian faith. It could also be synthesized with a Tory sense of continuity and hierarchy.[38] Indeed, his nephew recalled that 'he believed that our personality is immeasurably ancient, that it may be born again and again'. In particular, Haggard 'believed that he had lived before; as an ancient Egyptian, as a Zulu, as a Norseman.'[39] In his autobiography, he hesitated between describing his 'visions' of these lives, flashes of embodied memory, as possibly previous incarnations, deep race memories, or merely as subconscious confabulations. In ancient Egypt, it seemed, he remembered or imagined himself in 'quaint and beautiful robes wound rather tightly around the body,' as if he were psychically alive there yet already wrapped in mummy cloth.[40]

Elsewhere, he thought it worth recording that a mystic friend had forwarded 'to me a list of my previous incarnations... Two of these were Egyptian, one as a noble at the time of Pepi II... and the second as one of the minor Pharaohs.'[41] In print, he suspended any opinion about these claims. In private, Haggard was less ambiguous, believing that he could identify amongst visitors to Norfolk those who had been reincarnated from Ancient Egyptian times.

In a letter to the 'psychic' artist William T. Horton, who worked from his own visionary experiences, Haggard once opined that 'I suppose there isn't any receipt for getting oneself back to old Egypt? How do you do it? *I* should like to go.'[42] Yet in many ways, Haggard consistently imagined himself into ancient or 'primitive' worlds by processes of intense empathetic projection, a form of *feeling into* that for many of his contemporaries did indeed border on the supernatural, so 'authentic' did his fiction feel.[43] 'And your Egyptology!' one enthusiastic fan wrote to Haggard. 'Only reincarnation can account for it.'[44] His ambivalence about spiritual mediumship may have been latterly because it was simply too close to the manner in which his own creativity worked, since both seemed to use forms of psychic automatism.

Haggard's imagination tended to develop around material places and things, physical objects that then provoked his flights of romantic fancy. His own Norfolk home, Ditchingham House, rapidly became stuffed with objects acquired on his travels. A piece in the *Strand Magazine* in 1892 recorded that 'every nook and cranny of the house has some reminder of a career which has been in many ways remarkable,' and called the study 'a perfect treasure house of curios'.[45] He had to travel in southern Africa, getting caught up in debates about the origin of the actual mysterious ruins found at Great Zimbabwe in the late 1860s, before envisaging them as the legendary mines of King Solomon mentioned in the Bible. He collected Zulu spears and spent bullets from the site of Isandlwana, the melancholy locale where English troops had been massacred by the Zulus in 1879. These travels would inspire not only his multivolume imagining into Zulu history, tracing the history of the Zulus' ultimately fatal encounter with white settlers, but also, more famously, a slew of lost African civilizations ruled by last representatives of ancient races. Encouraged by Andrew Lang to rewrite the Icelandic sagas, Haggard had to visit Iceland to imbibe the atmosphere for the writing of *Eric Brighteyes*. Central American adventures followed his aborted trip to Mexico in the early 1890s. The Museum at Didlington Hall had already given him opportunities for feeling into Ancient Egyptian artefacts, and his personal experience with the mummy of Nesmin also took place before he had set foot in Egypt. Travelling there, however, would each time prompt further Egyptian fictions.

Haggard travelled four times to Egypt, in 1887, 1904, 1912 and 1924. On the first visit, he took in the royal mummies at the Cairo Museum, and witnessed excavations of very ancient remains, before mummification became a funerary process, near the pyramids at Giza. These encounters made him 'wonder how we dare to meddle with those hallowed relics'.[46] Subsequent encounters with mummies were also fraught, or rather this was the kind of anecdote Haggard deemed worthy of recording about Egypt. After he had travelled down the Nile as far as Aswan, following the conventional tourist trail, he visited a newly discovered mummy pit which contained, his very brief diary notes recounted, 'hundreds of dead'.[47] He panicked underground thinking it might be a plague pit and was nearly suffocated in a sand-fall. On the return leg, he recorded that a friend in his party was nearly killed after an ascent of the Great Pyramid. Haggard also purchased a number of antiquities, presumably on the grey market, somewhere between official and unofficial dealings. In 1886, he had been presented with a pharaonic ring by the dealer Reverend Loftie, one of a pair (the other was presented to Andrew Lang). It was inscribed as belonging to the 'Royal Son of the Sun', and it had featured centrally as Leo Vincey's ring in *She*, the device by which Vincey proves his direct lineal descent from ancient Egypt. This gift clearly started a predilection to collect rings. In Egypt, he purchased another signet ring with the cartouche of Akhenaten, the heretic pharaoh. He also bought a Coptic amulet with the Greek legend 'One God in Heaven' and several magical gems and amulets that he presented to the British Museum. On his return to England, he composed *Cleopatra* at his usual lightning pace, a book that Lang criticized as being stalled narratively under the weight of its antiquarian detail. The narrative was framed as the translation of a papyrus that had been discovered by Arabs in a coffin whose 'mummy...had moved with violence *since it was put in the coffin*,' revealed finally to be a transgressor who had been buried alive.[48]

By 1904, Haggard was a very famous man. He was also a profoundly melancholic figure, brooding privately on the fall of dynasties since the death of his only son Jock in 1891, which plunged him into several years of crippling grief. There is evidence that William Haggard, his father, was obsessed with tracing the family pedigree and coat of arms back to Danish aristocratic ancestry.[49] Rider Haggard's psychology was also deeply dynastic, and his surviving daughters could not compensate for the loss of the patrilineal line. Biblical and other curses were often visited on sons and Egypt's dynastic king lists must have gained added resonance for Haggard.

Haggard wrote very little Egyptian fiction during the 1890s, and returned to the country only after extensive travels around the world and intensive journeys across Britain to assess the crisis in farming, county by county, in *Rural England*. He came to feel that Britain was falling apart, farm by farm.

He was commissioned by the *Daily Mail* to print his thoughts on returning to Egypt, and these pieces were marked by a melancholic narrative of decline, complaining that both Cairo and Aswan had lost their early romance and become vulgar tourist towns, full of people who 'know nothing and care less about Egypt'.[50] He was careful to praise the tireless work of English imperial improvers, yet failed to make any connection between the British occupation and the denunciations he made under the headline 'The Trade in the Dead'. He considered the new display of royal mummies in Cairo 'repulsive' and spoke about mummy and mummy fragments on sale in Luxor for a few piastres, leaving 'scarcely a grave in Egypt…unrifled'.[51] He plainly did not associate himself with such acts, even though one of the high points of his trip was to be conducted by Howard Carter into the newly discovered tomb of Queen Nefertari, wife of Rameses II. They were, he claimed, the first white men to enter the tomb (although the body was long gone). Carter gave Haggard a heart scarab, inscribed with phrases from the Book of the Dead on the reverse, and Haggard purchased others on the trip for his burgeoning private collection. When he returned to England, he composed *The Way of the Spirit* (1906), about a resolute British officer in Egypt who had fought at Tel-el-Kebir in 1882 and alongside Herbert Stewart at Abu Klea in 1885. His disgrace is engineered by rivals and Ullershaw ends up far into the trackless desert as the platonic partner of the last queen of a race directly descended from the Ancient Egyptians, unsullied by the racial dilutions of centuries of occupation and conquest. In this novel, Haggard fantasized a spiritual, asexual union between Ancient Egypt and the British Empire that transcended the taint of any intervening colonial history.

Two novels featuring Egypt came after this trip. *Queen Sheba's Ring* (1910) is a fantasy about a lost Egyptian race written in the corners of the struggle against the Mahdi uprising in Sudan. It begins, however, with an interview in London, amongst the Egyptian collection of Ptolemy Higgs, 'an extraordinary collection of antiquities, including a couple of mummies with gold faces arranged in their coffins against the wall'. '"Nothing gives me such an appetite as unrolling mummies; it involves so much intellectual wear and tear, in addition to the physical labour,"' he opines.[52] The scene, and the mummy, surely echo Haggard's own study in Gunterstone Road. *Morning Star* (1910) was a dynastic struggle set entirely in ancient Egypt, without a modern framing device, and was dedicated to Ernest Wallis Budge. In his autobiography, Haggard praised Wallis Budge in his highest terms: he was a 'great believer in the Old Egyptians; indeed…he has been so long of their company in spirit that almost he has become one of them.'[53] One of Haggard's later visits to the British Museum was disturbed by 'a horde of young women pouring down the staircase', about which he complained to *The Times*, probably because, as he put it in his diary in the same year, 'there is nothing that I enjoy more than a talk with Budge and a solitary walk in the Museum.'[54]

The mention of Wallis Budge prompts Haggard to recall particular versions of the curse stories of Thomas Douglas Murray and Walter Herbert Ingram, as we've seen, presumably because he heard them through his association with the Keeper of Egyptian Antiquities. Writing his autobiography in 1912,

Haggard may have known that Douglas Murray had died, and thus the circulation of anonymous accounts of his curse were beginning to add his real name to the story. After recounting the fate of Douglas Murray and Ingram, Haggard adds: 'I asked Budge if he believed in the efficacy of curses. He hesitated to answer.' This is probably a record of Wallis Budge's strategic calculation of what he thought Haggard would like to hear. Wallis Budge offered a typically skilful sidestep:

> At length he said that in the East men believed that curses took effect, and that he had always avoided driving a native to curse him. A curse launched into the air was bound to have an effect if coupled with the word of God, either on the person cursed or on the curser. [Wallis Budge added:] 'I have always feared to curse a man.'[55]

The answer, and Haggard's record of it, is a typical displacement of belief onto Eastern credulity, a willing suspension of judgment masked as liberal respect for (but also superiority over) the other.

Haggard's third trip in 1912 was a winter trip to help treat a dose of bronchitis. He visited the mummy of the recently discovered pharaoh, Meneptah – presumed to be the pharaoh at the time of the Jewish Exodus – in the company of the eminent Egyptologist, Gaston Maspero. With the same rhythm, the journey prompted Haggard to write, this time one of his later great successes, *The Moon of Israel* (1918), about the Jewish flight from Egypt to escape the tyranny of a usurper pharaoh that Haggard fictively inserted into the dynastic king lists. The book was dedicated to Maspero. He also began to draft *The Ancient Allan*, which would find an iteration of Haggard's recurrent hero Allan Quatermain back in Egypt. More immediately, Haggard composed 'Smith and the Pharaohs', a long story that appeared in the *Strand Magazine* over the Christmas and New Year 1912–13 editions. This was Haggard's crucial contribution to the Egyptian Museum Gothic.

Thunderstruck by a beautiful statuette of an unknown queen in the Egyptian Rooms of the British Museum, the spiritually dead banker James Smith is compelled by an uncontrollable artefactual desire to become an excavator in Egypt. He works every winter digging season until he finds, or is supernaturally directed to find, the lost tomb of Ma-Mee (even the characters in the tale find this unlikely name amusingly transparent). The mummy has been destroyed by fire but Smith finds the severed hand of the queen, complete with pharaonic rings, dropped by the ancient tomb robber at the exit. Along with an arresting statuette of the queen, he trades these for all the jewels he has found with the director of the Cairo Museum. Smith's vindication for his deeds comes when he is locked in overnight in the Museum. He is called to judgment by the entire lineage of the assembled pharaohs of Ancient Egypt, a gathering that includes Queen Ma-Mee. He is saved from death because Smith is recognized as the reincarnation of Horu, of royal blood and once the court artist who fell in love with Ma-Mee and was exiled. The story in effect redeems the modern collector and excavator: transgressing tombs and stealing body parts are not violations but vindications of undying love. It essentially rewrites earlier stories by Grant Allen or Conan Doyle into Haggard's own distinctive framework of reincarnation as legitimation.

The story, in which two rings on the mummy hand seem to switch places, was also prompted by the death of his friend Andrew Lang in 1912. Lang's will presented Haggard with the pharaonic ring of Queen Taia, one of the two that the Reverend Loftie had given to Lang and Haggard in 1886, and probably stolen by Arab dealers from a tomb in Amarna. Lang's ring was inscribed with the figure of the god Bes, just as it is in the story. 'The ring has been anciently much worn,' the cataloguer of Haggard's collection noted.[56] Haggard would later give an ancient Egyptian ring to Kipling. Like Masonic rings, or the rings that Freud had forged for his Secret Committee to preserve the institution of psychoanalysis, these exchanges of rings were emblematic of secrecy, brotherhood and an eternal bond.[57]

Interestingly, when Haggard told the story of these rings in a letter to *The Times* in 1922, he recorded in his diary that he had received a letter that 'reviles me as a receiver of goods which I knew to be stolen with these words: "Hand back the stolen goods."' Haggard reflected merely that this was 'typical of much of the mentality of our age. Its writer is probably a person of more or less generous mind … But he entirely lacks knowledge. When he tells me to hand back certain rings, his intelligence doesn't realise that the thing is impossible. How can I hand back to bodies that have been destroyed? Nor does he realise that without such relics we should know nothing.'[58] Haggard clearly had no conception of Egyptian ownership or wider cultural rights.

After 1912, Haggard was appointed a commissioner to investigate the state of the settler colonies, and travelled around the world via New Zealand and Canada, although the work was disrupted by the outbreak of the Great War. It was over ten years before he could return to Egypt. By then, Haggard knew his visit to Egypt in 1924, at the age of 68, would likely be his last, and he was ultimately relieved to escape the vulgar modernity of newly independent Cairo for an Egypt of memory, nostalgia and imagination.

As his date of departure for Egypt approached, Haggard was full of foreboding about the horrifying prospect of a Labour Prime Minister, the first in history. He wrote an anguished letter to *The Times* announcing that 'utter ruin draws near with revolution at its heels, or so many of us believe'. The letter ended with the apocalyptic question: 'After the up-building of a thousand years must England crash, in its fall dragging down the Empire?' He decided to withdraw the letter from publication, in part because of his imminent departure to Egypt.[59]

Egypt, though, symbolized everything that was wrong with imperial policy. A Labour government was 'practically abandoning [Egypt] to its fate', following the same route as the granting of Irish independence. He expected a catastrophe in which millions would die of starvation once British expertise in irrigation and farming technology were withdrawn.[60] He eagerly recorded the lamentations of Egyptian servants and other local officials on the departure of the British. Already, the hue of tourists was changing from the British to brash Americans and 'Jews in battalions'.[61] For all his complaints about respect for the dead and the sensitivity of the antiquities situation, Haggard still purchased ancient pieces illegally. Of a wooden statuette purchased from a custodian guarding an ancient cemetery, Haggard airily proclaimed 'I am glad to have rescued it from the dealers', utterly blind to his own contribution to the black market.[62]

The politics of independence was evident in Howard Carter's ghastly entanglements with a newly aggressive Antiquities Service over the tomb of Tutankhamun. In Luxor, Haggard met Carter, who looked 'tired and worn', but was able to usher Haggard and his daughter into the Tomb of Tutankhamun, a place Haggard professed 'small' and 'mean'.[63] He visited Abydos and Tel el Amarna (the city built by the pharaoh Akhenaten), and on return to Luxor took a moonlit ride into the Valley of the Kings, where work on Tutankhamun's disputed tomb had now been left suspended by political wrangling. The lid of the king's sarcophagus had been left literally hanging on ropes above the body when Carter's rage against the authorities stopped work again. In the Valley of the Kings, Haggard asked his daughter Lilias if the spirits of the pharaohs were angry at the rotten state of Egypt, but she could only reply that the valley held no atmosphere of 'wrath and terror'.[64] On return to Cairo, he stayed at the Mena House Hotel near the pyramids, a place now disturbed by the roar of the motorcars of German and American tourists. He visited excavations with Alan Gardiner, but was 'sad to see the bones and grave wrappings of some of them dragged from the death-pits'.[65] He left Egypt for the last time on 23 March 1924: 'I never expect to look on it again and, indeed, do not wish to do so ... If the old Pharaohs and their courts and people could behold it now in all its hateful and brazen vulgarity I think they would go mad!'[66] The first thing Haggard did on his return to England was to lunch with Lord Curzon, the colonial administrator, where he presented him with a ring with the cartouche of the pharaoh Amenophis III. His last Egyptian novel came in the wake of this trip, *Queen of the Dawn* (1925). It was set entirely in Ancient Egypt, banishing any consideration of the post-imperial world that loomed so calamitously for Haggard. His diary grimly tracked the record of assassinations and attacks in Egypt, presuming the place too dangerous now for the English to travel, and even wondered if murderous attacks would begin in London: 'there are plenty of Egyptian students in London of the worst and most dangerous order'.[67]

Haggard died in May 1925. His son-in-law Major Cheyne placed the death-bed scene within an almost inevitable frame of reference: 'The window-blind was up, and the blaze from a large building on fire was visible in the distance. Rider rose up in bed, and pointed to the conflagration with an arm outstretched, the red glow upon his dying face. "My God!" said Cheyne to himself, "an old Pharaoh!"'[68] As Haggard died, his relative fulfilled the writer's desire to merge with the ancient past.

Although it was the colonial policy and wars of southern Africa that forged Haggard's identity, Egypt was always at the crux of his political, religious and imaginative life. It was also surely significant that two of Haggard's brothers, Andrew and Arthur, not only fought in the army in Egypt, but also published extensively about their experiences, in both memoirs and literary fictions. These texts have been almost entirely overlooked, yet they are worth consider-ing as part of Rider Haggard's encounter with Egypt, since they deepened and complicated his engagement with the country.

## Lieutenant-Colonel Andrew Haggard and Major E. Arthur Haggard in Egypt

Andrew Haggard's army career was impressive. He joined the King's Own Bor-derers at the age of nineteen, serving in India and Aden. It was because he had picked up a smattering of Arabic that he was transferred to the Army Staff in Egypt. He arrived a matter of days after the famous battle of Tel-el-Kebir that launched the British invasion of Egypt in 1882, thus missing his chance of glory. After the successful occupation of Cairo, Haggard was then hand-picked by Sir Evelyn Wood as one of twenty-three British officers who would raise, train and command a new native Egyptian army. This group included Francis Grenfell and Herbert Kitchener, who would later both take overall command of forces in Egypt at critical battles against the Sudanese uprising and be ennobled for their efforts. Andrew Haggard was rapidly promoted to Lieutenant-Colonel, in com-mand of an Egyptian army battalion. Egypt was not the distant sublime or super-ficial encounter that it was for many foreign tourists or career soldiers: for months, Andrew Haggard travelled alone with a mix of Egyptian officers of different races and tribes. His memoirs even strongly hinted at sexual relationships with the women of the East, coyly recalling 'the times when beautiful dark eyes flash on the passing cavalier'.[69] As officers of the Egyptian army, the officers observed Eastern custom, and as a result were often regarded with distrust by the British army. Andrew Haggard's position, in effect, demanded that he go native.

In 1884, Haggard was attached to the Royal Navy at the crucial strategic port of Suakim on the Red Sea, following the catastrophe in which Valentine Baker was slaughtered by Mahdi rebels who destroyed an under-trained native force of over two thousand men. A handful of British officers trained a new native force to build up defences there. Suakim would prove to be the centre of battles against Osman Digna, leader of Mahdi forces in the East. These were fierce fights, as the memoirs of the soldier and Tory politician Guy Dawnay recounted, thousands of dead littering the battlefields.[70] Haggard held the port whilst the Gordon Relief Expedition took the lengthier route down the Nile, ultimately only to fail. Months after the death of General Gordon, Andrew Haggard went south to take part in frontier defence, although this was only a prelude to what he contemptuously referred to as 'the shameful policy of scuttle', the British withdrawal from Sudan.[71] Haggard rescued wounded and dying under heavy fire at the Battle of Ginnis, for which he was mentioned in dispatches. His memoir gives an inadvertently comical portrait of gentlemanly behaviour of officers at war. The famous Edward Montagu-Stuart-Wortley ('Wortles' to his chums) had voluntarily come south to find some decent fighting. Haggard fondly recalled: 'I thought he looked superb, as, faultlessly attired with white kid gloves...he sat on his horse, and, with the utmost nonchalance, lighted his cigarette under a hail of bullets, while calmly discussing with me the prospects of our having "a good bag." '[72] It was during this trip, at Akhmim, that he purchased the mummy of Nesmin sent back to his brother Rider who was disconsolately training to be a lawyer in London.

Andrew Haggard began writing in the late 1880s, after Rider Haggard's stunning successes (although he had offered artistic advice to his brother on the plodding manuscript of his first novel, *Dawn*, years before). He wrote novels, history books, travel notes, memoirs and poetry. In 1889, his novel *Dodo and I*, opened in the middle of the Battle of Tamai, with that rare bird Alexander 'Dodo' Ross saving the narrator from certain death on the battlefield. After a posting to Suakim, Cuninghame, the narrator, is soon involved in Cairene scrapes, caught between the beautiful slave-girl Zuleikha and the occultist Lady Aidée Featherstone, with her 'strange' power and 'mesmeric influence'.[73] Andrew Haggard uneasily combines realism and romance in an uninvolving way. In 1891, he published *A Strange Tale of the Scarabaeus*, a long narrative poem in quatrains, about the soldier Lord Angus who, after his campaigns in Egypt, finds a scarab in the Great Pyramid, and presents it to the object of his desire, Mathilde, mounted on a ring. This declaration opens a magical access to Ancient Egypt, since it repeats that of Cheops to his lover Nepthe thousands of years before. Angus becomes a commander of the pharaoh's troops but is caught in another love triangle at the court of Cheops, which suggests a kind of eternal recurrence, though also rather more than that, since this magical resuscitation of the ancient court depends on Angus and Mathilde breaking the Victorian social codes that hold them apart: 'When a white man takes a wife/With this gem, then thou shalt reign,/When the seal be crushed in strife,/Thou and thine be dust again.'[74] Ultimately, the scarabaeus is destroyed and

Angus and Mathilde lose their visionary access to their Egyptian existence. They return to the present day, only to find a small coffin case carrying the child born to them in their vision. The mummified corpse implicitly marks their renunciation of their illicit union as a deathly choice. The poem oddly intertwines with the recurrent themes of Rider Haggard's books, but it also loosely intersects with the Biblical story of Potiphar's wife, the pharaoh's wife who tempts with transgression. Was Andrew Haggard persuaded to buy his mummy in Akhmim, 'popularly supposed to be that of Potiphar's wife', because he was already harping on stories of transgressive desire? The story of Joseph and Potiphar's wife resembles, according to John Yohannan, one of the oldest story forms – the seductive stepmother – told and retold in Egyptian, Jewish, Christian and Islamic texts.[75] When it arrives in the fiction of Rider Haggard, he shares his brother's renunciation of this desire, yet also mourns its loss.

Edward Arthur Haggard was Rider Haggard's only younger brother, born in 1860, and educated at Shrewsbury school and Cambridge. He joined the King's Shropshire Light Infantry and served in Egypt at Suakim with Andrew in 1884 and throughout the British occupation of Egypt until 1886. He later served in the Second Boer War, and retired as a Major. He wrote fiction as Arthur Amyand, although the pseudonym was often exposed on title pages, suggesting conflicting attempts to distance himself from but also capitalize on his brother's fame. *With Rank and File* (1895) were Kiplingesque attempts to tell barrack-room stories about the average soldier, two of which were set in Egypt. 'Poor Valentine: A Story of Suakim' relates the sacrifice of a salt-of-the-earth plucky new recruit in night skirmishes with the dastardly forces of Osman Digna beyond the defences of the port. He is found the morning after providing cover for lost troops 'on his back pinned to the ground by his own bayonet, which the savages had thrust through his two hands, crossed above his heart.'[76] A second story, 'How He Was Buried' is the serio-comic account of a soldier at Suakim who catches enteric fever with hundreds of other troops arriving in that 'terrible unhealthy spot'. His identity is confused with a soldier on the neighbouring bed who dies. After his recovery from fever, the military bureaucracy continues to insist on pronouncing him dead for several weeks, such that he returns home from the war in a curious posthumous state, a dead man walking.[77]

With *The Kiss of Isis*, a few years later, Arthur Haggard produced a full-scale contribution to the Egyptian Gothic. The novel is set in Cairo, in 1883, the British on the veranda at Shepheard's Hotel surrounded by an embittered occupied population as skirmishes with Mahdist hordes escalate towards the massacre of the frontier forces commanded by Colonel William Hicks in the Sudan. The hero, Godfrey Owen, shares quarters in Cairo with a fellow officer who exerts 'a strange fascination', and proves to be a dabbler in ancient magical arts.[78] On his deathbed, this man confesses to Owen that he has conjured an ancient 'Spirit of Evil' that will now attach itself to Owen: 'I have been the means of transmitting to another the evil influence by which I am possessed.'[79] This nameless thing owes something to Richard Marsh's *The Beetle* and has more than a passing resemblance to Kali, the Hindu goddess of destruction, but it is explicitly declared to be a force more primal than Ancient Egypt. In Owen, it appears to represent the death drive, kept in check by Isis, goddess of love. Owen's wrestling with this malign spirit leads him to Ben Hasan, a keeper of the ancient Hermetic wisdom and a man with 'occult powers' who extends his protection to Owen with the gift of a scarabaeus ring. Just as we would expect from a Haggard brother narrative, it was 'a scarabaeus of great antiquity, the cartouche on the reverse side of which was deeply cut in hieroglyphs.'[80] The ring is a sign of protection that will allow Owen to enter the hidden world of Isis worship, continued unbroken since ancient times in a secret temple in Memphis. Here, Ben Hasan is revealed to be Amosis, immortal high priest of the cult of Isis, firm in the belief that Owen is one of the few moderns worthy of entry into the cult. The culmination of *The Kiss of Isis* is the reverse of *She*: Owen's last test is a trial by fire. Rather than destruction, Owen survives and unites with the object of his desire, Ena, set up from her first entry into the narrative to be an incarnation of Isis. The tone thus finally shifts from Gothic menace to the romance of immortal love.

Rider Haggard's fictions are woven in and out of his brothers' military experiences and literary fantasies of Egypt. The army careers of his brothers show that the family had a much more intimate engagement with Egypt than run-of-the-mill tourism or a brief military campaign could ever give. It is evident that all three brothers shared the same circuits of gossip and rumour about Egypt, and were equally fascinated by a kind of supernatural supplement that washed across Egyptian landscapes, ruins and objects – not least in the mummy that passed through Andrew and Rider's possession so early in their writing careers. But I think Rider Haggard's romances had a different emphasis precisely because he did not live for any sustained time in Egypt. Instead, he had to conjure Egypt through the objects that he accumulated around him at Ditchingham House in Norfolk.

## Rider Haggard's artefactual fictions

In 1917, Aylward Blackman listed for the *Journal of Egyptian Archaeology* the most significant pieces in Haggard's Egyptian collection, including bronze reliquaries, a statue of Isis, heart scarabs and three signet rings. But much earlier, in 1892, the *Strand Magazine* had lavishly illustrated a report on the curios of Haggard's home, with its tumble of ostrich eggs, Egyptian bows, African horns, Zulu shields, Mexican combs and Charles Dickens's desk, purchased from the Gad's Hill sale after the author's death. Ditchingham House was less an orderly museum collection than an older cabinet of curiosities, a mark of Haggard's 'maniac and absolutely anti-categorical' collecting.[81] Even so, the process of transporting these bewilderingly diverse objects into a single space, collapsing the globe into rural Norfolk, made them resonate with new significance. Cabinets were, after all, designed to be mystical arrays built on a logic of sympathetic magic, the objects collapsing time and space and allowing 'communication between worlds' or between the visible and the invisible.[82]

If artefaction is the process of turning unruly things into museum artefacts, Haggard adopted a parallel process of turning objects into fictions. For such a fantastical writer, his imagination was often utterly material, starting out with a literal handling of objects. At one moment in his autobiography, he recalls visiting Famagusta in Cyprus on his return journey from Egypt, picking up some medieval cannon balls from the Turkish attack, adding 'I hold one of them in my hand as I write.'[83] He would have twirled the pharaonic signet rings on his fingers as he composed *She* or *Queen Sheba's Ring*. Perhaps he knew of Madame Blavatsky's definition of the power of psychometry, 'the faculty which enables any object held in the hand or against the forehead [to produce] impressions of the character or appearance of the individual, or any other object with which it has previously been in contact.' It was called by another writer the power to call up 'the soul of things.'[84]

Haggard even went to great lengths to manufacture fictional artefacts for his early novels. One of Haggard's sisters created and artificially aged the ancient map that points the way to *King Solomon's Mines* in the novel. The potsherd of Amenartas, the family heirloom in *She* that tells the story of Leo Vincey's ancestors in ancient Greek, Roman and medieval Latin, was a joint project of Haggard's scholarly friends, and was manufactured and displayed at his home. This was not just because a youthful writer required stage props to jolt his imagination. At the end of his career, in 1922, *Virgin of the Sun*, a romance about an unrecorded early modern English encounter with the Incas, was composed only after he had finally acquired the Inca ring that one of his schoolmasters had owned. For Haggard, it seemed that ownership of this object, which he bought from a down-at-heel descendant of the Reverend Graham, was vital before he could tell its formative story:

> When I was a boy of nine...I was sent to a private tutor, the Reverend Mr. Graham...Mr. Graham wore a thick gold ring engraved in a curious, but rather conventional frieze pattern with symbols in it that may have been meant to represent the sun. He told me that an old friend of his who had business in Peru or Central America had opened some burial place and in it found a chamber wherein, round a stone table, sat a dead and mummified man at the head and about a dozen or so other persons ranged around the table...[T]he

discoverer of the tomb took it thence and gave it to Mr. Graham in after years (I seem, however, to recall that he said that after the tomb was opened all its inmates crumbled into dust, but of this I am not sure). The tale made a deep impression on my youthful mind and, in fact, first turned it towards Romance.[85]

The romance he wrote, once in possession of the ring, purported to be a manuscript that had been discovered under the feet of this mummy. This constituted another iteration of Haggard's skill at writing artefactual fiction.

In the 1920s and '30s, the materialist critic Walter Benjamin took on the task of tracking the rise of commodity culture in the nineteenth century, often tracing it through the objects and interiors of the bourgeois home. His intent was to break open the surface of these interiors, to show the social relations of exploitation that they concealed. For evidence, Benjamin contended that detective fiction that emerged in the Victorian period offered 'the only adequate description of' the 'horror of apartments'.[86] In a short piece entitled 'Manorially Furnished Ten-Room Apartment' in *One-Way Street*, Benjamin argued that 'The bourgeois interior of the 1860s to the 1890s, with its gigantic sideboards distended with carvings, the sunless corners where palms stand... and the long corridors with their singing gas flames, fittingly houses only the corpse.'[87] The generic detail is always, Benjamin notes, exotic and strange, 'that rank Orient inhabiting their interiors: the Persian carpet and the ottoman, the hanging lamp and the genuine Caucasian dagger,' the last curio always used as the gruesome murder weapon.[88] Glossing this insight, Carlo Salzani explains that for Benjamin the cluttered interior of the Victorian home was 'soulless and lifeless, built as a trap and inhabited by corpses, from which any living thing is expelled, annihilated, or murdered by the cult of lifeless and ageless commodities.'[89] Even if Haggard was anxious to expel the literal presence of the mummified dead from Ditchingham House, his cabinet of curiosities and the artefactual fictions he spun from them literalize this deathly view. The curios that bolstered his identities as writer, squire and servant of Empire, were often records of violent or deathly social relations, whether traces of conquered or vanished peoples, mementos of battle, rare pieces bought from auctions of possessions of the dead, or family heirlooms. If Haggard's work was dominated by tones of nostalgia or melancholy, it was fostered by the way his museal interiors were conflated with the mausoleum.

The inherent deathliness of imperial possession played out in the fiction too, but not in the obvious tropes of the Egyptian Gothic. The coffin of Nesmin was expelled from Rider Haggard's cabinet very early in his writing and collecting life. Later, throughout his romance writing, Haggard certainly dallied with curse narratives and the possibility of supernatural punishment for transgressing a proper reverence for the dead, but this was always trumped by the romance of immortality or reincarnation, of the *continuity beyond death* that is the quintessence of Haggard's conservatism. This stance led him to his most sublime moments and most rapturous prose. Yet I think it is significant that the mummy always returns in Haggard's romances not as a single, shuffling avenger, but passively in massed or multiplied form. There is a repeated primal scene in Haggard's fiction, the discovery of underground rooms or tombs, caverns where the perfectly preserved mummified body is multiplied into legions of undead. It was there from the start in *Dawn*, Mildred Carr's domestic world hiding the Egyptian mummies in the cavern beneath her home. In *King Solomon's Mines*, one of the last revelations of the intrepid voyagers into the interior of the mountains is to find that the dead kings of the Kukuanas are sternly seated in perpetual conference underground, transformed over the centuries into (un)living rock: 'They were human forms indeed, or rather had been human forms; now they were *stalactites*. This was the way in which the Kukuana people had from time immemorial preserved their royal dead. They petrified them.'[90] *She* repeats the scene of the discovery that the massed undead undergird a barely living society. The Tombs of Kôr are described as 'a honeycomb of sepulchres', and the adventurers find that 'the whole mountain is full of dead'.[91] It is there that Leo Vincey virtually defines the uncanny long before Freud, confronting the perfectly preserved corpse of his exact double, the ancestor that he reincarnates, Kallikrates. In *Queen Sheba's Ring*, the lost civilization at Mur conceals another primal scene in the caves beneath it: 'A great stone chair and, piled upon its seat and upon its base, human bones.'[92] Here, the old kings are sent to the beyond with a large entourage of massacred attendants. This was a scene that Haggard used again in *Virgin of the Sun*, presented as a manuscript that has been recovered from beneath the feet of a perfectly mummified noblewoman, 'surrounded by a number of other women, perhaps her servants who were brought to be buried with her'.[93] This was the primal story Haggard claimed in later life to have been at the origin of his first stirrings of interest in the romance form.

Can anxiety or fear, paradoxically, be managed not by eliminating the threat, but rather by *multiplying* it? This was Freud's peculiar explanation for the writhing snakes of the Medusa's Head, where multiplication was the busy attempt to disguise the fear of castration whilst simultaneously building a monument to it.[94] Haggard's mummies are sometimes read in this way, targets of Haggard's 'archaeological desire', the sexual economy of the fiction an 'intimate part of the structures of meaning surrounding the grave'.[95] But Haggard's legions of mummies are ambivalent in a rather less obvious way. On the one hand, they represent the dead weight of an oppressive history, strangling the last living representatives of once noble civilizations. On the other hand, they act as emblems of preserved tradition, forms of conservation that are menaced by modernity. Haggard's melancholia is the product of the desire to own these vanishing signs and a dawning sense that possession is a deathly act. Their liminal status breaks open the sheen of artefaction; they are things that expose true horror, the deathly social networks at the heart of colonial occupation.

What did this welter of late Victorian and Edwardian popular fictions about Egypt contribute to the circulation of the mummy curse? Popular fictions bind floating emotional states into cohesive narratives, their templates and icons short-cuts for complex and contradictory feelings. The Egyptian Gothic doubles the critical encounter of Britain with Egypt, intensifying dark stories from the 1860s and exploding after the British occupation of 1882. The crudest form of the Egyptian Gothic is the unmotivated, relentless avenger, the mummy as murderous drive, a mirror to imperial ideology, haunting the corridors of the metropolitan museum or private collection. This did much to hammer home a popular image of the mummy avenger, later reinforced by Hollywood films that progressively unravelled any nuance from the shuffling monster. But at the time this figure rarely appeared unalloyed. The immortal romance, the textual and sexual resuscitation of the mummy, is nearly always twined around the curse, exquisitely coupling love with death in an exemplary decadent manner.

The Egyptian fictions of Rider Haggard and Algernon Blackwood ultimately seem the most complex and over-determined literature of this encounter. Blackwood transcends the violence of magazine mummies, ultimately transforming Egypt in his insular tales into a figurative landscape for a metaphysical descent into the 'layered personality'. The ambiguous virtue of Haggard's materialist and artefactual Egyptian corpus is that his fictions always return us to the scene of the crime, with artefacts that break open in uncanny ways and return to speak the secret histories of things from beyond the grave.

It should be becoming clear that the curse of the mummy comes into shape in the late Victorian period through multiple vectors. Supernatural fictions achieve their best shivery effects when they rely on a penumbra of uncertainty between fact and fiction, Gothic fantasy and archaeological knowledge. This was the place that Ernest Wallis Budge strategically occupied, leaving a zone of uncertainty around the status of curse stories that circled around the Egyptian Rooms. It was the hesitation that effective horror writers like Bram Stoker consistently used, planting his fictions at the vanishing points of normal and supernormal science.

In the late Victorian period another crucial context for the spread of curse rumours was the emerging science around hypnosis, trance and the depredations of free will. This area of research was located somewhere between orthodox science and the supernatural, a space swarming not just with men of science but the magicians of the occult revival. What if the hypnotist could command with an imperious gaze? What if the trained magical adept could kill with a glance or speak Words of Power that could crush their enemies? What if Ancient Egyptian magic had mastered the 'science' of mesmeric command? Could not the curse be a version of these deathly gazes?

# 8

# Evil Eyes, Punitive Currents and the Late Victorian Magic Revival

'Everything is worse...if you think something is looking at you.'

Shirley Jackson[1]

I have been trying to suggest that in nineteenth-century Britain, Egypt is figured on a cusp, the balance shifting as the century progresses away from the sublime, and more definitively towards horror. If architecture, commercial entertainment and world's fair spaces began by emphasizing the spectacle and wonder of a vanished past and an exploitable present, a more forward imperial policy and the subsequent colonial wars darkened the imagination, the ruins of Egypt instead occupied by fanatical dervishes, distrustful colonial subjects and vengeful spirits of the ancient dead. In the popular literature of the Gothic revival the imagination curdles into oriental phantasms. The mummy shuffles along the border of rumour and knowledge, appearing as the shadowy double to the emerging science of Egyptology, occupying a space of unnerving hesitancy, allowing the spectral to leak from the Gothic into archaeology, into the very encounter with Egypt and the rubble of its past. This final chapter explores a last set of contexts from the late Victorian period that decidedly associates Egypt with threat and menace: magic.

Sax Rohmer's *The Green Eyes of Bâst* (1920) revolves around a plot to unseat the Coverleys from their ancestral home. The likely heirs are being systematically murdered, each body discovered with a small idol of the Ancient Egyptian goddess Bubastis left beside it. Around the time of every death, too, a pair of luminous, horrifying cat's eyes is seen swelling out of the darkness. Suspicions converge on the half-caste medic, Dr Geefe, personal physician to Lady Coverley since her husband had served in the government of Egypt. Geefe's library in the rotting family seat is cluttered with old books and antiquities: tablets, papyri, coffins and unravelled mummy parts. Once more, ancestral English landscape suffers an ominous oriental intrusion. Geefe's final confession explains the mystery: he researches 'psycho-hybrids', weird and uncanny chimeras of human and animal. The murderer is Lord Coverley's rejected and now vengeful daughter, conceived in Egypt near the ancient centre of worship to Bubastis and somehow a psycho-physical fusion of West and East, human and cat. Nahéma must wear a veil to hide her terrifying '*chatoyant* eyes'.[2] A monster of colonial hybridity, she toys with then kills her family prey.

Rohmer's melodrama feeds off a terror we have encountered before. Remember the enormous, compelling eyes in *The Beetle*. Every mummy in Gothic fiction has those 'dull, steadily staring eyes [that] had a sort of hypnotic effect'.[3] Recall how Cheiro, the palm-reader who claimed to have read Thomas Douglas Murray's fate in the lines of his hand, reported Douglas Murray's reaction to the Egyptian antiquity that he had purchased: 'As I looked into the carved face of the Priestess on the outside of the mummy case, her eyes seemed to come to life, and I saw such a look of hate in them that my very blood seemed to turn to ice.'[4] Later, when the Edwardian press was reporting on strange things afoot in the Egyptian Rooms, the psychic Elliott O'Donnell visited only to be pursued by 'strange dark faces... always with the same baffling and peculiar enigmatical expression in their long and glittering eyes'.[5] When it comes to curses, the eyes have it.

The eye is central to many ancient Egyptian myths. Everywhere, the Eye of Horus stares out from monuments and friezes, is marked on doors and coffins, makes the shape of the most ubiquitous protective amulets. Horus, son of Isis and Osiris, rules with two eyes, the right eye the sun, the left the moon. Horus loses his eye in a struggle with Seth, brother-enemy of Ra; it is reassembled through the magic of Thoth. The *wedjat* eye – meaning the 'whole one' – becomes the protective sign and also the wrathful emblem of godly and pharaonic power over the forces of chaos. In the Book of the Dead, 'The Eye of Horus prevails over the accursed soul and shade of Apep, and the flame of the Eye of Horus shall gnaw into that enemy of Ra.'[6] Apep or Apopis, the serpent and agent of chaos, has the evil eye, like all snakes and crocodiles, the one that covets and envies. There were many rituals ways of fending off this evil eye: aside from the protective hex of the Eye of Horus, in one ritual the pharaoh would hit away a ball that symbolized the eye of Apopis.[7]

Ancient Egyptians appeared to believe in the extromissive theory of vision, the idea that the gaze fired something *from* the eye, a flame or ray of energy that would strike out. Although Plato and other Greek philosophers held this view, Aristotle's rejection proved more influential in the West. The early Arab scholar Yaqub ibn Ishaq al-Kindi, however, wrote a manual on optics in the ninth

Figure 8.1 Boris Karloff as Imhotep in *The Mummy*, 1932 (AKG Images).

century that maintained the extromissive view, a theory of radiation that 'binds the world into a vast network in which everything acts upon everything else to produce natural effects'.[8] This influential text found its way back into Western thought, Francis Bacon for instance regarding envy as 'an ejaculation, or irradiation of the eye'.[9] In the Renaissance, the ability to fascinate, to bewitch or enchant, was also associated with optical effluvia, a poison that magicians could ejaculate through the eye. After Franz Mesmer postulated his theory of 'animal magnetism' in 1779, the notion that the mesmerist directed invisible magnetic energies through their enthralling gaze was a common, if commonly contested, theory. And despite the dominance of intromissive theory in optics since Kepler (the mechanical view that the eye is only a lens that receives light), marginal extromissive belief has continued. A contemporary researcher, Rupert Sheldrake, in his study of 'the sense of being stared at', still holds to the possibility that a powerful influence can be projected outward from the eye. It is why we physically feel the touch of the concentrated gaze of others, Sheldrake contends.[10]

The insistence on malevolent eyes in many mummy curse stories therefore seems to intersect with the notion that certain gazes can fire a malefic influence on those who covet or envy. It can even be accommodated to Christian ethics, since both the New and Old Testaments of the Bible invoke the tradition of the evil eye.[11] But there is a complex cluster of factors that comes together in the late Victorian period that helps render the evil eye one of the privileged vehicles for mummy curses.

First, there was a surge of interest in the facts of hypnotism. After nearly one hundred years of being marginalized as quackery, the folk practice of healing by trance induced by the gaze of the mesmerist was sanctioned as the objective medical condition of 'artificial somnambulism' in the 1880s by respected medical research centres, particularly in France. The greatest neurologist of the age, Jean-Martin Charcot, began experimenting with hypnotic treatments for hysteria, and began reporting some deeply weird phenomena associated with trance states. Hypnosis remained controversial in England, with Ernest Hart of the British Medical Association campaigning against its use throughout the 1890s. This was mainly because hypnosis seemed inextricably linked to claims about supernatural powers. The key advocates of hypnosis in England were psychical researchers who considered that the heightened sensitivity of trance states 'proved' the existence of telepathy. They also continued to speculate on what ethereal substance might be passed in the rapport between mesmerist and mesmerized. Soon enough, what Hart called 'the new witchcraft' caused public panic over what unscrupulous hypnotists could do to the innocent merely through suggestions exercised by their compelling gaze. The question of hypnosis was also always a question of race. Mesmerists were regularly depicted as foreigners, Jews from the East, Arabs from the South, men able to prey on innocent English women and weak-willed effeminate modern men. In the popular imagination, the racial aspect of rapport dangerously subverted colonial power.

Second, anthropologists became interested in documenting instances of belief in 'the evil eye', particularly in North Africa and the Middle East, where the superstition seemed most pervasive. Frederick Elsworthy's study appeared in 1895, whilst Siegfried Seligmann's two-volume *Der Böse Blick* was published in 1910. Elsworthy noted that 'abundant testimony exists in the oldest monuments in the world that among the ancient Egyptians belief in and dread of the evil eye were ever present.'[12] The belief evidently survived among the credulous fellaheen of present-day Egypt. The point was that the evil eye was a frustrating 'survival' of a primitive superstition, a stubborn form of magical thinking that 'still exists among all savage nations, and even here in England in our very midst'.[13] Elsworthy confirmed that 'no science, no religion, no laws have been able to root out this fixed belief; and no power has ever been able to eradicate it from the human mind.'[14] Edward Tylor, the first academic anthropologist in England, had defined the task of the nascent science as 'to expose the remains of crude old culture which have passed into harmful superstition, and to mark these out for destruction'.[15] Yet theorists of primitive magic, belief in influences exerted at a distance through unseen channels, could only record its brute survival through every stage of cultural evolution. This is still the case.[16] In the 1890s, it seemed that the findings of Egyptology confirmed the ancient and pervasive nature of the belief.

But third, and most importantly, there was a full-scale magical revival in the late Victorian period which was heavily invested in recovering the lost wisdom and supposedly immense supernatural powers of the ancient Egyptian priests. Where anthropologists saw evidence of savage thought, theosophists from the 1880s and the self-authored magicians of the Hermetic Order of the Golden Dawn in the 1890s and after regarded Ancient Egypt as the seat of a lost lore of fabulous magical powers. These could be recovered through devoted study and careful decoding of the fragmentary evidence that survived. The occultist was defined as 'the disciple of one or all of these secret sciences' (in contrast with the mystic, who sought only inner experience, not the systematic knowledge suggested by alchemy, astrology, divination or magic).[17] The occult knowledge of the Hermetic tradition was founded on a belief that the magic books of the *Corpus Hermeticum* were written in Ancient Egypt, by the scribe and magician Hermes Trismegistus (Hermes 'the thrice blessed'), a later instantiation of the god Thoth, or perhaps a powerful priest who was later deified. The books were first translated in the fifteenth century by Ficino for the court of the Medicis, and manuscripts of books circulated secretly around Europe and placed magic at the heart of the Renaissance revival of classical learning.[18] Hermetic influences entered England through figures like the Elizabethan scholar John Dee.[19] The origin story for Hermes was mistaken: the *Corpus* is a composite collection of books written by multiple hands four centuries into the Christian era. But many continued to believe that the *Corpus* was a key to ancient mysteries. For those prepared to study the magical texts of Ancient Egypt, they promised illimitable supernatural powers, ultimately over life and death.

Before long, this fractious and eccentric group of Victorian and Edwardian occultists was beaming 'punitive currents' of energy at each other across the astral plane, modern day curses conjured by magical rite. This bizarre world constantly spilled over into the popular press at the turn of the century. The most notorious of these magi was Aleister Crowley, the mad staring prophet of his own cosmology, the self-proclaimed Antichrist who was never far from public scandal. Crowley was repeatedly depicted in Gothic novels as a manipulator of vast magical powers, commanding weaklings with mesmerism and cruelly cursing his enemies. Indeed, every villain of the Egyptian Gothic has access to supernatural magical and mesmeric powers gleaned from the study of the ancients that have been foolishly dismissed by Western science. These narratives fed back into the self-mythology of magi and mystics, in a place where the boundaries between truth and fiction were often entirely blurred.

It is the context of the magic revival, I think, that helps supercharge the idea of the mummy curse at the turn of the century. Magic was a marginal subculture, no doubt, but the medical study of hypnosis and the anthropology of magic helped push the notion of lost Egyptian 'science' into a realm of hesitancy, that place where rumour and gossip could circulate spooky stories on the cusp between belief and disbelief, the natural and the supernatural. In this sphere, the curse was not an ancient story but an active possibility, an agency alive and operating in the world. It's among the occultists, then, that we need to start.

## Late Victorian Hermeticism: Blavatsky's Theosophical Society

In 1881, the journalist Alfred Sinnett published a small book called *The Occult World*, which proved very popular. A former editor of *The Pioneer* newspaper in India, Sinnett proposed to reintroduce the reader to various branches of thought that modernity, in its headlong rush, had apparently forgotten. His typically syncretic list included Ancient Egyptian theology, Chaldean magic, Gnostic Christianity, and Neoplatonist philosophy. In a classic statement of occult belief, Sinnett claimed that 'the wisdom of the ancient world...was a reality, and it still survives...It was already a complete system of knowledge that had been cultivated in secret, and had been handed down to initiates for ages.'[20] These arcana had been held by the elite priesthood of Ancient Egypt and the Greek keepers of the Mysteries in the sanctuaries of cult centres and had been passed on as a living tradition in contemporary India among the 'Hindoos'. In Tibet, a territory completely closed to outsiders and long a space of fantasy investment in the West, Sinnett claimed that there were 'secluded Orientals [who] may understand more about electricity than Faraday'.[21] The knowledge of this secret brotherhood, if received and understood, promised spectacular powers. This initiation into the supernatural had nothing to do with the mass movement of spiritualism. To be a medium was merely to be a passive receiver, open to anyone prepared to suspend their will, and indeed spiritualism had many links to radical democratic and plebeian movements.[22] Occult initiation, in contrast, was for an elite, who must pass through hierarchical stages of training, open only to those ultimately capable of exercising power actively 'by the force of their own will'.[23]

Sinnett was espousing the belief of the Theosophical Society, the occult movement that had been established by the mercurial Russian émigré Madame Helena Blavatsky in New York in 1875. She travelled to India in 1880 to set up a study centre there, and Sinnett was an early convert. Blavatsky, famed for her blazing, mesmeric eyes and charismatic presence, claimed in her first major book, *Isis Unveiled*, that she had travelled for years seeking wisdom in the East, and had finally unlocked the secret of a grand synthesis of science and religion, revealed to her by 'the sages of the Orient'.[24] It synthesized Darwinian theory in a grand history of human spiritual development. The title of her book placed her in a tradition of mystery religions, stretching back to the Isiac cults of Alexandria, and which spread to Greece and through the Roman Empire, centred on Isis as mother goddess. Mystery rites typically were focused on 'gaining esoteric wisdom after the endurance of ordeals', and although much of the actual content of the ceremonies was kept hidden except to initiates, rituals included the symbolic unveiling of the statue of Isis.[25] Blavatsky therefore also placed herself in the Hermetic tradition, recovering knowledge known by many ancient cultures including the Egyptians but which had been carefully secreted then lost after centuries of Christian erasure and persecution. An early name for her venture in setting up a new religion had been the 'Brotherhood of Luxor', another clue that an idea of Egyptian magic was important for Blavatsky.

Her movement was therefore part of a Western tradition that Erik Hornung calls Egyptosophy: 'the study of an *imaginary* Egypt viewed as the profound source of all esoteric lore. This Egypt is a timeless *idea* bearing only a loose relationship to the historical reality.'[26] Out of the *Corpus Hermeticum* and the magical powers ascribed to the Egyptian hieroglyph, 'Creative readers could stitch together whatever variegated quilts they liked from Hermetic revelations,' thus ensuring that 'the ancient Near East became the home of the cryptic, the uncanny, and the profound'.[27]

Amongst these lost sciences, so Blavatsky claimed, was an active theurgy practised in Egyptian temples and Greek Mystery cults: 'The purpose of it was to make spirits visible to the eyes of mortals.'[28] Proper training in this recovered knowledge would result in mastery of many things deemed 'supernatural' by blinkered modern sceptics: astral travel, mesmerism, or various forms of psychic sensitivity. She also hinted at a 'Goetic theurgy', a black magic that shadowed these practices. Discussing powers to project 'the force of the will', she claimed that the astral plane 'can be used to direct, so to speak, a bolt of fluid against a given object, with fatal force. Many a dark revenge has been taken that way; and in such cases the coroner's inquest will never disclose anything but sudden death, apparently resulting from heart-disease, an apoplectic fit, or some other natural, but still not veritable cause.' Blavatsky also avowed that 'despite materialist scepticism, man does possess such a power' and it would only be a short time before the evidence would persuade Europeans 'of the weird and formidable potency existing in the human will and imagination'.[29] Such powers, presumably including the menacing evil eye, could only be revealed by submitting to the teachings of Blavatsky the hierophant. She alone had access to the still-living Mahatmas, as the elected intermediary to the communicants of this lost tradition, who were hidden away in the fastness of Tibet. Blavatsky further communicated their philosophy in her next tome, *The Secret Doctrine*.

Blavatsky briefly visited London in 1884, and then lived her final years there between 1887 and 1891, securing a small but fractious world of occult scholars in the imperial metropolis. A three-month investigation of Blavatsky by the Society of Psychical Research in 1885, at a time when this new society was keen to establish its sober scientific and sceptical credentials, lambasted her claims. Alleged messages from the Mahatmas that drifted down from the astral plane appeared to be glued to the ceiling and pulled by strings. Writings that miraculously appeared in a sealed safe could be explained by a concealed back door in the safe accessed from the adjoining room. The SPR report memorably concluded that the Theosophical Society was 'but the aloe-blossom of a woman's monomania', and 'the strange, wild, passionate, unconventional Madame Blavatsky' had but 'a morbid yearning for notoriety' in perpetuating such an obvious fraud.[30] Her syncretic scholarship, merging the holy books of Egypt, India and early Christianity with modern science was also dismissed as inaccurate and fallacious by the leading comparative philologist of the time, Max Müller.[31]

These attacks did little to dent her influence among seekers of spiritual enlightenment. Sinnett's little book on her ideas was passed by William Stead to the radical social campaigner and atheist Annie Besant; to the astonishment of her contemporaries, firebrand Besant converted to theosophy after a year of secretive experiments with hypnotism and séances. In her autobiography she recalled visiting Blavatsky in Notting Hill, struck by 'the compulsion of that yearning voice, her compelling eyes'.[32] Besant went on to run the Society after Blavatsky's death, eventually leaving England to become a prominent nationalist politician in India.

Another convert was the antivivisectionist Anna Kingsford, the first woman in England to qualify as a medical doctor. She had trained in Paris – since women were excluded from the profession in England – largely to give authority to her campaign against animal experiments. Kingsford was also an inspirational writer, writing automatic texts in trance states, and was deeply imbued with the Christian mystical tradition. She became head of the London Lodge of the Theosophical Society in 1883, but soon left to form her own Hermetic Society, concerned that theosophy was too anti-Christian and 'Eastern' in outlook. Her book written with her collaborator Edward Maitland, *The Perfect Way* (1882), proved influential on the trajectory of English occultism. After her early death, Maitland revealed that Kingsford was a firm believer in the projection of her will. Indeed, she claimed that she had killed the vivisector Claude Bernard, after being 'provoked to launch a malediction at him' for his contemptuous, godless materialism, 'hurling her whole spiritual being at him with all her might'.[33] She was astounded to hear of his death soon afterwards (from Bright's disease), but after searching her conscience continued to use this unconventional weapon in her campaign against the chilling experimentalists who tortured animals. On reading this account, William Stead excitedly termed Kingsford a 'killer-willer' and cited other testimony to the effect that 'force or power or influence or principle is no fiction. It is a terrible truth.'[34] Kingsford took authority for her claim from the Renaissance occultist Paracelsus, who boasted that 'my spirit, without the help of my body, may, through a fiery will alone and without a sword, stab and wound others'.[35] Kingsford always had fragile health, but the effect of making 'a spiritual thunderbolt of oneself' on the astral plane apparently exhausted her. She died after catching pneumonia in a downpour outside the laboratories of Louis Pasteur. She was only 41. It was suspected that Pasteur had parried her killer-will with his own fatal 'shock in return'.[36]

This was an undoubtedly eccentric belief, but it is worth recalling that these events took place in 1880s Paris, where marvels associated with hypnotic powers were being demonstrated and widely discussed by the authoritative doctors of the Salpêtrière Hospital. Two of them, Alfred Binet and Charles Féré, wrote a guide to the latest research in which they warned that trance states could be 'induced without the aid of the subject's imagination, against his will, and without his knowledge'.[37] In this 'morbid state of receptivity', the will of another could impose negative and harmful suggestions, inducing paralysis, blindness and perhaps even worse. Normal science vanished into supernaturalism around this peculiar power of suggestion, Binet and Féré confessing that 'we do not think it can be explained by any psychical facts now known to us'.[38] One English introduction called *Hypnotism and Suggestion* suggested that it was the 'encroachment' of men of science 'upon this former *terra incognita* which has transformed magic in all its forms into science, and the supernatural into the reign of law.'[39] Another breathless guide cut through the scientific controversies about the agency of hypnotism to state: 'I should advise all experimenters to act as if such influence existed. That in every move and *pass,* look or *gaze,* act as if they were throwing out something… all looks and passes being but vehicles to conduct the *specific influence.*'[40] Whilst Jean-Martin Charcot limited suggestion to hysterics and degenerates who inherited a weak will, the so-called 'Nancy School' formed around Hippolyte Bernheim argued for universal susceptibility to suggestion, however strong the will. The stance of the Nancy School prompted panics about hypnosis used to force the innocent to commit crimes under nefarious influences. In a sensational trial in 1889, Gabrielle Bompard used the defence that she was not a responsible agent in a gruesome murder because she had acted under the hypnotic command of her accomplice Michel Eyraud (a defence that was rejected). As these sensational claims swirled around France, even Ernest Hart's stolid English rejection of these credulous assertions about the power of suggestion borrowed the language of the occult, denouncing hypnosis as 'the new witchcraft', and Hart probably composed the leader in the *British Medical Journal* that called for the outlawing of this 'dangerous mental poison'.[41] In 1894, British popular culture was swept with a craze around the publication of George du Maurier's *Trilby,* a novel that introduced the figure of Svengali, the Jewish impresario who proves to be animating his singer Trilby through his mesmeric force of will. The craze fused criminal suggestion with the tradition of the evil eye of the dastardly foreigner.[42] Anna Kingsford may have had weird beliefs, but she was hardly alone.

Another important figure involved in theosophy was A. R. Orage. Orage was the editor of *The New Age* from 1908, which became an important vehicle for Modernist writers and for transmitting the philosophy of Bergson and Nietzsche into English cultural circles. It also had a mystical bent. This was unsurprising, since before becoming editor, Orage wrote for the *Theosophical Review* and published the short book *Consciousness* through a theosophical imprint. The book praised any training that intensified the focus of mental attention. This could lift the mind beyond the 'ordinary world' into a new stage of mental evolution. 'The main problem of the mystics of all ages has been the problem of how to develop superconsciousness, of how to become superhuman,' Orage said.[43] His concern to empower the will of the 'active mind' diffused theosophy into Nietzschean and other strands of Modernist thought. It seemed to work on some: one contributor recalled Orage's 'hypnotic effect' and the way 'he cast a spell upon his hearers', enthusing them to write for a journal jocularly known as *The No Wage*.[44] Orage abandoned *The New Age* in 1922 to proselytize for another charismatic Eastern mystic, the spiritual leader George Gurdjieff.[45]

Theosophy could stand as the blueprint for post-traditional religious movements. It regarded the institutions of worship with suspicion and although providing a rigid hierarchy of spiritual insight it effectively psychologized religious feeling, locating authenticity finally in interior spiritual experience rather than in the external authority of doctrine or church institution.[46] It confronted modern doubt by apparently fusing new scientific discoveries in physics with ancient magics. Darwin's biology was spiritualized. It was a syncretic melange of diverse sources, outflanking restrictive Catholic or Protestant doctrines and claiming greater illumination either by looking to their heterodox margins or by relativizing Christianity by embedding it in a plural and cosmopolitan religious history. It provided an origin story, a history of profound ancient wisdom lost in diaspora, but one that could be reassembled, promising a transformed spiritual future. Theosophy offered strange reversals, placing primitive magic before modern theology or science, and subordinating Western seekers to Eastern masters, inverting the relation of power between colonial centre and margin. It was an odd kind of cosmopolitanism, Gauri Viswanathan has suggested, in which 'the otherworldliness of the occult offered alternative possibilities for imaging colonial relations outside a hierarchical framework.'[47] But if there was a chance for an anti-colonial politics to emerge from commitment to theosophy (as in Annie Besant's career), it also reinforced certain racial stereotypes, including conceptions of a threatening black magic exercised by oriental magicians who could unleash the dark energies of their fatal will.

Blavatsky's emphasis on the East caused problems for some. Anna Kingsford wished to pursue the Western mystical Christian tradition, and this prompted a divergent strand of occult study averse to orientalism, which was the path taken by seekers such as A. E. Waite, G. R. S. Mead and the influential writer on mysticism, Catholic and otherwise, Evelyn Underhill. Blavatsky was also suspicious of too much interest in the practice of ritual magic and tried to suppress it as a danger. Such was the interest in London, however, that she allowed a secretive 'Esoteric Section' to be established within the Theosophical Society. Centrally involved in this study centre was the poet William Butler Yeats. He retained a lifelong interest in Indian philosophy, but in 1890 he moved the focus of his occult studies to the newly established Hermetic Order of the Golden Dawn. This group was similarly syncretic, but the revival of Egyptian magic was at its heart.

## Hermetic Order of the Golden Dawn: *Haute magie* and low comedy

The origins of the Golden Dawn were shrouded in fog, and histories of the Order remain heavily invested in obscure factional disputes.[48] It was founded in 1887 by three men, William Woodman, a surgeon and long-term student of the occult, William Wynn Westcott, an expert in the Hermetic tradition who also served as the official coroner for north London, and Samuel Mathers, a scholar of the occult in reduced circumstances who haunted the Reading Room of the British Museum and had garnered respect for his translation of works on the Jewish Kabbalah. All three were involved in Freemasonry, the more mystical end of which had always 'claimed to guard knowledge passed down from Ancient Egypt'.[49] Since the 1780s, as French and English involvement in Egypt grew, there was an acceleration in the uses of Egyptian symbols and architectural motifs in Masonic Lodges whilst the origin myth of the movement took on an increasingly Hermetic tone. Woodman, Westcott and Mathers had also dabbled in Kingsford's Hermetic Society and on the edges of theosophy. Woodman, the eldest, had direct links to the French magician Eliphas Lévi, who had died in 1875. Lévi (pen-name and self-creation of the writer Alphonse Constant) was the man most responsible for generating a European revival of ritual magic in the nineteenth century, through his book *Dogme et rituel de la haute magie* (1853), a 'transcendental magic' that had its roots, so he claimed, in Egypt. Lévi had performed magical rituals in London with Edward Bulwer Lytton, novelist and occultist. Woodman had also been Supreme Magus of the Masonic sect Societas Rosicruciana in Anglia for many years. Rosicrucianism was a secret Protestant mystical society that had been built on carefully fabricated documents with baffling allegorical meanings in seventeenth-century Germany. The Rosicrucians, whose secrets centred on the truths hidden in the tomb of the allegorical figure Christian Rosencreutz, claimed to have decoded Hermetic secrets and mastered the meanings of the 'monas hieroglyphica', the magical symbol created by the Elizabethan magician John Dee that allegedly revealed the unity that ordered the world.[50] Training in the Hermetic tradition promised that the Rosicrucian 'who mastered these formulae could move up and down the ladder of creation, from terrestrial matter, through the heavens, to the angels and God.'[51] The creators of the Golden Dawn therefore followed several magical models, and all of these secret societies offered good training in obscuring their own origins.

Woodman, it was said, had discovered magical scripts amongst papers he had inherited from an associate of Lévi. Once decoded, they appeared to point to a group of powerful master magicians in Germany. Woodman contacted their representative and was given permission to set up the Hermetic Order of the Golden Dawn in England. These documents were obviously faked to establish a supernal authority that could not be challenged. Just like Madame Blavatsky's Mahatmas, then, the Order had its own hidden masters, called the Secret Chiefs, whom only the leaders could contact and which gave the group strict hierarchy. The prospect of access to a secret world promises, as the sociologist Georg Simmel observed, an 'enormous extension of life': 'Secrecy secures ... the possibility of a second world alongside of the obvious world.'[52]

The name of the Order invoked Egypt twice, in its reference to Hermes and to the sacred rays of the rising sun, embodying the power of sun-god Ra. The first temple in London was called the Isis-Urania Temple, located in rooms in Fitzroy Street (it later moved to Blythe Road). As the movement grew an Osiris Temple appeared in Weston-super-Mare, a Horus Temple in Bradford, and an Amen-Ra Temple in Edinburgh (where a full-scale neo-pharaonic Masonic meeting hall, the Supreme Grand Lodge Royal Arch and Chapter of Scotland, with friezes depicting Isis and Osiris, also opened on Queen Street in 1901, suggesting a concentration of interest in the city). The room for rituals and initiation at the Isis-Urania Temple was evidently arranged with a melange of astrological, Kabbalistic, Rosicrucian and magical signs, but there was also a veil behind the altar where the goddesses Isis and Nephthys were placed. Some rituals involved a tearing of this veil, or symbolic unveilings and reveilings of the goddess. The figure of Thoth-Hermes also featured prominently. This was not mere decoration: ancient mysteries were rituals meant to bring the very gods down to earth in their idols.

As Francis King observes, 'The motivating power ... in all magical operations is the trained will of the magician.'[53] The Order was therefore insistent that it refused 'any persons accustomed to submit themselves as Mediums to the Experiments of Hypnotism, Mesmerism, or Spiritualism; or who habitually allow themselves to fall into a completely passive condition of will.'[54] This emphasized their distance from the passivity of automatists, spiritualists or inspired mystics. Instead, they asserted that their focus was the active training and projection of will. They learnt to exercise this will, but always under the threat of a greater Will that could punish serious transgressions of secrecy or heresy.

The Order took initiates through ten progressive stages of magical knowledge, one revelation leading to the next, the levels based on the Kabbalistic tree of knowledge. Those who joined began as a Neophyte in the 'Outer Order'. They were given a lecture on the 'official history' of the Golden Dawn composed by Westcott, and instructed that they had joined a society dedicated to 'the principles of Occult Science and the Magic of Hermes'.[55] Westcott appealed to the 'revival of mysticism', but saw this as 'but a new development of the vastly older wisdom of the Qabalistic Rabbis, and of that very ancient secret knowledge, the Magic of the Egyptians'.[56] After several stages which were essentially crammers in the Hermetic tradition, initiates who made it to the Inner Order were called Adepts and could begin exercises in practical magic. Here, the learning of active magical powers was promised. This introduction to ceremonial magic involved, amongst other things, learning that 'to WILL is the key to the kingdom' and how the concentration of will was a 'terrific labour' that could be elevated to levels of awesome power.[57] Adepts were trained in the invocation of spiritual entities, good and bad, and in storing curative or punitive energies in talismans. The last three stages, beyond the Second Order, took these adepts into the realm of the Magus and (highest stage) Ipsissimus, on a level with the Secret Chiefs. One effectively needed to transcend puny human limits before arriving at these heights. Very few would make it.

The content of the rituals were meant to be closely guarded secrets, although Aleister Crowley disdainfully started publishing them in 1909, declaring them (rather richly it must be said) 'verbose and pretentious nonsense'.[58] In the first ritual, the Neophyte was sworn to secrecy, kneeling:

> He then swears to observe the above under the awful penalty of submitting 'myself to a deadly and hostile current of will set in motion by the chiefs of the order, by which I should fall slain or paralysed without visible weapon, as if blasted by the lightning flash!' As the candidate affirmeth his own penalty should he prove a traitor to the Order, the evil triad riseth up in menace, and the avenger of the Gods, Horus, layeth the blade of his sword on the point of the D'aäth junction (i.e. of the brain with the spine).[59]

This solemn oath was pronounced when bound up in a rope, 'like the mummified form of Osiris'.[60] The evil eye, the Eye of Horus, and the prospect of punitive, projective curses, were all swept into this heady brew formulated around rituals of coming into light that were probably based on versions of the Eleusinian Mysteries recreated in Freemasonry.

The language of Egyptian magic and gods was never far away in the Golden Dawn because Samuel and Moina Mathers dominated the Order. Woodman died in 1891 and Westcott, already warned by his civil service bosses that his occult activities interfered with his role as coroner, entirely resigned from the Order in 1897. Samuel Mathers was a deeply eccentric man, instructed, so he claimed, by the Secret Chiefs to move to Paris in 1892 where he directed affairs in London with a disdainful and autocratic hand. In Paris, he claimed Scottish aristocratic descent and took to wearing Highland regalia, marching around in a kilt and calling himself Comte Macgregor of Glenstrae. This self-fashioning was entirely consistent with a faith in the magical assertion of will. In 1890, he married Mina Bergson, the sister of the philosopher Henri Bergson, whom he had met in the Egyptian Rooms of the British Museum. Mina, now the mystical Moina, had studied art at the Slade with Annie Horniman. The couple were financially supported by Annie, the wealthy granddaughter of the Horniman tea importers, the family that had opened the Horniman Museum in south London, where Mathers was briefly the curator. The Egyptian portion of the collection had been substantially built up in the 1890s. Annie Horniman's money presumably also helped the Golden Dawn to keep afloat; Macgregor angrily expelled her from the Order when she stopped paying his bills in 1896.

In Paris, in the Rue Mozart, Samuel and Moina Mathers established a Temple of Isis, where they became Hierophant Rameses and High Priestess Anari. This venture received some publicity in 1899, when they performed 'The Rites of Isis' as paid, public performances. Comtesse Macgregor explained to a reporter rather transfixed by this 'dreamy' woman: 'we are possessed of certain traditional, occult knowledge. We have many traditional truths which are unknown nowadays, except to a very few people. But this hidden knowledge we can only impart to those who consent to be initiated.'[61] In these performances, Isis worship seemed to relax into vague feminine Nature-worship, the ladies of the 'fashionable Parisian audience' throwing flowers, whilst Priestess Anari claimed that 'Woman is the magician born of Nature by reason of her great natural sensibility.'[62] Membership of the Hermetic Order of the Golden Dawn had been predominantly women (Masonic lodges and other magical orders barred women), so this was a strategic shift of marketing.

For some, Moina Mathers was not the dreamy figure of a benign Isiac cult ritual, however. In 1930, the novelist and sensitive Dion Fortune (pen-name of Violet Evans) published *Psychic Self-Defence*, a manual for protection from magical attacks. It began with a record of Fortune's own experience in 1919 of suffering psychic terrorism at the hands of the unnamed Moina Mathers, by then head of a subsequent Golden Dawn magical order. Fortune detailed the exercise of a crushing mesmeric power that 'left me with shattered health' for three years, and stated: 'I am convinced that hypnotic methods are very largely used in Black Magic, and that telepathic suggestion is the key to a large proportion of its phenomena.'[63] Although she managed to escape with her life from this mesmeric attack, 'all the time,' she recorded, 'I was obsessed by the fear that this strange force, which had been applied to me so effectually, would be applied again.'[64] Part of the persecution had involved being menaced by slime and by black cats, including a terrifyingly large beast that she assumed was a projected negative 'thought-form' that manifested on her stairs. Since Fortune believed that 'we live in the midst of invisible forces whose effects alone we perceive', she was a firm believer in the mummy's curse too.[65] When Carter and Carnarvon opened Tutankhamun's tomb, 'I said to myself "If the mummy's curse does not work in this case, I shall lose my faith in occultism." We all know how it has worked.'[66] Ten years later, Fortune accused Moina Mathers of the psychic murder of an initiate, Netta Fornario, who had been found dead in mysterious circumstances amongst ruins on the island of Iona, her body discovered naked beneath her cloak, a cross scored into the ground, perhaps part of some magical ritual.

Oddly for a book that demonstrates such extreme paranoia, Fortune's sensational account is full of eminently sensible warnings that 'we have to be sure that the person who complains of a psychic assault is not hearing the reverberation of his own dissociated complexes.'[67] This awareness reflected her training in psychology. At the time of her initiation into the occult group Alpha et Omega in 1919, she was also an analyst at the pioneering Medico-Psychological Clinic in Bloomsbury. In these early years, psychoanalysis and the occult were frequently coupled, technical concepts like transference introduced by Freud bearing the trace of spooky mesmeric rapport and other supernatural resonances.[68]

Another influential woman in the Hermetic Order of the Golden Dawn was Florence Farr, who eventually rose to become its Chief Adept. Farr was an actress at the heart of the controversial New Drama of the 1890s, playing Rebecca in the first English production of Henrik Ibsen's *Rosmersholm*. Part of the bohemian settlement in Bedford Park, she had an affair with George Bernard Shaw, who wrote the part of Louka in *Arms and the Man* for her. She was also very close to Yeats, and appeared in his plays in Dublin at the Abbey Theatre. Ezra Pound recalled her 'Strange spars of knowledge' in 'Portrait d'une femme' in 1912.[69] It was perhaps her taste for the theatrical element of magical ritual that pushed her occult interests towards an explicit adoption of Egyptian magic. She also used this to cross-pollenate an interest in new assertions of female sexuality in Ibsenite drama with occult mythology. With Olivia Shakespear, she wrote and performed in two 'Egyptian' plays, *The Beloved of Hathor* and *The Shrine of the Golden Hawk*. As Yeats described them, these were 'less plays than fragments of a ritual – the ritual of a beautiful forgotten worship…Copied or imitated from old Egyptian poems' and enunciated 'as one thinks the Egyptian priestesses must have spoken them', the plays were performed in striking poses against a plain backcloth, like a living frieze.[70]

There was occult theory behind this practice. In 1896, Farr published *Egyptian Magic*, part of William Westcott's multivolume *Collectanea Hermetica*. She typically claimed that behind the exoteric public religion of Ancient Egypt was an esoteric magic for an elite, an Isiac cult that included powerful women such as Queen Hatshepsut. To train in this tradition was to train the will to exercise immense powers: 'a great part of Egyptian Magic lay in a species of Hypnotism, called by later magicians, Enchantment, Fascination, and so forth.'[71] Beyond these vulgar skills, however, lay another order of magical practice that focused on the 'Shining Body', the *ka* or spirit or 'real Ego' that could be trained to transcend the limits of the physical body and travel on the astral plane. She set up a group within the Golden Dawn to explore this practice. Farr's investigations seemed essentially benign, but the idea of astral projection seemed to become continually mixed up in dark and paranoid versions of Egyptian magic. Her book spoke of becoming 'Osirified', an esoteric reading of the Book of the Dead suggesting that the *ka* could re-enter 'mummified form to seek and to save that which was lost'.[72] Others spoke of black magic emerging from sacred books as a product of Egypt's long decline until 'sunk very low indeed'.[73] This secret order within the Order, a fragmentation of authority and collective focus, was eventually to lead to Farr's expulsion from the Golden Dawn. As the movement shifted its focus increasingly towards Western Hermeticism and the Christian mystical tradition, Yeats came to regard Farr's Eastern interests as unhelpful, the Egyptological focus disrupting the exercise of the Order's 'group mind'. Farr shifted closer to the orientalism of the Theosophical Society and eventually moved to Ceylon to teach, following Annie Besant away from London and beyond the colonial frontier.

If the Golden Dawn has survived at all in cultural memory, it is largely because the development of the poetry of W. B. Yeats is incomprehensible without grasping his extensive participation in the occult movement. Yeats's occultism has long been marginalized as embarrassing or irrelevant, but scholarship on his investment in theosophy, ritual magic, spiritualism and psychical research now grasps them as unavoidably interwoven with his poetry and cultural nationalism.[74] Yeats had first encountered the exoticism of the occult when the Hindu theosophist Mohini Chatterjee visited Dublin in 1885. By the end of the year, Yeats was leading the Dublin Hermetic Society. He read Sinnett's *The Occult World* and met Blavatsky in London in 1887, joining the newly established Esoteric Section of the Theosophical Society. In the late 1880s, he also recounted that he had experienced visions of past lives or what he took to be 'symbolical histories' of race memory during incantations spoken by Samuel and Moina Mathers.[75] In March 1890 he was initiated into the Hermetic Order of the Golden Dawn, where he would eventually hold the post of Instructor in Mystical Philosophy. By this point, Yeats was already becoming interested in the notion that magic and poetry shared an access to a 'great mind and great memory [that] can be evoked by symbols'.[76] This took on a racial aspect, too, Yeats believing that these symbols could be evoked and shaped into inspiring Irish national myths, thus linking his fascination with Celtic folklore, superstition and the incantation of symbolical poetry to the elite world of ceremonial magic. Yeats became close to Samuel Mathers because they shared this Celtic interest. As Yeats explained in his *Autobiographies*, 'I planned a mystical Order' centred on Castle Rock near Roscommon, which would 'buy or hire the castle, and keep it as a place where its members could retire for a while for contemplation, and where we might establish mysteries like those of Eleusis and Samothrace'.[77] Throughout the 1890s, Yeats visited Mathers in Paris to work on establishing distinct rituals for this Celtic Mystical Order that would help establish 'an Irish literature which, though made by many minds, would seem the work of a single mind, and turn our places of beauty or legendary association into holy symbols'.[78] The project was never realized.

With this focus, however, Yeats was increasingly uncomfortable with orientalist elements of theosophy and with Florence Farr's fascination with Egypt. These confused the racial underpinnings of the magical and poetic symbol. He also objected to factions or groups within the Golden Dawn because they undermined his firm belief that a coherent, disciplined and hierarchical order was in fact 'an Actual Being, an organic life' that, collectively, amplified their magical power. 'Ancient unity' was for Yeats better than 'anarchic diversity'.[79]

Yeats, then, resisted the Egyptian turn and professed no interest in it. Nevertheless, in 1900, as the Golden Dawn began to disintegrate into factions, he became involved in a battle of magical energies over the soul of the movement with the young turk of the group, Aleister Crowley. Crowley had been initiated in 1898, at the age of 21, following a spiritual crisis that had led him to read A. E. Waite's *Book of Black Magic and of Pacts*. Crowley became a firm believer in the powers invested in magical orders with access to Hermetic secrets. An heir to a large fortune that he burned through within ten years largely on magical pursuits, Crowley progressed rapidly through the levels of the Outer Order, hungry for the practical magic of the Inner Order. He was refused leave to progress to Adeptus Minor stage, however, deemed 'unsuitable' by Florence Farr. Crowley was already notorious for his collection of verse, *White Stains*, published by the Decadent and pornographer Leonard Smithers. Scandals gathered around his treatment of his mistresses, and the rumours of bisexual magical practices undertaken in his Chancery Lane rooms had allegedly reached the ears of the police in an era of homosexual panic in the wake of the imprisonment of Oscar Wilde. Crowley was already 'a person of unspeakable life'.[80]

Incensed at his rejection, Crowley travelled to Paris and appealed to Samuel Mathers to overrule London. This was excellent timing, since Mathers had recently been made the subject of a committee investigation established by Farr to investigate the authenticity of the cipher scripts that had established the Golden Dawn in 1887. The founding fraud was about to be exposed. Mathers had already warned the rebels in London 'that I shall formulate my request to the Highest Chiefs for the Punitive Current to be prepared' if they did not disband this inquiry, although 'nobody seemed a penny the worse' for these hostile astral attacks, as Crowley laconically noted.[81] Instead, Mathers sent Crowley as his envoy to take back physically the Isis-Urania Temple, now controlled by Yeats and Farr. Crowley was warned that dangerous magical current would be aimed at him. On the April night that he ventured to Blythe Road in London, Crowley believed that he saw evidence of these magical attacks everywhere: when he tried to hire a cab, several horses bolted. Once in a cab, the cab-lamps caught fire and had to be doused, but not before his own coat caught alight. Fire elementals were being invoked to impede him. 'I was very badly obsessed' by rival magicians, he claimed.[82] He arrived at the doors of the temple in a kilt, wearing the mask of Osiris and, with a hired ruffian, tried to gain entry. Yeats considered this young emissary simply insane. Over the next few days Farr and Yeats saw him off with the rather mundane agency of a policeman and the threat of legal proceedings. Meanwhile, in Paris, Mathers tried to curse his rivals using sympathetic magic aimed at some dried peas that represented his enemies in the Golden Dawn.

This comical Battle of Blythe Road presaged the end of the Golden Dawn. Its true end came with a farcical trial which, salaciously reported in the tabloid press, subjected the secret rituals and paltry rivalries of these magicians to public ridicule. In autumn 1901, police raided 99 Gower Street, headquarters of the Order of Theocratic Unity, a movement headed by Theo and Laura Horos, the magical monikers of a couple of swindlers called Frank and Editha Jackson. This husband and wife team had already tricked an American widow out of a fortune and been imprisoned. In Paris, Madame Horos had bamboozled Samuel Mathers and had stolen many secret documents detailing the rituals of the Hermetic Order of the Golden Dawn, a name the Jacksons began to use for their own fake magical organizations. They tried to set up in South Africa, but had to leave rather sharpish. The Gower Street operation back in London had a darker purpose. Frank Jackson was put on trial for the rape of a 16-year-old girl, Daisy Adams, who had been persuaded that an initiation rite involving mutual masturbation and then intercourse were part of a communion with God. This was one of several teenage initiates found by placing small ads in newspapers. The court was read documents, lifted entirely from Golden Dawn initiation rituals, that warned of 'hostile currents' that would kill transgressors. There was some talk that the young girl witnesses could be controlled across the courtroom by the powerful mesmeric glares of Theo or Laura. Worryingly, Samuel Mathers was mentioned in court proceedings. At the end of the trial, Frank Jackson was sentenced to fifteen years in jail.[83] The reputation of the Hermetic Order was fatally damaged, even in press more likely to be sympathetic to supernatural beliefs. One correspondent to the spiritualist journal *Light* asked why Mathers had not punished the Jacksons with his alleged command of punitive magical powers. Mathers responded, rather ingeniously, that:

> Had an occult current then been sent against them, it would have only caused them to exchange the well-merited living death of penal servitude for the comforts of the penal infirmary; and had they been slain by the same means, they would have become dangerous entities on the astral plane.[84]

Yeats had already resigned by the time this material appeared in the press and was involved in establishing a new magical order, Stella Matutina. He soon largely abandoned ceremonial magic and shifted his attention to the séance table and to revelations generated by automatic writing, both of which practising magicians were meant to forgo. After 1909, Yeats began an extensive dialogue, through various mediums and his own subliminal consciousness, with a spirit who took the name Leo Africanus. After many years of emphasizing Celticism and racial unity of the group mind in the Golden Dawn, Yeats's alter ego at the séance table was a Muslim slave from North Africa, who had been captured by Venetian pirates and taken to Italy where he had published *A Geographical History of Africa Written in Arabicke and Italian* in 1600. John Leo was a historical figure, but this version was the product of orientalist fantasy, an imaginary construct rather disarmingly acknowledged by Yeats himself. In his 'dialogue' with Leo Africanus, both sides of which were composed by Yeats, the poet understood the spirit as a symbolic anti-Self, who was asking him to work by imagining through the absolute other: 'You were my opposite. By association with one another we should each become more complete.'[85] At the end of their exchange, after extensive descriptions of 'the sand, & many Arab cities', Yeats still told Leo 'I am not convinced that in this letter there is one sentence that has come from beyond my own imagination.'[86] It was a commonplace for mediums to mark the otherness of spirits called to the table by stark racial differences or gender inversions. For Yeats, who always raised imagination above reason, Leo Africanus was a half-knowing subconscious construct, created from the imagistic rubble of theosophy and the orientalist leanings of the Golden Dawn. Farr's heretical Egyptology perhaps got to him after all.

For Yeats's rather more material alter ego, Aleister Crowley, Egypt soon became an actual destination in his magical self-fashioning. The Egyptian pantheon had always swirled through Crowley's poetry and magical practice, although he had criticized the Golden Dawn for their mishmash of deities, 'a kind of buffoonish carnival of Gods which in the sane can only provoke laughter'.[87] Crowley seemed most indebted to the 'Enochian' magic pursued by the Elizabethan magus John Dee in his angelic conversations, and Dee was one of the leading Hermetic scholars. In 1901, Crowley published the verse collection, *The Soul of Osiris*, and he wintered in Cairo in 1902, returning again the following year, where he honeymooned with Rose Kelly. Crowley claimed to have hired the King's Chamber in the Great Pyramid for one night to consecrate the wedding magically, reading invocations to the gods. During the ritual, 'The King's Chamber was aglow as if with the brightest tropical moonlight', he later claimed.[88] It was on this visit, in more sedate rooms hired opposite the Cairo Museum, that Rose began to receive automatic messages in trance states. Initially from Horus, these modulated into a different control called Aiwass, an angel, who dictated to Rose the text that would form the basis of Crowley's 'thelemic' magic, *The Book of Law*. The exercise and extension of the will remained absolutely central to Crowley's practice. Unsure about the authenticity of the messages, Crowley tested Rose by asking her to identify Horus amongst the artefacts of the Cairo Museum. She pointed correctly at a small stele that also happened to be catalogue item 666, the allegorical Number of the Antichrist in the Revelation of St John and long Crowley's transgressive point of self-identification. A few years later, with the poet and initiate Victor Neuberg, Crowley travelled into the desert in Algeria to conduct a sequence of rituals and conjurations. These involved intense sexual acts that helped conjure demonic forces, Neuberg or Crowley sometimes 'hosting' these beings.[89] This 'sexual illuminism' would increasingly form part of Crowley's magical organization, Ordo Templi Orientis, and his notorious Abbey of Thelema, where the physical and sexual degradation of his initiates earned Crowley the epithet of 'the wickedest man in the world' in the 1920s.

It is hard to grasp Crowley's place in the Edwardian imagination. He was a comical and eccentric figure, working hard on his invisibility spells in the Café Royal, staging his mad 'Rites of Eleusis' in a public hall in 1910, and appearing in scandalous gossip over unpaid bills and debased mistresses. *Equinox* caught him up in a preposterous court action over the ownership of secrets that the judge ultimately deemed worthless. Arnold Bennett called him the Mahatma in *Paris Nights*, a man 'wearing a heavily jewelled waistcoat and the largest ring I ever saw on a human hand...Without any preface he began to talk supernaturally.'[90] He appears in many memoirs of the time and his exploits amongst London Decadent and Modernist circles could fill many pages, a mythology that has been further encouraged since the 1960s counter-cultural revival of interest in Crowley.[91] He drifts through Anthony Powell's autobiographical novel sequence of London life, *A Dance to the Music of Time*, as Doctor

Trelawney. In *The Kindly Ones*, Trelawney booms out magical epigrams ('The Essence of the Will is the Godhead of the True'), but is also cherished as a genuine English eccentric: 'What will happen to people like him as the world plods on to standardisation?' someone mournfully asks.[92] Powell's deep conservatism embraced Crowley's resistance to modern democracy in a novel sequence held together by the idea of occulted patterns of meaning and 'secret harmonies'.

Yet Crowley also seemed to generate genuine fear in some. Crowley believed that his investigations into black magic meant that his 'house in London became charged with such an aura of evil that it was scarcely safe to visit it...Weird and terrible figures were often seen moving about his rooms, and in several cases workmen and visitors were struck senseless by a kind of paralysis and by fainting fits.'[93] Many were prepared to give credence to these dark associations. He was certainly a sexual terrorist, and the damage he inflicted on his many partners was decidedly unfunny. His release of secret documents and open discussion of magical practice seemed to energize the Gothic imagination of the period. Algernon Blackwood, who would have directly encountered Crowley during his time in the Golden Dawn, dramatized Crowley's magical researches in Chancery Lane in his short story 'Smith: An Episode in a Lodging House'. The portrait of Smith by a terrified neighbour begins, of course, with his searing eyes, 'a sinister light in them that lent to the whole face an aspect almost alarming. Moreover, they were the most luminous optics I think I have ever seen in a human being.'[94] Smith, it transpires, has been conducting magical practices based on occult researches and found the '"words of Power", which, when uttered with the vehemence of a strong will behind them, were supposed to produce physical results'.[95] These conjure invisible forces of immense power that the narrator can only sense. Crowley, too, lurks somewhere behind the demonic figure of Karswell in M. R. James's short story about practical curses, 'Casting the Runes'.[96] In the serial stories about the psychic detective Carnacki, published by William Hope Hodgson in *The Idler* in 1910, the talk of black magic rituals in the ugly technical prose of psychical research, and the use of electric pentangles to fend off demonic intrusions, owe much to the then ongoing release of Golden Dawn materials by Crowley in *Equinox*.[97] Crowley is also depicted as the dastardly mesmeric Magus Oliver Haddo in Somerset Maugham's *The Magician* (1908). Maugham had encountered Crowley in Paris in 1903, where he took an 'immediate dislike to him' yet was greatly entertained by his talk. 'He had fine eyes,' Maugham recalled, 'and a way, whether natural or acquired I do not know, of so focusing them that, when he looked at you, he seemed to look behind you. He was a fake, but not entirely a fake.'[98] This feeds into the portrait of Haddo as a vengeful sexual terrorist, who uses his mesmeric stare as vehicle for a limitless demonic energy to first capture, then morally corrupt and finally physically destroy a helpless flower of

English innocence, Margaret Dauncey. Haddo grows into an appalling corpulent creature, bulging with perverse desires and a secret plan to conjure homunculi into obscene life. The attempt to fend off his magical powers is aided by a student of the occult, Dr Porhoët, now retired from a life principally spent in Egypt and who is thus steeped in supernatural lore. Margaret dies but England is avenged when Haddo goes up in a conflagration at his country house. Crowley was inevitably delighted by this libellous portrait, and added Oliver Haddo to his many pseudonyms.

Crowley became fixed in popular culture at his most demonic in Dennis Wheatley's *The Devil Rides Out* (1934). He appears as the sinister diabolist Mocata, memorably described as 'a pot-bellied, bald-headed person of about sixty with large, protuberant, fishy eyes, limp hands, and a most unattractive lip. He reminded me of a large white slug.'[99] A mesmeric tug of war, a battle of white and black magic, takes place in the unlikely settings of Mayfair and St John's Wood, Mocata's devilry consistently located in hypnotic eyes that 'stripped and flayed' anyone caught by them, 'threatening a thousand unspeakable abominations'.[100] The black magicians of Charles Williams's novels *War in Heaven* (1930) and *All Hallow's Eve* (1945), oozing menace and exercising a demonic will over those with weak Christian faith, also owe much to the reputation of Crowley. Williams knew this subculture, having joined a version of the Golden Dawn in 1917, although he was a pious Christian mystic rather than a magician. In his study *Witchcraft*, he documented 'that perverted way of the soul which we call magic, or (on a lower level) witchcraft', in which 'malefical wizards' attempt to direct the Supernatural Will.[101] His novels convey a genuine metaphysical dread of the potential catastrophic rifts black magic might produce in the order of the world, as dark forces plot Armageddon in dusty backstreets of Holborn.

Although a semi-comic figure, then, the very public persona of Crowley as magus, master adept of Hermetic or Egyptian rites and black magic, fed into an atmosphere in which the notion of the curse was not just something attached to unruly objects in museums but was also a form of the punitive current being actively used in the bohemian underworlds of London. Crowley's ambiguous status, a self-proclaimed Antichrist simultaneously mocked and feared, was perfectly at one with the ambivalence of mummy curse rumours.

## Magical thinking and curse logic

How are we to read this late Victorian magical revival and its insistent Egyptological tinge? One could simply dismiss this subculture, as Frances Yates did, as a 'bottomless bog' of obfuscation that 'deservedly sinks below the notice of the serious historian'.[102] Many of its adherent's intellectual contemporaries felt the same, viewing belief in magic as evidence of the superstitious survival of primitive thought. The armchair anthropologist J. G. Frazer, author of *The Golden Bough*, an important evolutionary synthesis of primitive mythology, published a second edition in 1900 with a long preface and additional chapters that systematically divided magic from religion: 'Magic, as representing a lower intellectual stratum, has probably everywhere preceded religion.'[103] Magic was 'a spurious system of natural law', a misunderstanding of causation that produced 'a false science' and an 'abortive art'.[104] Religion, in contrast, was 'a propitiation or conciliation of powers superior to man which are believed to direct and control the course of nature and human life'.[105] It was therefore a system of order, structure and natural law, and as such marked a sophisticated intellectual advance.

Frazer went on to categorize the various forms of primitive magic, the theoretical pseudo-science of magic informing the practical pseudo-arts of positive magic (sorcery) and negative magic (taboo). In his view, the essence underlying the whole system was based on sympathy, the mistaken assumption that 'things act on each other at a distance through a secret sympathy, the impulse being transmitted from one to the other by means of what we may conceive as a kind of invisible ether.'[106] Sympathetic magic worked on the law of similarity in which like could affect like from afar. This explained homoeopathy and imitative magical rites. Contagious magic, on the other hand, worked metonymically, operating on a part to affect the whole, such as witches using hairs or fingernails for nefarious ends. A logic and system were discernible in this practice, but operated on an entirely fallacious premise. Proper understanding of natural laws ought to abolish magic. It was a measure of the arrested and degenerate state of contemporary Egypt that the modern population, particularly the fellaheen, continued to be dominated by superstitious fears left unchanged across millennia. Edward William Lane's *An Account of the Manners and Customs of the Modern Egyptians* (1836), read as an authoritative guide to the country by generations of English travellers, devoted two lengthy chapters to Egyptian superstition. Later, these beliefs were what anthropological fieldwork in Egypt on jinns, afreets and ghouls or on spirit possession continued to attest.[107]

Frazer's view, built on Edward Tylor's theory of superstitious survivals, was highly influential. Yet recognized scholars of Ancient Egypt, like Ernest Wallis Budge, struggled to fit their particular archaeological evidence to this evolutionary schema, because in Egypt magic and religion seemed to be entirely intertwined throughout the history of their civilization. In his 1899 book *Egyptian Magic*, Wallis Budge explored magical beliefs of the Ancient Egyptians as typical of 'most early nations'.[108] These involved the extensive use of magical actions at a distance, protective amulets and projective ritual utterances that aimed at 'destroying their enemies by the recital of a few words possessed of magical power'.[109] There was also a much degraded peasant version of these beliefs. He confessed that these elements of Ancient Egyptian culture looked 'savage', whilst Egyptian religion was 'beautiful', 'noble' and 'sublime', yet had to acknowledge that primitive, 'pre-Dynastic' magic continued to be practised rather than being superseded.[110] The French Egyptologist Alexandre Moret had similar difficulties. 'Magic gave an unstable character to that Egyptian religion which proclaimed under other circumstances so lofty a moral ideal,' he said, before concluding that 'Ancient Egypt reveals, notwithstanding her very advanced civilisation, a mental state that, in some respects, was still on a level with savage peoples.'[111]

This continuity of magic rather frustratingly lent support to counterclaims that the practice was in fact the trace of a lost Hermetic wisdom, purer the earlier one went. Wallis Budge's translations and commentaries were constantly cited by occultists like Florence Farr, and thus fed supernatural interpretations of museum objects. In fact, Frazer had been forced into a second edition to clarify the proper sequence of magic and religion by the growing conviction of the rival anthropologist Andrew Lang that evidence from savage tribes proved not only that abstract theological ideas arrived very early, but also that magical practices were not at all superstitions since they were being objectively 'proved' by the new science of psychical research. We have already encountered Lang as a close ally of Rider Haggard in the romance revival, conservative politics and tendency towards supernatural belief. Lang contested Frazer's theories in august journals and published his counter-argument *Magic and Religion* in 1901. It left Frazer concluding bitterly that belief in the 'efficacy of magic' was still maintained by 'the dull, the weak, the ignorant, and the superstitious, who constitute, unfortunately, the vast majority of mankind'. For Frazer, superstition seemed to reach up through the cracks, for all the world like an undead thing restless in a tomb: 'We seem to move on a thin crust which may at any moment be rent by the subterranean forces slumbering below.'[112]

When it comes to the broad spectrum of occult beliefs at the end of the nineteenth century, historians have largely stopped just dismissing them, or ascribing them to personal biographical foibles, and have instead begun to ask questions about the cultural work they achieved for the minority who so passionately invested in them. There is a view that the heterodox theologies of the late Victorian period were specific compromise formations, pressured into odd and provisional shapes between the collapsing foundations of the Established Church – exposed to the rigours of historical criticism and cultural comparativism – and the growing cultural authority of science. In Max Weber's famous formulation, the advance of rationalization 'means that principally there are no mysterious incalculable forces that come into play, but rather that one can, in principle, master all things by calculation. This means that the world is disenchanted.'[113] However, the common thesis that modernity means progressive secularization throughout the nineteenth century has been put under some pressure.[114] Certainly, many forms of late Victorian occultism set about re-enchanting the world, taking account of the changed conditions of belief to adopt very heterodox modes of expression. Re-enchantment becomes a way of rebinding onself affectively to a world otherwise emptied out of meaning.[115]

Spiritualists had often been driven out of the punitive forms of Christianity espoused by evangelicals, yet were still motivated by a genuine terror of purely materialistic conceptions of life. They pointed to the séance as offering empirical, scientific evidence of an ultramundane world, where spirit survived the transient bruteness of matter. Theosophy and Hermeticism presented a synthesis that outflanked both orthodox religion and science by embedding them in longer trajectories that diminished the claims of modern scepticism. This stance was 'proved' by biological, anthropological and comparativist methodologies. In a different way, Alex Owen has suggested that the magicians of the Golden Dawn were involved in producing an internal critique of narrow conceptions of rationality, 'a re-working of the idea of reason through a radical engagement with self-consciousness as a necessary route to an interiorised encounter with the divine'.[116] Magical explorations of the self can thus be seen in parallel with, but using a different language from, new investigations of the subconsciousness or subliminal mind in researches into hypnotism or in therapeutics such as psychoanalysis.

Psychical researchers, meanwhile, exploited the vanishing points in contemporary energy physics or dynamic psychology to suggest that instances of 'supernatural' communication and strange influences at a distance were merely operating in realms that normal science would shortly reach and confirm. Beyond these small circles, Simon During has suggested that this era was marked by the growth of mass appeal for 'secular magic', forms of popular culture that left the supernatural hovering uncertainly between entertainment and the full force of the old convictions. Modern secular magic is a fuzzy set, with unclear boundaries. It might include literature, 'because both stood outside the dominant regimes of utility and rationality' and relied on the suspension of disbelief.[117] It certainly included the circuits of rumour and gossip that housed the simultaneously menacing yet comical figures like Aleister Crowley or the curse stories that circled around the Priestess of Amen-Ra.

Magical thinking was once meant to be located in the mind of savages only, and then as a developmental phase of cognition in children. More recent psychological research has acknowledged that magical thinking, that 'general set of invisible, insensible forces that can cause illness, death, disaster and social effects might constitute a cognitive domain with its own relevant set of rules and principles'. This is a framework that has 'stubbornly resisted the aggressive expansion of modern science' because it provides some useful, adaptive functions, particularly as a means of dealing with loss, grief and death.[118]

Yet all of these rationalizations are rather paradoxical, ultimately. They are hard at work searching for interpretations of precisely those beliefs that escape reason. The jargon of secularization, disenchantment and re-enchantment can sometimes make you lose sight of how simply bug-out crazy many of the beliefs of the inner circle of secret societies like the Hermetic Order of the Golden Dawn were. These beliefs, as Thomas Laqueur gently reminds us, might have been formed under the peculiar pressures of modernity, but were often distinctly anti-modern.[119] Perhaps it is exactly what is *out* of control that could take us to another level of insight.

## Closing in: The evil eye looks back

When Thomas Douglas Murray's blood was turned to ice by the gaze of the Priest-ess of Amen-Ra, many lines of magical thinking converged and were powerfully reinforced. In mythology, the Eye of Horus guards and punishes the covetous. The gaze of the Medusa petrifies those who look upon her face. Animistic belief holds that the case would be the locus for the astral double of the priestess or the invisible elementals that guard it. Occult revivalists would insist that the case was an ancient coffin, made for an initiate of an esoteric elite. It might well be sur-rounded by forgotten magical powers, able to act at a distance, across space and time. If the lost magic of the Egyptians could be revived, might punitive currents of negative energy be blasted at enemies, even down to the present day, as the war-ring magicians of the Golden Dawn and the melodrama of Gothic fiction seemed to prove? Douglas Murray's spiritualist convictions would have further enhanced these associations, since objects and places could hold the psychic residues of the departed, although we might infer from his oddly playful relationship with British Museum catalogue number 22542, revealed in the minutes of the Ghost Club, that he also understood the ambiguous pleasures of 'secular magic'.

But perhaps what binds all of these levels together, and ensures their reinforcement is something that escapes these contextualizations. Belief in a nefarious curse strongly suggests a structure of paranoia. In a paranoid world, enemies orchestrate actions undetectably and seem to possess supernatural knowledge and power that everywhere threatens disaster. Borders have been systematically overrun; infiltration by foreign bodies is always already well ad-vanced. The paranoiac interprets the world as a place shot through with malign influences and occult forces. In persecutory delusions, the condition is struc-tured by a belief in patients 'that someone, or some organization, or some force or power, is trying to harm them in some way; to damage their reputation, to cause them bodily injury, to drive them mad or bring about their death.'[120] These are not chaotic views: if anything, paranoid thinking is over-coherent, with no space left for the arbitrary or accidental. Everything shines with hidden meaning; everything is magically connected.[121]

Paranoia is classically understood as a form of psychic defence that works by projecting subjective states onto the objective world. This is how Freud defined the core mechanism: 'An internal perception is suppressed, and, instead, its content, after undergoing certain kinds of distortion, enters consciousness in the form of an external perception.' In short, 'What was abolished internally returns from without', often in exaggerated or monstrous form.[122] Freud later discussed this structure in relation to the evil eye. In his essay 'The Uncanny', an anecdote about a neurotic patient who believed he had cursed a man and caused his death leads in to a discussion of a dread of the evil eye. 'There never seems to have been any doubt about the source of this dread', Freud argues. 'Whoever possesses something that is at once valuable and fragile is afraid of other people's envy, in so far as he projects on to them the envy he would have felt in their place.'[123] This is a structure confirmed in later anthropology, where the evil eye is seen as a cycle of charm and counter-charm, where a 'gaze or suspected gaze' is met with the 'gazee's raising of a protection, and thereby the deflection of the gazer (or his power) from seizure, expropriation, or destruction'.[124] In this account, there is something inherently reversible about the evil eye: what was subjective or interior is now objective or exterior; where you were is now where I stand.

The Surrealist Roger Caillois, in his eccentric study of the power of hypnotic eye-like patterns and the fear they inspire, grasped this essential reversibility, which he claimed was shared by many species:

> Almost everywhere we see in man this tenacious, almost ineradicable, fear of the eye whose gaze paralyses, roots him to the spot, suddenly deprives him of thought, movement and will. He is afraid of finding himself in front of this circular device, which can bring unconsciousness or death, which can kill or turn to stone. He is terrified of it, but at the same time tries to use this instrument of terror so as to be master of it in his turn.[125]

'The evil eye,' Caillois argued,

> projects bad luck, it carries a curse. One must fly from its baleful regard and protect oneself from it by a suitable counter-magic. The best way is to turn it against itself and to interpose between the adversary and oneself the same fearful power of an eye charged with the same evil influence.[126]

This seizing and reversal of the evil eye is embedded in many myths, such as the slaying of the Medusa by Perseus. Perseus avoids the direct gaze of the monster by using a mirror, beheads the creature, then allows Athena to incorporate the gorgon's gaze by placing the Medusa head on her own shield and using it to petrify her enemies. The logic of reversal explains the wide use of the Gorgoneion, a stone image of the gorgon head, which was used as an apotropaic device in Greek culture, placed at doorways and thresholds to ward off danger. Exactly the same idea operated with the protective Eye of Horus in Ancient Egypt. 'The exercise of fascination always meets and provokes its prophylactic,' Steven Connor has observed, 'the mask, talisman, shield or screen...both absorbs and averts the consuming eye' – and also tries to assume the power of the other's gaze, always at the risk of a reversal of fortune.[127]

This logic of projection and persecutory return in malign, amplified forms captures something about the way the occultists of the late Victorian and Edwardian revival in magic always tottered on the brink of losing their alleged mastery of will to a greater force that could threaten annihilation with punitive currents of murderously directed willpower. This fear, articulated within a very specific occult language and framework of belief, could also be read as a version of a wider anxiety about the reversibility often ascribed to hypnotic rapport. Men of science always distrusted mesmeric phenomena, even after its respectable conversion into hypnotism. The spooky inversions between the hypnotist and hypnotized, a confusing collapse of distinction between subject and object typical of trance states, wreaked havoc with scientific protocols. Enchantment, fascination or magic is all about losing boundaries. Even someone as far out on the fringes of orthodox medicine as the Viennese doctor Sigmund Freud always claimed he only found the proper method of psychoanalysis once he abandoned hypnosis.[128]

What does this odd set of reversals associated with the evil eye help to reveal about the mummy's curse? It is that all those magic Horus talismans and the eyes painted on Egyptian objects are not there to curse, but to protect. They are trying to ward off what is, through projection, your own envious and acquisitive gaze. In this reading, what is looking back at you, as a Victorian or Edwardian gentleman, is the malignancy of your own desire and the violence you are prepared to commit to satisfy that desire. The hand that Thomas Douglas Murray stretched out to take the mummy case from Arab traders in Luxor was shattered by his own bullet. Walter Ingram's involvement in the slaughter of Zulus at the Battle of Ulundi or in his relentless firing into the ranks of Mahdist forces at Abu Klea and on the Nile five years later was what made the eyes on the coffin of Nesmin shine, reflecting the fervour of his own violent acts of domination and acquisition. The evil eye is the supernatural supplement, an uncanny revenge on colonial power. In the end, reversing the trajectory, the evil eye is the colonial gaze that defeats all those protective hexes and turns ancient objects into modern artefacts for private collections and museums, part of the intrinsic expropriation of surplus value that drives imperialism. What was it that cursed these men, Thomas Douglas Murray, Walter Herbert Ingram, the Fifth Earl of Carnarvon? Their own desire. They were caught in the beams of their own covetous gaze.

But I wonder too if there isn't something that ultimately escapes this hermeneutic interpretation of the mummy's curse. It is possible to conceive of another order of paranoia that exceeds this loop of subjective projection and return. The science fiction writer Philip K. Dick once observed: 'The ultimate paranoia is not when everyone is against you, it's when *everything* is against you. Instead of "My boss is plotting against me", it would be "My boss's phone is plotting against me." '[129] This continues the thoughts of the Gothic writer M. R. James in his essay 'The Menace of Inanimate Objects'. Some thinkers have lately begun to address the sparky, independent life of objects beyond the control of human subjects. Steven Connor has devoted himself to the study of every day magical objects, things 'that we allow and expect to do things back to us' in a rather wondrous way.[130] With more menace, Jean Baudrillard has observed that 'We have always lived off the splendour of the subject and the poverty of the object', but then asks: 'Who has ever sensed the foreboding of the particular and sovereign potency of the object?'[131] Where Baudrillard conceived of a 'revenge of the object', a simple ironic inversion of the binary, others have looked to an 'object-oriented philosophy' where objects are actors that deserve to be given a conception of their own complex agency.[132] Jane Bennett has proposed an analysis of the *thing-power* of 'vibrant matter', proclaiming that things are 'vivid entities not entirely reducible to the contexts in which human subjects set them, never entirely exhausted by their semiotics'.[133] Graham Harman wishes to dethrone anthropocentric readings of the object world, to move well beyond the 'typical, futile half-measure of saying that the human subject is not all-powerful but meets with resistance from the world'.[134]

Maybe, then, the curse of the mummy is actually a record of the refusal of objects to obey subjects, a mark of their lively but unfathomable agency, in the way I have suggested that these antiquities refuse to stabilize into artefacts. Oddly enough, then, object-oriented thought might end up, philosophically at least, concurring with the possibility that some objects might, after all, be out to curse some subjects. In this sense, curses become the record of objectal acts of dethronement. Now *that*, as they say, really would be magic.

# Afterword

T HE AR-RABI AL-ARABIYY, the Arab Spring or Awakening, began in
Tunisia with the self-immolation of Mohamed Bouazizi on 17 December
2010. In January 2011, it spread to Egypt. After eighteen days of mass protests in
Tahir Square, the thirty-year rule of Hosni Mubarak came to an end amidst
delirious celebratory scenes. Mubarak resigned on 11 February 2011; he was
subsequently arrested and brought to trial. Throughout 2011, however, the revolutionaries struggled repeatedly with entrenched counter-revolutionary
forces in Egypt and beyond. The Mubarak regime was replaced by the Supreme
Council of the Armed Forces (SCAF), headed by Field Marshal Muhammed
Hussein Tantawi, meant to be a transitional ruling council of twenty army officials. The army was initially praised by protestors for swinging behind the
revolution, but SCAF increasingly used 'security concerns' to try to suppress
dissent, and imprisoned thousands of people through military courts. At the
time of writing, elections have been held but a democratic outcome hangs in
the balance.[1]

The early reaction of the British and American governments to the Arab
Spring was notably ambivalent, swaying often hour by hour between support
for democracy and concern at the overnight erasure of the West's long-term
geopolitical strategy in the region. Mubarak's regime, a repressive one-party
rule using 'emergency' powers to suppress opposition, was supported by successive Western European and American governments. Egypt's brutal intelligence services are thought to have been used for 'extraordinary rendition', to
torture suspects on behalf of America in the wake of 9/11.

In the midst of the nightly occupations of Tahir Square by protestors, the Cairo Museum was broken into at the end of January 2011 by a small group, and looted of a number of objects from the collection. Several cases were smashed and about fifty items, including a gilded statuette of Tutankhamun, were stolen. There was also the news that two mummies had been ripped apart, their heads wrenched off and bones scattered. A rumour circulated that these might be Yuya and Tuya, Tutankhamun's great-grandparents, among the best-preserved and most scientifically valuable mummies in the collection (this proved to be untrue). Web-page news reports and bloggers from the community of Egyptologists were horrified, perhaps anticipating the scale of looting of museums that accompanied the invasion of Iraq by American forces in 2003. The obsession was with documenting the damage and gathering catalogue numbers of the missing artefacts.

As some of the objects were recovered over the next few weeks, there was open suspicion of, and contempt for, Zahi Hawass, then Minister of Antiquities, and rumours that it was all an 'inside job'.[2] The stereotype of the untrustworthy Arab was barely suppressed in some of these accounts. 'What is surprising,' the museologist Christina Riggs commented, 'is the response from the academic community, which has focused on objects rather than politics, as if the two can be separated. "Heartbreaking", "a catastrophe", "shameful", laments the blogosphere – but with little mention of protests or people.'[3] There was little comment, either, on just how emblematic one of the looted items was: a gilded bronze and wooden trumpet from the tomb of Tutankhamun. When it was recovered in April 2011, undamaged, Nervine al-Aref reported that the trumpet was claimed by one curator at the Museum to have magical powers: 'According to [Hala] Hassan, whenever someone blows into it a war occurs. A week before the revolution, during a documenting and photographing process, one of the museum's staff had blown into it and a week after revolution broke out. The same thing had happened before the 1967 war and prior to the 1991 gulf war.'[4]

The point of this book has been to argue that if we pay attention to superstitions about artefacts – the stories that exceed the mere documentation of antiquities – they often possess meaningful political and historical traces. In this case, the story of the trumpet recalls the way in which the discovery of the tomb of Tutankhamun was inextricably intertwined with national liberation in 1922. As Elliott Colla has observed: 'It is impossible to overestimate the degree to which the discovery of King Tutankhamun's tomb changed everything about how Egyptian national elites looked at their past.'[5] The place of Tutankhamun in national consciousness was still significant in the 2011 Arab Spring.

My study has aimed to unpick the knot of stories of the mummy's curse in order to unravel significant strands of the West's relationship with the Middle East. The mummy's curse has been pushed to the margins of legitimate

Egyptology as a mess of falsehood, misinterpretation and superstition. Serious scholars in the field still mostly consider that such stories should only be dismissed. Consequently, this journey to uncover the lost history buried behind the sensational discovery of Tutankhamun, the stories of Thomas Douglas Murray and Walter Ingram, has forced me to look askance at the record of what survives of the wisps of the rumours about these men. I have fished in the uncatalogued annual tomes of letters to the British Museum, deciphered thousands of pages of handwritten minutes of the Ghost Club, felt a little queasy rifling through old departmental papers in dusty filing cabinets in the basement of the Institute of Archaeology, seen a square of mummy wrapping slide out of old 'Mummy' Pettigrew's papers onto the table in front of me in the Wellcome Institute and listened to the family stories that resonate down the generations in the inheritors of Walter Ingram's legacy. This has been an exploration of what marginal knowledge institutions might hold, unknown to themselves, strange stories that can only be gathered from the gaps between the zeros and ones of computerized catalogues and other systems of formalized knowledge. Perhaps all this effort has recovered just a marginal history at best, a footnote. Some historians fear that the focus on the more eccentric passages of British history has ended up returning to 'parochial antiquarianism'.[6] But I think that such micro-histories can also operate as telling symptoms of much greater shifts in culture.

As the nineteenth century progressed, the consequences of imperial occupation blackened the blood of the English body politic. The belief that Empire was a benign exercise in enlightenment, carried on the saintly wings of abolitionism, democracy and Christian charity, had increasingly to confront the murderous logic of colonial expropriation. From the widest historical perspective, it seems likely that the Indian Mutiny of 1857 was the major cultural turning point, not just because it showed the extent of violent resistance to the benign narrative that the British had told themselves about Empire, but also because it unleashed a virtually uncontrollable frenzy of revenge amongst the British command in India. Whilst the atrocities of the mutineers were exaggerated and endlessly recycled by the hysterical British press, the suppression also revealed that the British too could indulge in acts of depravity and give themselves up to the unholy frenzy of 'exterminating vengeance'.[7] The violent suppression and exorbitant acts of revenge against the rebels in the Jamaican uprising in 1865 was another source of horror and controversy. By the 1880s, the military suppression of the Urabi revolt and the British occupation of Egypt led to a similar circulation of real and phantasmal narratives of atrocity between colonized and colonizer. Once the specific details of each instance of the mummy's curse are unravelled, they reveal themselves as cogent narratives of the intrinsic violence of colonialism. It leads to this structural principle: wherever there is imperial occupation, there is a reserve of supernaturalism, an occult supplement to allegedly enlightened rule that becomes a currency for acknowledging and even negotiating the consequences of this colonial violence.

This legacy is still not over, given the structural inequalities built into the geopolitical condition of the Middle East. In 2009, Rabab El-Mahdi and Philip Marfleet reported that Egypt was buckling under the pressure of nearly thirty years of Hosni Mubarak's oppressive State of Emergency. Fifteen million people in Egypt were estimated to be living on less than $2 a day, with forty per cent of the urban population living in slums. During Mubarak's regime, social inequality increased, with a parallel world of privilege existing for those in the political elite and the military-industrial complex. For El-Mahdi and Marfleet, the problem resided in the harsh economic policies demanded by the International Monetary Fund since the 1970s, which had turned Egypt into a 'laboratory for neoliberalism'.[8] Super-power realpolitik cynically ensured support for Mubarak's corrupt and oppressive but stable government. The region had gone through formal decolonization but, as Perry Anderson has observed, this 'has been accompanied by a virtually uninterrupted sequence of imperial wars and interventions in the post-colonial period.'[9]

To my now oddly attuned ears, the initial hesitancy of Barack Obama and the British Foreign Secretary William Hague over the revolt of the Egyptian people in the early days of the Arab Spring sounded like the shuffling of something undead through Western policy. It was an uncanny return of all those troubled Victorian reflections of imperial powers over 'the Egyptian Question', musings from lofty heights on the undifferentiated and unruly multitudes of the Middle East. Yet contemporary popular culture in the West continues to be stuffed with figures of the undead, with vindictive ghosts, post-apocalyptic zombies, feral vampires and shuffling mummies. Each of these has its own highly specific set of historical origins and allegorical resonances, but all are a trace, I would argue, of a history of violence that returns to haunt modernity's idealist aims. Unravel the mummy and what we finally encounter is the agony that travels as a secret sharer within modernity.

# NOTES

## Chapter 1

1. Howard Carter and A. C. Mace, *The Tomb of Tut-Ankh-Amen, Discovered by the Late Earl of Carnarvon and Howard Carter*, 3 vols (1923–33; New York: Cooper Square, 1963), I, 86.
2. Carter and Mace, *Tomb,* I, 90.
3. Carter and Mace, *Tomb,* I, 95–6. Carnarvon's more prosaic version of this exchange appeared in *The Times* of London: 'Well, what is it?' 'There are some marvellous objects here.' 'The Egyptian Treasure. Story of the Discovery. A Graphic Account by Lord Carnarvon', *The Times* (11 Dec 1922), 13. This is also the version of the exchange in the typewritten account preserved in the British Museum archive AES Ar.347.
4. Carter and Mace, *Tomb* I, 99.
5. Carter and Mace, *Tomb* I, 97–8.
6. 'An Egyptian Treasure', *The Times* (30 Nov 1922), 13.
7. 'Cairo Outrages: A Grave Situation', *The Times* (20 Nov 1922), 11.
8. 'A Marvellous Discovery', *The Times* (30 Nov 1922), 13.
9. Alan Gardiner, 'The Egyptian Treasure. Importance of the Find', *The Times* (4 Dec 1922), 7.
10. Elliott Colla, *Conflicted Antiquities: Egyptology, Egyptomania, Egyptian Modernity* (Durham, NC: Duke University Press, 2007), 177.
11. 'Tutankhamen's Tomb. Treasures in Peril', *Morning Post* (12 Jan 1923), 9.
12. 'Luxor Tomb and Publicity. Lord Carnarvon's Attitude to the Press', *Morning Post* (15 Jan 1923), 6.
13. Cited H. V. F. Winstone, *Howard Carter and the Discovery of the Tomb of Tutankhamun* (London: Constable, 1991), 180.
14. 'The Luxor Find', *The Times* (15 Jan 23), 11.
15. *Illustrated London News* (10 Feb 1923), 196–7.
16. Headline, *Morning Post* (22 Jan 1923), 7.
17. 'The Lighter Side at Luxor', *Morning Post* (19 Jan 1923), 7 and 8.
18. Letter P. Kyticas (1 Feb 1923), British Museum, *Correspondence.*
19. Carter and Mace, *Tomb,* I, 186.
20. Marie Corelli, 'Pharaoh Guarded by Poisons', *Daily Express* (24 March 1923), 5.
21. Letter Marie Corelli to Wallis Budge (8 April 1923), British Museum, Budge Correspondence File, E: Miscellaneous, Department of Ancient Egypt and Sudan,

AES Ar.603. The letter included an unsourced newspaper cutting, 'British Museum Officials Reply to Miss Corelli.'

22. 'Lord Carnarvon's Last Hours', *Daily Express* (6 April 1923), 1.
23. H. V. Morton, 'The Tragedy of Lord Carnarvon', *Daily Express* (6 April 1923), 4.
24. 'Egyptian Collectors in a Panic', *Daily Express* (7 April 1923), 1.
25. Letter, H. Dallas to Wallis Budge (7 May 1923), BM *Correspondence*, 1923.
26. Memo, H. H. [H. R. Hall] to Wallis Budge (7 April 1923), BM *Correspondence*, 1923.
27. 'A Great Egyptologist', *Morning Post* (6 April 1923), 6
28. *Morning Post* cited Christopher Frayling, *The Face of Tutankhamun* (London: Faber, 1992), 46.
29. 'The Hand of the Pharaohs. French Occultists Comment', *Morning Post* (6 April 1923), 7.
30. Algernon Blackwood, 'Superstition and the Magic "Curse"', *Daily Express* (9 April 1923), 6.
31. 'The Talk of Magic. Sir Rider Haggard Condemns it as Nonsense', *Morning Post* (7 April 1923), 7.
32. 'King Tutankhamen. Reburial in the Great Pyramid. Sir Rider Haggard's Plan', *The Times* (13 Feb 1923), 13.
33. Ernest Crawley, *Oath, Curse, and Blessing and Other Studies in Origins* (London: Watts, 1934), 12.
34. 'Mr Howard Carter's Return to Luxor', *The Times* (16 April 1923), 11.
35. Arthur Weigall, *Tutankhamen, and Other Essays* (New York: George Doran, 1924), 89. It has been suggested that Weigall made this comment to his fellow reporter H. V. Morton.
36. Weigall, *Tutankhamen*, 157.
37. Weigall, *Tutankhamen*, 140.
38. Weigall, *Tutankhamen*, 151.
39. Weigall, *Tutankhamen*, 144.
40. These images are discussed in Jay Winter, *Sites of Memory, Sites of Mourning: The Great War in European Cultural History* (Cambridge: Cambridge University Press, 1995).
41. Weigall, *Tutankhamen*, 145.
42. Weigall, 'The Ghosts of the Valley of the Tombs of the Queens', *Pall Mall Magazine* (June 1912), 766.
43. Cited Julie Hankey, *A Passion for Egypt: Arthur Weigall, Tutankhamun and the 'Curse of the Pharaohs'* (London: I. B. Taurus, 2001), 138.
44. Weigall, *Tutankhamen*, 317.
45. Hans-Joachim Neubauer, *The Rumour: A Cultural History*, trans. C. Brown (London: Free Association Books, 1999), 2.
46. Neubauer, *Rumour*, 21.
47. Neubauer, *Rumour*, 22.
48. Charles Breasted, *Pioneer to the Past: The Story of James Henry Breasted, Archaeologist, Told by his Son* (1943; Chicago: University of Chicago Press, 1977), 342–3. Weigall also reports this rumour at the beginning his essay 'The Malevolence of Ancient Egyptian Spirits', only to undercut the existence of curses, *Tutankhamen*, 136.
49. Philipp Vandenberg, *The Curse of the Pharaohs*, trans. T. Weyr (London: Hodder & Stoughton, 1975), 20.

50. Henry Field, *The Track of Man: Adventures of an Anthropologist* (London: Peter Davies, 1955), 43.

51. See [Sixth] Earl of Carnarvon, *No Regrets* (London: Weidenfeld & Nicolson, 1976), 127.

52. Sir Archibald Reid's obituary appeared in the *British Medical Journal* (26 Jan 1924), with no mention of Tutankhamun.

53. Obituary of Lord Westbury, *The Times* (22 Feb 1930), 17.

54. 'Suicide of Lord Westbury: Fall From Bedroom Window', *The Times* (22 Feb 1930), 4.

55. Report cited Barry Wynne, *Behind the Mask of Tutankhamen* (London: Corgi, 1972), 169. For the reliability of this account, see comments below.

56. 'News in Brief', *The Times* (26 Feb 1930), 30.

57. *Daily Express* (3 and 4 Jan 1934).

58. Gerald O'Farrell, *The Tutankhamun Deception: The True Story of the Mummy's Curse* (London: Sidgwick and Jackson, 2001).

59. Reported in Simon Cox and Susan Davies, 'Curses', *An A to Z of Ancient Egypt* (Edinburgh: Mainstream, 2006), 70.

60. Anne Campbell, 'Is Boy, 3, Latest King Tut Victim?', *Metro* (19 June 2006), unpaginated cutting.

61. Cheiro, *Cheiro's Memoirs: The Reminiscences of a Society Palmist* (London: William Rider, 1912), 15.

62. Cheiro, cited Wynne, *Behind the Mask*, 79.

63. Velma, the Seer, *My Mysteries and my Story: A Book on Palmistry* (London: John Long, 1929), 97 and 98.

64. Carnarvon, *No Regrets*, 128.

65. Carnarvon, *No Regrets*, 128.

66. Antonia Lant, 'The Curse of the Pharaoh, or How Cinema Contracted Egyptomania', *October* 59 (1992), 103. Her earliest citation of a trick film reanimating a mummy is *The Haunted Curiosity Shop* (dir. Walter Booth, 1901).

67. John Balderston, 'Tutankhamen's Royal Gems Dazzle Explorers', *The World* (13 Nov 1923), 1–2.

68. The cycle included *The Mummy's Hand* (dir. Christy Labanne, 1940), *The Mummy's Tomb* (dir. Harold Young, 1942), *The Mummy's Ghost* (dir. Reginald LeBorg, 1944) and *The Mummy's Curse* (dir. Leslie Goodwin, 1944).

69. See, for instance, the commentary in Michael Brunas, John Brunas and Tom Weaver, *Universal Horrors: The Studio's Classic Films, 1931–46* (London: McFarland, 1990).

70. Evelyn Waugh, *Labels: A Mediterranean Journey* (Harmondsworth: Penguin, 1985), 88.

71. Salima Ikram and Aidan Dodson, *The Mummy in Ancient Egypt: Equipping the Dead for Eternity* (London: Thames & Hudson, 1998), 72.

72. Charlotte Booth, *The Curse of the Mummy and Other Ancient Mysteries of Egypt* (Oxford: Oneworld, 2009), 187.

73. Margaret A. Murray, 'Curses', *The Splendour that was Egypt: A General Survey of Egyptian Culture and Civilization* (London: Sidgwick & Jackson, 1949), 218.

74. Katarina Nordh, *Aspects of Ancient Egyptian Curses and Blessings: Conceptual Background and Transmission* (Uppsala: Uppsala University Press, 1996), 31 and 3.

75. Booth, *Curse of the Mummy,* 201.

76. Carter Lupton, ' "Mummymania" for the Masses: Is Egyptology Cursed by the Mummy's Curse?', in S. MacDonald and M. Rice (eds), *Consuming Ancient Egypt* (London: UCL Press, 2003), 38.

77. Lupton, 'Mummymania', 44.

78. Frank Holt, 'Egyptomania: Have we Cursed the Pharaohs?', *Archaeology* (March–April 1986), 62.

79. Mark R. Nelson, 'The Mummy's Curse: Historical Cohort Study', *British Medical Journal* 325 (2002), 1482.

80. Carol Nemeroff and Paul Rozin, 'The Makings of the Magical Mind: The Nature and Function of Sympathetic Magical Thinking', in K. Rosengren et al. (eds), *Imagining the Impossible: Magical, Scientific, and Religious Thinking in Children* (Cambridge: Cambridge University Press, 2000), 5.

81. Nemeroff and Rozin, 'Makings of the Magical Mind', 25.

82. Carter and Mace, *Tomb,* I, 141.

83. Breasted, *Pioneer to the Past,* 345.

84. Jasmine Day, *The Mummy's Curse: Mummymania in the English Speaking World* (London: Routledge, 2006), 56 and 92.

85. Day, *Mummy's Curse,* 65–6.

86. Freud, 'The Uncanny', *Art and Literature,* Penguin Freud Library vol. 14 (Harmondsworth: Penguin, 1985), 365.

87. Julia Kristeva, *Powers of Horror: An Essay in Abjection,* trans. L. Roudiez (New York: Columbia University Press, 1984), 4.

88. Nicholas Daly, 'That Obscure Object of Desire: Victorian Commodity Culture and Fictions of the Mummy', *Novel* 28/1 (1994), 27.

89. See, for instance, Franco Moretti, 'The Dialectic of Fear', in *Signs Taken for Wonders: Essays in the Sociology of Literary Forms* (London: Verso, 1983). For zombies, see my discussion in 'Public Sphere, Counter-Publics and the Zombie Apocalypse', in D. Glover and S. McCracken (eds), *The Cambridge Companion to Popular Fiction* (Cambridge: Cambridge University Press, 2012).

90. Winifred Burghclere, 'Biographical Sketch of the Late Lord Carnarvon', in Carter and Mace, *Tomb,* I.

91. Charles R. Beard, *Lucks and Talismans: A Chapter of Popular Superstition* (London: Sampson and Low, 1934), 99.

92. Beard, *Lucks,* xvi.

93. Edward Lovett, 'The Folk Lore of London', *Journal of the London Society* 23 (1920), 8–12.

94. J. G. Lockhart, *Curses, Lucks and Talismans* (London: Geoffrey Bles, 1938), 41.

95. Crawley, *Oath, Curse, and Blessing,* 38.

96. 'Sale of the Hope Diamond', *The Times* (25 June 1909), 5.

97. 'Sale of Hope Diamond', 5.

98. Richard Kurin, *Hope Diamond: The Legendary History of a Cursed Gem* (New York: HarperCollins, 2006), 15.

99. For background, see Paul Young, '"Carbon, Mere Carbon": The Kohinoor, the Crystal Palace, and the Mission to Make Sense of British India', *Nineteenth-Century Contexts* 29/4 (2007), 343–58.

100. Thorstein Veblen, *The Theory of the Leisure Class* (1899; New York: Dover, 1994), 79.

101. Veblen, *Leisure Class*, 46.

102. Veblen, *Leisure Class*, 171 and 177.

## Chapter 2

1. 'The "Ghost" Anyone May See at the British Museum', *Illustrated London News* (26 Feb 1927), 342–3.

2. 'Mummies at the Museum. Egyptian Gallery Changes', *The Times* (28 March 1921), 11.

3. 'The Unlucky Mummy', single-page British Museum Information Sheet (1995).

4. Letter, Bertram Fletcher Robinson to Wallis Budge (undated), British Museum, *Correspondence,* 1904.

5. Bertram Fletcher Robinson, 'A Priestess of Death,' *Daily Express* (3 June 1904), 1.

6. 'Priestess, Dead Centuries Ago, Still Potent to Slay and Afflict', *Atlanta Constitution* (20 June 1904).

7. Archibald Marshall, *Out and About: Random Reminiscences* (London: John Murray, 1933), 6.

8. Douglas Sladen, *Twenty Years of my Life* (London: Constable, 1915), 274.

9. Sladen, *Twenty Years,* 275.

10. See, for instance, his South African tale, 'A True Ghost Story', *Daily Express* (18 April 1904), 4.

11. A complete bibliography is included in Brian W. Pugh and Paul Spiring, *Bertram Fletcher Robinson: A Footnote to the Hound of the Baskervilles* (London: MX Publishing, 2008), 193–221. Biographical details can also be accessed at www.bfronline.biz, a site dedicated to Robinson.

12. G. St. Russell, 'The Mysterious Mummy', *Pearson's Magazine* 28 ( July–Dec 1909), 163.

13. The report was in the *San Francisco Examiner,* 15 August 1909. A clipping was sent to the British Museum by A. Edwards, who called the story 'hardly credible', yet still requested a photograph of the mummy case. BM *Correspondence,* 1909.

14. Details in this paragraph derive from Pugh and Spiring, *Bertram Fletcher Robinson.*

15. Arthur Conan Doyle, *The Hound of the Baskervilles* (1902; Harmondsworth: Penguin, 1981), 6. The first British edition read: 'My Dear Robinson, it was to your account of a West-Country legend that this tale owes its inception.' Some claim that Robinson's role in the writing was more substantial than this. Indeed, Rodger Garrick-Steele charged in *The House of the Baskervilles* (2003) that Doyle engineered the murder of Robinson, supplying Robinson's wife, Gladys, with poison, in order to conceal both his dependence on Robinson's ideas and his affair with Gladys. Pugh and Spiring's biography of Robinson was written as a riposte to this

theory. In 2006, Paul Spiring and some of Bertram Fletcher Robinson's descendants petitioned the diocese of Exeter for an exhumation of the body to disprove death by poisoning.

16. Doyle, *Hound*, 126.
17. 'Lot No. 249' appeared first in *Harper's Monthly Magazine* in September 1894 and then in *Round the Red Lamp*. It is reprinted in *Late Victorian Gothic Tales*, ed. R. Luckhurst (Oxford: Oxford World's Classics, 2005), 109–40.
18. 'Sir A. Conan Doyle's Theory. "Elementals"', *Daily Express* (7 April 1923), 1.
19. 'Fear of a Curse. Relics Showered on the British Museum', *Daily Express* (7 April 1923), 1.
20. Robinson, 'A Priestess of Death', 1.
21. Russell, 'Mysterious Mummy', 163–4.
22. Robinson, 'A Priestess of Death', 1.
23. Ada Goodrich-Freer, 'The Priestess of Amen-Ra: A Study in Coincidences', *Occult Review* 17 (Jan 1913), 11.
24. Biographical details, mixed with much speculation and venomous character assassination, are in Trevor Hall, *The Strange Story of Ada Goodrich Freer* (London: Duckworth, 1980). The book was part of Hall's feud with the Society for Psychical Research, so is unreliable.
25. Goodrich-Freer, 'The Priestess', 14.
26. Goodrich-Freer, 'The Priestess', 14.
27. Goodrich-Freer, 'The Priestess', 16.
28. Goodrich-Freer, 'The Priestess', 16.
29. J. G. Lockhart, 'The Fatal Mummy Case', in *Curses, Lucks and Talismans* (London: Geoffrey Bles, 1938), 179.
30. Goodrich-Freer, 'The Priestess', 16.
31. Winifred Gordon, FRGS, was an expert on the Balkans, writing several books. In one, she recalls the story of a séance held by W. T. Stead in early 1903 with the medium Mrs Burchell, who predicted the murder of the Serbian king three months later. She also took great interest in peasant superstitions. These might suggest a certain openness to stories about mummy curses. See *A Woman in the Balkans* (London: Hutchinson, 1916), 50–2.
32. Horace Leaf, letter to editor, *Occult Review* (March 1909), 170.
33. Elliott O'Donnell, *Haunted Houses of London* (London: Eveleigh Nash, 1909), 88.
34. O'Donnell, *Haunted Houses*, 92.
35. O'Donnell, *Haunted Houses*, 92.
36. O'Donnell, *Haunted Houses*, 94.
37. O'Donnell, *Haunted Houses*, 95.
38. Cheiro, *True Ghost Stories* (London: London Publishing Co., n.d. [date-stamped by BM, 1928]), 48.
39. Cheiro, *True Ghost Stories*, 48.
40. Cheiro, *True Ghost Stories*, 52.
41. Cheiro, *True Ghost Stories*, 54.
42. H. Rider Haggard, *The Days of my Life: An Autobiography*, 2 vols (London: Longmans, 1926), II, 32.

43. See entry in *Alumni Oxonienses, 1715–1886* (Oxford: Parker, 1888), IV, 1534.

44. Montague Summers, *Witchcraft and Black Magic* (New York: Dover, 2000), 109.

45. Summers, *Witchcraft*, 110.

46. Letter Elizabeth Bowen to Wallis Budge (1 December 1909), BM *Correspondence,* 1909.

47. Letter SPG to Wallis Budge (27 November 1909), BM *Correspondence,* 1909.

48. 'Comments on the Paragraphs' (5 March 1909), Budge Correspondence Files, 1906–13, copy number 5754, British Museum Department of Ancient Egypt and Sudan. Wallis Budge's responses to correspondents are on thin carbon copy paper. This page is damaged and the name of his respondent, Lady B----, is unreadable.

49. Letter L. W. King to Miss G. Tysen (5 October 1909), Budge Correspondence Files, 1906–13.

50. George Digby, telegram to Wallis Budge (18 March 1909), BM *Correspondence,* 1909.

51. Memo from *Al-Muktataf* to Wallis Budge (20 November 1909), BM *Correspondence,* 1909.

52. Letter Ernest Brain to Wallis Budge (28 Sept 1909), BM *Correspondence,* 1909.

53. Wallis Budge, 'Response to Ernest Brain' (30 September 1909), Budge Correspondence Files, 1906–13, British Museum Department of Ancient Egypt and Sudan Archive.

54. Ernest A. Wallis Budge, *By Nile and Tigris: A Narrative of Journeys in Egypt and Mesopotamia on Behalf of the British Museum between the Years 1886 and 1913,* 2 vols (London: Murray, 1920), II, 391.

55. Wallis Budge, *By Nile and Tigris,* 392.

56. J. G. Lockhart, citing Wallis Budge, *Curses, Lucks and Talismans,* 178. He claims this is from a *Sunday Times* article in 1934, but I have been unable to locate this source.

57. The Countess de Contardone was at the heart of the establishment, the sister of the imperial soldier and diplomat Sir Edward Durand. Mrs Gerald Wellesley was the widow of the Dean of Windsor, one of Queen Victoria's most trusted advisors. Lady Hunter might well have been the widow of Sir William Hunter, eminent civil servant in India and a historian of the subcontinent. Mrs Patrick Campbell, the actress, had been made famous by her appearance in Pinero's *The Second Mrs Tanqueray* in 1893.

58. Letter Thomas Douglas Murray to Wallis Budge (23 August 1900), BM *Correspondence,* 1900.

59. Letter Thomas Douglas Murray to Wallis Budge (7 November 1900), BM *Correspondence,* 1900.

60. Letter W. T. Stead to Wallis Budge (5 March 1909), BM *Correspondence,* 1909.

61. W. T. Stead, 'Ghost of Mummy Haunts the British Museum', *San Francisco Examiner* (15 Aug 1909), in BM *Correspondence,* 1909, filed under the sender, A. Edwards.

62. *Review of Reviews* May 1912, cited Frederick Whyte, *The Life of W. T. Stead,* 2 vols (London: Jonathan Cape, 1925), II, 315.

63. 'The Sinking of the *Titanic.* Some Notable Victims. Mr W. T. Stead's Career', *The Times* (18 April 1912), 12.

64. James Coates, *Has W. T. Stead Returned?* (London: L. N. Fowler, 1913).

65. See Grace Eckley, *Maiden Tribute: A Life of W. T. Stead* (Philadelphia: XLibris, 2007), 379ff.

66. Cited 'W. T. Stead', *Westminster Gazette* (19 April 1912), pasted entry in British Library Stead obituaries cuttings file.

67. Typewritten rebuttal in envelope marked 'Mummy Coffin of the Priestess of Amen-Ra', BM, Department of Ancient Egypt and Sudan, Department Lists 1923–56, item 97.

68. Philipp Vandenberg, *The Curse of the Pharaohs* (London: Hodder & Stoughton, 1975), 197.

69. John Richard Stephens, 'The Truth of the Mummy's Curse', in Stephens (ed.), *Into the Mummy's Tomb* (New York: Berkley Books, 2001), 11.

70. Margaret Murray, *My First Hundred Years* (London: William Kimber, 1963), 177.

71. Murray, *My First Hundred Years*, 178.

72. Lockhart, 'The Fatal Mummy Case', 173.

73. Charles Pellegrino, *Unearthing Atlantis: An Archaeological Odyssey* (New York: Vintage, 1993), 298–9.

74. See, for starters, 'The Mummy on the *Titanic*' at www.catchpenny.org/titanic.html

75. The Victoria and Albert Archive contains the full record of memos and correspondence relating to the Captain H. B. Murray Bequest. For a useful discussion of this bequest and the problems it created, see Sarah E. M. Farley, 'The Bequest of Captain H. B. Murray (1843–1910) to the Victoria and Albert Museum', MA dissertation, Courtauld Institute of Art, 2001.

76. Sir Wyndham Murray, *A Varied Life* (Winchester: Warren & Son, 1925), 130.

77. Frank died in February 1928, leaving his estate to his wife, Mina Darling Murray. Annie Mabel Murray died in January 1936 and does not appear to have married.

78. 'The Horse Show at Islington', *Land and Water* (5 June 1869), 353.

79. See reports in the *Country Gentleman*, 19 March 1881 and 13 May 1882.

80. Douglas Murray wrote to Sir William Mackinnon 'I will call for you at Burlington Hotel ... and we will go to call on Millais': letter (11 July 1890), William Mackinnon Archive, SOAS, Personal File 32. Letter Douglas Murray to James Whistler (21 Feb 1885), *The Correspondence of James Whistler*, http://www.whistler.arts.glas.ac.uk/correspondence, catalogue number M499.

81. Louise Jopling, *Twenty Years of my Life 1867–87* (London: John Lane, 1925), 205.

82. 'Court Circular', *The Times* (29 April 1890).

83. Letter Douglas Murray to Mackinnon (11 Sept 1890), William Mackinnon Archive, SOAS, Personal File 32.

84. Alfred E. Lomax, *Sir Samuel Baker: His Life and Adventures*, Splendid Lives Series (London: Sunday School Union, 1894). Thomas Douglas Murray and A. Silva White, *Sir Samuel Baker: A Memoir* (London: Macmillan, 1895).

85. See David Waller, *The Magnificent Mrs Tennant* (New Haven: Yale University Press, 2009).

86. For histories of the Society for Psychical Research, see Frank M. Turner, *Between Science and Religion: The Reaction to Scientific Naturalism in Late Victorian England* (New Haven: Yale University Press, 1974), Janet Oppenheim, *The Other World: Spiritualism and Psychical Research in England, 1850–1914* (Cambridge: Cambridge University Press, 1985), and Roger Luckhurst, *The Invention of Telepathy* (Oxford: Oxford University Press, 2002).

87. 'The Ghost Club 1882–1936', Ghost Club archive, British Library, Add MSS 52273, 2.

88. Letter Stainton Moses to C. C. Massey (2 November 1882), Ghost Club Records and Correspondence, Add MSS 52770.

89. Ghost Club rules, Ghost Club minutes, Vol I, BL Add MSS 52258, 7.

90. For the class variants of Victorian spiritualism, see Logie Barrow, *Independent Spirits: Spiritualism and English Plebeians 1850–1910* (London: Routledge, 1986).

91. 'The Ghost Club. Story of Mr Churton Collins and a Compact', *The Observer* (20 September 1908), 5. The story revealed that the recently deceased Collins was a member of a club that was awaiting a communication from his departed spirit. 'It is evidence of the interest in the occult that is taken in high quarters that the majority of the members of the Ghost Club are exceedingly well known.' The only named person in the article was an occasional guest, not a member: the explorer Henry Stanley. The story was recycled two days later as 'Messages for the Dead. Late Professor's Compact with Ghost Club', *Daily Mail* (22 September 1908), 4.

92. William Crookes, *Psychic Force and Modern Spiritualism* (London: Longmans, 1871).

93. William Crookes, 'Spirit-Forms', March 1874, reprinted in *Researches into the Phenomena of Spiritualism* (London: J. Burns, 1874), 106.

94. Unsigned letter, 'The Suez Canal', *Land and Water* (15 January 1870), 52.

95. See Trevor Mostyn, *Egypt's Belle Epoque: Cairo and the Age of the Hedonists* (London: Tauris Parke Paperbacks, 2006) for a lively account of this era.

96. Thomas Douglas Murray, 'Egypt, and a Christmas Week at Thebes', *Land and Water* (11 July 1868), 386.

97. Thomas Douglas Murray, 'A Christmas Week at Thebes I', *Land and Water* (25 July 1868), 3.

98. Lucie Duff Gordon, *Letters from Egypt* (London: Virago, 1983), 111. The letters were first published in 1865, then considerably expanded after her death in the 1875 edition.

99. Thomas Douglas Murray, 'A Christmas Week at Thebes II', *Land and Water* (1 Aug 1868), 24.

100. Thomas Douglas Murray, 'A Christmas Week at Thebes IV', *Land and Water* (22 Aug 1868), 69.

101. Douglas Murray, 'Thebes IV', 70.

102. Thomas Douglas Murray, 'The Traveller on the Nile – The Temple of Dendera', *Land and Water* (27 March 1869), 206.

103. Thomas Douglas Murray, 'On the Nile – Theban Mummies', *Land and Water* (3 April 1869), 222.

104. Douglas Murray, 'Theban Mummies', 222.

105. Douglas Murray, 'Theban Mummies', 222.

106. Thomas Douglas Murray, 'Africa an Island – The Suez Canal', *Land and Water* (17 April 1869), 251.

107. Editorial, *Land and Water* (28 November 1868), 289.

108. Ghost Club minutes, November 1894, Vol III, 38.

109. The notorious spirit communications of Sir Richard Burton had been published in Stead's occult journal *Borderland,* then being edited by Goodrich-Freer under the signature 'Miss X.' *Borderland* recorded the full story after Lady Isabel Burton

died in 1896. See Miss X, 'Some Thoughts on Automatism', *Borderland* (April 1896), 157–71.

110. Ghost Club Minutes, June 1896, Vol III, 224–5.

111. Ghost Club minutes, June 1898, Vol III, 432.

112. Ghost Club minutes, December 1902, Vol IV, 372.

113. Ghost Club minutes, March 1898, Vol III, 390.

114. Ghost Club minutes, April 1898, Vol III, 404 and 405.

115. Ghost Club minutes, July 1900, Vol IV, 86.

116. Ghost Club minutes, July 1900, Vol IV, 86 and 88.

117. Letter, Thomas Douglas Murray to Wallis Budge (14 March 1904), BM *Correspondence*, 1904.

118. Letter, Thomas Douglas Murray to Wallis Budge (14 October 1905), BM *Correspondence*, 1905.

119. Ghost Club minutes, November 1900, Vol IV, 114.

120. Ghost Club minutes, November 1900, Vol IV, 114 and 116.

121. Ghost Club minutes, June 1904, Vol V, 44.

122. Ghost Club minutes, June 1904, Vol V, 52.

123. Ghost Club minutes, July 1905, Vol V, 124.

124. Letter W. Usborne Moore to Wallis Budge (22 January 1909), asking for the Keeper's opinion about the psychic photograph. The following day, he added a note that 'I think that we have mutual friends such as Douglas Murray who will testify to you that I am as sane as most people.' Indeed, Douglas Murray wrote to Wallis Budge on 3 February 1909 to declare Moore as 'one of the soundest headed, most sensible men that ever trod a quarter deck.' By 2 March, however, Douglas Murray suggested he forget Moore's 'confounded picture', clearly embarrassed by the whole thing. BM *Correspondence*, 1909.

125. Douglas Murray reports on these séances in April 1907 and May 1908.

126. Ghost Club minutes, December 1907, Vol VI, 39.

127. Ghost Club minutes, December 1907, Vol VI, 40.

128. Ghost Club minutes, December 1907, Vol VI, 42.

129. See W. T. Stead's report, 'The Arts and Crafts of Spirit Materialisation', *Review of Reviews* (February 1909), 120–3.

130. Ghost Club minutes, June 1909, Vol VI, 400.

131. See W. T. Stead, 'Julia's Bureau: An Attempt to Bridge the Grave', *Review of Reviews*, (May 1909), 433.

132. Ghost Club minutes, June 1909, Vol VI, 400.

133. Ghost Club minutes, June 1909, Vol VI, 401.

134. Ghost Club minutes, May 1912, Vol VII, 153.

135. Ghost Club minutes, Nov 1898, Vol III, 452, and June 1897, Vol III, 322.

136. Ghost Club minutes, March 1903, Vol IV, 414.

137. Will of Thomas Douglas Murray, *CGPLA* 1912 (IV). Murray initially left £1000. In a codicil, this money was reduced to £200 owing to the collapse of the value of Douglas Murray's investments in railway stock. University College have no surviving records of the establishment of the fund and the Flinders Petrie Museum there has no surviving records of any written exchanges between Douglas Murray

and Flinders Petrie. The uncatalogued departmental papers of the Edwards Professor of Archaeology, H. S. Smith, contains a slim file titled 'Douglas Murray Scholarship', with paperwork back to 4 March 1936, when the secretary of the college wrote in a memo: 'I am afraid that under present conditions it is impossible to make an award which conforms to the will and is, at the same time, such as any candidate would wish to hold.' It did, however, survive a rocky start, and the scholarship is still awarded. I am grateful to Rachael Sparks at the Institute of Archaeology archive, UCL, for digging out this file.

138. Margaret S. Drower, *Flinders Petrie: A Life in Archaeology* (London: Gollancz, 1985), xxii.
139. See Margaret S. Drower, 'The Early Years', in T. G. H. James (ed.), *Excavating in Egypt: The Egypt Exploration Society 1882–1983* (London: British Museum, 1983), 9–36. The Egypt Exploration Society has no record of Thomas Douglas Murray being a member.
140. Jopling, *Twenty Years*, 122–3.
141. For details of Lootie, see Rumer Godden, *The Butterfly Lions: The Story of the Pekingese in History, Legend and Art* (London: Macmillan, 1977). On discussion of the notorious looting of the Palace, see James L. Hevia, 'Loot's Fate: The Economy of Plunder and the Moral Life of Objects from the Summer Palace of the Emperor of China', *History and Anthropology* 6/4 (1994), 319–45.
142. Thomas Douglas Murray, 'The Ancient Palace Dogs of China', in L. C. Smythe ('Lady Betty'), *The Pekingese: A Monograph on the Pekingese Dog: Its History and Points* (London: 'The Kennel', 1909), 5.
143. Godden, *The Butterfly Lions*, 153.
144. Thomas Douglas Murray, 'Ancient Palace Dogs', 6. The taxidermized Ah Cum now resides in the Zoological Museum at Tring, the annex of the Natural History Museum and formerly the famous private zoological collection of Walter Lionel Rothschild.
145. Harriet Ritvo, *The Animal Estate: The English and Other Creatures in the Victorian Age* (London: Penguin, 1990), 84.
146. See 'History' pages of the Pekingese Club UK, www.thepekingeseclub.co.uk/history.htm
147. Thorstein Veblen, *The Theory of the Leisure Class* (1899; New York: Dover, 1994), 86 and 80.
148. The Hon. Mrs Neville Lytton, *Toy Dogs and their Ancestors* (London: Duckworth, 1911), 248, 249 and 253.
149. 'Mr T. D. Murray', *The Times* (22 Nov 1911), 11.
150. A. Silva White, 'The Late Mr Douglas Murray', *The Times* (23 Nov 1911), 11.
151. Murray, *A Varied Life*, 159–61.
152. Murray, *A Varied Life*, 161.
153. Letter Wyndham Murray to Sir Cecil Harcourt-Smith (30 August 1910), 'Captain H. B. Murray Bequest', V&A Archive. Wyndham Murray continued to badger the V&A for the rest of his life about the bequest, causing some exasperation to section heads in the Museum.
154. Summers, *Witchcraft and Black Magic*, 109–110. Summers gives no date or source for this letter.

155. This document was probably the eight-page pamphlet, *Premature Burial, with Sir Benjamin Ward Richardson's Signs and Proofs of Death,* issued by the Association for the Prevention of Premature Burial (London: Denton-Ingham, 1908).

156. Ghost Club minutes, July 1913, Vol VIII, 250–1.

157. W. B. Yeats, 'All Souls' Night' (written 1920), *The Poems,* ed. Daniel Albright (London: Dent, 1990), 282.

## Chapter 3

1. Kipling to Haggard, undated letter 1889, in Morton Cohen (ed.), *Rudyard Kipling to Rider Haggard: The Record of a Friendship* (Rutherford: Farleigh Dickinson University Press, 1965), 28.

2. H. Rider Haggard, *The Days of my Life: An Autobiography,* 2 vols (London: Longmans, 1926), II, 32.

3. See the illustrated front pages of both papers (21 April 1888).

4. William G. Fitzgerald, 'Illustrated Interviews. No. XLVIII – Lord Charles Beresford', *Strand Magazine* (July 1896), 25–6.

5. See, for instance, 'The Mummy's Curse. A Romance of Real Life', *Hampshire Telegraph and Sussex Chronicle* (25 July 1896).

6. Ada Goodrich-Freer, 'The Priestess of Amen-Ra', 19.

7. Ghost Club minutes, June 1904, Vol V, 58.

8. Ghost Club minutes, June 1904, Vol V, 58.

9. Letter Ralph Shirley to Wallis Budge (2 July 1909), British Museum, *Correspondence,* 1909.

10. Ernest A. Wallis Budge, *Some Account of the Collection of Egyptian Antiquities in the Possession of Lady Meux of Theobalds Park, Waltham Cross* (London: Harrison, 1893), 31. Privately printed in 200 copies.

11. See Ernest A. Wallis Budge, *Some Account,* 2nd edn (London: Harrison, 1896).

12. Ronald Mott, 'Theobalds Park 1820–1951' in P. E. Rooke (ed.), *Theobalds through the Centuries: The Changing Fortunes of a Hertfordshire House and Estate* (Waltham Cross: Broxbourne Press, 1980), 14.

13. This sequence of acquisitions has been traced by John Larson, archivist at the Oriental Institute of the University of Chicago, who sent me his account written up for the International Mummy Database in 1995 by email.

14. Henry Field, *The Track of Man: Adventures of an Anthropologist* (London: Peter Davies, 1955), 43.

15. Edward Meyer email to author (23 Nov 2008).

16. Isabel Bailey, *Herbert Ingram Esq., M.P., of Boston* (Boston, Lincolnshire: Richard Key, 1996), 194. This detail is repeated in Bailey's entry for Herbert Ingram in the *Oxford Dictionary of National Biography.*

17. Maudie Ellis, *The Squire of Bentley (Mrs Cheape): Memory's Milestones in the Life of a Great Sportswoman* (London: Blackwood, 1926), 44. Mrs Cheape was Maudie Hemming, Ethelinda's eldest sister.

18. Ellis, *The Squire of Bentley,* 46.

19. Ellis, *The Squire of Bentley,* 47.

20. Susan Grace Galassi and Helen M. Burnham, 'Lady Henry Bruce Meux and Lady Archibald Campbell', in Margaret MacDonald et al. (eds), *Whistler, Women, and Fashion* (New Haven: Yale University Press, 2003), 161.

21. Biographical information derived from 'Meux Family' entry, *Oxford Dictionary of National Biography* and Virginia Surtees, *The Actress and the Brewer's Wife: Two Victorian Vignettes* (Wilby: Michael Russell, 1997).

22. Lady Meux to Whistler, letter of 1892, cited Galassi and Burnham, 'Lady Henry Bruce Meux' 178.

23. Surtees, *The Actress*, 119.

24. 'Lady Meux Dead, Rich Patron of Art', *New York Times* (22 December 1910).

25. Letter Lady Meux to Wallis Budge (8 February 1901), British Museum, Budge Correspondence File D, Department of Ancient Egypt and Sudan, AES Ar. 603.

26. Letter Lady Meux to Wallis Budge (22 November 1906), Budge Papers, British Library, Add MSS 58211.

27. After much recalculation, Lady Meux's estate was finally settled to be £862,253: probate 17 Jan 1911, *CGPLA England and Wales*.

28. See 'Meux Sale To-Day', *New York Times* (15 May 1911). On the previous day, the paper had identified an Elizabethan oak staircase and the mummy and coffin of Nes-Amsu as the most significant lots.

29. AFROMET, the Association for the Return of the Maqdala Ethiopian Treasures, was founded in 1999 to campaign for restitution of these artefacts, which were looted by British troops in 1868.

30. The estate was left to his wife Ethelinda. Probate 4 March 1889, *CPGLA England and Wales*.

31. Melton Prior, in Ron Lock and Peter Quantrill (eds), *The 1879 Zulu War, Through the Eyes of the Illustrated London News* (Kloof, South Africa: Q-Lock Publications, 2003), 179. For a history of this period, see Jeff Guy, *The Destruction of the Zulu Kingdom: The Civil War in Zululand, 1879–84* (London: Longman, 1979).

32. John Dunn is briefly sketched in *Illustrated London News* reports, see Lock and Quantrill (eds), *The 1879 Zulu War*, 91.

33. *Narrative of the Field Operations Connected with the Zulu War of 1879* (London: HMSO, 1881), 116.

34. F. E. Colenso, *History of the Zulu War* (London: Chapman & Hall, 1880), 448.

35. Citations from editorials in the *Illustrated London News* (23 Feb 1884), 170 and (26 Jan 1884), 74.

36. Melton Prior, *Campaigns of a War Correspondent* (London: Edward Arnold, 1912), 206.

37. See Case 22676, Royal Humane Society, awarded at committee meeting, 19 May 1885. The citation reads that the boat capsized in a strong current, forty yards from the shore. 'Mr Ingram first handed an oar to Mitchell and then swam ashore but on seeing Mitchell becoming exhausted, he ran down the bank, swam out again and seized hold of the drowning man, he had just strength enough to bring him ashore.' Royal Humane Society Case Book (October 1883–December 1885), London Metropolitan Archives, 4517/B/01/01/014.

38. Luisa Villa, 'The Breaking of the Square: Late Victorian Representations of Anglo-Sudanese Warfare', *Cahiers Victoriens et Edouardiens* 66 (2007), 116.

39. G. A. Henty, *The Dash for Khartoum: A Tale of the Nile Expedition* (1892; Glouces-ter: Dodo Press reprint edn, n.d.), 184.

40. Henry Newbolt, 'Vitai Lampada', *Collected Poems 1897–1907* (London: Nelson, n.d.), 132.

41. Undated cutting from *Morning Post*, 'Walter Ingram' album of cuttings, private collection.

42. Count Gleichen, *With the Camel Corps up the Nile* (London: Chapman & Hall, 1888), 120 and 137.

43. Gleichen, *With the Camel Corps*, 197.

44. For a history of the Relief, see Julian Symons, *England's Pride: The Story of the Gordon Relief Expedition* (London: Hamish Hamilton, 1965). For a trenchant mili-tary critique of the Relief, see Adrian Preston's introduction to *In Relief of Gordon: Lord Wolseley's Campaign Journal of the Khartoum Relief Expedition 1884–5* (London: Hutchinson, 1967), xiii–xliv.

45. Colonel Sir Charles W. Wilson, *From Korti to Khartum: A Journal of the Desert March from Korti to Gubat, and of the Ascent of the Nile in General Gordon's Steamers*, 4th edn (London: Blackwood, 1886), 120–1.

46. Wilson, *From Korti to Khartum*, 121.

47. Wilson, *From Korti to Khartum*, 177.

48. Charles Beresford, *The Memoirs of Admiral Lord Charles Beresford*, 2 vols (London: Methuen, 1914), II, 309–10.

49. Prior, *Campaigns*, 220.

50. Flyer for the event, held on 24 June 1885, in Walter Ingram family album.

51. Wolseley, letter of October 1884, cited Symons, *England's Pride*, 118.

52. Ritvo, *The Animal Estate*, 254.

53. Ritvo, *The Animal Estate*, 247–8.

54. James Sutherland, *The Adventures of an Elephant Hunter* (London: Macmillan, 1912), x.

55. See, for instance, 'Death of Walter Ingram', *Fishing Gazette* (14 April 1888).

56. Sir Samuel Baker, *Wild Beasts and their Ways: Reminiscences of Europe, Asia, Africa, and America*, 2 vols (London: Macmillan, 1889), I, 48–9.

57. Baker, *Wild Beasts*, I, 128.

58. Baker, *Wild Beasts*, I, 120.

59. C. V. A. Peel, *Somaliland, Being an Account of Two Expeditions into the Far Interior* (London: F. E. Robinson, 1900), 301.

60. F. L. James, *The Unknown Horn of Africa: An Exploration from Berbera to the Leopard River* (London: George Philip, 1888), vii and 7.

61. Sir Alfred E. Turner, *Sixty Years of a Soldier's Life* (London: Methuen, 1912), 88.

62. Turner, *Sixty Years*, 104.

63. Ghost Club minutes, Vol VI, April 1907 and May 1908.

64. Louisa May Alcott, 'Lost in a Pyramid, or the Mummy's Curse', in J. R. Stephens (ed.), *Into the Mummy's Tomb* (New York: Berkley Books, 2001).

65. The story that American books and newspapers produced in the 1850s and 1860s might be made from paper derived from mummy rags is controversial in book his-tory. Dard Hunter explored the oral history of this Egyptian story in *Papermaking:*

*The History and Technique of an Ancient Craft* (1943).Joseph Dane called 'The Curse of the Mummy Paper' a piece of 'urban mythology' in *The Myth of Print Culture: Essays on Evidence, Textuality, and Biographical Method* (Toronto: University of Toronto Press, 2003), 170. However, Nicholson Baker later takes these claims very seriously: 'There is a fair chance, I think, that some of the remaining bound volumes of the biggest New York dailies from 1855 through, say, 1870, entomb more than the history of the United States.' *Double Fold: Libraries and the Assault on Paper* (New York: Random House, 2001), 63.

66. See Warren R. Dawson, 'Pettigrew's Demonstrations upon Mummies: A Chapter in the History of Egyptology', *Journal of Egyptian Archaeology* 20 (1934), 170–82.

## Chapter 4

1. Citations, Donald R. Knight and Alan. D. Sabey, *The Lion Roars at Wembley: British Empire Exhibition Sixtieth Anniversary* (New Barnet: D. R. Knight, 1984), 12–13.

2. These replicas were sold to the industrialist Albert Reckitt when the Wembley exhibition closed in 1925 and were then presented to the City of Hull Museum, where they still reside.

3. 'Doubly Interesting since the "Strike" and "Lock-Out"', *Illustrated London News* (23 Feb 1923), 310.

4. See T. G. H. James, *Howard Carter: The Path to Tutankhamen* (London: Kegan Paul, 1992), 307.

5. 'The First Photograph of Tutankhamen's Shrouded Coffin', *Illustrated London News* (26 April 1924), 731.

6. *The Tomb of Tut-Ankh-Amen, British Empire Exhibition* (London: Haycock, 1924), n. p. This pamphlet is in the British Empire Collection of the Brent Museum and Archives.

7. Alexander C. T. Geppert, 'True Copies: Time and Space Travels at the British Imperial Exhibitions, 1880–1930', in H. Berghoff et al. (eds.), *The Making of Modern Tourism: The Cultural History of British Experience, 1600–2000* (Basingstoke: Palgrave, 2002), 236.

8. C. E. Briggs, 'The Seeker', in *The Tomb of Tut-Ankh-Amen*, n. p.

9. Henri Lefebvre, *The Production of Space*, trans. D. Nicholson-Smith (Oxford: Blackwell, 1991), 33.

10. Lefebvre, *The Production of Space*, 42.

11. The key sources are Nikolaus Pevsner and S. Lang, 'The Egyptian Revival', *Architectural Review* 119 (1956) and J. S. Curl, *The Egyptian Revival: Ancient Egyptian Inspiration for Design Motifs in the West*, revised edn (London: Routledge, 2005). Patrick Conner expresses scepticism about the extent of this 'revival' in 'The Egyptian Style 1790–1830', in Conner (ed.), *The Inspiration of Egypt: Its Influence on British Artists, Travellers and Designers 1700–1900* (Brighton: Brighton Borough Council, 1983).

12. Thomas Hope, *Household Furniture and Interior Design* (1807; London: Alec Tiranti, 1970), 27.

13. See Abigail Harrison Moore, '*Voyage*: Dominique-Vivant Denon and the Transference of Images of Egypt', *Art History* 25/4 (2002), 531–49.

14. See M. H. Port, *Imperial London: Civil Government Building in London 1850–1915* (New Haven: Yale University Press, 1995).

15. Curl, *The Egyptian Revival*, 260.

16. 1813 description, cited in Conner, *Inspiration of Egypt*, 53.

17. Robert Southey, *Letters from England*, ed. J. Simmons (London: Cresset, 1951), Letter 71, 449.

18. Soane, cited by Alex Werner, 'Egyptian London – Public and Private Displays in the Nineteenth Century Metropolis', in J.-M. Hubert and C. Price (eds), *Imhotep Today: Egyptianizing Architecture* (London: UCL Press, 2003), 79. Ackermann cited by Conner, *Inspiration of Egypt*, 40.

19. W. Macqueen-Pope, *Carriages at Eleven: The Story of Edwardian Theatre* (London: Hutchinson, 1947), 208.

20. Detailed commentary on the Egyptian Hall is in *Survey of London*, XXIX: *Parish of St. James Westminster* (London: Athlone, 1960), 266–70, and in Aleck Abrahams, 'The Egyptian Hall, Piccadilly, 1813–73', *Antiquary* 42 (1906), 61–4, 139–44 and 225–30. Only the statues of Isis and Osiris survive. They were bought by a salvage company in 1905, then sold on to a family who used them as garden ornaments for their house outside Edinburgh before their provenance was rediscovered in 1987. They were purchased by the Museum of London in 1994.

21. Leigh Hunt, *A Saunter through the West End* (London: Hurst and Blackett, 1861), 43.

22. Cited Michael P. Costeloe, *William Bullock: Connoisseur and Virtuoso of the Egyptian Hall: Piccadilly to Mexico, 1773–1849* (Bristol: HiPLAM, 2008), 50.

23. Abrahams, 'The Egyptian Hall', 62.

24. Robert Altick, *The Shows of London* (Cambridge, MA: Harvard University Press, 1978), 250.

25. Their responses to Belzoni are discussed in Judith Pascoe, *The Hummingbird Cabinet: A Rare and Curious History of Romantic Collectors* (Ithaca: Cornell University Press, 2006), 119–20.

26. Biographical information in this paragraph derives in the main from Alberto Siliotti, 'Giovanni Belzoni in Nineteenth-Century Egypt', in Giovanni Belzoni, *Belzoni's Travels: Narrative of the Operations and Recent Discoveries in Egypt and Nubia*, ed. Siliotti (London: British Museum, 2001) and Stanley Mayes, *The Great Belzoni: The Circus Strongman who Discovered Egypt's Treasures* (London: Taurus Parke, 2003).

27. Belzoni, *Belzoni's Travels*, 110.

28. 'Belzoni's Travels', *The Times* (28 Dec 1820), 3.

29. In April 1822, Belzoni wrote to *The Times* to record his offence at not being recognized and turned out of his seat at a Charity Ball at the King's Theatre.

30. Belzoni, *Description of the Egyptian Tomb, Discovered by G. Belzoni* (London: John Murray, 1821), 5.

31. Belzoni, *Description*, 15.

32. See, for instance, 'The Belzoni Sarcophagus', *The Times* (28 March 1825), 5. The poet Samuel Taylor Coleridge attended one of these nights with the painter of Egyptian scenes Benjamin Robert Haydon.

33. 'Exhibition of the Egyptian Tombs', *The Times* (1 April 1825), 2.

34. 'Mrs Belzoni', *The Times* (10 Nov 1825), 2.

35. Gillen D'Arcy Wood, *The Shock of the Real: Romanticism and Visual Culture, 1760–1860* (Basingstoke: Palgrave, 2001), 12.

36. Susan M. Pearce, 'Giovanni Battista Belzoni's Exhibition of the Reconstructed Tomb of Pharaoh Seti I in 1821', *Journal of the History of Collections* 12/1 (2000), 117–8.

37. [Lady Blessington], 'The Tomb', in *The Magic Lantern, or, Sketches of Scenes in the Metropolis* (London: Longman, 1823), 60.

38. Lady Blessington, *Magic Lantern*, 58 and 69.

39. Lady Blessington, *Magic Lantern*, 65.

40. [Edward Upham], *Memoranda, Illustrative of the Tombs and Sepulchral Decorations of the Egyptians; with a Key to the Egyptian Tomb now Exhibiting in Piccadilly. Also, Remarks on Mummies, and Observations on the Process of Embalming* (London: Thomas Boys, 1822), 62.

41. Upham, *Memoranda*, iv–v.

42. Belzoni, *Narrative*, 168.

43. Belzoni, *Narrative*, 169.

44. Belzoni, *Narrative*, 180.

45. Belzoni, *Narrative*, 148 and 100.

46. Pettigrew's commonplace book includes a copy of Horace Smith's poem 'Address to the Mummy at Belzoni's Exhibition' and a 'Fragment on Mummies' which he initially ascribed to the seventeenth-century naturalist Sir Thomas Browne. The commonplace book is MS 3861 in the Pettigrew Papers held in the Wellcome Institute archive. The best summary of Pettigrew's career remains Warren R. Dawson, 'Pettigrew's Demonstrations upon Mummies: A Chapter in the History of Egyptology', *Journal of Egyptian Archaeology* 20 (1934), 170–82. I have also relied on the excellent unpublished paper by Gabriel Moshenska, 'Unrolling Egyptian Mummies in Nineteenth Century Britain', which focuses on the career of Pettigrew.

47. See A. R. David and E. Tapp, *The Mummy's Tale: The Scientific and Medical Investigation of Natsef-Amun, Priest in the Temple of Karnak* (London: Michael O'Mara, 1992). The 1828 unrolling is detailed in William Osburn, *An Account of an Egyptian Mummy, Presented to the Museum of the Leeds Philosophical and Literary Society by the Late John Blayds* (Leeds: Robinson and Hernaman, 1828).

48. John Davidson, *An Address on Embalming Generally, Delivered at the Royal Institution on the Unrolling of a Mummy* (London: Ridgway, 1833), 23.

49. See 'The Royal Institution', *Morning Chronicle* (30 May 1836), 5.

50. 'The College Mummy', *Lancet* (18 Jan 1834), 693 and 694.

51. Thomas Joseph Pettigrew, *A History of Egyptian Mummies, and an Account of the Worship and Embalming of Sacred Animals by the Egyptians* (London: Longman, 1834), 29.

52. See Alison Winter, *Mesmerized: The Powers of Mind in Victorian Britain* (Chicago: University of Chicago Press, 1998).

53. Thomas Pettigrew, *On Superstitions Connected with the History and Practice of Medicine and Surgery* (London: John Churchill, 1844), 165.

54. See Pettigrew's section on 'physical history' in his *History of Egyptian Mummies*.

55. Robert J. C. Young, 'Egypt in America: The Confederacy in London', in *Colonial Desire: Hybridity in Theory, Culture and Race* (London: Routledge, 1994).

56. Ernest Wallis Budge, *Prefatory Remarks Made on Egyptian Mummies on the Occasion of Unrolling the Mummy of Bak-Rom* (London: Harrison, 1890), 5–6.

57. 'Egyptian Antiquities', *Literary Gazette and the Journal of Belles Lettres* (11 March 1837), 163.

58. 'Unrolling a Mummy', *Morning Chronicle* (13 April 1837), 3.

59. 'Scientific Mummery', *Figaro in London* (1837), cited by Moshenska, 'Unrolling Egyptian Mummies.'

60. See Iwan Rhys Morus, *Michael Faraday and the Electrical Century* (Cambridge: Icon, 2004) for discussion of this artisanal world beyond the realm of the Royal Society or Royal Institution.

61. 'Deed of Settlement of the Corporation Called "The Royal Panopticon of Science and Art"', 21 February 1850, London Metropolitan Archives, LMA B/WGL/36/9.

62. Pettigrew Papers, Wellcome Institute archive, MS 5371/41.

63. James Secord, 'Extraordinary Experiment: Electricity and the Creation of Life in Victorian England', in D. Gooding et al. (eds.), *The Uses of Experiment: Studies in the Natural Sciences* (Cambridge: Cambridge University Press, 1989), 337–83.

64. 'Obsequies of the Duke of Hamilton', *The Times* (7 Sept 1852), 6. The Duke had married one of the daughters of William Beckford, who famously spent millions on his fake Gothic folly, Fonthill Abbey, which we will encounter in Chapter 6 below.

65. 'Obsequies of the Duke of Hamilton', 6.

66. Augustus Pugin, *Apology for the Revival of Christian Architecture in England* (London: John Weale, 1843).

67. See Catharine Arnold, *Necropolis: London and its Dead* (London: Pocket Books, 2007), 86–7.

68. See Herbert C. Andrews, 'The Leicester Square and Strand Panoramas: Their Proprietors and Artists', *Notes and Queries* 159 (1930), 57–61 and 75–8.

69. Dufourroy, cited by Bernard Comment, *The Panorama*, trans. A-M. Glasheen (London: Reaktion, 1999), 101.

70. See R. Derek Wood, 'The Diorama in Great Britain in the 1820s', *History of Photography* 17/3 (1993), 284–95.

71. William Wordsworth, *The Prelude*, Book VII (1805 version), lines 248–9 and 254–5.

72. See Dana Arnold, 'Panoptic Visions of London: Possessing the Metropolis', *Art History* 32/2 (2009), 332–50.

73. Comment cited in Martin Zerlang, 'London as a Panorama', in M. Zerlang (ed.), *Representing London* (Copenhagen: Spring Publishers, 2001), 35.

74. Altick, *Shows of London*, 136.

75. Wordsworth, *Prelude*, VII, 236, 241–3.

76. Wordsworth, *Prelude*, VII, 269.

77. This panorama is discussed in Nicky Levell, *Oriental Visions: Exhibitions, Travel and Collecting in the Victorian Age* (London: Horniman Museum, 2000), 33.

78. M. Phipps-Jackson, 'Cairo in London: Carl Haag's Studio', *Art Journal* (March 1883), 74.

79. Comment, *The Panorama*, 8.
80. Timothy Mitchell, *Colonising Egypt* (Berkeley: University of California Press, 1991), 23–4.
81. Walter Benjamin, 'Paris, the Capital of the Nineteenth Century' (1935), in *The Arcades Project*, trans. H. Eiland and K. McLaughlin (Cambridge, MA: Harvard University Press, 1999), 13.
82. J. Taylor, *A Month in London,* cited Zerlang, 'London as Panorama', 45.
83. Account cited by Marina Warner, *Phantasmagoria: Spirit Visions, Metaphors, and Media into the Twenty-first Century* (Oxford: Oxford University Press, 2006), 150.
84. Charles Dickens, 'Some Account of an Extraordinary Traveller' (1850) in *Dickens' Journalism*, vol. 2: *'The Amusements of the People' and Other Papers*, ed. Michael Slater (London: Dent, 1996), 207–8.
85. Edward Walford, *Old and New London*, vol. 4: *Westminster and the Western Suburbs* (London: Cassell, 1891), 170–1.
86. *Catalogue of the Oriental Museum at the Great Globe, Leicester Square* (London: James Wyld, 1857).
87. 'Deed of Settlement', London Metropolitan Archives, LMA B/WGL/36/9.
88. 'Royal Panopticon of Science and Art', *Illustrated London News* (31 July 1852), 96.
89. For the history of the building, see *Survey of London*, xxxiv (London: Athlone, 1966), 492–5. See also Victor Glasstone, *Victorian and Edwardian Theatres: An Architectural and Social Survey* (London: Thames and Hudson, 1975).
90. Macqueen-Pope, *Carriages at Eleven,* 214.
91. Macqueen-Pope, *Carriages at Eleven,* 215.
92. See Joseph Bristow, '"Sterile Ecstasies": The Perversity of the Decadent Movement', in Laurel Brake (ed.), *The Endings of Epochs*, Essays and Studies (Cambridge: D. S. Brewer, 1995), 57–79.
93. Macqueen-Pope, *Carriages at Eleven,* 179.
94. Edward Ziter, *The Orient on the Victorian Stage* (Cambridge: Cambridge University Press, 2003), 154.
95. Ziter, *The Orient*, 164.
96. Harris's melodramas were unpublished, but the scripts passed through the Lord Chamberlain's Office for licensing approval and are now lodged in the British Library: *Human Nature* (1881), Add. MS 53342H.
97. A summary text of *Khartoum! or, The Star of the East* was published by William Muskerry and John Jourdain in 1885. The full handwritten script is in the Lord Chamberlain's collection, British Library, Add. MS 5334B.
98. Russell Jackson, 'Cleopatra "Lilyised": *Antony and Cleopatra* at The Princess's 1890', *Theatrephile* 2/8 (1985), 37.
99. Michael Booth, 'Soldiers of the Queen: Drury Lane Imperialism', in M. Hays and A. Nikolopoulou (eds), *Melodrama: The Cultural Emergence of a Genre* (New York: St Martin's Press, 1996), 3.
100. Émile Zola, *Au bonheur des dames,* trans. as *The Ladies' Paradise* (Berkeley: University of California Press, 1992), 75.
101. Zola, *Bonheur,* 78.
102. Zola, *Bonheur,* 79.

103. Rosalind Williams, *Dream Worlds: Mass Consumption in Late Nineteenth-Century France* (Berkeley: University of California Press, 1982), 73.

104. Cited Erika Diane Rapoport, *Shopping for Pleasure: Women in the Making of London's West End* (Princeton: Princeton University Press, 2000), 21.

105. Liberty's Catalogue, *The Bazaar* (1898), cited by Sarah Cheang, 'Selling China: Class, Gender and Orientalism at the Department Store', *Journal of Design History* 20/1 (2007), 10.

106. For details, see chapters 2 and 3 of Mica Nava, *Visceral Cosmopolitanism: Gender, Culture and the Normalisation of Difference* (Oxford: Berg, 2007).

107. Rudi Laermans, 'Learning to Consume: Early Department Stores and the Shaping of Modern Consumer Culture (1860–1914)', *Theory, Culture and Society* 10/4 (1993), 91.

108. Virginia Woolf, 'Oxford Street Tide', in *The London Scene* (London: Snowbooks, n.d.), 32.

109. Description cited by Ralph Hyde and Pieter van der Merwe, 'The Queen's Bazaar', *Theatrephile* 2/8 (1985), 11.

110. 'The Philosophy of Shopping', *Saturday Review* (16 Oct 1875), 488.

111. Quote from 'The Philosophy of Shopping', 488. For investigations of women as entranced shoppers, see Rachel Bowlby, *Carried Away: The Invention of Modern Shopping* (New York: Columbia University Press, 2001).

112. Malek Alloula, *The Colonial Harem,* trans. M and W. Gozich (Manchester: Manchester University Press, 1986), 95.

113. See Daniel Pick, *Svengali's Web: The Alien Enchanter in Modern Culture* (New Haven: Yale University Press, 2000). This theme is picked up in chapter 8, below.

114. See Williams, *Dream Worlds,* 67.

115. See Relli Shechter, 'Selling Luxury: The Rise of the Egyptian Cigarette and the Transformation of the Egyptian Tobacco Market, 1880–1914', *International Journal of Middle East Studies* 35 (2003), 51–75.

116. Ivan Davidson Kalmar, 'The *Houkah* in the Harem: On Smoking and Orientalist Art', in S. Gilman and Z. Xun (eds.), *Smoke: A Global History* (London: Reaktion, 2004), 218–29.

117. For a discussion of London's opium dens, see Marek Kohn, *Dope Girls: The Birth of the British Drug Underground* (London: Granta, 1992), Anne Witchard, *Thomas Burke's Dark Chinoiserie: Limehouse Nights and the Queer Spell of Chinatown* (Aldershot: Ashgate, 2009), and Barry Milligan, 'The Opium Den in Victorian London', in Gilman and Xun, *Smoke: A Global History* (London: Reaktion, 2004), 118–25.

118. Kate Chopin, 'An Egyptian Cigarette', in E. Showalter (ed.), *Daughters of Decadence: Women Writers of the Fin de Siècle* (London: Virago, 1993), 1 and 2.

119. Chopin, 'An Egyptian Cigarette', 4.

120. See discussion in Chris Elliott, Katherine Griffis-Greenberg and Richard Lunn, 'Egypt in London – Entertainment and Commerce in the Twentieth Century Metropolis', in J. M. Humbert and C. Price (eds), *Imhotep Today: Egyptianizing Architecture* (London: UCL Press, 2003), 106–9.

121. Karl Marx, *Capital: A Critique of Political Economy,* trans. B. Fowkes, 3 vols (Harmondsworth: Penguin, 1976), I, 167.

## Chapter 5

1. Edward A. Freeman, *A History of Architecture* (London: Joseph Masters, 1849), 74.

2. Freeman, *History of Architecture*, 271–2.

3. John Ruskin, *Stones of Venice,* cited Mark Crinson, *Empire Building: Orientalism and Victorian Architecture* (London: Routledge, 1996), 50.

4. John Ruskin, *The Two Paths,* cited Mark Crinson, *Empire Building,* 60.

5. See M. H. Port, *Imperial London: Civil Government Building 1850–1915* (New Haven: Yale University Press, 1995).

6. Edward Ziter, *The Orient on the Victorian Stage* (Cambridge: Cambridge University Press, 2003), 118.

7. Reverend Thomas Boyles Murray, *A Day in the Crystal Palace,* 2nd edn (London: SPCK, 1852), 8.

8. For details of these commissions, see Michael Darby, *The Islamic Perspective: An Aspect of British Architecture and Design in the Nineteenth Century* (London: Leighton House Gallery, 1983).

9. These are listed in the *Short Version of the Official Catalogue* (1851). Egypt's place is discussed in Francesca Vanke, 'Degrees of Otherness: The Ottoman Empire and China at the Great Exhibition of 1851', in J. Auerbach and P. Hoffenberg (eds), *Britain, the Empire, and the World at the Great Exhibition of 1851* (Aldershot: Ashgate, 2008), 191–205.

10. Nicky Levell, *Oriental Visions: Exhibitions, Travel, and Collecting in the Victorian Age* (London: Horniman, 2000), 33. The best visual record are the forty-seven photographic prints made by Philip Delamotte, and purchased by English Heritage in 2004. See Ian Leith, *Delamotte's Crystal Palace: A Victorian Pleasure Dome Revealed* (London: English Heritage, 2005).

11. Owen Jones, 'Preface' to Jones and Joseph Bonomi, *Description of the Egyptian Court Erected in the Crystal Palace* (London: Crystal Palace Company, 1854), 3.

12. Tony Bennett, *The Birth of the Museum: History, Theory, Politics* (London: Routledge, 1995), 10.

13. Carol Duncan and Alan Wallach, 'The Universal Survey Museum', *Art History* 3/4 (1980), 450–1.

14. Lieutenant-General Pitt-Rivers, 'Typological Museums, as Exemplified by the Pitt-Rivers Museum at Oxford and his Provincial Museum at Farnham, Dorset', *Journal of the Society of Arts* 40 (18 Dec 1891), 116. His principles are discussed further by William Ryan Chapman, 'Arranging Ethnology: A. H. L. F. Pitt Rivers and the Typological Tradition', in George W. Stocking (ed.), *Objects and Others: Essays on Museums and Material Culture* (Madison: University of Wisconsin Press, 1985), 75–111.

15. David Murray, *Museums: Their History and their Use* (Glasgow: MacLehose, 1904), 269.

16. Nerval, cited Timothy Mitchell, *Colonising Egypt* (Berkeley: University of California Press, 1991), 29.

17. Mitchell, 'Preface to Papberback Edition', *Colonising Egypt,* xv.

18. Edward W. Said, *Orientalism* (London: Peregrine, 1985), 92–3.

19. Walter Benjamin, *The Arcades Project,* trans. H. Eiland and K. McLaughlin (Cambridge, MA: Harvard University Press, 1999), 201.

20. *The Times* (17 March 1851), cited by Paul Young, *Globalization and the Great Exhibition: The Victorian New World Order* (Basingstoke: Palgrave, 2009), 3.

21. Thackeray, cited Hermione Hobhouse, *The Crystal Palace and the Great Exhibition: Art, Science and Productive Industry: A History of the Royal Commission for the Exhibition of 1851* (London: Athlone, 2002), 46.

22. See the opening pages of Henry Mayhew and George Cruikshank, *1851, or, The Adventures of Mr and Mrs Sandboys and Family, who Came up to London to 'Enjoy Themselves' and to see the Great Exhibition* (London: Bogue, 1851).

23. See Jeffrey A. Auerbach's chapter 'Nationalism and Internationalism', in *The Great Exhibition of 1851: A Nation on Display* (New Haven: Yale University Press, 1999).

24. Paul Hoffenberg, *An Empire on Display: English, Indian and Australian Exhibitions from the Crystal Palace to the Great War* (Berkeley: University of California Press, 2001), 18.

25. Ward, cited Auerbach, *The Great Exhibition*, 95. Letter Thomas Carlyle to Ralph Waldo Emerson (8 July 1851), cited Hoffenberg, *An Empire on Display*, 14 (full text of letter available online at http://carlyleletters.dukejournals.org).

26. Auerbach, *The Great Exhibition*, 94–5.

27. George Routledge, *Routledge (One Shilling) Guide to the Crystal Palace* (London: Routledge, 1854), 32.

28. *Routledge Guide*, 32.

29. *Routledge Guide*, 33–4 and 41.

30. *Routledge Guide*, 70.

31. Hippolyte Taine, *Notes on England*, trans. E. Hyams (London: Thames and Hudson, 1957), 188–9.

32. George Augustus Sala, *Paris herself Again in 1878–9*, 2 vols (London: Remington, 1880), II, 237.

33. Paul Greenhalgh, *Ephemeral Vistas: The Expositions Universelles, Great Exhibitions and World's Fairs, 1851–1939* (Manchester: Manchester University Press, 1988), 2.

34. Kiralfy's career is discussed in Greenhalgh and in John M. Mackenzie, 'The Imperial Exhibitions', in *Propaganda and Empire: The Manipulation of British Public Opinion 1880–1960* (Manchester: Manchester University Press, 1984).

35. J. R. Morell, *Bradshaw's Handbook to the Paris International Exhibition of 1867* (London: Bradshaw, 1867), 50.

36. *Bradshaw's Handbook*, 109.

37. For detailed description, see Zeynep Çelik, *Displaying the Orient: Architecture of Islam at Nineteenth-Century World's Fairs* (Berkeley: University of California Press, 1992). Egypt at Paris 1867 is also given cultural context in Trevor Mostyn, *Egypt's Belle Epoque: Cairo and the Age of the Hedonists* (London: Tauris Parke, 2007), 56–60.

38. Gautier, cited Çelik, *Displaying the Orient*, 62.

39. Cited Levell, *Oriental Visions*, 84.

40. *Colonial and Indian Exhibition Official Guide* (London: William Clowes, 1886), 9.

41. See H. Trueman Wood, *Colonial and Indian Exhibition, London, 1886: Reports on the Colonial Sections of the Exhibition* (London: William Clowes, 1887).

42. *Colonial and Indian Exhibition Official Guide*, 12.

43. *Colonial and Indian Exhibition Official Guide*, lxxxix.

44. Cited Greenhalgh, *Ephemeral Vistas*, 88.

45. See Pascal Blanchard et al. (eds), *Human Zoos: Science and Spectacle in the Age of Colonial Empires*, trans. T. Bridgeman (Liverpool: Liverpool University Press, 2008).

46. This is viewable in electronic form at Rice University's Travellers in the Middle East Archive project, http://scholarship.rice.edu/jsp/xml/1911/9168/165/DegRu Ca.tei-timea.html#index-div1-N10784. Accessed 23 August 2010.

47. Cited Çelik, *Displaying the Orient*, 76.

48. Greenhalgh, *Ephemeral Vistas*, 103.

49. Lorrain, cited Philippe Julian, *The Triumph of Art Nouveau: Paris Exhibition 1900* (London: Phaidon, 1974), 87 and 163.

50. Lorrain, cited Julian, 167.

51. Robert Ross wrote to More Adey about Wilde's time in the exotic cafés, recalling Wilde saying that 'he was responsible for the failure of the Exhibition, the English having gone away when they saw him so well-dressed and happy.' Letter (14 December 1900), as epilogue to *The Complete Letters of Oscar Wilde,* ed. Merlin Holland and Rupert Hart-Davis (London: Fourth Estate, 2000), 1212.

52. See 'Greater Britain Exhibition African Village and Mud Huts Cyprus Street and Cairo Street, 1899', London Metropolitan Archives, LCC/AR/TH/02/028.

53. 'The Greater Britain Exhibition', *The Times* (9 May 1899), 14.

54. 'The Greater Britain Exhibition', *The Times* (9 May 1899), 14.

55. Darby, *The Islamic Perspective*, 134.

56. Guy Mauve, 'Architecture', in F. G. Dumas (ed.), *The Franco-British Exhibition: Illustrated Review* (London: Chatto, 1908), 10 and 13.

57. J. Nixon Horsfield, 'The Franco-British Exhibition of Science, Arts, and Industries, London, 1908', *Journal of the Royal Institute of British Architects* 15 (1907–8), 551.

58. Horsfield, 'The Franco-British Exhibition', 546.

59. H. S., 'The Indian Pavilion', in Dumas (ed.), *The Franco-British Exhibition*, 266.

60. Paul Laforgue, 'Palace of the Colonies', in Dumas (ed.), *The Franco-British Exhibition,* 280.

61. See files of the London Council's Architecture Department on the Great White City, 1908, London Metropolitan Archives, AR/TH/4/1.

62. 'Countless Other Attractions: The Sideshows', in Dumas (ed.), *The Franco-British Exhibition,* 296.

63. Letter from architect E. White to Buildings Committee, 6 Aug 1908, in Great White City, 1908 file, London Metropolitan Archives, AR/TH/4/1.

64. See visitor figures listed in 'The Franco-British Exhibition: The Closing Ceremony', *The Times* (31 Oct 1908), 13.

65. David M. Wilson, *The British Museum: A History* (London: British Museum Press, 2002), 39. Details in this paragraph are also derived from T. G. H. James, *The British Museum and Ancient Egypt* (London: British Museum Press, 1989).

66. Cited Ian Jenkins, *Archaeologists and Aesthetes in the Sculpture Galleries of the British Museum 1800–1939* (London: British Museum Press, 1992), 107.

67. Bruno Latour, *Science in Action: How to Follow Scientists and Engineers through Society* (Cambridge, MA: Harvard University Press, 1987), 228.

68. See T. G. H. James, 'Samuel Birch (1813–85)', *Oxford Dictionary of National Biography*.

69. This portrait of Birch is in the 'Prolegomena' of Sir E. A. Wallis Budge, *By Nile and Tigris: A Narrative of Journeys in Egypt and Mesopotamia on Behalf of the British Museum between the Years 1886 and 1913*, 2 vols (London: John Murray, 1920), I, 21.

70. For a critical reading of Wallis Budge's career, see Donald Malcolm Reid, *Whose Pharaohs? Archaeology, Museums, and Egyptian National Identity from Napoleon to the First World War* (Berkeley: University of California Press, 2002). Robert Morell's *'Budgie': The Life of Sir E. A. T. Wallis Budge* (Nottingham: privately printed, 2002), the only biography to date, defends Wallis Budge's methods.

71. Wallis Budge, *By Nile and Tigris*, I, 82.

72. Wallis Budge, *By Nile and Tigris*, I, 111.

73. This assistance is revealed in Wallis Budge's letters from the field written back to Sir Edward Maunde Thompson, Director of the British Museum from 1888 to 1909.

74. Letter Wallis Budge to Sir Edward Maunde Thompson (16 October 1892), Budge Papers box file, British Museum archive.

75. Letters Wallis Budge to Sir Edward Maunde Thompson (16 October 1892 and 20 October 1890), Budge Papers box file, BM archive.

76. Wallis Budge, *By Nile and Tigris*, I, 351ff.

77. Violet Markham, 'Sir Ernest Budge: An Appreciation', *The Times* (26 Nov 1934), 14.

78. See Margaret S. Drower, *Flinders Petrie: A Life in Archaeology* (London: Gollancz, 1985).

79. Wallis Budge, *By Nile and Tigris*, I, 300.

80. 'Egyptian Collectors in a Panic', *Daily Express* (7 April 1923), 1.

81. See Ernest A. Wallis Budge, *Prefatory Remarks Made on Egyptian Mummies on the Occasion of Unrolling the Mummy of Bak-Ran* (London: Harrison, 1890).

82. Markham, 'Sir Ernest Budge', 14.

83. Barbara J. Black, *On Exhibit: Victorians and their Museums* (Charlottesville: University of Virginia Press, 2000), 24.

84. Black, *On Exhibit*, 34.

85. See, for instance, the correspondence about the refusal of the Javanese collection of Lady Raffles, *Copy of all Communications made by the Officers and Architect of the British Museum to the Trustees, Respecting the Want of Space for Exhibiting the Collections in that Institution, and the Removal of Part of those Collections . . . and of the Minutes of the Trustees Thereon*, House of Commons Papers, 126 (1859).

86. *Report from the Select Committee on the British Museum*, House of Commons Papers (1860), vi and 2.

87. Pitt-Rivers, 'Typological Museums', 115.

88. Paul Valéry, 'The Problem of Museums' (1923), *Collected Works*, ed. J. Matthews, vol. 12 (London: Routledge and Kegan Paul, 1960), 203.

89. Edward Tylor, *Primitive Culture: Researches into the Development of Mythology, Philosophy, Religion, Art and Custom*, 2 vols (London: Murray, 1871), II, 2.

90. Tylor, *Primitive Culture*, II, 452.

91. James Clifford, 'Objects and Selves – An Afterword', in George W. Stocking (ed.), *Objects and Others: Essays on Museums and Material Culture* (Madison: University of Wisconsin Press, 1985), 244.

92. Lorraine Daston and Katherine Park, *Wonders and the Order of Nature 1150–1750* (New York: Zone, 1998), 13.

93. See Krzysztof Pomain, *Collectors and Curiosities, Paris and Venice, 1500–1800*, trans. E. Wiles-Portier (Cambridge: Polity, 1990).

94. Ambrose Parey, 'A Discourse on *Mumia*, or Mummie', in *The Works of that Famous Chirurgion Ambrose Parey* (London: Cotes and Young, 1634), 448. For context, see Karl Dennefeldt, 'Egypt and Egyptian Antiquities in the Renaissance', *Studies in the Renaissance* 6 (1959), 7–27.

95. Details in Arthur MacGregor, 'The Cabinet of Curiosities in 17th-century Britain', in O. Impey and A. MacGregor (eds), *The Origins of Museums: The Cabinet of Curiosities in Sixteenth- and Seventeenth-Century Europe* (London: House of Stratus, 2001), 201–16.

96. Cited Altick, *The Shows of London*, 14.

97. Daston and Park, *Wonders and the Order of Nature*, 360.

98. Wallis Budge, *By Nile and Tigris*, I, 35–6.

99. Walter Besant, *All Sorts and Conditions of Men* (Oxford: Oxford University Press, 1997), 214.

100. For anti-Catholic agitation, see Dominic Janes, 'The Rites of Man: The British Museum and the Sexual Imagination in Victorian Britain', *Journal of the History of Collections* 20/1 (2008), 101–12. For occultists interested in Egyptian magic, see chapter 8 below.

101. H. R. Pinching informed Wallis Budge that 'I have obtained Masonic evidence that there is a secret entrance to the platform of the Great Pyramid from the interior, of which the Masons have proof.' Letter (11 March 1908). The psychometrist, G. Billing, in a letter to Wallis Budge (25 January 1923), explained that he had taken psychic readings from a small Egyptian statuette, and enclosed his automatic writing script, which, he confessed, 'may be simple rubbish'. An open letter, 'Concerning the claims of the "Merry" family of Warwickshire and Derbyshire, to be direct descendants of the Egyptian "Pharaoh-Mery" Line' was received by Wallis Budge in March 1923. BM *Correspondence*, 1908 and 1923.

102. Elliott O'Donnell, 'The Oriental Department of the British Museum', *Haunted Houses of London* (London: Eveleigh Nash, 1909), 95.

103. 'The "Ghost" Anyone May See at the British Museum', *Illustrated London News* (26 Feb 1927), 342–3.

104. Jonah Siegel, *Haunted Museum: Longing, Travel and the Art-Romance Tradition* (Princeton: Princeton University Press, 2005), 4.

105. Jacques Derrida, 'Archive Fever: A Freudian Impression', *Diacritics* 25/2 (1995), 9–63.

106. For a discussion of Soane's sarcophagus, see Colin Davies, 'Architecture and Remembrance', *Architectural Review* 175 (Feb 1984), 49–55.

107. Cited Levell, *Oriental Visions*, 316.

108. See Nicholas Reeves, 'The Sigmund Freud Collection of Egyptian Antiquities', *KMT: A Modern Journal of Ancient Egypt* 11/4 (2000–1), 31–9, and Peter Ucko, 'Unprovenanced Material Culture and Freud's Collection of Antiquities', *Journal of Material Culture* 6/3 (2001), 269–322.

109. For more detailed discussion of this London topography, see my essay, 'An Occult Gazetteer of Bloomsbury: An Experiment in Method', in A. Witchard and L. Phillips (eds), *London Gothic: Place, Space and the Gothic Imagination* (London: Continuum, 2010).

110. Wallis Budge, *By Nile and Tigris*, II, 390.

111. Mary Bouquet and Nuno Porto, 'Introduction' to Bouquet and Porto (eds), *Science, Magic and Religion: The Ritual Processes of Museum Magic* (New York: Berghahn Books, 2005), 9.

112. Elliott Colla, *Conflicted Antiquities: Egyptology, Egyptomania, Egyptian Modernity* (Durham, NC: Duke University Press, 2007), 16.

113. Susan Stewart, *On Longing: Narratives of the Miniature, the Gigantic, the Souvenir, the Collection* (Durham, NC: Duke University Press, 1993), 148.

114. Colla, *Conflicted Antiquities*, 29.

115. Bill Brown, 'Thing Theory', *Critical Inquiry* 28 (2001), 1–16.

116. Brian Curran et al., *Obelisk: A History* (Cambridge, MA: Burndy Library, 2009). 7.

117. Hargrave Jennings, *The Obelisk: Notices of the Origin, Purpose and History of Obelisks* (London: Bursill, 1877), 39.

118. Adrian Ball, *Cleopatra's Needle: The Story of One Hundred Years in London* (Havant: Kenneth Mason, 1978), 17.

119. Details of Captain Carter's statement on the voyage and a final reckoning of the costs of the removal of Cleopatra's Needle to England are in the London Metropolitan Archives, Q/CN/13 & 14.

120. *The Times* cutting (10 Oct 1878), LMA Q/CN/7.

121. See Curran et al., *Obelisk: A History*, chapter 6.

122. James Curtis, *The Gilt Kid* (London: London Books, 2007), 16.

123. See the brief account of Cleopatra's Needle ghosts in James Clark, *Haunted London* (Stroud: Tempus, 2007), 63–5.

124. See Charlotte A. Roberts, *Human Remains in Archaeology: A Handbook* (Ann Arbor: University of Michigan Press, 2009).

125. Ian Jenkins, *Archaeologists and Aesthetes in the Sculpture Galleries of the British Museum 1800–1939* (London: British Museum Press, 1992), 9.

126. William St Clair, *Lord Elgin and the Marbles: The Controversial History of the Parthenon Sculptures,* 3rd edn (Oxford: Oxford University Press, 1998), 166.

127. John Keats, 'On Seeing the Elgin Marbles' in *The Complete Poems*, ed. John Barnard (Penguin: Harmondsworth, 1988), 99–100, quote from line 11.

128. St Clair, *Lord Elgin and the Marbles*, 255.

129. Lord Byron, 'English Bards and Scotch Reviewers', *Complete Poetical Works*, vol. 1, ed. J. McGann (Oxford: Clarendon Press, 1980), l. 1030–1.

130. Cited by St Clair, *Lord Elgin and the Marbles*, 181.

131. Byron, *Childe Harold's Pilgrimage, The Complete Poetical Works*, vol. 2, ed. J. McGann (Oxford: Clarendon Press, 1980), l. 100–1.

132. Byron, *Childe Harold's Pilgrimage*, l. 129–35.

133. Byron, 'Notes', *Childe Harold's Pilgrimage*, l. 190–1.

134. St Clair, *Lord Elgin and the Marbles*, 199.

135. Byron, 'The Curse of Minerva', *Complete Poetical Works,* vol. l, ed. McGann, l. 163–6.

136. Byron, 'The Curse of Minerva', l. 199 and l. 202.

137. Byron, 'The Curse of Minerva', l. 221–4.

138. Byron, 'The Curse of Minerva', l. 306–9.

139. Sheldon Annis, 'The Museum as Staging Ground for Symbolic Action', *Museum* 151 (1986), 168–71. This notion is pursued further in Gaynor Kavanagh, *Dream Spaces: Memory and the Museum* (London: Leicester University Press, 2000).

140. Caroline Franklin, *Byron: A Literary Life* (Basingstoke: Macmillan, 2009), x.

## Chapter 6

1. Chris Baldick, 'The End of the Line: The Family Curse in Shorter Gothic Fiction', in V. Tinkler-Villani and P. Davidson (eds), *Exhibited by Candlelight: Sources and Developments in the Gothic Tradition* (Amsterdam: Rodopi, 1995), 149.

2. Horace Walpole, *The Castle of Otranto: A Gothic Story* (1764), ed. E. J. Clery (Oxford: Oxford World's Classics, 1998), 17.

3. Anonymous, 'The Curse', published in *Fraser's Magazine* 6 (Nov 1832), and collected in John Polidori, *The Vampyre and Other Tales of the Macabre,* ed. Robert Morrison and Chris Baldick (Oxford: Oxford World's Classics, 1997), 120.

4. Alicia Weisberg-Roberts, 'Singular Objects and Multiple Meanings' in Michael Snodin (ed.), *Horace Walpole's Strawberry Hill* (New Haven: Yale University Press, 2009), 89.

5. J. W. Oliver, *The Life of William Beckford* (Oxford: Oxford University Press, 1932), 88, 89 and 91.

6. William Beckford, *Vathek,* ed. Roger Lonsdale (Oxford: Oxford World's Classics, 1998), 42.

7. See Anne Nellis Richter, 'Spectacle, Exoticism, and Display in the Gentleman's House: The Fonthill Auction of 1822', *Eighteenth-Century Studies* 41/4 (2008), 543–64.

8. Arthur Conan Doyle, 'Lot No. 249' (1894), in Roger Luckhurst (ed.), *Late Victorian Gothic Tales* (Oxford: Oxford World's Classics, 2005), 114 and 115.

9. Doyle, 'Lot No. 249', 129.

10. Doyle, 'Lot No. 249', 132.

11. Richard Freeman, 'The Mummy in Context', *European Journal of American Studies* 1 (2009), http://ejas.revues.org/7566.

12. Arthur Conan Doyle, 'Egypt in 1896', in *Memories and Reflections* (London: Greenhill, 1988), 130.

13. Details of his Egyptian stay are recounted in Andrew Lycett, *Conan Doyle: The Man who Created Sherlock Holmes* (London: Weidenfeld & Nicolson, 2007), 219ff.

14. Arthur Conan Doyle, *The Tragedy of the Korosko* (London: Hesperus Press, 2003), 4.

15. Conan Doyle, *The Tragedy of the Korosko,* 111.

16. For an important staking out of this territory, see Patrick Brantlinger's chapter on the Imperial Gothic in his *Rule of Darkness: British Literature and Imperialism 1830–1914* (Ithaca: Cornell University Press, 1988).

17. Robert Miles, *Gothic Writing 1750–1820: A Genealogy* (London: Routledge, 1993), 32.

18. See Dominic Montserrat, 'Louisa May Alcott and the Mummy's Curse', *KMT: A Modern Journal of Ancient Egypt* 9/2 (1998), 70–5. The wider cluster is discussed in Jasmine Day, *The Mummy's Curse: Mummymania in the English-Speaking World* (London: Routledge, 2006), 46–7, and further excavation of the 1860s has been undertaken by Ailise Bulfin in 'The Fictions of Gothic Egypt and British Imperial Paranoia: The Curse of the Suez Canal', *English Literature in Transition* 54/4 (2011), 411–43.

19. See, for instance, David Keys, 'Curse (and Revenge) of the Mummy Invented by Victorian Writers', *The Independent* (31 Dec 2000), which summarizes the work of Dominic Montserrat. Article reproduced at http://www.rense.com/general6/curse.htm

20. A discussion of *Vathek* ends Ros Ballaster's *Fabulous Orients: Fictions of the East in England 1662–1785* (Oxford: Oxford University Press, 2007). See also Martha Pike Conant, *The Oriental Tale in England in the Eighteenth Century* (New York: Columbia University Press, 1908). The impact of the first English translation of the Arabian Nights is dealt with by Marina Warner, *Stranger Magic: Charmed States and the Arabian Nights* (London: Chatto, 2011).

21. Robert Southey, *Poetical Works 1793–1810*, vol. 4: *The Curse of Kehama*, ed. Daniel Sanjiv Roberts (London: Pickering and Chatto, 2004), II, 160–1 and 168–9.

22. See Carol Bolton, *Writing the Empire: Robert Southey and Romantic Colonialism* (London: Pickering and Chatto, 2007).

23. Thomas De Quincey, *Confessions of an English Opium-Eater and other writings*, ed. Grevel Lindop (Oxford: Oxford World's Classics, 1985), 73.

24. De Quincey, 'The System of the Heavens as Revealed by Lord Rosse's Telescopes', *Tait's Edinburgh Magazine* (1846), quoted from full text online at http://www.readbookonline.net/readOnLine/38345/

25. De Quincey, 'The System of the Heavens'.

26. John Barrell, *The Infection of Thomas De Quincey: A Psychopathology of Imperialism* (New Haven: Yale University Press, 1991), 15. There is also helpful commentary on this passage in Josephine McDonagh, *De Quincey's Disciplines* (Oxford: Clarendon Press, 1994).

27. Barrell, *Infection*, 19.

28. Jane Loudon, *The Mummy! A Tale of the Twenty-Second Century* (1827), ed. Alan Rauch (Ann Arbor: University of Michigan Press, 1994), 69.

29. Loudon, *The Mummy!* 88–89.

30. Edgar Allan Poe, 'Some Words with a Mummy', *Complete Stories and Poems* (New York: Dover, 1966), 456.

31. For commentary, see Charles D. Martin, 'Can the Mummy Speak? Manifest Destiny, Ventriloquism, and the Silence of the Ancient Egyptian Body', *Nineteenth-Century Contexts* 31/2 (2009), 113–28.

32. Poe, 'Some Words', 462.

33. Grant Allen, 'My New Year's Eve Among the Mummies', first published in *Belgravia* in January 1880. Text available at http://gaslight.mtroyal.ab.ca/newmummy.htm

34. Théophile Gautier, 'The Mummy's Foot' in *The Mummy's Foot and Other Tales* (Los Angeles: Aegypan Press, n.d. [2010]), 9.

35. Gautier, 'The Mummy's Foot', 11.

36. Théophile Gautier, *The Romance of a Mummy*, trans. M. Young (London: John & Robert Maxwell, 1886), 39.

37. Sigmund Freud, 'Fetishism' (1927) in *On Sexuality*, Penguin Freud Library, vol. 7 (London: Penguin, 1987).

38. See Gautier, 'One of Cleopatra's Nights' in *The Mummy's Foot and Other Tales*, 19–46.

39. See Nicholas Daly's reading of the mummy story as 'narrativised commodity theory' in his *Modernism, Romance and the Fin de Siècle* (Cambridge: Cambridge University Press, 1999).

40. Quote from Dominic Montserrat, 'Unidentified Human Remains: Mummies and the Erotics of Biography', in D. Montserrat (ed.), *Changing Bodies, Changing Meanings: Studies on the Human Body in Antiquity* (London: Routledge, 1998), 162.

41. Gautier, 'The Mummy's Foot', 12.

42. Gustave Flaubert, *Flaubert in Egypt: A Sensibility on Tour*, compiled and translated by Francis Steegmuller (London: Penguin, 1996), 170–1.

43. Theo Douglas, *Iras: A Mystery* (London: William Blackwood, 1896), 61, 51 and 54.

44. Douglas, *Iras*, 59.

45. Douglas, *Iras*, 175–6.

46. Judith Thurman, *Secrets of the Flesh: A Life of Colette* (London: Bloomsbury, 1999), 171. The scandal of the Moulin Rouge is also discussed in detail in Yvonne Mitchell, *Colette: A Taste for Life* (London: Weidenfeld and Nicolson, 1975).

47. Louisa May Alcott, 'Lost in a Pyramid, or The Mummy's Curse' (1869), in J. R. Stephens (ed.), *Into the Mummy's Tomb* (New York: Berkley Books, 2001), 38.

48. Alcott, 'Lost in a Pyramid,' 42.

49. 'Mr Grubbe's Night with Memnon', *Putnam's Monthly Magazine* 10/56 (Aug 1857), 196.

50. Nicholas Daly, *Sensation and Modernity in the 1860s* (Cambridge: Cambridge University Press, 2009), 90.

51. See Dard Hunter, 'Stanwood and his Mummy Paper' in *Papermaking: The History and Technique of an Ancient Craft*, 2nd edn (London: Pleiades Books, 1967). The story of the import of mummies relies on oral history. It is debunked in Joseph A. Dane, 'The Curse of the Mummy Paper', in *The Myth of Print Culture: Essays on Evidence, Textuality, and Bibliographical Method* (Toronto: University of Toronto Press, 2003).

52. Morley in 'Sir Charles Dilke on Egypt', *African Review* 6 (19 Oct 1895), 659, cited by Bulfin, 'The Fictions of Gothic Egypt', 417.

53. Guy Boothby, 'A Professor of Egyptology', originally published in *The Graphic*, reprinted in *The Lady of the Island* (London: John Long, 1904), 41.

54. Guy Boothby, *Pharos the Egyptian* (London: Ward, Lock, 1899). 27.

55. Boothby, *Pharos*, 56.

56. For an eyewitness account of the war, see Winston Spencer Churchill, *The River War: An Historical Account of The Reconquest of The Soudan*, ed. Col. F. Rhodes, 2 vols (London: Longmans, Green, 1899).

57. Stephen Arata, 'The Occidental Tourist: *Dracula* and the Anxiety of Reverse Colonization', *Victorian Studies* 33 (1990), 623.

58. See Daniel Pick, *Svengali's Web: The Alien Enchanter in Modern Culture* (New Haven: Yale University Press, 2000).

59. For more context, see my 'Trance Gothic 1882–1897', in Ruth Robbins and Julian Wolfreys (eds), *Victorian Gothic* (Basingstoke: Palgrave, 2000), 148–67.

60. See the discussion of Fu-Manchu's 'mingled' Eastern physiognomy in Urmila Seshagiri, 'Modernity's (Yellow) Peril: Dr Fu-Manchu and English Race Paranoia', *Cultural Critique* 62 (2006), from which these quotes derive, 176–7.

61. Sax Rohmer, *The Romance of Sorcery* (1914; Rockville, MD: Wildside Press, 2003), 9.

62. For background, see Anne Witchard, *Thomas Burke's Dark Chinoiserie: Limehouse Nights and the Queer Spell of Chinatown* (Aldershot: Ashgate, 2009).

63. See Cay Van Ash and Elizabeth Sax Rohmer, *Master of Villainy: A Biography of Sax Rohmer* (Bowling Green: Bowling Green University Popular Press, 1972).

64. Sax Rohmer, *The Brood of the Witch-Queen* (London: Pearson, 1918), 3 & 6.

65. Rohmer, *Brood*, 23.

66. Rohmer, *Brood*, 28.

67. Rohmer, *Brood*, 147.

68. Rohmer, *Brood*, 103.

69. Rohmer, *Brood*, 194.

70. Rohmer, *Brood*, 196.

71. Robert Bloch, 'The Brood of Bubastis', *Weird Tales* (March 1937), 274–85. The Cornwall setting is a nod to the end of Stoker's *The Jewel of Seven Stars*, as we shall see. *Weird Tales* often exploited the aura of the uncanny around the King Tut discovery, and regularly published curse tales after 1923.

72. Sax Rohmer, *Tales of Secret Egypt* (1918; Amsterdam: Fredonia, 2002), 13.

73. Rohmer, *Tales of Secret Egypt*, 43.

74. Rohmer, *Tales of Secret Egypt*, 57.

75. Rohmer, *The Dream Detective: Being Some Account of the Methods of Moris Klaw* (London: Jarrolds, 1920), 82 and 48.

76. Rohmer, *Tales of Secret Egypt*, 215

77. See the opening sections of Edward Said, *Orientalism* (London: Penguin, 1985).

78. The best background introduction to Marsh is Minna Vuohelainen, 'Introduction', *The Beetle* (Kansas: Valancourt Books, 2008), vii–xli.

79. Richard Marsh, *The Beetle*, edited Julian Wolfreys (Peterborough: Broadview, 2004), 147.

80. Marsh, *The Beetle*, 53.

81. Marsh, *The Beetle*, 303.

82. Marsh, *The Beetle*, 105.

83. Marsh, *The Beetle*, 140.

84. Marsh, *The Beetle*, 150–1.

85. Minna Vuohelainen, '"Cribb'd, Cabined, and Confined": Fear, Claustrophobia and Modernity in Richard Marsh's Urban Gothic Fiction', *Journal of Literature and Science* 3/1 (2010), 24.

86. Judith Halberstam, *Skin Shows: Gothic Horror and the Technology of Monsters* (Durham, NC: Duke University Press, 1995), 21.

87. Kelly Hurley, *The Gothic Body: Sexuality, Materialism and Degeneration at the Fin de Siècle* (Cambridge: Cambridge University Press, 1996), 3–4. See also Julian Wolfreys, 'The Hieroglyphic Other: *The Beetle*, London, and the Abyssal Subject', in Lawrence Phillips (ed.), *A Mighty Mass of Brick and Smoke: Victorian and Edwardian Representations of London,* (Amsterdam: Rodopi, 2007), 169–92.

88. Richard Marsh, *The Goddess: A Demon* (London: F. V. White, 1900).

89. William R. Wilde, *Narrative of a Voyage to Madeira, Teneriffe, and Along the Shores of the Mediterranean, including a Visit to Algiers, Egypt, Palestine, Tyre, Rhodes, Telmessus, Cyprus and Greece*, 2 vols (Dublin: William Curry, 1840), I, 369, 370 and 387.

90. See Joyce Tyldesley, *Hatchepsut: The Female Pharaoh* (London: Penguin, 1998). In June 2007, the then Secretary General of the Supreme Council of Antiquities, Dr Zahi Hawass, announced that he had identified the 'missing' mummy of Hatshepsut.

91. Bram Stoker, *The Jewel of Seven Stars,* ed. Kate Hebblethwaite (London: Penguin, 2008), 35.

92. Stoker, *Jewel*, 124.

93. For some useful insights on this trajectory, see Meilee D. Bridges, 'Tales from the Crypt: Bram Stoker and the Curse of the Egyptian Mummy', *Victoria Institute Journal* 36 (2008), 137–65. The most sustained work on *Jewel* remains David Glover's *Vampires, Mummies and Liberals: Bram Stoker and the Politics of Popular Fiction* (Durham, NC: Duke University Press, 1996).

94. M. R. James, 'The Malice of Inanimate Objects' (1933), reprinted in *Casting the Runes and Other Ghost Stories,* ed. Michael Cox (Oxford: Oxford World's Classics, 1987), 288.

95. M. R. James, 'The Mezzotint' (1904) and '"Oh, Whistle, and I'll Come to You, My Lad"' (1904).

96. K. and Hesketh Prichard, *Ghosts: Being the Experiences of Flaxman Low* (London: Pearson, 1899), 95.

97. Prichard, *Ghosts,* 87.

98. Prichard, *Ghosts,* 97.

99. Jonah Siegel, *Haunted Museum: Longing, Travel and the Art-Romance Tradition* (Princeton: Princeton University Press, 2005), 4.

100. M. R. James, 'Casting the Runes' (1911). The manuscript of this story, appropriately enough, is in the British Library archive.

101. Sabine Baring-Gould, *A Book of Ghosts* (London: Methuen, 1904).

102. James Douglas, 'In the Reading Room', in *Adventures in London* (London: Cassell, 1909), 374, 375.

103. Edith Nesbit, *The Story of the Amulet* (London: Puffin, 1996), 145.

104. Nesbit, *Story of the Amulet,* 146.

105. See Julia Briggs, *A Woman of Passion: The Life of E. Nesbit 1858–1924* (London: Penguin, 1989), 245ff.

106. Jude Hill, 'The Story of the Amulet: Locating the Enchantment of Collections', *Journal of Material Culture* 12/1 (2007), 75. See also Karen Sands-O'Connor, 'Impertinent Miracles at the British Museum: Egyptology and Edwardian Fantasies for Young People', in *Journal of the Fantastic in the Arts* 19/2 (2008), 224–37.

107. See Mike Ashley, *Starlight Man: The Extraordinary Life of Algernon Blackwood* (London: Constable, 2001).

108. H. P. Lovecraft, *Supernatural Horror in Literature* (New York: Dover, 1973), 15 and 95.

109. China Miéville, 'Weird Fiction', in Mark Bould et al. (eds), *The Routledge Companion to Science Fiction* (London: Routledge, 2009), 511.

110. See Algernon Blackwood, *John Silence, Physician Extraordinary* (London: Eveleigh Nash, 1908).

111. Algernon Blackwood, 'Egypt: An Impression', *Country Life* (8 Nov 1913), 625.

112. Blackwood, 'Egypt: An Impression', 626.

113. Blackwood, 'Egypt: An Impression', 626.

114. Blackwood, 'Egypt: An Impression', 628.

115. Blackwood, 'Egyptian Sorcery', in *The Wolves of God and Other Fey Stories* (London: Cassell, 1921); 'By Water' and 'The Wings of Horus', along with 'An Egyptian Hornet', appeared in *Day and Night Stories* (London: Cassell, 1917).

116. Blackwood, 'Sand', in *Pan's Garden* (1912; Leyburn: Tartarus Press, 2000), 121.

117. Blackwood, 'Sand', 124.

118. Blackwood, 'Sand', 160.

119. For details, see Richard Kaczynski, *Perdurabo: The Life of Aleister Crowley* (Tempe, AZ: New Falcon, 2002), 157–9. Crowley will reappear in chapter 8.

120. Blackwood, 'Sand', 178.

121. Blackwood, 'A Descent into Egypt', *Incredible Adventures* (London: Macmillan, 1914), 247.

122. Blackwood, 'A Descent', 278.

123. Blackwood, 'A Descent,' 258 and 270.

124. Blackwood, 'A Descent', 318.

125. Blackwood, 'A Descent', 325.

126. Blackwood, 'A Descent', 275.

127. See my discussion of these links in *The Invention of Telepathy* (Oxford: Oxford University Press, 2002), 269ff.

128. Blackwood, *The Wave: An Egyptian Aftermath* (London: Macmillan, 1916), 184.

129. Blackwood, *The Wave*, 186.

130. Blackwood, *The Wave*, 186.

131. See, for instance, Norman A. Etherington, 'Rider Haggard, Imperialism, and the Layered Personality', *Victorian Studies* 22/1 (1978), 71–87.

132. Sigmund Freud, 'The Aetiology of Hysteria' (1896), *The Standard Edition of the Complete Psychological Works of Sigmund Freud*, ed. J. Strachey, vol. 3 (London: Hogarth, 1962), 189–221, 192.

133. The term 'introjection', as defined in a technical dictionary of psychoanalytic terms, occurs when, 'in phantasy, the subject transposes objects and their inherent qualities from the "outside" to the "inside" of himself'. J. Laplanche and J.-B. Pontalis, *The Language of Psychoanalysis*, trans. D. Nicholson-Smith (London: Karnac Books, 1988), 229.

134. F. W. H. Myers, 'The Subliminal Consciousness', *Proceedings of the Society for Psychical Research* 7 (1891–2), 329.

135. André Breton, 'The Automatic Message' (1933), in *What is Surrealism? Selected Writings*, ed. F. Rosemont (London: Pluto, 1978), 100.

## Chapter 7

1. Rider Haggard, 'King Tutankhamen. Reburial in Great Pyramid. Sir Rider Haggard's Plea', *The Times* (13 Feb 1923) 13.

2. Rider Haggard, 'Desecrating the Dead – A Protest', *Sunday Express* (18 Feb 1923), reproduced in Shirley M. Addy, *Rider Haggard and Egypt* (Accrington: AL Publications, 1998), 81.

3. Rider Haggard, Diary, 20 March 1923, vol. 20, Norfolk Record Office, MS4694/1/20.

4. Rider Haggard, Diary, 22 March 1923, vol. 20.

5. Rider Haggard, Diary, 22 March 1923, vol. 20.

6. Rider Haggard, undated cutting pasted into diary, 7 April 1923, vol. 20.

7. Rider Haggard, *The Private Diaries of Sir Rider Haggard 1914–25*, ed. D. S. Higgins (London: Cassell, 1980), 102.

8. Tom Pocock, *Rider Haggard and the Lost Empire* (London: Weidenfeld and Nicolson, 1993), 69–70. Pocock's chapter ends with this ellipsis, leaving the status of the story suspended.

9. Warren R. Dawson, 'A Note on the Egyptian Mummy in the Castle Museum Norwich', *Journal of Egyptian Archaeology* 15/3–4 (1929), 188.

10. Andrew Haggard, *Under Crescent and Star* (Edinburgh: Blackwood, 1895), 339.

11. Aylward M. Blackman, 'The Nugent and Haggard Collection of Egyptian Antiquities', *Journal of Egyptian Archaeology* 4/1 (1917), 39–46.

12. H. Rider Haggard, *The Days of my Life: An Autobiography*, 2 vols (London: Longmans, 1926), I, 245.

13. H. Rider Haggard, *She*, ed. Daniel Karlin (Oxford: Oxford World's Classics, 1991), 142.

14. Rider Haggard, *She*, 155.

15. Rider Haggard, *She*, 227.

16. Rider Haggard, *She*, 256.

17. Rider Haggard, *She*, 294.

18. Rider Haggard, *Days of my Life*, I, 257.

19. Andrew Lang, 'Realism and Romance' (1886), in Sally Ledger and Roger Luckhurst (eds), *The Fin de Siècle: A Reader in Cultural History c. 1880–1920* (Oxford: Oxford University Press, 2000), 102.

20. Sigmund Freud, *The Interpretation of Dreams, Standard Edition of the Complete Psychological Works of Sigmund Freud*, ed. J. Strachey, vol. 5 (London: Hogarth,

1958) 453–5. In his essay 'Psychology and Literature' (1930), Carl Jung names Haggard as his example for the view that 'it is the non-psychological novel that offers the richest opportunities for psychological elucidation': in *Collected Works*, trans. R. F. C. Hull, vol. 15 (London: Routledge and Kegan Paul, 1971), 88. In *The Archetypes and the Collective Unconscious*, Jung defines the anima via Haggard's fiction as a figure that is 'unconditional, dangerous, taboo, magical...She likes to appear in historic dress, with a predilection for Greece and Egypt': *Collected Works*, trans. R. F. C. Hull, vol. 9 part 1 (London: Routledge and Kegan Paul, 1968), 28.

21. C. S. Lewis, 'The Mythopoeic Gift of Rider Haggard', in *Essay Collection and Other Short Pieces*, ed. L. Walmsley (London: HarperCollins, 2000), 560.

22. For a critique of Haggard as ideologue of empire, see Wendy R. Katz, *Rider Haggard and the Fiction of Empire: A Critical Study of British Imperial Fiction* (Cambridge: Cambridge University Press, 1987). A more supportive account is Gerald H. Monsman, *H. Rider Haggard on the Imperial Frontier: The Political and Literary Contexts of his African Romances* (Greensboro: ELT Press, 2006).

23. Rider Haggard, *Dawn*, 3 vols (London: Hurst and Blackett, 1884), II, 136.

24. Rider Haggard, *Dawn*, II, 186–7.

25. Letter Kipling to Haggard, late 1889 (undated), in Morton Cohen (ed.), *Rudyard Kipling to Rider Haggard: The Record of a Friendship* (Rutherford: Fairleigh Dickinson University Press, 1965), 29.

26. Haggard, *Days of my Life*, I, 5.

27. John Lee's collection at his home outside Aylesbury was one of the most famous in mid-Victorian Britain. It was catalogued by Joseph Bonomi, *Catalogue of the Egyptian Antiquities in the Museum of Hartwell House* (London: W. M. Watts, 1858).

28. A. C. Haddon, *Brandon and Didlington Hall* (Cambridge: British Association, 1904). This was a guidebook printed for those taking the day trip associated with the British Association for the Advancement of Science that year.

29. T. G. H. James, *Howard Carter* (New York: I. B. Taurus, 2006), 12.

30. See Angela Reid's memoir at http://www.amhersts-of-didlington.com/taodh2.html.

31. See the Sotheby's list for *The Amherst Collection of Egyptian and Oriental Antiquities* reproduced at http://www.griffith.ox.ac.uk/gri/gif-files/Amherst_13.jpg.

32. See the report in *Medium and Daybreak* (26 May 1871), 167.

33. Rider Haggard, *Days of my Life*, I, 37.

34. Rider Haggard, *Days of my Life*, I, 38.

35. Rider Haggard, *Days of my Life*, I, 41.

36. Haggard claimed to have received a message from his dog, a retriever, as it lay dying after being hit by a train. He discussed this dream in a letter to *The Times* (21 July 1904) and it was later reported in the *Journal of the Society for Psychical Research*. It is recalled in *Days of my Life*, II, 161–2.

37. For background, see Joscelyn Godwin, *The Beginnings of Theosophy in France* (London: Theosophical History Centre, 1989). A typical Caithness occult publication was *The Mystery of All Ages Contained in the Secret Doctrine of All Religions* (London: C. Wallace, 1887).

38. See Carolyn Burdett, 'Romance, Reincarnation and Rider Haggard', in Nicola Bown, Carolyn Burdett and Pam Thurschwell (eds), *The Victorian Supernatural* (Cambridge: Cambridge University Press, 2004), 217–35.

39. Godfrey Haggard, 'Foreword' in Lilias Rider Haggard, *The Cloak that I Left: A Biography of the Author Henry Rider Haggard K. B. E. by his Daughter* (London: Hodder, 1951), 19 and 20.

40. Rider Haggard, *Days of my Life,* II, 169.

41. Rider Haggard, *Days of my Life,* I, 254.

42. Cited Morton Cohen, *Rider Haggard: His Life and Works* (London: Hutchinson, 1960), 150.

43. Empathy, the process of 'feeling into', was coined in English from German art theory by Haggard's contemporary, the aesthete and occasional ghost-story writer Vernon Lee. That she explored aesthetic empathy in strange experiments in museums and art galleries also has many parallels with Haggard. See, for instance, Vernon Lee 'Aesthetic Empathy and its Organic Accompaniments', in *Beauty and Ugliness, and Other Studies in Psychological Aesthetics* (London: John Lane, 1912), 45–76.

44. Letter Courtenay Mansel to Haggard, 30 July 1922, pasted into Haggard's diary, vol. 19, Norfolk Record Office MS4694/1/19, at 121.

45. Harry How, 'Illustrated Interviews – Mr H. Rider Haggard,' *Strand Magazine* (Jan 1892), 4, 7.

46. Rider Haggard, *Days of my Life,* I, 257.

47. Cited, Addy, *Haggard and Egypt,* 5.

48. Rider Haggard, *Cleopatra,* facsimile reprint of 1889 edn (Gillette: Wildside Press, 1999), 6.

49. Arthur Haggard went to Copenhagen in September 1889 to trace the genealogy of Sir Andrew Ogard, clearly at his father's request. Norfolk Record Office HAG 167/602/x3.

50. Rider Haggard, 'Egypt Today: The Land of Cleopatra', *Daily Mail* (23 April 1904), reproduced in Addy, *Haggard and Egypt,* 42.

51. Rider Haggard, 'The Trade in the Dead', *Daily Mail* (22 July 1904), reproduced in Addy, *Haggard and Egypt,* 51.

52. Rider Haggard, *Queen Sheba's Ring* (1910; London: Newnes, 1913), 7 and 10.

53. Rider Haggard, *Days of my Life,* II, 30.

54. Rider Haggard, 'The British Museum', *The Times* (24 Jan 1920), 8, and Haggard diary entry (8 Oct 1920) in *The Private Diaries,* 204.

55. Rider Haggard, *Days of my Life,* II, 33.

56. See Blackman, 'The Nugent and Haggard Collections', 44, including a long narrative of how Loftie gave the rings to Lang and Haggard, 45.

57. Freud issued these rings in May 1913. Phyllis Grosskurth, *The Secret Ring: Freud's Inner Circle and the Politics of Psychoanalysis* (Reading, MA: Addison-Wesley, 1991).

58. Rider Haggard, Diary entry 20 Dec 1922, vol. 20, Norfolk Record Office MS4694/1/20.

59. Rider Haggard, Diary 31 Dec 1923, vol. 21, NRO MS4694/1/21.

60. Rider Haggard, Diary, 2 Feb 1923, vol. 22, NRO MS4693/1/22.

61. Rider Haggard, Diary, 8 Feb 1923, vol. 22, NRO MS4693/1/22.

62. Rider Haggard, Diary, 24 Jan 1923, vol. 22, NRO MS4693/1/22.

63. Rider Haggard, Diary, 2 Feb 1923, vol. 22, NRO MS4693/1/22.

64. Rider Haggard, Diary, 20 Feb 1923, vol. 22, NRO MS4693/1/22.

65. Rider Haggard, Diary, 5 March 1923, vol. 22, NRO MS4693/1/22.

66. Rider Haggard, Diary, 23 March 1923, vol. 22, NRO MS4693/1/22.

67. Rider Haggard, Diary, 5 Dec 1923, vol. 22, NRO MS4693/1/22.

68. Godfrey Haggard, 'Foreword' to Lilias Haggard, *The Cloak that I Left*, 21.

69. Andrew Haggard, *Under Crescent and Star*, 75.

70. Guy C. Dawnay, *Campaigns: Zulu 1879, Egypt 1882, Suakim 1885* (Cambridge: Kent Trotman, 1989), journals printed for private circulation. Dawnay, like Walter Ingram, was killed big game hunting in 1889.

71. Andrew Haggard, *Under Crescent and Star*, 120.

72. Andrew Haggard, *Under Crescent and Star*, 370–1.

73. Andrew Haggard, *Dodo and I: A Novel* (Edinburgh: Blackwood, 1889), 22.

74. A. C. P. Haggard, *A Strange Tale of the Scarabaeus* (London: Kegan Paul, 1891), 164.

75. John D. Yohannan, *Joseph and Potiphar's Wife: An Anthology of the Story of the Chaste Youth and the Lustful Stepmother* (New York: New Directions, 1968).

76. Arthur Amyand, *With Rank and File, or Sidelights on the Soldier's Life* (London: Osgood, 1895), 73.

77. Amyand, *With Rank and File*, 146.

78. Arthur Amyand, *The Kiss of Isis* (London: Hurst & Blackett, 1900), 11.

79. Amyand, *Kiss of Isis*, 16.

80. Amyand, *Kiss of Isis*, 119.

81. Marilena Parlati, 'Memories of Exoticism and Empire: Henry Rider Haggard's *Wunderkammer* at Ditchingham House', in Harald Hendrix (ed.), *Writers' Houses and the Making of Memory* (London: Routledge, 2008), 178.

82. See, for very helpful formulations, Krzysztof Pomain, *Collectors and Curiosities, Paris and Venice, 1500–1800*, trans. E. Wiles-Portier (Cambridge: Polity, 1990), 24.

83. Rider Haggard, *Days of my Life*, I, 259.

84. H. P. Blavatsky, *Isis Unveiled: A Master-Key to the Mysteries of Ancient and Modern Science and Theology*, 2 vols (New York: J. W. Bouton, 1877), I, 182. Blavatsky references W. Denton's *The Soul of Things* (1873).

85. Rider Haggard, *Private Diaries*, 209.

86. Walter Benjamin, *One-Way Street*, trans. E. Jephcott and K. Shorter (London: Verso, 1997), 48.

87. Walter Benjamin, *One-Way Street*, 48–9.

88. Walter Benjamin, *One-Way Street*, 49. Benjamin's next section is called 'Chinese Curios', continuing the theme.

89. Carlo Salzani, 'The City as Crime Scene: Walter Benjamin and the Traces of the Detective', *New German Critique* 100 (2007), 179.

90. H. Rider Haggard, *King Solomon's Mines*, ed. Dennis Butts (Oxford: Oxford World's Classics, 2006), 167.

91. Rider Haggard, *She*, 214 and 170.

92. Rider Haggard, *Queen Sheba's Ring*, 139.

93. H. Rider Haggard, *Virgin of the Sun* (London: Cassell, 1922), 13.

94. Sigmund Freud, 'Medusa's Head' (1922), *Standard Edition of the Complete Psychological Works of Sigmund Freud*, ed. J. Strachey, vol. 18 (London: Hogarth, 1955), 273–4.

95. Richard Pearson, 'Archaeology and Gothic Desire: Vitality Beyond the Grave in H. Rider Haggard's Ancient Egypt', in Ruth Robbins and Julian Wolfreys (eds), *Victorian Gothic: Literary and Cultural Manifestations in the Nineteenth Century* (Basingstoke: Palgrave, 2000), 242. Patrick Brantlinger has also discussed *She* as offering 'the consolations of necrophilia' in his 'Mummy Love: *She* and Archaeology', in Tania Zulli (ed.), *She: Explorations into a Romance* (Rome: Aracne, 2009), 49.

## Chapter 8

1. Shirley Jackson, *The Haunting of Hill House* in *Novels and Stories* (New York: Library of America, 2010), 327.

2. Sax Rohmer, *The Green Eyes of Bâst* (London: Cassell, 1920), 280.

3. Riccardo Stephens, *The Mummy* (London: Eveleigh Nash, 1912), 284.

4. Cheiro, *True Ghost Stories* (London: London Publishing Company, 1928), 52.

5. Elliott O'Donnell, *Haunted Houses of London* (London: Eveleigh Nash, 1909), 92.

6. Cited by Ernest A. Wallis Budge, *Egyptian Magic* (1899; London: Routledge and Kegan Paul, 1972), 79–80.

7. J. F. Bourghouts, 'The Evil Eye of Apopis', *Journal of Egyptian Archaeology* 59 (1973), 114–30.

8. David C. Lindberg, *Theories of Vision from Al-Kindi to Kepler* (Chicago: University of Chicago Press, 1976), 19.

9. Francis Bacon, 'On Envy' *The Essays*, ed. J. Pitcher (Harmondsworth: Penguin, 1985), 83.

10. Rupert Sheldrake, *The Sense of Being Stared At, and Other Aspects of the Extended Mind* (London: Arrow, 2004).

11. See Deuteronomy 28.54 or Galatians 3.1.

12. Frederick Thomas Elsworthy, *The Evil Eye: An Account of this Ancient and Widespread Superstition* (London: John Murray, 1895), 6.

13. Elsworthy, *Evil Eye*, 3.

14. Elsworthy, *Evil Eye*, 6.

15. Edward Tylor, *Primitive Culture: Researches into the Development of Mythology, Philosophy, Religion, Art and Custom*, 2 vols (London: John Murray, 1871), II, 453.

16. See Alan Dundes (ed.), *The Evil Eye: A Casebook* (Madison: University of Wisconsin Press, 1992).

17. A. E. Waite, 'The Life of the Mystic', *Occult Review* 1 (1905), 29.

18. The classic account is Frances Yates, *Giordano Bruno and the Hermetic Tradition* (London: Routledge, 2002).

19. See Stephen Clucas (ed.), *John Dee: Interdisciplinary Studies in English Renaissance Thought* (Dordecht: Springer, 2006).

20. A. P. Sinnett, *The Occult World*, (London: Trubner, 1881), 4.

21. Sinnett, *The Occult World*, 5. On Tibet as a 'sanitorium for the recuperation of an exhaustive body of knowledge that was always in danger of entropy, loss, or destruction' see Thomas Richards, *The Imperial Archive: Knowledge and the Fantasy of Empire* (London: Verso, 1993), 12.

22. See Logie Barrow, *Independent Spirits: Spiritualism and English Plebeians 1850–1919* (London: Routledge, 1986).

23. Sinnett, *The Occult World*, 12.
24. H. P. Blavatsky, *Isis Unveiled: A Master-Key to the Mysteries of Ancient and Modern Science and Theology*, 2 vols (New York: J. W. Bouton, 1877), I, vi.
25. R. E. Witt, *Isis in the Ancient World* (Baltimore: Johns Hopkins University Press, 1971), 153. See also Hugh Bowden, *Mystery Cults in the Ancient World* (London: Thames & Hudson, 2010), which suggests that the ceremonies were less about imparting a doctrine than experiencing an 'imagistic' disorientation of darkness and confusion coming into light.
26. Erik Hornung, *The Secret Lore of Egypt: Its Impact on the West*, trans. D. Lorton (Ithaca: Cornell University Press, 2001), 3.
27. Brian Curran et al., *Obelisk: A History* (Cambridge, MA: Burndy Library, 2009), 88.
28. Blavatsky, *Isis Unveiled*, I, xlii.
29. Blavatsky, *Isis Unveiled*, I, 380 and 384.
30. 'Report of the Committee Appointed to Investigate Phenomena Connected with the Theosophical Society', *Proceedings of the Society for Psychical Research* 3 (1885), 313 and 314.
31. See Janet Oppenheim, *The Other World: Spiritualism and Psychical Research in England, 1850–1914* (Cambridge: Cambridge University Press, 1985).
32. Annie Besant, *An Autobiography* (London: Unwin, 1893), 341. She reported on her psychical researches in *Why I Became A Theosophist* (London: Freethought Publishing, 1889).
33. Edward Maitland, *Anna Kingsford: Her Life, Letters, Diary and Work*, 2 vols (London: Redway, 1896), I, 258 and 259.
34. W. T. Stead, 'Killing by Willing: Some Confessions by the Killer-Willers', *Borderland* 3 (April 1896), 212.
35. Maitland, *Kingsford*, I, 261.
36. See discussion of Kingsford in Mary K. Greer, *Women of the Golden Dawn: Rebels and Priestesses* (Rochester, VT: Park Street, 1995).
37. Alfred Binet and Charles Féré, *Animal Magnetism*, 3rd edn (London: Kegan Paul, 1891), 96.
38. Binet and Féré, *Animal Magnetism*, 206.
39. R. Osgood Mason, *Hypnotism and Suggestion in Therapeutics, Education and Reform* (London: Kegan Paul, 1901), 216.
40. James Coates, *How to Mesmerise: A Manual of Instruction in the History, Mysteries, Modes of Procedure, and Arts of Mesmerism* (London: Hay Nisbet, 1893), 39.
41. See leader article, *British Medical Journal* (31 May 1890), 1264.
42. For a history of the anti-Semitic inflection of evil eye beliefs, see Daniel Pick, *Svengali's Web: The Alien Enchanter in Modern Culture* (New Haven: Yale University Press, 2000).
43. A. R. Orage, *Consciousness: Animal, Human and Superhuman* (London: Theosophical Publishing Society, 1907), 72.
44. Paul Selver, *Orage and The New Age Circle: Reminiscences and Reflections* (London: Allen & Unwin, 1959), 15.
45. See Wallace Martin, *The New Age under Orage: Chapters in English Cultural History* (Manchester: Manchester University Press, 1967).

46. Formulations here have been aided by Paul Heelas, *The New Age Movement* (Oxford: Blackwell, 1996).

47. Gauri Viswanathan, 'The Ordinary Business of Occultism', *Critical Inquiry* 27 (2000), 2.

48. With this caveat, I have relied mainly on Mary K. Greer, *Women of the Golden Dawn*, Francis King, *Modern Ritual Magic: The Rise of Western Occultism* (1970; Bridport: Prism, 1989), Ellic Howe, *The Magicians of the Golden Dawn: A Documentary History of a Magical Order, 1887–1923* (London: Routledge and Kegan Paul, 1972) and R. A. Gilbert, *Revelations of the Golden Dawn: The Rise and Fall of a Magical Order* (London: Quantum, 1997).

49. J. S. Curl, *The Art and Architecture of Freemasonry* (London: Batsford, 1991), 22.

50. For discussion, see Peter French, *John Dee: the World of an Elizabethan Magus* (London: Ark, 1987).

51. Frances Yates, *The Rosicrucian Enlightenment* (London: Routledge, 1972), 253.

52. Georg Simmel, 'The Sociology of Secrecy and Secret Societies', *American Journal of Sociology* 11/4 (1906), 462.

53. King, *Modern Ritual Magic*, 55.

54. Cited Gilbert, *Revelations of the Golden Dawn*, 23.

55. Westcott, 'The Golden Dawn's Official History Lecture', Appendix G of King, *Modern Ritual Magic*, 212.

56. Westcott, 'Golden Dawn's Official History Lecture,' 213.

57. Aleister Crowley, 'The Temple of Solomon the King, part III', *Equinox* 1/3 (1910), 143, 148.

58. Aleister Crowley, 'The Temple of Solomon the King, part II', *Equinox* 1/2 (1909), 241.

59. Crowley, 'The Temple of Solomon II', 255.

60. Crowley, 'The Temple of Solomon II', 258.

61. Frederic Lees, 'Isis Worship in Paris: Conversations with Hierophant Rameses and the High Priestess Anari', *The Humanitarian* 16 (1900), 85–6.

62. Lees, 'Isis Worship in Paris', 83, 87.

63. Dion Fortune, *Psychic Self-Defence: A Study in Occult Pathology and Criminality* (Wellingborough: Aquarian Press, 1977), 9, 18.

64. Fortune, *Psychic Self-Defence*, 17.

65. Fortune, *Psychic Self-Defence*, 25.

66. Fortune, *Psychic Self-Defence*, 74.

67. Fortune, *Psychic Self-Defence*, 19.

68. I have discussed this connection in *The Invention of Telepathy* (Oxford: Oxford University Press, 2002), 270–6.

69. Ezra Pound, cited A. Walton Litz, 'Florence Farr: A "Transitional" Woman', in Maria D. Battista and Lucy MacDiarmid (eds), *High and Low Moderns: Literature and Culture, 1889–1939* (Oxford: Oxford University Press, 1996), 86.

70. W. B. Yeats, 'Egyptian Plays' (reviewed for *Star* in 1902), in *Collected Works*, vol. 10: *Later Articles and Reviews*, ed. Colton Johnson (New York: Scribner, 2000), 62, 63.

71. Florence Farr, *Egyptian Magic* (Wellingborough: Aquarian Press, 1982), 11.

72. Farr, *Egyptian Magic*, 16.

73. Irene E. Toye-Warner, 'Black Magic in Ancient and Modern Egypt', *Occult Review* 23 (1916), 144.

74. The pioneering book is George Mills Harper, *Yeats's Golden Dawn* (London: Macmillan, 1974). A helpful short summary is Margaret Mills Harper, 'Yeats and the Occult', in Marjorie Hawes and John Kelly (eds), *The Cambridge Companion to W. B. Yeats* (Cambridge: Cambridge University Press, 2006), 144–66.

75. W. B. Yeats, 'Magic' (1901) in *Essays and Introductions* (London: Macmillan, 1911), 36.

76. Yeats, 'Magic', 28.

77. W. B. Yeats, *Autobiographies* (1922), *Collected Works*, vol. 3, ed. W. H. O'Donnell and Douglas N. Archibald (New York: Scribner, 1999), 204.

78. Yeats, *Autobiographies*, 204–5.

79. W. B. Yeats, 'Is the Order of R. R. & A. C. to Remain a Magical Order?' (1901), as Appendix K in Harper, *Yeats's Golden Dawn*, 263.

80. Cited Lawrence Sutin, *Do What thou Wilt: A Life of Aleister Crowley* (New York: St Martin's, 2000), 72.

81. Mathers cited Richard Kaczynski, *Perdurabo: The Life of Aleister Crowley* (Tempe, AZ: New Falcon, 2002), 63, and Aleister Crowley, 'The Temple of Solomon III', 266.

82. Crowley, 'The Temple of Solomon III', 264. These incidents are related from Yeats's perspective in Harper, *Yeats's Golden Dawn*, but also in R. F. Foster, *W. B. Yeats: A Life*, vol. 1: *The Apprentice Mage 1865–1914* (Oxford: Oxford University Press, 1998).

83. The trial is discussed by Gilbert, *Revelations of the Golden Dawn*, and King, *Modern Ritual Magic*. The tone of the reporting is well instanced in the stories filed for the *Evening News* in October 1901. 'The Horos Creed. In most of the mystic religions the world has seen there is peculiar significance in the number seven. This fact was probably in the minds of the two Horoses when they entered the dock at Marylebone Police-court today for the seventh time.' *Evening News* (17 Oct 1901), 3.

84. Cited Gilbert, *Revelations of the Golden Dawn*, 17.

85. W. B. Yeats, 'The Manuscript of "Leo Africanus"', in Steve Adams and George Mills Harper (eds), *Yeats Annual* 1 (1982), 21.

86. Yeats, 'Manuscript of "Leo Africanus"', 38.

87. Crowley, 'The Temple of Solomon II', 289.

88. Crowley, cited Sutin, *Do What thou Wilt*, 115.

89. For discussion of these rituals, see Alex Owen, 'The Sorcerer and his Apprentice: Aleister Crowley and the Magical Exploration of Edwardian Subjectivity', *Journal of British Studies* 36 (1997), 99–133.

90. Arnold Bennett, *Paris Nights* (New York: Doran, 1913), 36.

91. See Gary Lachman, *Turn Off your Mind: The Mystic Sixties and the Dark Side of the Age of Aquarius* (London: Sidgwick and Jackson, 2001).

92. Anthony Powell, *The Kindly Ones* (1962) in *A Dance to the Music of Time*, 4 vols (London: Arrow, 2000), II, 504, 559. Powell said that Trelawney was a composite, including Crowley but also recalling the eccentric cult leader of an ancient Greek cult revival before the Great War, Dr Oyler.

93. Crowley, 'The Temple of Solomon II', 214.

94. Algernon Blackwood, 'Smith: An Episode in a Lodging House', in *The Empty House* (London: Eveleigh Nash, 1906), 189.

95. Blackwood, 'Smith', 198.

96. The similarities and potential biographical links are discussed in Ron Weighall, 'Dark Devotions: M. R. James and the Magical Tradition', in S. T. Joshi and Rosemary Pardoe (eds), *Warnings to the Curious: A Sheaf of Criticism on M. R. James* (New York: Hippocampus, 2007), 129–30.

97. William Hope Hodgson, *Carnacki, the Ghost-Finder* was published in book form in 1913, and reissued in 'The Dennis Wheatley Library of the Occult' (London: Sphere, 1974).

98. Somerset Maugham, 'A Fragment of Autobiography', published as Preface to *The Magician* (London: Vintage, 2000), vii, viii.

99. Dennis Wheatley, *The Devil Rides Out* (London: Heron, 1972), 4.

100. Wheatley, *Devil Rides Out*, 170.

101. Charles Williams, *Witchcraft* (London: Faber, 1941), 9, 35.

102. Yates, *The Rosicrucian Enlightenment*, 262.

103. James George Frazer, *The Golden Bough: A Study in Magic and Religion,* Part 1: *The Magic Art*, vol. 1, 3rd edn (London: Macmillan, 1932), xx.

104. Frazer, *Golden Bough*, I, 53.

105. Frazer, *Golden Bough*, I, 222.

106. Frazer, *Golden Bough*, I, 119.

107. See, for instance, Constance E. Padwick, 'Notes on the Jinn and the Ghoul in the Peasant Mind of Lower Egypt', *Bulletin of the School of Oriental Studies* 3/3 (1924), 421–46. See also Hans Alexander Winkler's 1936 study *Ghost Riders of Upper Egypt: A Study of Spirit Possession,* trans. N. Hopkins (Cairo: American University in Cairo Press, 2009).

108. Ernest A. Wallis Budge, *Egyptian Magic* (1899; London: Routledge and Kegan Paul, 1972), ix.

109. Wallis Budge, *Egyptian Magic,* 6.

110. Wallis Budge, *Egyptian Magic,* 1. Frazer's schema is explicitly abandoned by subsequent specialists. See, for instance, Geraldine Pinch, *Magic in Ancient Egypt* (Austin: University of Texas Press, 1994).

111. Alexandre Moret, *In the Time of the Pharaohs,* trans. Mme Moret (New York: Putnam's, 1911), 297, 303.

112. Frazer, *Golden Bough*, I, 236, 237.

113. Max Weber, 'Science as a Vocation', in *From Max Weber: Essays in Sociology,* trans. H. H. Gerth and C. Wright Mills (London: Routledge and Kegan Paul, 1948), 139.

114. For Victorian specifics, see Frank M. Turner, *Contesting Cultural Authority: Essays in Victorian Intellectual Life* (Cambridge: Cambridge University Press, 1993). For a broad-sweep counter-thesis that argues that there was a change in the conditions of religious belief but not belief itself, see Charles Taylor, *A Secular Age* (Cambridge, MA: Harvard University Press, 2007).

115. See Jane Bennett, *The Enchantment of Modern Life: Attachments, Crossings, and Ethics* (Princeton: Princeton University Press, 2001).

116. Alex Owen, *The Places of Enchantment: British Occultism and the Culture of the Modern* (Chicago: Chicago University Press, 2004), 255.

117. Simon During, *Modern Enchantments: The Cultural Power of Secular Magic* (Cambridge, MA: Harvard University Press, 2002), 24.

118. Carol Nemeroff and Paul Rozin, 'The Makings of the Magical Mind: The Nature and Function of Sympathetic Magical Thinking', in Karl S. Rosengren et al. (eds), *Imagining the Impossible: Magical, Scientific, and Religious Thinking in Children* (Cambridge: Cambridge University Press, 2000), 25. On grief and magical thinking, see my 'Reflections on Joan Didion's *The Year of Magical Thinking*', *New Formations* 67 (2009), 91–100.

119. Thomas Laqueur, 'Why the Margins Matter: Occultism and the Making of Modernity', *Modern Intellectual History* 3/1 (2006), 111–35.

120. World Health Organization definition, cited by Daniel Freeman and Philippa Garety, *Paranoia: The Psychology of Persecutory Delusions* (Hove: Psychology Press, 2004), 9.

121. These formulations have been assisted by Richard Hofstadter's classic account, *The Paranoid Style in American Politics and Other Essays* (London: Cape, 1966).

122. Sigmund Freud, 'Psychoanalytic Notes on An Autobiographical Account of a Case of Paranoia (Dementia Paranoides)' (1911), in *Case Histories II,* Penguin Freud Library, vol. 11 (Harmondsworth: Penguin, 1979), 204, 210.

123. Freud, 'The Uncanny' (1919), in *Art and Literature,* Penguin Freud Library, vol. 14 (Harmondsworth: Penguin, 1985), 362.

124. Vivian Garrison and Conrad Arensberg, 'The Evil Eye: Envy or Risk of Seizure? Paranoia or Rational Dependency?' in Clarence Maloney (ed), *The Evil Eye* (New York: Columbia University Press, 1976), 293.

125. Roger Caillois, *The Mask of Medusa,* trans. G. Ordish (London: Gollancz, 1964), 101.

126. Caillois, *Mask of the Medusa,* 97.

127. Steven Connor, 'Fascination, the Skin and the Screen,' *Critical Quarterly* 40/1 (1998), 21.

128. On Freud's persistent trouble with hypnosis, see Mikkel Borch-Jacobsen, *The Emotional Tie: Psychoanalysis, Mimesis and Affect,* trans. D. Brick (New Haven: Yale University Press, 1993).

129. Philip K. Dick, 'Colony' in *Beyond Lies the Wub* (London: Gollancz, 1988), 404.

130. Steven Connor, *Paraphernalia: The Curious Lives of Magical Things* (London: Profile, 2011), 4.

131. Jean Baudrillard, *Fatal Strategies,* trans. P. Beitchman and W. G. J. Niesluchowski (New York: Semiotext(e), 1990), 111.

132. 'Object-oriented philosophy' is a term associated with the philosopher Graham Harman, developing the ideas of Bruno Latour. For an introduction, see Harman, *Towards Speculative Realism: Essays and Lectures* (Winchester: Zero Books, 2010). Harman's most detailed elaboration of his position is in *Prince of Networks: Bruno Latour and Metaphysics* (Melbourne: Re:Press, 2009).

133. Jane Bennett, *Vibrant Matter: A Political Ecology of Things* (Durham, NC: Duke University Press, 2010), 5.

134. Graham Harman, 'Autonomous Objects', *New Formations* 71 (2011), 30.

# Afterword

1. See Adam Shatz, 'Whose Egypt?', *London Review of Books* (5 Jan 2012), 15–17.

2. See, for instance, the CultureGrrl blog at the *Arts Journal*, 'Damaged King Tut, Three Other Missing Objects, Recovered by Egyptian Museum', http://www.artsjournal.com/culturegrrl/2011/04/harpooning_tut_three_other_mis.html.

3. Christina Riggs, 'We've Been Here Before', *Times Higher Education* (24 Feb 2011), http://www.timeshighereducation.co.uk/story.asp?storycode=415262.

4. Nervine el-Aref, 'Missing Artefacts from the Egyptian Museum Returned,' http://english.ahram.org.eg/NewsContentP/9/9871/Heritage/Missing-artifacts-from-the-Egyptian-Museum-retriev.aspx.

5. Elliott Colla, *Conflicted Antiquities: Egyptology, Egyptomania, Egyptian Modernity* (Durham, NC: Duke University Press, 2007), 177.

6. James A. Secord, 'Knowledge in Transit', *Isis* 95 (2004), 659.

7. Christopher Herbert, *War of No Pity: The Indian Mutiny and Victorian Trauma* (Princeton: Princeton University Press, 2008), 45.

8. Rabab El-Mahdi and Philip Marfleet, 'Introduction', El-Mahdi and Marfleet (eds), *Egypt: The Moment of Change* (London: Zed Books, 2009), 2.

9. Perry Anderson, 'On the Concatenation in the Arab World', *New Left Review* 68 (March/April 2011), 6.

# BIBLIOGRAPHY

## Manuscript Sources

British Museum, Department of the Middle East Archive
British Museum, Department of Ancient Egypt and Sudan Archive
Ghost Club Papers, British Library
Henry Rider Haggard Papers, Norfolk Public Record Office
Walter Ingram Papers, private collection
London Metropolitan Archives
Sir William Mackinnon Papers, School of Oriental and African Studies
Captain H. B. Murray Bequest Papers, Victoria and Albert Museum

## Unpublished Sources

Farley, Sarah E. M., 'The Bequest of Captain H. B. Murray (1843–1910) to the Victoria and Albert Museum', MA dissertation, Courtauld Institute of Art, 2001.

## Printed Sources

Abrahams, Aleck, 'The Egyptian Hall, Piccadilly, 1813–73', *Antiquary* 42 (1906), 61–4, 139–44 and 225–30.
Addy, Shirley M., *Rider Haggard and Egypt* (Accrington: AL Publications, 1998).
Alcott, Louisa May, 'Lost in a Pyramid, or the Mummy's Curse' (1869), in J. R. Stephens (ed.), *Into the Mummy's Tomb* (New York: Berkley Books, 2001), 33–42.
Allen, Grant, 'My New Year's Eve Among the Mummies' (1880), http://gaslight.mtroyal.ab.ca/newmummy.htm
Alloula, Malek, *The Colonial Harem*, trans. M. and W. Gozich (Manchester: Manchester University Press, 1986).
Altick, Robert, *The Shows of London* (Cambridge, MA: Harvard University Press, 1978).
Amyand, Arthur, *The Kiss of Isis* (London: Hurst & Blackett, 1900).
—— *With Rank and File, or Sidelights on the Soldier's Life* (London: Osgood, 1895).
Anderson, Perry, 'On the Concatenation in the Arab World', *New Left Review* 68 (March/April 2011), 5–15.
Andrews, Herbert C., 'The Leicester Square and Strand Panoramas: Their Proprietors and Artists', *Notes and Queries* 159 (1930), 57–61 and 75–8.

Annis, Sheldon, 'The Museum as Staging Ground for Symbolic Action', *Museum* 151 (1986), 168–71.

Arata, Stephen, 'The Occidental Tourist: *Dracula* and the Anxiety of Reverse Colonization', *Victorian Studies* 33 (1990), 621–45.

Arnold, Catharine *Necropolis: London and its Dead* (London: Pocket Books, 2007).

Arnold, Dana, 'Panoptic Visions of London: Possessing the Metropolis', *Art History* 32/2 (2009), 332–50.

Ash, Cay Van and Rohmer, Elizabeth Sax, *Master of Villainy: A Biography of Sax Rohmer* (Bowling Green: Bowling Green University Popular Press, 1972).

Ashley, Mike, *Starlight Man: The Extraordinary Life of Algernon Blackwood* (London: Constable, 2001).

Auerbach, Jeffrey A., *The Great Exhibition of 1851: A Nation on Display* (New Haven: Yale University Press, 1999).

Bacon, Francis, 'On Envy' (1625), *The Essays*, ed. J. Pitcher (Harmondsworth: Penguin, 1985), 83–8.

Bailey, Isabel, *Herbert Ingram Esq., M. P., of Boston* (Boston, Lincolnshire: Richard Key, 1996).

Baker, Nicholson, *Double Fold: Libraries and the Assault on Paper* (New York: Random House, 2001).

Baker, Sir Samuel, *Wild Beasts and their Ways: Reminiscences of Europe, Asia, Africa, and America*, 2 vols (London: Macmillan, 1891).

Balderston, John, 'Tutankhamen's Royal Gems Dazzle Explorers', *The World* (13 Nov 1923), 1–2.

Baldick, Chris, 'The End of the Line: The Family Curse in Shorter Gothic Fiction', in V. Tinkler-Villani and P. Davidson (eds), *Exhibited by Candlelight: Sources and Developments in the Gothic Tradition* (Amsterdam: Rodopi, 1995), 147–57.

Ball, Adrian, *Cleopatra's Needle: The Story of One Hundred Years in London* (Havant: Kenneth Mason, 1978).

Ballaster, Ros, *Fabulous Orients: Fictions of the East in England 1662–1785* (Oxford: Oxford University Press, 2007).

Baring-Gould, Sabine, *A Book of Ghosts* (London: Methuen, 1904).

Barrell, John, *The Infection of Thomas De Quincey: A Psychopathology of Imperialism* (New Haven: Yale University Press, 1991).

Barrow, Logie, *Independent Spirits: Spiritualism and English Plebeians 1850–1919* (London: Routledge, 1986).

Baudrillard, Jean, *Fatal Strategies,* trans. P. Beitchman and W. G. J. Niesluchowski (New York: Semiotext(e), 1990).

Beard, Charles R., *Lucks and Talismans: A Chapter of Popular Superstition* (London: Sampson and Low, 1934).

Beckford, William, *Vathek*, ed. Roger Lonsdale (Oxford: Oxford World's Classics, 1998).

Belzoni, Giovanni, *Belzoni's Travels: Narrative of the Operations and Recent Discoveries in Egypt and Nubia* (1820), edited and introduced by Alberto Siliotti (London: British Museum, 2001).

—— *Description of the Egyptian Tomb, Discovered by G. Belzoni* (London: John Murray, 1821).

Benjamin, Walter, *The Arcades Project*, trans. H. Eiland and K. McLaughlin (Cambridge, MA: Harvard University Press, 1999).

—— *One-Way Street*, trans. E. Jephcott and K. Shorter (London: Verso, 1997).

Bennett, Arnold, *Paris Nights* (New York: Doran, 1913).

Bennett, Jane, *The Enchantment of Modern Life: Attachments, Crossings, and Ethics* (Princeton: Princeton University Press, 2001).

—— *Vibrant Matter: A Political Ecology of Things* (Durham, NC: Duke University Press, 2010).

Bennett, Tony, *The Birth of the Museum: History, Theory, Politics* (London: Routledge, 1995).

Beresford, Charles, *The Memoirs of Admiral Lord Charles Beresford*, 2 vols (London: Methuen, 1914).

Besant, Annie, *An Autobiography* (London: Unwin, 1893).

—— *Reincarnation: Its Necessity* (Adyar: Theosophical Publishing House, 1915).

—— *Why I Became A Theosophist* (London: Freethought Publishing, 1889).

Besant, Walter, *All Sorts and Conditions of Men* (Oxford: Oxford University Press, 1997).

Binet, Alfred and Féré, Charles, *Animal Magnetism*, 3rd edn (London: Kegan Paul, 1891).

Black, Barbara J., *On Exhibit: Victorians and their Museums* (Charlottesville: University of Virginia Press, 2000).

Blackman, Aylward M., 'The Nugent and Haggard Collection of Egyptian Antiquities', *Journal of Egyptian Archaeology* 4/1 (1917), 39–46.

Blackwood, Algernon, *Day and Night Stories* (London: Cassell, 1917).

—— 'A Descent into Egypt', *Incredible Adventures* (London: Macmillan, 1914), 241–335.

—— 'Egypt: An Impression', *Country Life* (8 Nov 1913), 625–8.

—— 'The Egyptian Desert from Heluan I', *Country Life* (16 March 1908), 381–4.

—— 'Egyptian Sorcery', in *The Wolves of God and Other Fey Stories* (London: Cassell, 1921), 153–71.

—— *John Silence, Physician Extraordinary* (London: Eveleigh Nash, 1908).

—— 'Sand', in *Pan's Garden* (1912; Leyburn: Tartarus Press, 2000), 119–88.

—— 'Smith: An Episode in a Lodging House', in *The Empty House* (London: Eveleigh Nash, 1906), 186–217.

—— 'Superstition and the Magic "Curse"', *Daily Express* (9 April 1923), 6.

—— *The Wave: An Egyptian Aftermath* (London: Macmillan, 1916).

Blanchard, Pascal, Bancel, Nicolas, Boëtsch, Gilles, Deroo, Éric and Lemaire, Sandrine (eds), *Human Zoos: Science and Spectacle in the Age of Colonial Empires*, trans. T. Bridgeman (Liverpool: Liverpool University Press, 2008).

Blavatsky, H. P., *Isis Unveiled: A Master-Key to the Mysteries of Ancient and Modern Science and Theology*, 2 vols (New York: J. W. Bouton, 1877).

[Blessington, Lady], *The Magic Lantern, or, Sketches of Scenes in the Metropolis* (London: Longman, 1823).

Bloch, Robert, 'The Brood of Bubastis', *Weird Tales* (March 1937), 274–85.

Bolton, Carol, *Writing the Empire: Robert Southey and Romantic Colonialism* (London: Pickering and Chatto, 2007).

Bonomi, Joseph, *Catalogue of the Egyptian Antiquities in the Museum of Hartwell House* (London: W. M. Watts, 1858).

Booth, Charlotte, *The Curse of the Mummy and Other Ancient Mysteries of Egypt* (Oxford: Oneworld, 2009).

Booth, Michael, 'Soldiers of the Queen: Drury Lane Imperialism', in M. Hays and A. Nikolopoulou (eds), *Melodrama: The Cultural Emergence of a Genre* (New York: St Martin's Press, 1996), 3–20.

Boothby, Guy, *Pharos the Egyptian* (London: Ward, Lock, 1899).

—— 'A Professor of Egyptology', in *The Lady of the Island* (London: John Long, 1904), 37–72.

Borch-Jacobsen, Mikkel, *The Emotional Tie: Psychoanalysis, Mimesis and Affect,* trans. D. Brick (New Haven: Yale University Press, 1993).

Bouquet, Mary and Porto, Nuno (eds), *Science, Magic and Religion: The Ritual Processes of Museum Magic* (New York: Berghahn Books, 2005).

Bourghouts, J. F., 'The Evil Eye of Apopis', *Journal of Egyptian Archaeology* 59 (1973), 114–30.

Bowden, Hugh, *Mystery Cults in the Ancient World* (London: Thames & Hudson, 2010).

Bowlby, Rachel, *Carried Away: The Invention of Modern Shopping* (New York: Columbia University Press, 2001).

Brantlinger, Patrick, 'Mummy Love: *She* and Archaeology', in Tania Zulli (ed.), *She: Explorations into a Romance* (Rome: Aracne, 2009), 37–57.

—— *Rule of Darkness: British Literature and Imperialism 1830–1914* (Ithaca: Cornell University Press, 1988).

Breasted, Charles, *Pioneer to the Past: The Story of James Henry Breasted, Archaeologist, Told by his Son* (1943; Chicago: University of Chicago Press, 1977).

Breton, André, *What is Surrealism? Selected Writings,* ed. F. Rosemont (London: Pluto, 1978).

Bridges, Meilee D., 'Tales from the Crypt: Bram Stoker and the Curse of the Egyptian Mummy', *Victoria Institute Journal* 36 (2008): 137–65.

Briggs, Julia, *The Rise and Fall of the English Ghost Story* (London: Faber, 1977).

—— *A Woman of Passion: The Life of E. Nesbit 1858–1924* (London: Penguin, 1989).

Bristow, Joseph, '"Sterile Ecstasies": The Perversity of the Decadent Movement', in Laurel Brake (ed.), *The Endings of Epochs*, Essays and Studies (Cambridge: D. S. Brewer, 1995), 57–79.

Brown, Bill, 'Thing Theory', *Critical Inquiry* 28 (2001), 1–16.

Brunas, Michael, Brunas, John and Weaver, Tom, *Universal Horrors: The Studio's Classic Films, 1931–46* (London: McFarland, 1990).

Bulfin, Ailise, 'The Fictions of Gothic Egypt and British Imperial Paranoia: The Curse of the Suez Canal', *English Literature in Transition* 54/4 (2011), 411–43.

Burdett, Carolyn, 'Romance, Reincarnation and Rider Haggard', in Nicola Bown, Carolyn Burdett and Pam Thurschwell (eds), *The Victorian Supernatural* (Cambridge: Cambridge University Press, 2004), 217–35.

Burghclere, Winifred, 'Biographical Sketch of the Late Lord Carnarvon', in Howard Carter and A. C. Mace, *The Tomb of Tut-Ankh-Amen, Discovered by the Late Earl of Carnarvon and Howard Carter,* 3 vols (New York: Cooper Square, 1963), vol. 1, 1–40.

Byron, Lord, *The Complete Poetical Works,* ed. J. McGann, 7 vols (Oxford: Clarendon Press, 1980–93).

Caillois, Roger, *The Mask of Medusa*, trans. G. Ordish (London: Gollancz, 1964).

Caithness, Marie, Countess of, *The Mystery of All Ages Contained in the Secret Doctrine of All Religions* (London: C. Wallace, 1887).

Carnarvon, [Sixth] Earl of, *No Regrets* (London: Weidenfeld & Nicolson, 1976).

Carrott, Richard G., *The Egyptian Revival: Its Sources, Monuments and Meaning 1808–58* (Berkeley: University of California Press, 1978).

Carter, Howard and Mace, A. C., *The Tomb of Tut-Ankh-Amen, Discovered by the Late Earl of Carnarvon and Howard Carter*, 3 vols (1923–33; New York: Cooper Square, 1963).

*Catalogue of the Oriental Museum at the Great Globe, Leicester Square* (London: James Wyld, 1857).

Çelik, Zeynep, *Displaying the Orient: Architecture of Islam at Nineteenth-Century World's Fairs* (Berkeley: University of California Press, 1992).

Chapman, William Ryan, 'Arranging Ethnology: A. H. L. F. Pitt Rivers and the Typological Tradition', in George W. Stocking (ed.), *Objects and Others: Essays on Museums and Material Culture* (Madison: University of Wisconsin Press, 1985), 75–111.

Cheang, Sarah, 'Selling China: Class, Gender and Orientalism at the Department Store', *Journal of Design History* 20/1 (2007), 1–16.

Cheiro, *Cheiro's Memoirs: The Reminiscences of a Society Palmist* (London: William Rider, 1912).

Chopin, Kate, 'An Egyptian Cigarette', in E. Showalter (ed.), *Daughters of Decadence: Women Writers of the Fin de Siècle* (London: Virago, 1993), 1–5.

—— *True Ghost Stories* (London: London Publishing Company, 1928).

Churchill, Winston Spencer, *The River War: An Historical Account of The Reconquest of the Soudan*, ed. Col. F. Rhodes, 2 vols (London: Longmans, Green, 1899).

Clark, James, *Haunted London* (Stroud: Tempus, 2007).

Clifford, James, 'Objects and Selves – An Afterword', in George W. Stocking (ed.), *Objects and Others: Essays on Museums and Material Culture* (Madison: University of Wisconsin Press, 1985), 236–46.

Coates, James, *Has W. T. Stead Returned?* (London: L. N. Fowler, 1913).

—— *How to Mesmerise: A Manual of Instruction in the History, Mysteries, Modes of Procedure, and Arts of Mesmerism* (London: Hay Nisbet, 1893).

Cohen, Morton, *Rider Haggard: His Life and Works* (London: Hutchinson, 1960).

Cohen, Morton (ed.), *Rudyard Kipling to Rider Haggard: The Record of a Friendship* (Rutherford: Farleigh Dickinson University Press, 1965).

Colenso, F. E., *History of the Zulu War* (London: Chapman & Hall, 1880).

Colla, Elliott, *Conflicted Antiquities: Egyptology, Egyptomania, Egyptian Modernity* (Durham, NC: Duke University Press, 2007).

—— ' "Non, non! Si, si!": Commemorating the French Occupation of Egypt (1798–1801)', *MLN* 118 (2003), 1043–69.

—— 'Shadi Abd Al-Salam's *al-Mumiya*: Ambivalence and the Egyptian Nation-State', in Ali Abdullatif Ahmida (ed.), *Beyond Colonialism and Nationalism in the Maghrib* (Basingstoke: Palgrave, 2000), 109–43.

—— 'The Stuff of Egypt: The Nation, the State and their Proper Objects', *New Formations* 45 (2001), 72–90.

Comment, Bernard, *The Panorama*, trans. A-M. Glasheen (London: Reaktion, 1999).

Conan Doyle, Arthur, *The Hound of the Baskervilles* (1902; Harmondsworth: Penguin, 1981).

—— 'Lot No. 249', in Roger Luckhurst (ed.), *Late Victorian Gothic Tales* (Oxford: Oxford World's Classics, 2005), 109–40.

—— *Memories and Reflections* (London: Greenhill, 1988).

—— *The Tragedy of the Korosko* (London: Hesperus Press, 2003).

Conant, Martha Pike, *The Oriental Tale in England in the Eighteenth Century* (New York: Columbia University Press, 1908).

Conner, Patrick (ed.), *The Inspiration of Egypt: Its Influence on British Artists, Travellers and Designers 1700–1900* (Brighton: Brighton Borough Council, 1983).

Connor, Steven, 'Fascination, the Skin and the Screen,' *Critical Quarterly* 40/1 (1998), 9–24.

—— *Paraphernalia: The Curious Lives of Magical Things* (London: Profile, 2011).

Corelli, Marie, 'Pharaoh Guarded by Poisons', *Daily Express* (24 March 1923), 5.

Costeloe, Michael P., *William Bullock: Connoisseur and Virtuoso of the Egyptian Hall: Piccadilly to Mexico, 1773–1849* (Bristol: HiPLAM, 2008).

Cowie, Susan D. and Johnson, Tom, *The Mummy in Fact, Fiction and Film* (Jefferson, NC: McFarland, 2007).

Cox, Simon and Davies, Susan, 'Curses', *An A to Z of Ancient Egypt* (Edinburgh: Mainstream, 2006), 70–2.

Crawley, Ernest, *Oath, Curse, and Blessing and Other Studies in Origins* (London: Watts, 1934).

Crookes, William, *Psychic Force and Modern Spiritualism* (London: Longmans, 1871).

—— *Researches into the Phenomena of Spiritualism* (London: J. Burns, 1874).

Crinson, Mark, *Empire Building: Orientalism and Victorian Architecture* (London: Routledge, 1996).

Crowley, Aleister, 'The Temple of Solomon the King, part I', *Equinox* 1/1 (1909), 143–229.

—— 'The Temple of Solomon the King, part II', *Equinox* 1/2 (1909), 217–334.

—— 'The Temple of Solomon the King, part III', *Equinox* 1/3 (1910), 133–280.

Curl, J. S., *The Art and Architecture of Freemasonry* (London: Batsford, 1991).

—— *The Egyptian Revivial: Ancient Egyptian Inspiration for Design Motifs in the West*, revised edn (London: Routledge, 2005).

Curran, Brian, Grafton, Anthony, Long, Pamela and Weiss, Benjamin., *Obelisk: A History* (Cambridge, MA: Burndy Library, 2009).

Curtis, James, *The Gilt Kid* (London: London Books, 2007).

Daly, Nicholas, *Modernism, Romance and the Fin de Siècle* (Cambridge: Cambridge University Press, 1999).

—— *Sensation and Modernity in the 1860s* (Cambridge: Cambridge University Press, 2009).

—— 'That Obscure Object of Desire: Victorian Commodity Culture and Fictions of the Mummy', *Novel* 28/1 (1994), 24–51.

Dane, Joseph, *The Myth of Print Culture: Essays on Evidence, Textuality, and Biographical Method* (Toronto: University of Toronto Press, 2003).

Darby, Michael, *The Islamic Perspective: An Aspect of British Architecture and Design in the Nineteenth Century* (London: Leighton House Gallery, 1983).

Daston, Lorraine and Park, Katherine, *Wonders and the Order of Nature 1150–1750* (New York: Zone, 1998).

David, A. R. and Tapp, E., *The Mummy's Tale: The Scientific and Medical Investigation of Natsef-Amun, Priest in the Temple of Karnak* (London: Michael O'Mara, 1992).

Davidson, John, *An Address on Embalming Generally, Delivered at the Royal Institution on the Unrolling of a Mummy* (London: Ridgway, 1833).

Davies, Colin, 'Architecture and Remembrance', *Architectural Review* 175 (Feb 1984), 49–55.

Dawnay, Guy C., *Campaigns: Zulu 1879, Egypt 1882, Suakim 1885* (Cambridge: Kent Trotman, 1989).

Dawson, Warren R., 'A Note on the Egyptian Mummy in the Castle Museum Norwich,' *Journal of Egyptian Archaeology* 15/3–4 (1929), 186–90.

—— 'Pettigrew's Demonstrations upon Mummies: A Chapter in the History of Egyptology', *Journal of Egyptian Archaeology* 20 (1934), 170–82.

Day, Jasmine, *The Mummy's Curse: Mummymania in the English-Speaking World* (London: Routledge, 2006).

Deane, Bradley, 'Mummy Fiction and the Occupation of Egypt: Imperial Striptease', *English Literature in Transition* 51/4 (2008), 381–410.

Dennefeldt, Karl, 'Egypt and Egyptian Antiquities in the Renaissance', *Studies in the Renaissance* 6 (1959), 7–27.

De Quincey, Thomas, *Confessions of an English Opium-Eater and Other Writings*, ed. Grevel Lindop (Oxford: Oxford World's Classics, 1985).

—— 'The System of the Heavens as Revealed by Lord Rosse's Telescopes', *Tait's Edinburgh Magazine* (1846), http://www.readbookonline.net/readOnLine/38345/

Derrida, Jacques, 'Archive Fever: A Freudian Impression', *Diacritics* 25/2 (1995), 9–63.

Dick, Philip K., *Beyond Lies the Wub* (London: Gollancz, 1988).

Dickens, Charles, 'Some Account of an Extraordinary Traveller' (1850) in *Dickens's Journalism*, vol. 2: 'The Amusements of the People' and Other Papers, ed. Michael Slater (London: Dent, 1996), 201–11.

Douglas, James, *Adventures in London* (London: Cassell, 1909).

Douglas, Theo, *Iras: A Mystery* (London: William Blackwood, 1896).

Douglas Murray, Thomas, 'A Christmas Week at Thebes', *Land and Water* (25 July 1868), 3.

—— 'A Christmas Week at Thebes II', *Land and Water* (1 Aug 1868), 24.

—— 'A Christmas Week at Thebes III', *Land and Water* (8 Aug 1868), 40

—— 'A Christmas Week at Thebes IV', *Land and Water* (22 Aug 1868), 69–70.

—— 'A Christmas Week at Thebes V', *Land and Water* (19 Sept 1868), 132–3.

—— 'Africa an Island – The Suez Canal', *Land and Water* (17 April 1869), 251–2.

—— 'The Ancient Palace Dogs of China', in L. C. Smythe ('Lady Betty'), *The Pekingese: A Monograph on the Pekingese Dog: Its History and Points* (London: 'The Kennel', 1909), 3–10.

—— 'Egypt, and a Christmas Week at Thebes', *Land and Water* (11 July 1868), 386.

—— *Jeanne d'Arc, Maid of Orleans, Deliverer of France: Being the Story of her Life, her Achievements and her Death, as Attested on Oath and Set Forth in the Original Documents* (London: Heinemann, 1902).

—— 'On the Nile – Theban Mummies', *Land and Water* (3 April 1869), 222.

—— 'Philae and the First Cataract', *Land and Water* (10 April 1869), 237.

—— 'The Traveller on the Nile – The Temple of Dendera', *Land and Water* (27 March 1869), 206.

Douglas Murray, Thomas and Silva White, A., *Sir Samuel Baker: A Memoir* (London: Macmillan, 1895).

Drower, Margaret S., 'The Early Years', in T. G. H. James (ed.), *Excavating in Egypt: The Egypt Exploration Society 1882–1983* (London: British Museum, 1983), 9–36.

—— *Flinders Petrie: A Life in Archaeology* (London: Gollancz, 1985).

Duff Gordon, Lucie, *Letters from Egypt, 1875* (London: Virago, 1983).

Dumas, F. G. (ed.), *The Franco-British Exhibition: Illustrated Review* (London: Chatto, 1908).

Duncan, Carol and Wallach, Alan, 'The Universal Survey Museum', *Art History* 3/4 (1980), 448–69.

During, Simon, *Modern Enchantments: The Cultural Power of Secular Magic* (Cambridge, MA: Harvard University Press, 2002).

Eckley, Grace, *Maiden Tribute: A Life of W. T. Stead* (Philadelphia: XLibris, 2007).

Edwards, Amelia, *Pharaohs, Fellahs and Explorers* (London: Osgood, 1891).

Elliott, Chris, Griffis-Greenberg, Katherine and Lunn, Richard, 'Egypt in London – Entertainment and Commerce in the Twentieth Century Metropolis', in J. M. Humbert and C. Price (eds), *Imhotep Today: Egyptianizing Architecture* (London: UCL Press, 2003), 105–22.

Ellis, Maudie, *The Squire of Bentley (Mrs Cheape): Memory's Milestones in the Life of a Great Sportswoman* (London: Blackwood, 1926).

El-Mahdi, Rabab and Marfleet, Philip (eds), *Egypt: The Moment of Change* (London: Zed Books, 2009).

Elsworthy, Frederick Thomas, *The Evil Eye: An Account of this Ancient and Widespread Superstition* (London: John Murray, 1895).

Etherington Norman A., 'Rider Haggard, Imperialism, and the Layered Personality', *Victorian Studies* 22/1 (1978), 71–87.

Fagan, Brian, *The Rape of the Nile: Tomb Robbers, Tourists, and Archaeologists in Egypt* (Cambridge, MA: Westview Press, 2004).

Farr, Florence, *Egyptian Magic* (Wellingborough: Aquarian Press, 1982).

Field, Henry, *The Track of Man: Adventures of an Anthropologist* (London: Peter Davies, 1955).

Fitzgerald, William G., 'Illustrated Interviews. No. XLVIII – Lord Charles Beresford', *Strand Magazine* (July 1896), 15–27.

Flaubert, Gustave, *Flaubert in Egypt: A Sensibility on Tour,* compiled and translated by Francis Steegmuller (London: Penguin, 1996).

Fortune, Dion, *Psychic Self-Defence: A Study in Occult Pathology and Criminality* (Wellingborough: Aquarian Press, 1977).

Foster, R. F., *W. B. Yeats: A Life,* vol. 1: *The Apprentice Mage 1865–1914* (Oxford: Oxford University Press, 1998).

Franklin, Caroline, *Byron: A Literary Life* (Basingstoke: Macmillan, 2009).

Frayling, Christopher, *The Face of Tutankhamun* (London: Faber, 1992).

Frazer, James George, *The Golden Bough: A Study in Magic and Religion,* Part 1: *The Magic Art,* vol. 1, 3rd edn (London: Macmillan, 1932).

Freeman, Daniel and Garety, Philippa, *Paranoia: The Psychology of Persecutory Delusions* (Hove: Psychology Press, 2004).

Freeman, Edward A., *A History of Architecture* (London: Joseph Masters, 1849).

Freeman, Richard, '*The Mummy* in Context', *European Journal of American Studies* 1 (2009), http://ejas.revues.org/7566

Freud, Sigmund, 'The Aetiology of Hysteria' (1896), *The Standard Edition of the Complete Psychological Works of Sigmund Freud*, ed. J. Strachey, vol. 3 (London: Hogarth, 1962), 189–221.

—— 'Animism, Magic and the Omnipotence of Thoughts', *The Standard Edition of the Complete Psychological Works of Sigmund Freud*, ed. J. Strachey, vol. 13 (London: Hogarth, 1955), 75–99.

—— 'Fetishism' (1927), in *On Sexuality*, Penguin Freud Library, vol. 7 (London: Penguin, 1977), 345–57.

—— *The Interpretation of Dreams*, Standard Edition of the Complete Psychological Works of Sigmund Freud, ed. J. Strachey, vol. 5 (London: Hogarth, 1958).

—— 'Medusa's Head' (1922), *Standard Edition of the Complete Psychological Works of Sigmund Freud*, ed. J. Strachey, vol. 18 (London: Hogarth, 1955), 273–4.

—— 'Psychoanalytic Notes on An Autobiographical Account of a Case of Paranoia (Dementia Paranoides)' (1911), in *Case Histories II*, Penguin Freud Library, vol. 11 (Harmondsworth: Penguin, 1979), 129–223.

—— 'The Uncanny' (1919), in *Art and Literature*, Penguin Freud Library, vol. 14 (Harmondsworth: Penguin, 1985), 335–76.

Frost, Brian J., *The Essential Guide to Mummy Literature* (Lanham, MD: Scarecrow Press, 2008).

Galassi, Susan Grace and Burnham, Helen M., 'Lady Henry Bruce Meux and Lady Archibald Campbell', in Margaret MacDonald et al. (eds), *Whistler, Women, and Fashion* (New Haven: Yale University Press, 2003), 156–83.

Galbraith, John S., *Mackinnon and East Africa 1878–1895: A Study in the 'New Imperialism'* (Cambridge: Cambridge University Press, 1972).

Gardiner, Alan, 'The Egyptian Treasure. Importance of the Find', *The Times* (4 Dec 1922), 7.

Garrison, Vivian and Arensberg, Conrad, 'The Evil Eye: Envy or Risk of Seizure? Paranoia or Rational Dependency?' in Clarence Maloney (ed.), *The Evil Eye* (New York: Columbia University Press, 1976), 286–328.

Gautier, Théophile, *The Mummy's Foot and Other Tales* (Los Angeles: Aegypan Press, n.d. [2010]).

—— *The Romance of a Mummy*, trans. M. Young (London: John & Robert Maxwell, 1886).

Geppert, Alexander C. T., 'True Copies: Time and Space Travels at the British Imperial Exhibitions, 1880–1930', in H. Berghoff et al. (eds), *The Making of Modern Tourism: The Cultural History of British Experience, 1600–2000* (Basingstoke: Palgrave, 2002), 223–48.

Gilbert, R. A., *Revelations of the Golden Dawn: The Rise and Fall of a Magical Order* (London: Quantum, 1997).

Glasstone, Victor, *Victorian and Edwardian Theatres: An Architectural and Social Survey* (London: Thames and Hudson, 1975).

Gleichen, Count, *With the Camel Corps up the Nile* (London: Chapman & Hall, 1888).

Gliddon, George R., *An Appeal to the Antiquaries of Europe on the Destruction of the Monuments of Egypt* (London: James Maddon, 1841).

Glover, David, *Vampires, Mummies and Liberals: Bram Stoker and the Politics of Popular Fiction* (Durham, NC: Duke University Press, 1996).

Godden, Rumer, *The Butterfly Lions: The Story of the Pekingese in History, Legend and Art* (London: Macmillan, 1977).

Godwin, Joscelyn, *The Beginnings of Theosophy in France* (London: Theosophical History Centre, 1989).

Goodrich-Freer, Ada, 'The Priestess of Amen-Ra: A Study in Coincidences', *Occult Review* 17 ( Jan 1913), 11–19.

Gordon, Winifred, *A Woman in the Balkans* (London: Hutchinson, 1916).

Greenhalgh, Paul, *Ephemeral Vistas: The Expositions Universelles, Great Exhibitions and World's Fairs, 1851–1939* (Manchester: Manchester University Press, 1988).

Greer, Mary K., *Women of the Golden Dawn: Rebels and Priestesses* (Rochester, VT: Park Street, 1995).

Grosskurth, Phyllis, *The Secret Ring: Freud's Inner Circle and the Politics of Psychoanalysis* (Reading, MA: Addison-Wesley, 1991).

Guy, Jeff, *The Destruction of the Zulu Kingdom: The Civil War in Zululand, 1879–84* (London: Longman, 1979).

Habachi, Labib, *The Obelisks of Egypt: Skyscrapers of the Past* (London: Dent, 1978).

Haddon, A. C., *Brandon and Didlington Hall* (Cambridge: British Association, 1904).

Haggard, Andrew, *Dodo and I: A Novel* (Edinburgh: Blackwood, 1889).

—— *A Strange Tale of the Scarabaeus* (London: Kegan Paul, 1891).

—— *Under Crescent and Star* (Edinburgh: Blackwood, 1895).

Haggard, H. Rider, *Cleopatra*, facsimile reprint of 1889 edn (Gillette: Wildside Press, 1999).

—— *Dawn*, 3 vols (London: Hurst and Blackett, 1884).

—— *The Days of my Life: An Autobiography*, 2 vols (London: Longmans, 1926).

—— *King Solomon's Mines*, ed. Dennis Butts (Oxford: Oxford World's Classics, 2006).

—— 'King Tutankhamen. Reburial in the Great Pyramid: Sir Rider Haggard's Plea', *The Times* (13 Feb 1923), 13.

—— *The Private Diaries of Sir Rider Haggard 1914–25*, ed. D. S. Higgins (London: Cassell, 1980).

—— *Queen Sheba's Ring* (1910; London: Newnes, 1913).

—— *She*, ed. Daniel Karlin (Oxford: Oxford World's Classics, 1991).

—— 'Smith and the Pharaohs', in J. R. Stephens (ed.), *Into the Mummy's Tomb* (New York: Berkley Books, 2001), 137–78.

—— *Virgin of the Sun* London: Cassell, 1922).

—— *The Way of the Spirit* (London: Skeffington, n.d. [1906]).

Haggard, Lilias Rider, *The Cloak that I Left: A Biography of the Author Henry Rider Haggard K. B. E. by his Daughter* (London: Hodder, 1951).

Halberstam, Judith, *Skin Shows: Gothic Horror and the Technology of Monsters* (Durham, NC: Duke University Press, 1995).

Hall, Trevor, *The Strange Story of Ada Goodrich Freer* (London: Duckworth, 1980).

Hankey, Julie, *A Passion for Egypt: Arthur Weigall, Tutankhamun and the 'Curse of the Pharaohs'* (London: I. B. Taurus, 2001).

Harman, Graham, 'Autonomous Objects', *New Formations* 71 (2011), 25–30.

—— *Prince of Networks: Bruno Latour and Metaphysics* (Melbourne: Re:Press, 2009).

—— *Towards Speculative Realism: Essays and Lectures* (Winchester: Zero Books, 2010).

Harper, George Mills, *Yeats's Golden Dawn* (London: Macmillan, 1974).

Harper, Margaret Mills, 'Yeats and the Occult', in Marjorie Hawes and John Kelly (eds), *The Cambridge Companion to W. B. Yeats*, (Cambridge: Cambridge University Press, 2006), 144–66.

Heelas, Paul, *The New Age Movement* (Oxford: Blackwell, 1996).

Henty, G. A., *The Dash for Khartoum: A Tale of the Nile Expedition* (1892; Gloucester: Dodo Press reprint edn, n.d.).

Herbert, Christopher, *War of No Pity: The Indian Mutiny and Victorian Trauma* (Princeton: Princeton University Press, 2008).

Hevia, James L., 'Loot's Fate: The Economy of Plunder and the Moral Life of Objects from the Summer Palace of the Emperor of China', *History and Anthropology* 6/4 (1994), 319–45.

Hill, Jude, 'The Story of the Amulet: Locating the Enchantment of Collections', *Journal of Material Culture* 12/1 (2007), 65–87.

Hoberman, Ruth, 'In Quest of a Museal Aura: Turn of the Century Narratives about Museum-Displayed Objects', *Victorian Literature and Culture* 31 (2003), 467–82.

Hobhouse, Hermione, *The Crystal Palace and the Great Exhibition: Art, Science and Productive Industry: A History of the Royal Commission for the Exhibition of 1851* (London: Athlone, 2002).

Hodgson, William Hope, *Carnacki, the Ghost-Finder* (London: Sphere, 1974).

Hoffenberg, Paul, *An Empire on Display: English, Indian and Australian Exhibitions from the Crystal Palace to the Great war* (Berkeley: University of California Press, 2001).

Hofstadter, Richard, *The Paranoid Style in American Politics and Other Essays* (London: Cape, 1966).

Holt, Frank, 'Egyptomania: Have we Cursed the Pharaohs?', *Archaeology* (March–April 1986), 60–3.

Hope, Thomas, *Household Furniture and Interior Design* (1807; London: Alec Tiranti, 1970).

Hornung, Erik, *The Secret Lore of Egypt: Its Impact on the West*, trans. D. Lorton (Ithaca: Cornell University Press, 2001).

Horsfield, J. Nixon, 'The Franco-British Exhibition of Science, Arts, and Industries, London, 1908', *Journal of the Royal Institute of British Architects* 15 (1907–8), 546–56.

How, Harry, 'Illustrated Interviews – Mr H. Rider Haggard,' *Strand Magazine* (Jan 1892), 3–17.

Howe, Ellic, *The Magicians of the Golden Dawn: A Documentary History of a Magical Order, 1887–1923* (London: Routledge and Kegan Paul, 1972).

Hunt, Leigh, *A Saunter through the West End* (London: Hurst and Blackett, 1861).

Hurley, Kelly, *The Gothic Body: Sexuality, Materialism and Degeneration at the Fin de Siècle* (Cambridge: Cambridge University Press, 1996).

—— 'The Victorian Mummy-Fetish: H. Rider Haggard, Frank Aubrey and the White Mummy', in Marlene Tromp (ed.), *Victorian Freaks: The Social Context of Freakery in Britain* (Columbus: Ohio State University Press, 2008), 180–99.

Hyde, Ralph and van der Merwe, Pieter, 'The Queen's Bazaar', *Theatrephile* 2/8 (1985), 10–15.

Ikram, Salima and Dodson, Aidan, *The Mummy in Ancient Egypt: Equipping the Dead for Eternity* (London: Thames & Hudson, 1998).

Jackson, Russell, 'Cleopatra "Lilyised": *Antony and Cleopatra* at The Princess's 1890', *Theatrephile* 2/8 (1985), 37–40.

Jackson, Shirley, *Novels and Stories* (New York: Library of America, 2010).

James, F. L., *The Unknown Horn of Africa: An Exploration from Berbera to the Leopard River* (London: George Philip, 1888).

James, M. R., *Casting the Runes and Other Ghost Stories,* ed. Michael Cox (Oxford: Oxford World's Classics, 1987).

James, T. G. H., *The British Museum and Ancient Egypt* (London: British Museum Press, 1989).

—— *Howard Carter: The Path to Tutankhamen* (New York: I. B. Taures 2006).

Janes, Dominic, 'The Rites of Man: The British Museum and the Sexual Imagination in Victorian Britain', *Journal of the History of Collections* 20/1 (2008), 101–12.

Jenkins, Ian, *Archaeologists and Aesthetes in the Sculpture Galleries of the British Museum 1800–1939* (London: British Museum Press, 1992).

Jennings, Hargrave, *The Obelisk: Notices of the Origin, Purpose and History of Obelisks* (London: Bursill, 1877).

Jones, Owen and Bonomi, Joseph, *Description of the Egyptian Court Erected in the Crystal Palace* (London: Crystal Palace Company, 1854).

Jopling, Louise, *Twenty Years of my Life 1867–87* (London: John Lane, 1925).

Julian, Philippe, *The Triumph of Art Nouveau: Paris Exhibition 1900* (London: Phaidon, 1974).

Jung, Carl, 'Psychology and Literature' (1930), in *Collected Works,* trans. R. F. C. Hull, vol. 15 (London: Routledge and Kegan Paul, 1971), 84–105.

—— *The Archetypes and the Collective Unconscious* in *Collected Works,* trans. R. F. C. Hull, vol. 9 part 1 (London: Routledge and Kegan Paul, 1968).

Kaczynski, Richard, *Perdurabo: The Life of Aleister Crowley* (Tempe, AZ: New Falcon, 2002).

Kalmar, Ivan Davidson, 'The *Houkah* in the Harem: On Smoking and Orientalist Art', in S. Gilman and Z. Xun (eds), *Smoke: A Global History* (London: Reaktion, 2004), 218–29.

Katz, Wendy R., *Rider Haggard and the Fiction of Empire: A Critical Study of British Imperial Fiction* (Cambridge: Cambridge University Press, 1987).

Kavanagh, Gaynor, *Dream Spaces: Memory and the Museum* (London: Leicester University Press, 2000).

Keats, John. *The Complete Poems,* ed. John Barnard (Harmondsworth: Penguin, 1988).

Keys, David, 'Curse (and Revenge) of the Mummy Invented by Victorian Writers', *The Independent* (31 Dec 2000), http://www.rense.com/general6/curse.htm.

King, Francis, *Modern Ritual Magic: The Rise of Western Occultism* (1970; Bridport: Prism, 1989).

Knight, Donald R. and Sabey, Alan. D., *The Lion Roars at Wembley: British Empire Exhibition Sixtieth Anniversary* (New Barnet: D. R. Knight, 1984).

Kohn, Marek, *Dope Girls: The Birth of the British Drug Underground* (London: Granta, 1992).

Kristeva, Julia, *Powers of Horror: An Essay in Abjection,* trans. L. Roudiez (New York: Columbia University Press, 1984).

Kurin, Richard, *Hope Diamond: The Legendary History of a Cursed Gem* (New York: HarperCollins, 2006).

Lachman, Gary, *Turn Off your Mind: The Mystic Sixties and the Dark Side of the Age of Aquarius* (London: Sidgwick and Jackson, 2001).

Laermans, Rudi, 'Learning to Consume: Early Department Stores and the Shaping of Modern Consumer Culture (1860–1914)', *Theory, Culture and Society* 10/4 (1993), 79–102.

Lang, Andrew, 'Realism and Romance' (1886), in Sally Ledger and Roger Luckhurst (eds), *The Fin de Siècle: A Reader in Cultural History c.1880–1920* (Oxford: Oxford University Press, 2000), 99–104.

Lant, Antonia, 'The Curse of the Pharaoh, or How Cinema Contracted Egyptomania', *October* 59 (1992), 87–112.

Laplanche, J. and Pontalis, J.-B., *The Language of Psychoanalysis,* trans. D. Nicholson-Smith (London: Karnac Books, 1988).

Laqueur, Thomas, 'Why the Margins Matter: Occultism and the Making of Modernity', *Modern Intellectual History* 3/1 (2006), 111–35.

Latour, Bruno, *Science in Action: How to Follow Scientists and Engineers through Society* (Cambridge, MA.: Harvard University Press, 1987).

Lee, Vernon, 'Aesthetic Empathy and its Organic Accompaniments', in *Beauty and Ugliness, and Other Studies in Psychological Aesthetics* (London: John Lane, 1912), 45–76.

Lees, Frederic, 'Isis Worship in Paris: Conversations with Hierophant Rameses and the High Priestess Anari', *The Humanitarian* 16 (1900), 82–7.

Lefebvre, Henri, *The Production of Space,* trans. D. Nicholson-Smith (Oxford: Blackwell, 1991).

Leith, Ian, *Delamotte's Crystal Palace: A Victorian Pleasure Dome Revealed* (London: English Heritage, 2005).

Levell, Nicky, *Oriental Visions: Exhibitions, Travel and Collecting in the Victorian Age* (London: Horniman Museum, 2000).

Lewis, C. S., 'The Mythopoeic Gift of Rider Haggard ', in *Essay Collection and Other Short Pieces*, ed. L. Walmsley (London: HarperCollins, 2000), 559–62.

Lindberg, David C., *Theories of Vision from Al-Kindi to Kepler* (Chicago: University of Chicago Press, 1976).

Litz, A. Walton, 'Florence Farr: A "Transitional" Woman', in Maria D. Battista and Lucy MacDiarmid (eds), *High and Low Moderns: Literature and Culture, 1889–1939* (Oxford: Oxford University Press, 1996), 85–90.

Lock, Ron and Quantrill, Peter (eds), *The 1879 Zulu War, Through the Eyes of the Illustrated London News* (Kloof South Africa: Q-Lock Publications, 2003).

Lockhart, J. G., *Curses, Lucks and Talismans* (London: Geoffrey Bles, 1938).

Lomax, Alfred E., *Sir Samuel Baker: His Life and Adventures,* Splendid Lives Series (London: Sunday School Union, 1894).

Loudon, Jane, *The Mummy! A Tale of the Twenty-Second Century* (1827), ed. Alan Rauch (Ann Arbor: University of Michigan Press, 1994).

Lovecraft, H. P., *Supernatural Horror in Literature* (New York: Dover, 1973).

Lovett, Edward, 'The Folk Lore of London', *Journal of the London Society* 23 (1920), 8–12.

Luckhurst, Roger, 'Exhumed Tombs and Legendary Tales of Doom', *Times Higher Education* (14 July 2011), 40–2.

—— *The Invention of Telepathy* (Oxford: Oxford University Press, 2002).

—— 'The Mummy's Curse: A Study in Rumour', *Critical Quarterly* 52/3 (2010), 6–22.

—— 'An Occult Gazetteer of Bloomsbury: An Experiment in Method', in A. Witchard and L. Phillips (eds), *London Gothic: Place, Space and the Gothic Imagination* (London: Continuum, 2010), 51–62.

—— 'Public Sphere, Counter-Publics and the Zombie Apocalypse', in D. Glover and S. McCracken (eds), *The Cambridge Companion to Popular Fiction* (Cambridge: Cambridge University Press, 2012), 68–85.

—— 'Reflections on Joan Didion's *The Year of Magical Thinking*', *New Formations* 67 (2009), 91–100.

—— 'Trance Gothic 1882–1897', in Ruth Robbins and Julian Wolfreys (eds), *Victorian Gothic: Literary and Cultural Manifestations in the Nineteenth Century* (Basingstoke: Palgrave, 2000), 148–67.

Lupton, Carter, ' "Mummymania" for the Masses: Is Egyptology Cursed by the Mummy's Curse?', in S. MacDonald and M. Rice (eds), *Consuming Ancient Egypt* (London: UCL Press, 2003), 23–46.

Lycett, Andrew, *Conan Doyle: The Man who Created Sherlock Holmes* (London: Weidenfeld & Nicolson, 2007).

Lytton, The Hon. Mrs Neville, *Toy Dogs and their Ancestors* (London: Duckworth, 1911).

MacGregor, Arthur, 'The Cabinet of Curiosities in 17th-century Britain', in O. Impey and A. MacGregor (eds), *The Origins of Museums: The Cabinet of Curiosities in Sixteenth- and Seventeenth-Century Europe* (London: House of Stratus, 2001), 201–16.

Mackenzie, John M., *Propaganda and Empire: The Manipulation of British Public Opinion 1880–1960* (Manchester: Manchester University Press, 1984).

Macqueen-Pope, W., *Carriages at Eleven: The Story of Edwardian Theatre* (London: Hutchinson, 1947).

Maitland, Edward, *Anna Kingsford: Her Life, Letters, Diary and Work*, 2 vols (London: Redway, 1896).

Malley, Shawn, ' "Time Hath No Power Against Identity": Historical Continuity and Archaeological Adventure in H. Rider Haggard's *She*', *English Literature in Transition* 40/3 (1997), 275–97.

Marsh, Richard, *The Beetle* (1899), ed. Julian Wolfreys (Peterborough: Broadview, 2004).

—— *The Goddess: A Demon* (London: F. V. White, 1900).

Marshall, Archibald, *Out and About: Random Reminiscences* (London: John Murray, 1933).

Martin, Charles D., 'Can the Mummy Speak? Manifest Destiny, Ventriloquism, and the Silence of the Ancient Egyptian Body', *Nineteenth-Century Contexts* 31/2 (2009), 113–28.

Martin, Wallace, *The New Age under Orage: Chapters in English Cultural History* (Manchester: Manchester University Press, 1967).

Marx, Karl, *Capital: A Critique of Political Economy*, trans. B. Fowkes, 3 vols (Harmondsworth: Penguin, 1976).

Mason, R. Osgood, *Hypnotism and Suggestion in Therapeutics, Education and Reform* (London: Kegan Paul, 1901).

Maugham, Somerset, *The Magician* (London: Vintage, 2000).

Mayes, Stanley, *The Great Belzoni: The Circus Strongman who Discovered Egypt's Treasures* (London: Taurus Parke, 2003).

Mayhew, Henry and Cruikshank, George, *1851, or, The Adventures of Mr and Mrs Sandboys and Family, who Came up to London to 'Enjoy Themselves' and to see the Great Exhibition* (London: Bogue, 1851).

Miéville, China, 'Weird Fiction', in Mark Bould, Andrew Butler, Adam Roberts and Sherryl Vint (eds), *The Routledge Companion to Science Fiction* (London: Routledge, 2009), 510–15.

Miles, Robert, *Gothic Writing 1750–1820: A Genealogy* (London: Routledge, 1993).

Milligan, Barry 'The Opium Den in Victorian London', in S. Gilman and Z. Xun (eds), *Smoke: A Global History* (London: Reaktion, 2004), 118–25.

Mitchell, Timothy, *Colonising Egypt* (Berkeley: University of California Press, 1991).

Mitchell, Yvonne, *Colette: A Taste for Life* (London: Weidenfeld and Nicolson, 1975).

Monsman, Gerald, *H. Rider Haggard on the Imperial Frontier: The Political and Literary Contexts of his African Romances* (Greensboro: ELT Press, 2006).

Montserrat, Dominic, *Akhenaten: History, Fantasy, and Ancient Egypt* (London: Routledge, 2000).

——'Louisa May Alcott and the Mummy's Curse', *KMT: A Modern Journal of Ancient Egypt* 9/2 (1998), 70–5.

——'Unidentified Human Remains: Mummies and the Erotics of Biography', in D. Montserrat (ed.), *Changing Bodies, Changing Meanings: Studies on the Human Body in Antiquity* (London: Routledge, 1998), 162–97.

Moore, Abigail Harrison, '*Voyage*: Dominique-Vivant Denon and the Transference of Images of Egypt', *Art History* 25/4 (2002), 531–49.

Morell, J. R., *Bradshaw's Handbook to the Paris International Exhibition of 1867* (London: Bradshaw, 1867).

Morell, Robert, '*Budgie*': The Life of Sir E. A. T. Wallis Budge* (Nottingham: privately printed, 2002).

Moret, Alexandre, *In the Time of the Pharaohs*, trans. Mme Moret (New York: Putnam's, 1911).

Moretti, Franco, *Signs Taken for Wonders: Essays in the Sociology of Literary Forms* (London: Verso, 1983).

Morton, H. V., 'The Tragedy of Lord Carnarvon', *Daily Express* (6 April 1923), 4.

Morus, Iwan Rhys, *Michael Faraday and the Electrical Century* (Cambridge: Icon, 2004).

Mostyn, Trevor, *Egypt's Belle Epoque: Cairo and the Age of the Hedonists* (London: Tauris Parke, 2007).

Mott, Ronald, 'Theobalds Park 1820–1951' in P. E. Rooke (ed.), *Theobalds through the Centuries: The Changing Fortunes of a Hertfordshire House and Estate* (Waltham Cross: Broxbourne Press, 1980), 10–19.

'Mr Grubbe's Night with Memnon', *Putnam's Monthly Magazine* 10/56 (Aug 1857), 192–7.

Murray, David, *Museums: Their History and their Use* (Glasgow: MacLehose, 1904).

Murray, Margaret A., *My First Hundred Years* (London: William Kimber, 1963).

—— *The Splendour that was Egypt: A General Survey of Egyptian Culture and Civilization* (London: Sidgwick & Jackson, 1949).

Murray, Thomas Boyles, *Chronicles of a City Church, Being an Account of the Parish Church of St Dunstan in the East, in the City of London* (London: Smith, Elder, 1859).

—— *A Day in the Crystal Palace*, 2nd edn (London: SPCK, 1852).

—— *A Notice of Ely Chapel, Holborn, with Some Account of Ely Palace* (London: John Parker, 1840).

Murray, Sir Wyndham, *A Varied Life* (Winchester: Warren & Son, 1925).

Myers, F. W. H. 'The Subliminal Consciousness' (chapters 1 and 2), *Proceedings of the Society for Psychical Research* 7 (1891–2), 298–355.

*Narrative of the Field Operations Connected with the Zulu War of 1879* (London: HMSO, 1881).

Nava, Mica, *Visceral Cosmopolitanism: Gender, Culture and the Normalisation of Difference* (Oxford: Berg, 2007).

Nelson, Mark R., 'The Mummy's Curse: Historical Cohort Study', *British Medical Journal* 325 (2002), 1482–4.

Nelson, Nina, *Shepheard's Hotel* (London: Barrie and Rockliff, 1960).

Nemeroff, Carol and Rozin, Paul, 'The Makings of the Magical Mind: The Nature and Function of Sympathetic Magical Thinking', in Karl S. Rosengren et al. (eds), *Imagining the Impossible: Magical, Scientific, and Religious Thinking in Children* (Cambridge: Cambridge University Press, 2000), 1–34.

Nesbit, Edith, *The Story of the Amulet* (London: Puffin, 1996).

Neubauer, Hans-Joachim, *The Rumour: A Cultural History*, trans. C. Brown (London: Free Association Books, 1999).

Newberry, P. E., 'The Egyptian Cult-Object and the "Thunderbolt"', *Annals of Archaeology and Anthropology* 3 (1912), 50–3.

—— 'The Inscribed Tombs of Ekhmîm', *Annals of Archaeology and Anthropology* 4 (1912), 99–120.

Newbolt, Henry, *Collected Poems 1897–1907* (London: Nelson, n.d.).

Nordh, Katarina, *Aspects of Ancient Egyptian Curses and Blessings: Conceptual Background and Transmission* (Uppsala: Uppsala University Press, 1996).

O'Donnell, Elliott, *Haunted Houses of London* (London: Eveleigh Nash, 1909).

O'Farrell, Gerald, *The Tutankhamun Deception: The True Story of the Mummy's Curse* (London: Sidgwick and Jackson, 2001).

Oliver, J. W., *The Life of William Beckford* (Oxford: Oxford University Press, 1932).

Oppenheim, Janet, *The Other World: Spiritualism and Psychical Research in England, 1850–1914* (Cambridge: Cambridge University Press, 1985).

Orage, A. R., *Consciousness: Animal, Human and Superhuman* (London: Theosophical Publishing Society, 1907)

Osburn, William, *An Account of an Egyptian Mummy, Presented to the Museum of the Leeds Philosophical and Literary Society by the Late John Blayds* (Leeds: Robinson and Hernaman, 1828).

Ossian, Clair, 'The Egyptian Court of London's Crystal Palace', *KMT: A Modern Journal of Ancient Egypt* 18/3 (2007), 64–73.

Owen, Alex, *The Places of Enchantment: British Occultism and the Culture of the Modern* (Chicago: Chicago University Press, 2004).

—— 'The "Religious Sense" in a Post-War Secular Age', *Past and Present*, Supplement 1 (2006), 159–77.

—— 'The Sorcerer and his Apprentice: Aleister Crowley and the Magical Exploration of Edwardian Subjectivity', *Journal of British Studies* 36 (1997), 99–133.

Owen, Roger, *Lord Cromer: Victorian Imperialist, Edwardian Proconsul* (Oxford: Oxford University Press, 2004).

Padwick, Constance E., 'Notes on the Jinn and the Ghoul in the Peasant Mind of Lower Egypt', *Bulletin of the School of Oriental Studies* 3/3 (1924), 421–46.

Parey, Ambrose, 'A Discourse on *Mumia*, or Mummie', in *The Works of that Famous Chirurgion Ambrose Parey* (London: Cotes and Young, 1634), 447–9.

Parlati, Marilena, 'Memories of Exoticism and Empire: Henry Rider Haggard's *Wunderkammer* at Ditchingham House', in Harald Hendrix (ed.), *Writers' Houses and the Making of Memory* (London: Routledge, 2008), 175–85.

Pascoe, Judith, *The Hummingbird Cabinet: A Rare and Curious History of Romantic Collectors* (Ithaca: Cornell University Press, 2006).

Pearce, Susan M., 'Giovanni Battista Belzoni's Exhibition of the Reconstructed Tomb of Pharaoh Seti I in 1821', *Journal of the History of Collections* 12/1 (2000), 109–25.

Pearson, Richard, 'Archaeology and Gothic Desire: Vitality Beyond the Grave in H. Rider Haggard's Ancient Egypt', in Ruth Robbins and Julian Wolfreys (eds), *Victorian Gothic: Literary and Cultural Manifestations in the Nineteenth Century* (Basingstoke: Palgrave, 2000), 218–44.

Peel, C. V. A., *Somaliland, Being an Account of Two Expeditions into the Far Interior* (London: F. E. Robinson, 1900).

Pellegrino, Charles, *Unearthing Atlantis: An Archaeological Odyssey* (New York: Vintage, 1993).

Pels, Dick, Hetherington, Kevin, and Vandenberohe, F., 'The Status of the Object: Performances, Mediations and Techniques', *Theory, Culture and Society* 19/5–6 (2002), 1–21.

Petrie, W. M. Flinders, 'The Races of Early Egypt', *Journal of the Anthropological Society of Great Britain and Ireland* 31 (1901), 248–55.

Pettigrew, Thomas Joseph, *A History of Egyptian Mummies, and an Account of the Worship and Embalming of Sacred Animals by the Egyptians* (London: Longman, 1834).

—— *On Superstitions Connected with the History and Practice of Medicine and Surgery* (London: John Churchill, 1844).

Pevsner, Nikolaus and Lang, S., 'The Egyptian Revival', *Architectural Review* 119 (1956), 242–56.

Phipps-Jackson, M., 'Cairo in London: Carl Haag's Studio', *Art Journal* (March 1883), 72–5.

Pick, Daniel, *Svengali's Web: The Alien Enchanter in Modern Culture* (New Haven: Yale University Press, 2000).

Pinch, Geraldine, *Magic in Ancient Egypt* (Austin: University of Texas Press, 1994).

Pitt-Rivers, Lieutenant General, 'Typological Museums, as Exemplified by the Pitt-Rivers Museum at Oxford and his Provincial Museum at Farnham, Dorset', *Journal of the Society of Arts* 40 (18 Dec 1891), 115–22.

Pocock, Tom, *Rider Haggard and the Lost Empire* (London: Weidenfeld and Nicolson, 1993).

Poe, Edgar Allan, 'Some Words with a Mummy', *Complete Stories and Poems* (New York: Dover, 1966), 450–62.

Polidori, John, *The Vampyre and Other Tales of the Macabre*, ed. Robert Morrison and Chris Baldick (Oxford: Oxford World's Classics, 1997).

Pomain, Krzysztof, *Collectors and Curiosities, Paris and Venice, 1500–1800*, trans. E. Wiles-Portier (Cambridge: Polity, 1990).

Port, M. H., *Imperial London: Civil Government Building in London 1850–1915* (New Haven: Yale University Press, 1995).

Powell, Anthony, *A Dance to the Music of Time*, 4 vols (London: Arrow, 2000).

Preston, Adrian (ed.), 'Introduction', Garnet Joseph Wolseley, *In Relief of Gordon: Lord Wolseley's Campaign Journal of the Khartoum Relief Expedition 1884–5* (London: Hutchinson, 1967), xiii–xliv.

Prichard, K. and Prichard, Hesketh, *Ghosts: Being the Experiences of Flaxman Low* (London: Pearson, 1899).

Prior, Melton, *Campaigns of a War Correspondent* (London: Edward Arnold, 1912).

Pugh, Brian W. and Spiring, Paul, *Bertram Fletcher Robinson: A Footnote to the Hound of the Baskervilles* (London: MX Publishing, 2008).

Pugin, Augustus, *Apology for the Revival of Christian Architecture in England* (London: John Weale, 1843).

Rapoport, Erika Diane, *Shopping for Pleasure: Women in the Making of London's West End* (Princeton: Princeton University Press, 2000).

Reeves, Nicholas, *The Complete Tutankhamun: The King, the Tomb, the Royal Treasure* (London: Thames and Hudson, 1990).

—— 'The Sigmund Freud Collection of Egyptian Antiquities', *KMT: A Modern Journal of Ancient Egypt* 11/4 (2000–1), 31–9.

Reid, Donald Malcolm, 'The 'Urabi Revolution and the British Conquest 1879–82', in W. M. Daly (ed.), *The Cambridge History of Egypt*, vol. 2: *Modern Egypt, from 1517 to the End of the Twentieth Century* (Cambridge: Cambridge University Press, 1998), 217–38.

—— *Whose Pharaohs? Archaeology, Museums, and Egyptian National Identity from Napoleon to the First World War* (Berkeley: University of California Press, 2002).

'Report of the Committee Appointed to Investigate Phenomena Connected with the Theosophical Society', *Proceedings of the Society for Psychical Research* 3 (1885), 200–400.

Richards, Thomas, *The Imperial Archive: Knowledge and the Fantasy of Empire* (London: Verso, 1993).

Richter, Anne Nellis, 'Spectacle, Exoticism, and Display in the Gentleman's House: The Fonthill Auction of 1822', *Eighteenth-Century Studies* 41/4 (2008), 543–64.

Ritvo, Harriet, *The Animal Estate: The English and Other Creatures in the Victorian Age* (London: Penguin, 1990).

Roberts, Charlotte A., *Human Remains in Archaeology: A Handbook* (Ann Arbor: University of Michigan Press, 2009).

Robinson, Bertram Fletcher, 'A Priestess of Death', *Daily Express* (3 June 1904), 1.

—— *The Trail of the Dead, etc.* (London: Ward, Lock, 1904).

—— 'A True Ghost Story', *Daily Express* (18 April 1904), 4.

Rohmer, Sax, *The Brood of the Witch-Queen* (London: Pearson, 1918).

—— *The Dream Detective: Being Some Account of the Methods of Moris Klaw* (London: Jarrolds, 1920).

—— *The Green Eyes of Bâst* (London: Cassell, 1920).

—— *The Romance of Sorcery* (1914; Rockville, MD: Wildside Press, 2003).

—— *Tales of Secret Egypt* (1918; Amsterdam: Fredonia, 2002).

Romer, John, *Valley of the Kings* (London: Michael Joseph, 1981).

Routledge, George, *Routledge (One Shilling) Guide to the Crystal Palace* (London: Routledge, 1854).

Ruskin, John, *The Two Paths* in *The Works of John Ruskin,* ed. E. T. Cook and Alexander Wedderburn, vol. 16 (London: George Allen, 1903).

Russell, G. St., 'The Mysterious Mummy', *Pearson's Magazine* 28 (July–Dec 1909), 162–72.

Said, Edward W., *Orientalism* (London: Peregrine, 1985).

St Clair, William, *Lord Elgin and the Marbles: The Controversial History of the Parthenon Sculptures,* 3rd edn (Oxford: Oxford University Press, 1998).

Sala, George Augustus, *Paris herself Again in 1878–9,* 2 vols (London: Remington, 1880).

Salzani, Carlo, 'The City as Crime Scene: Walter Benjamin and the Traces of the Detective', *New German Critique* 100 (2007), 165–87.

Sands-O'Connor, Karen, 'Impertinent Miracles at the British Museum: Egyptology and Edwardian Fantasies for Young People', in *Journal of the Fantastic in the Arts* 19/2 (2008), 224–37.

Secord, James, 'Extraordinary Experiment: Electricity and the Creation of Life in Victorian England', in D. Gooding, T. Pinch and S. Shaffer (eds), *The Uses of Experiment: Studies in the Natural Sciences* (Cambridge: Cambridge University Press, 1989), 337–83.

Selver, Paul, *Orage and The New Age Circle: Reminiscences and Reflections* (London: Allen & Unwin, 1959).

Seshagiri, Urmila, 'Modernity's (Yellow) Peril: Dr Fu-Manchu and English Race Paranoia', *Cultural Critique* 62 (2006), 162–94.

Shafer, Byron E. (ed.), *Religion in Ancient Egypt: Gods, Myth, and Personal Practice* (Ithaca: Cornell University Press, 1991).

Shechter, Relli, 'Selling Luxury: The Rise of the Egyptian Cigarette and the Transformation of the Egyptian Tobacco Market, 1880–1914', *International Journal of Middle East Studies* 35 (2003), 51–75.

Sheldrake, Rupert, *The Sense of Being Stared At, and Other Aspects of the Extended Mind* (London: Arrow, 2004).

Siegel, Jonah, *Haunted Museum: Longing, Travel and the Art-Romance Tradition* (Princeton: Princeton University Press, 2005).

Simmel, Georg, 'The Sociology of Secrecy and Secret Societies', *American Journal of Sociology* 11/4 (1906), 441–98.

Sinnett, A. P., *The Occult World,* (London: Trubner, 1881).

Sladen, Douglas, *Twenty Years of my Life* (London: Constable, 1915).

Smith, Warren Sylvester, *The London Heretics 1870–1914* (London: Constable, 1967).

Soane, Sir John, *Description of the Residence of Sir John Soane, Architect* (London: James Moyes, 1832).

Southey, Robert, *Letters from England,* ed. J. Simmons (London: Cresset, 1951).

—— *Poetical Works 1793–1810*, vol. 4: *The Curse of Kehama,* ed. Daniel Sanjiv Roberts (London: Pickering and Chatto, 2004).

Stead, W. T., 'The Arts and Crafts of Spirit Materialisation', *Review of Reviews* (February 1909), 120–3.

—— 'Julia's Bureau: An Attempt to Bridge the Grave', *Review of Reviews* (May 1909), 433.

—— 'Killing by Willing: Some Confessions by the Killer-Willers', *Borderland* 3 (April 1896), 211–13.

Stephens, John Richard, 'The Truth of the Mummy's Curse', in Stephens (ed.), *Into the Mummy's Tomb* (New York: Berkley Books, 2001), 1–15.

Stephens, Riccardo, *The Mummy* (London: Eveleigh Nash, 1912).

Stewart, Susan, *On Longing: Narratives of the Miniature, the Gigantic, the Souvenir, the Collection* (Durham, NC: Duke University Press, 1993).

Stoker, Bram, *The Jewel of Seven Stars,* ed. Kate Hebblethwaite (London: Penguin, 2008).

Strathern, Paul, *Napoleon in Egypt* (London: Vintage, 2008).

Sullivan, Jack, *Elegant Nightmares: The English Ghost Story from LeFanu to Blackwood* (Athens: Ohio University Press, 1978).

Summers, Montague, *Witchcraft and Black Magic* (NY: Dover, 2000).

Surtees, Virginia, *The Actress and the Brewer's Wife: Two Victorian Vignettes* (Wilby: Michael Russell, 1997).

Sutherland, James, *The Adventures of an Elephant Hunter* (London: Macmillan, 1912).

Sutin, Lawrence, *Do What thou Wilt: A Life of Aleister Crowley* (New York: St Martin's, 2000).

Symons, Julian, *England's Pride: The Story of the Gordon Relief Expedition* (London: Hamish Hamilton, 1965).

Taine, Hippolyte, *Notes on England,* trans. E. Hyams (London: Thames and Hudson, 1957).

Taylor, Charles, *A Secular Age* (Cambridge, MA: Harvard University Press, 2007).

Thomas, Julian, 'Archaeology's Place in Modernity', *Modernism/Modernity* 11/1 (2004), 17–34.

Thompson, Brian, *Imperial Vanities: The Adventures of the Baker Brothers and Gordon of Khartoum* (London: HarperCollins, 2002).

Thurman, Judith, *Secrets of the Flesh: A Life of Colette* (London: Bloomsbury, 1999).

Toye-Warner, Irene E., 'Black Magic in Ancient and Modern Egypt', *Occult Review* 23 (1916), 138–45.

Turner, Sir Alfred E., *Sixty Years of a Soldier's Life* (London: Methuen, 1912).

Turner, Frank M., *Between Science and Religion: The Reaction to Scientific Naturalism in Late Victorian England* (New Haven: Yale University Press, 1974).

—— *Contesting Cultural Authority: Essays in Victorian Intellectual Life* (Cambridge: Cambridge University Press, 1993).

Tyldesley, Joyce, *Hatchepsut: The Female Pharaoh* (London: Penguin, 1998).

Tylor, Edward, *Primitive Culture: Researches into the Development of Mythology, Philosophy, Religion, Art and Custom*, 2 vols (London: John Murray, 1871).

Ucko, Peter, 'Unprovenanced Material Culture and Freud's Collection of Antiquities', *Journal of Material Culture* 6/3 (2001), 269–322.

[Upham, Edward], *Memoranda, Illustrative of the Tombs and Sepulchral Decorations of the Egyptians; with a Key to the Egyptian Tomb now Exhibiting in Piccadilly. Also, Remarks on Mummies, and Observations on the Process of Embalming* (London: Thomas Boys, 1822).

Valéry, Paul, 'The Problem of Museums' (1923), *Collected Works*, ed. J. Matthews, vol. 12 (London: Routledge and Kegan Paul, 1960), 202–6.

Vandenberg, Philipp, *The Curse of the Pharaohs*, trans. T. Weyr (London: Hodder & Stoughton, 1975).

Vanke, Francesca, 'Degrees of Otherness: The Ottoman Empire and China at the Great Exhibition of 1851', in J. Auerbach and P. Hoffenberg (eds), *Britain, the Empire, and the World at the Great Exhibition of 1851* (Aldershot: Ashgate, 2008), 191–205.

Veblen, Thorstein, *The Theory of the Leisure Class* (1899; New York: Dover, 1994).

Velma, the Seer, *My Mysteries and my Story: A Book on Palmistry* (London: John Long, 1929).

Villa, Luisa, 'The Breaking of the Square: Late Victorian Representations of Anglo-Sudanese Warfare', *Cahiers Victoriens et Edouardiens* 66 (2007), 111–28.

Viswanathan, Gauri, 'The Ordinary Business of Occultism', *Critical Inquiry* 27 (2000), 1–20.

Vuohelainen, Minna, ' "Cribb'd, Cabined, and Confined": Fear, Claustrophobia and Modernity in Richard Marsh's Urban Gothic Fiction', *Journal of Literature and Science* 3/1 (2010), 23–36.

—— 'Introduction', Richard Marsh, *The Beetle* (Kansas: Valancourt Books, 2008), vii–xli.

Waite, A. E., 'The Life of the Mystic', *Occult Review* 1 (1905), 29–34.

Walford, Edward, *Old and New London*, vol. 4: *Westminster and the Western Suburbs* (London: Cassell, 1891).

Waller, David, *The Magnificent Mrs Tennant* (New Haven: Yale University Press, 2009).

Wallis Budge, Ernest A., *By Nile and Tigris: A Narrative of Journeys in Egypt and Mesopotamia on Behalf of the British Museum between the Years 1886 and 1913*, 2 vols (London: Murray, 1920).

—— *Egyptian Magic* (1899; London: Routledge and Kegan Paul, 1972).

—— *Prefatory Remarks Made on Egyptian Mummies on the Occasion of Unrolling the Mummy of Bak-Ran* (London: Harrison, 1890).

Wallis Budge, Ernest A., *Some Account of the Collection of Egyptian Antiquities in the Possession of Lady Meux of Theobalds Park, Waltham Cross* (London: Harrison, 1893; 2nd edn 1896).

Walpole, Horace, *The Castle of Otranto: A Gothic Story* (1764), ed. E. J. Clery (Oxford: Oxford World's Classics, 1998).

Warner, Marina, *Phantasmagoria: Spirit Visions, Metaphors, and Media into the Twenty-first Century* (Oxford: Oxford University Press, 2006).

—— *Stranger Magic: Charmed States and the Arabian Nights* (London: Chatto, 2011).

Warner, Nicholas, *An Egyptian Panorama: Reports from the 19th Century British Press* (Cairo: Zeitouna, 1994).

Waugh, Evelyn, *Labels: A Mediterranean Journey* (Harmondsworth: Penguin, 1985).

Weber, Max, 'Science as a Vocation', in *From Max Weber: Essays in Sociology*, trans. H. H. Gerth and C. Wright Mills (London: Routledge and Kegan Paul, 1948), 196–244.

Weigall, Arthur, 'The Ghosts of the Valley of the Tombs of the Queens', *Pall Mall Gazette* (June 1912), 753–66.

—— *Tutankhamen, and Other Essays* (New York: George Doran, 1924).

Weighall, Ron, 'Dark Devotions: M. R. James and the Magical Tradition', in S. T. Joshi and Rosemary Pardoe (eds), *Warnings to the Curious: A Sheaf of Criticism on M. R. James* (New York: Hippocampus, 2007), 124–37.

Weisberg-Roberts, Alicia, 'Singular Objects and Multiple Meanings', in Michael Snodin (ed.), *Horace Walpole's Strawberry Hill* (New Haven: Yale University Press, 2009), 87–105.

Werner, Alex, 'Egyptian London – Public and Private Displays in the Nineteenth Century Metropolis', in J.-M. Hubert and C. Price (eds), *Imhotep Today: Egyptianizing Architecture* (London: UCL Press, 2003), 75–104.

Westcott, William Wynn, 'The Golden Dawn's Official History Lecture' (1887), reprinted as Appendix G in Francis King, *Modern Ritual Magic: The Rise of Western Occultism* (1970; Bridport: Prism, 1989), 212–17.

Whale, John, 'Sacred Objects and the Sublime Ruins of Art', in Stephen Copley and John Whale (eds), *Beyond Romanticism: New Approaches to Texts and Contexts 1780–1832* (London: Routledge, 1992), 218–36.

Wheatley, Dennis, *The Devil Rides Out* (London: Heron, 1972).

Whyte, Frederick, *The Life of W. T. Stead*, 2 vols (London: Jonathan Cape, 1925).

Wilde, Oscar, *The Complete Letters of Oscar Wilde*, ed. Merlin Holland and Rupert Hart-Davis (London: Fourth Estate, 2000).

Wilde, William R., *Narrative of a Voyage to Madeira, Teneriffe, and Along the Shores of the Mediterranean, including a Visit to Algiers, Egypt, Palestine, Tyre, Rhodes, Telmessus, Cyprus and Greece*, 2 vols (Dublin: William Curry, 1840).

Williams, Charles, *Witchcraft* (London: Faber, 1941).

Williams, M. J., 'The Egyptian Campaign of 1882', in Brian Bond (ed.), *Victorian Military Campaigns* (London: Hutchinson, 1967), 241–78.

Williams, Rosalind, *Dream Worlds: Mass Consumption in Late Nineteenth-Century France* (Berkeley: University of California Press, 1982).

Wilson, Sir Charles W., *From Korti to Khartum: A Journal of the Desert March from Korti to Gubat, and of the Ascent of the Nile in General Gordon's Steamers*, 4th edn (London: Blackwood, 1886).

Wilson, David M., *The British Museum: A History* (London: British Museum Press, 2002).

Wingate, Major F. R., 'The Rise and Wane of the Mahdi Religion in the Sudan', *Transactions of the Ninth International Congress of Orientalists*, 2 vols (London: Committee of the Congress, 1893), II, 339–59.

Winkler, Hans Alexander, *Ghost Riders of Upper Egypt: A Study of Spirit Possession*, trans. N. Hopkins (Cairo: American University in Cairo Press, 2009).

Winstone, H. V. F., *Howard Carter and the Discovery of the Tomb of Tutankhamun* (London: Constable, 1991).

Winter, Alison, *Mesmerized: The Powers of Mind in Victorian Britain* (Chicago: University of Chicago Press, 1998).

Winter, Jay, *Sites of Memory, Sites of Mourning: The Great War in European Cultural History* (Cambridge: Cambridge University Press, 1995).

Witchard, Anne, *Thomas Burke's Dark Chinoiserie: Limehouse Nights and the Queer Spell of Chinatown* (Aldershot: Ashgate, 2009).

Witt, R. E., *Isis in the Ancient World* (Baltimore: Johns Hopkins University Press, 1971).

Wolfreys, Julian, 'The Hieroglyphic Other: *The Beetle*, London, and the Abyssal Subject', in Lawrence Phillips (ed.), *A Mighty Mass of Brick and Smoke: Victorian and Edwardian Representations of London* (Amsterdam: Rodopi, 2007), 169–92.

Wood, Gillen D'Arcy, *The Shock of the Real: Romanticism and Visual Culture, 1760–1860* (Basingstoke: Palgrave, 2001).

Wood, R. Derek, 'The Diorama in Great Britain in the 1820s', *History of Photography* 17/3 (1993), 284–95.

Woolf, Virginia, *The London Scene* (London: Snowbooks, n.d.).

Wordsworth, William, *The Prelude* (1805 version), ed. Stephen Gill (Oxford: Oxford University Press, 1986), 375–590.

Wynne, Barry, *Behind the Mask of Tutankhamen* (London: Corgi, 1972).

Yates, Frances, *Giordano Bruno and the Hermetic Tradition* (London: Routledge, 2002).

—— *The Rosicrucian Enlightenment* (London: Routledge, 1972).

Yeats, W. B., *Autobiographies* (1922), *Collected Works*, vol. 3, ed. W. H. O'Donnell and Douglas N. Archibald (New York: Scribner, 1999).

—— 'Egyptian Plays' (1902), in *Collected Works*, vol. 10: *Later Articles and Reviews*, ed. Colton Johnson (New York: Scribner, 2000), 62–3.

—— 'Is the Order of R. R. & A. C. to Remain a Magical Order?' (1901), as Appendix K in George Mills Harper, *Yeats's Golden Dawn* (London: Macmillan, 1974), 259–68.

—— 'Magic' (1901), in *Essays and Introductions* (London: Macmillan, 1911), 28–52.

—— 'The Manuscript of "Leo Africanus"', in Steve Adams and George Mills Harper (eds), *Yeats Annual* 1 (1982), 3–47.

—— *The Poems*, ed. Daniel Albright (London: Dent, 1990).

Yohannan, John D., *Joseph and Potiphar's Wife: An Anthology of the Story of the Chaste Youth and the Lustful Stepmother* (New York: New Directions, 1968).

Young, Paul, ' "Carbon, Mere Carbon": The Kohinoor, the Crystal Palace, and the Mission to Make Sense of British India', *Nineteenth-Century Contexts* 29/4 (2007), 343–58.

—— *Globalization and the Great Exhibition: The Victorian New World Order* (Basingstoke: Palgrave, 2009).

Young, Robert J. C., *Colonial Desire: Hybridity in Theory, Culture and Race* (London: Routledge, 1994).

Zerlang, Martin, 'London as a Panorama', in M. Zerlang (ed.), *Representing London* (Copenhagen: Spring Publishers, 2001), 30–56.

Ziter, Edward, *The Orient on the Victorian Stage* (Cambridge: Cambridge University Press, 2003).

Zola, Émile, *Au bonheur des dames*, trans. as *The Ladies' Paradise* (Berkeley: University of California Press, 1992).

# INDEX

Orientalist shops 115–16
in panoramas 106
public mummy unwrappings 98–102
London Museum 93
*see also* Egyptian Hall
looting
of Maqdala 74
of the Parthenon 148–51
of the Summer Palace 57, 150
of Ulundi 76
Lorrain, Jean 131
Loudon, Jane 83, 159, 161
Louvre 123, 136, 157
Lovecraft, H. P. 16, 178
Lovett, Edward 21
luck 23
'lucks' 21, 74, 154
Lupton, Carter 18
*Lusitania* 41
Lythgoe, Albert 14
Lytton, Edward Bulwer 219

Macalister, Alexander 138
Mace, Arthur 14
MacKinnon, William 44
Maclean family curse 22
magic
Ancient Egyptian 168, 209
in anthropology 231–2
and secularism 232–3, 234
magic revival 213, 219, 221, 223–4
and public scandal 226–7, 229
magical thinking 18–19, 55, 124, 145, 212,
231, 233
Mahdi 77–80, 82, 113, 157, 158, 199
Maitland, Edward 216
Maqdala 74
Marfleet, Philip 242
Mariette, Claude 129
Markham, Victoria 140
Marsh, Richard 147, 156, 171–3
Marshall, Archibald 28
Marx, Karl 20, 118
Maskelyne, John Neville 94
Maspero, Gaston 196

Mathers, Moina 222–3, 225
Mathers, Samuel 144, 219, 225, 226, 227
Maugham, Somerset 229–30
Mayhew, Henry 125
Medusa's head 205, 235–6
Memnon, *see* Rameses II
Mesmer, Franz Anton 211
mesmerism 100, 168, 171–2, 173, 207, 211,
223, 229–30
Meux, Sir Henry 63
Meux, Susan, Lady 64, 65–6
dubious reputation of 70–2
Egyptian collection 138, 143
and Walter Ingram curse 66
Whistler's portraits of 71–2
will provisions 74
Mitchell, Timothy 108, 123–4
Montagu-Stuart-Wortley, Edward 200
Moret, Alexandre 232
Morgan, J. Pierpont 57
Morley, John 166
Morton, H. V. 9
Moshenska, Gabriel 102
Mubarak, Hosni 239, 242
Müller, Max 216
mummies
in cabinets of curiosities 142–4,
175–6
in London 95
as medicine 100, 142
as museum artefacts 141, 145–6, 175–7
pits 49, 98
psychic possession by 174–5, 180–1
rags used for paper 165–6, 256 n. 65
and revenge of 156–7, 165, 167, 171, 176,
178, 180, 206
romances with 162–4
and satire 161–2
unwrapping of 83, 98–102, 144
*Mummy, The* (film, 1932) 16, 157
*Mummy, The* (film, 1959) 18
*Mummy, The* (film, 1999) 18
*Mummy's Curse, The* (film, 1944) 157
*Mummy's Hand, The* (film, 1940) 17, 157
*Mummy's Tomb, The* (film, 1942) 157